DEFEATED FLESH

MANCHESTER
UNIVERSITY PRESS

Defeated flesh

Welfare, warfare and the making of modern France

BERTRAND TAITHE

✻

Manchester University Press

Copyright © Bertrand Taithe 1999

The right of Bertrand Taithe to be identified as the editor of this work has been asserted by her in accordance with the Copyright, Designs and Patents Act 1988.

Published by Manchester University Press
Oxford Road, Manchester M13 9NR, UK
and Room 400, 175 Fifth Avenue, New York, NY 10010, USA
www.manchesteruniversitypress.co.uk

Distributed exclusively in the USA by
Palgrave, 175 Fifth Avenue, New York NY 10010, USA

Distributed exclusively in Canada by
UBC Press, University of British Columbia, 2029 West Mall, Vancouver, BC, Canada V6T 1Z2

British Library Cataloguing-in-Publication Data
A catalogue record for this book is available from the British Library

Library of Congress Cataloging-in-Publication Data
A catalog record for this book is available from the Library of Congress

ISBN: 0 7190 8126 2 paperback

ISBN 13: 978 0 7190 8126 2

First published 1999 by Manchester University Press

First digital, on-demand edition produced by Lightning Source 2010

Contents

List of figures and tables	page vii
Acknowledgements	ix
List of abbreviations	xi

1 Memories of war: 1870–71   1
    Meanings attributed to the war   4
    Defeated flesh   18

2 The Franco-Prussian war, revolution and Commune: an overview   25
    The origin debates   26
    Immediate causes of the war   29
    The war and defeat   30
    Politics and the Commune   40
    Conclusion   43

3 The politics of social practice: medicine, war and revolution in Paris   46
    French medicine in 1870   48
    Health in Paris in 1870   53
    Revolution and medicine   61

4 Militarisation and war effort: Paris, the 'giant hospital'   71
    Military medicine   75
    The 'giant hospital'   83
    Discipline and space   89
    Post-war   96

5 The politics of care and order   99
    To free Paris   101
    To feed Paris   106
    The politics of food   114
    The politics of care   121

6 Revolutionary society and medicine   130
    Towards secular medicine   132
    Doctors against the Commune   141
    The agony of the Commune   146
    Conclusion   150

7 **The dynamics of humanitarianism and the making of the Red Cross**	155
Humanitarianism	157
Official movements	164
Voluntary movements	170
Ideology	174
Conclusion	177
8 **Defeat embodied: the severed limbs of the nation**	180
Bodyloss	181
Outliving war	193
Conclusion	206
9 **Seeds of defeat: alcohol and syphilis**	208
From the cabaret to the grave	210
Syphilis	217
Shifting regulation	222
Symbolic regulation and prohibition	227
Conclusion	229
10 **Conclusion: war stories**	233
Bibliography	241
Index	287

Figures and tables

Figures

1. A. de Neuville, *The House of the Last Cartridge at Balan*, 1873 (photoengraving by Goupil & Cie, in E. Montrosier, *Les Peintres Militaires*, Librairie Artistique Launette, 1881, p. 4) — *page* 7
2. Souvenir of the siege of Paris c. summer 1871 (author's collection) — 9
3. The ceremony to honour Canon Faller (*L'illustration* 10 August 1910, p. 113) — 18
4. Paris in 1870–71 — 45
5. Paris region in 1870 (*La Guerre illustrée*, offprint, n.d.) — 45
6. A. Brouillet, *The Ambulance of the Comédie Française*, c. 1885 (in A. Dayot, *L'Invasion, le siège et la Commune*, Stusi, 1901, p. 142) — 87
7. Lange & Verdeil, *Skeleton of a Marauder Shot Among the Cabbages* (*La Guerre illustrée*, 48, 7 January 1871, p. 380) — 122
8. Cham, *Don't blame the Commune, it was about to solve the housing and rent problem!* 1871 (in A. Dayot, *L'Invasion, le siège et la Commune*, Stusi, 1901, p. 243) — 133
9. A. Darjou, *The Looting and Massacre of Bazeilles by the Bavarians* (in E. Wachter, *La Guerre de 1870–1871*, E. Lachaud, 1873, p. 408) — 161
10. A. Darjou, *Wissembourg – Massacre of the Wounded in Farms Converted in Ambulances* (in E. Wachter, *La Guerre de 1870–1871*, E. Lachaud, 1873, p. 155) — 161
11. Steinler, *Le Mur des Fédérés: You need regiments to guard corpses like these!* [il faut des régiments pour garder ces morts là!], 1873 (in A. Dayot, *L'Invasion, le siège et la Commune*, Stusi, 1901, p. 320) — 197
12. The hand as tool: 'Crochet-pince' (in Comte de Beaufort, *Recherches sur la prothèse des membres*, P. Asselin, 1867, p. 91) — 200
13. The wooden limb as ornament (in Comte de Beaufort, *Recherches sur la prothése des membres*, P. Asselin, 1867, p. 67) — 202
14. and 15 Labourers' arms (in Comte de Beaufort, *Questions philanthropiques – transport des blessés – hôpitaux – appareils. Assistance aux mutilés pauvres, etc.*, Imprimerie Nationale, 1875, pp. 108 and 112) — 202
15. The fortieth anniversary of the first fight of 1870: the German Colonel von Villiez honours the grave of French NCO Pagnier (*L'Illustration*, 30 July 1910, p. 68) — 239

Tables

1	Mortality in Parisian hospitals and hospices	page	57
2	Breakdown of the mortality by disease declared in Paris, 1869–71		57
3	Mortality and discharges in Parisian hospitals		59
4	Mortality after major war surgery in 1870–71		60
5	Soldiers admitted in the major civilian hospitals of Paris		91
6	Soldiers admitted in the major military hospitals of Paris		91
7	Entries to the Bicêtre military hospital, 1870–71		92
8	The civilian war effort in Paris: number of soldiers treated in civilian hospitals		93
9	The Assistance Publique's bread production, 1870–72		109
10	The rationing legislation of 1870–71		111
11	Comparative table of the meat available through the Central Butchery		118
12	Social analysis of the inhabitants of La Cité-des-Fleurs		120
13	Soup kitchens in Paris		123
14	The type of help delivered to paupers: analytical breakdown by *arrondissement*		124
15	Pension rights awarded after the war		203
16	Breakdown of the people evicted from Paris in August 1870		221

All illustrations and tables are the author's property

Acknowledgements

Spending six or seven years of one's life on twelve months of history makes one a peculiar type of historian with an uncommon ability to reduce all major issues to a footnote of the 1870–71 war, a tendency I had to deplore in myself while pestering my colleagues. Many people have thus heard or read chunks of this research, some have had kind things to say and all were encouraging. Roger Cooter, Ruth Harris, Mark Jenner (and how further remote could one's research interest be!), John Pickstone and David Taylor have given good advice and have often been conscientious and friendly readers. I have exposed some of my views at many conferences: the cultural history conference at the University of York in 1995, the *fin des siècles* conference at Bath Spa University College in 1995, the Social History Society conference in York in 1995, the social history of medicine conference at the Wellcome Institute in 1995, yet another conference on the *fin de siècle* in London in 1997, more recently at the French History Society conference etc. I have also to thank the audience of the many seminars I have had the opportunity to bore over the years at the Centre for the History of Science, Technology and Medicine in Manchester, and in Huddersfield, Warwick and York. A shorter version of Chapter 7 has appeared with a different emphasis in R. Cooter, S. Sturdy and M. Harrison (eds), *Medicine, War and Modernity* (Sutton Publishing, 1998) and is used here with the editors' kind authorisation.

    I have other, often more literal, debts: first of all the Wellcome Trust for funding the research fellowship which fostered this project from 1992 to 1994, second the French army for being lenient during my military service and employing me as a historian, and third General Bazot of the Service de santé des armées for authorising me to benefit from the archives in spite of the refurbishment works affecting the archives of the Val-de-Grâce. The many weeks I have spent there alone with the conservationist and the occasional cleaner in the dusty ground floor of the archives are a very precious memory for me. My department at the University of Huddersfield has been friendly and generous with travel funds and research time, and I hope this book will pay back some of my debts. Marie-Armelle and Georges Bayard have long understood that research on a shoe-string meant frequent gatecrashing and long visits in their Parisian flat. They have never complained openly and I am forever (and the next book will need yet more thanks I am afraid) indebted to them for their hospitality.

    Over the years I have frequently used the following archives and libraries and I have always found the archivists and librarians patient, helpful and friendly:

Archives Nationales, Archives du Département de la Seine et de la Ville de Paris, Bibliothèque Historique de la Ville de Paris, Bibliothèque Administrative de la Ville de Paris, Archives de la Préfecture de Police de Paris, Archives Épiscopales de l'Archevéché de Paris, Archives du Grand Orient de France, Archives du Service de Santé des Armées de Terre, Archives des Armées de Terre of Vincennes, Archives de l'Assistance Publique de Paris, Archives Départementales de l'Hérault, de la Creuse, de la Corrèze, de la Haute Vienne, du Rhône, the Bibliothèque Nationale, the British Library, the John Rylands Library at Manchester University, the Brotherton Library at Leeds University, the University of Huddersfield Library and their interlibrary loan service. Among my book providers I must thank all the dealers who sold me myriad invaluable books. In particular, I would like to thank Andrew Jones of Deddington, who never knowingly overpriced a book and indeed often is a philanthropist rather than a bookseller. On the domestic front Vicky is the long-suffering companion on book chases, the patient victim of my ranting and the source of all the stability I have ever had.

This book is dedicated to my father, who fought so many wars until his ultimate defeat and early death as this book was nearing completion, and to my mother, who had to live through all these hard times and now has to carry on alone. We all miss my father, and as I wrote this book for him it seems fitting that it is dedicated to his memory.

Abbreviations

AAP   Archives de l'Assistance Publique de Paris
ADC   Archives Départementales de la Corrèze
ADCr   Archives Départementales de la Creuze
ADH   Archives Départementales de l'Hérault
ADHV   Archives Départementales de la Haute-Vienne
ADR   Archives Départementales du Rhône
AEP   Archives Épiscopales de la Ville de Paris
AGOF   Archives du Grand Orient de France
AN   Archives Nationales
APdP   Archives de la Préfecture de Police de Paris
ASSAT   Archives du Service de Santé des Armées de Terre
AVdP   Archives du Département de la Seine et de la Ville de Paris
BAIM   *Bulletin de l'Académie Impériale de Médecine*
BAVP   Bibliothèque Administrative de la Ville de Paris
BHVP   Bibliothèque Historique de la Ville de Paris
GMP   *La Gazette médicale de Paris*
JORC   *Journal officiel de la république, édition de la Commune*
SHAT   Archives des Armées de Terre de Vincennes

IN MEMORIAM GULIO TAITHE (1925–97)

...

Un soldat jeune, bouche ouverte, tête nue,
Et la nuque baignant dans le frais cresson bleu,
Dort; il est étendu dans l'herbe, sous la nue,
Pâle dans son lit vert où la lumière pleut.

Les pieds dans les glaïeuls, il dort. Souriant comme
Sourirait un enfant malade, il fait un somme :
Nature, berce-le chaudement : il a froid.

Les parfums ne font pas frissonner sa narine;
Il dort dans le soleil, la main sur sa poitrine
Tranquille. Il a deux trous rouges au côté droit.

Arthur Rimbaud, *Le Dormeur du Val,* October 1870.

1 Memories of war: 1870–71

The Franco-Prussian war and the Commune have exerted an enduring attraction on historians of Europe. Paradoxically for such a short period, the two wars have customarily been treated separately. The complexity of a military defeat on an unprecedented scale for the French armies and the political mystery of the Commune have scared most historians conscious of word limits and publishing imperatives. These competing sequences of *l'année terrible* have each enjoyed alternating periods of historiographical attention. From 1870 to 1914, or even for some years after the war, the Franco-Prussian war was overwhelmingly the focus of study. Since the 1920s, however, the growth of a specific Communist historiography in France and abroad ensured that the Commune has increasingly become the centre of interest.[1] Since the 1970–71 commemorations, which produced a wave of popular and scholarly works discussed in Chapter 2 of this book, trickles of mostly academic texts have dealt with some aspects of either the Franco-Prussian war or the Commune. Everything seemed to have been said and written; as the Commune political experience seemed to lose its relevance to contemporary politics, one had to wait for the development of new approaches and questions to witness the current revival of interest.[2]

A reason for this relative silence in the age of post-modern and new cultural histories is that the sources are not easy to use or deconstruct. There are two major obstacles to an easy incursion into this moment of French and European history: the first is the very invasive form of epic and retrospective narratives encountered in virtually all the literature; the second is the issue of duration. The well-documented minutiae of both the war and the Commune make for an imposing jungle of details. The day-to-day accounts, the precise chronologies and intimate details give a peculiar intensity to a study of 1870–71.[3] The stuffiness of an ever more precise but not necessarily meaningful archival and literary mass can, at times, be overpowering.

---

1 R. Le Quillec, *La Commune de Paris, bibliographie critique* (La Boutique de l'histoire, 1997).
2 Citizenship is at the heart of this revival, for instance: R. V. Gould, *Insurgent Identities: Class, Community and Protest in Paris from 1848 to the Commune* (Chicago University Press, 1996); P. Nord, *The Republican Moment: Struggles for Democracy in Nineteenth-Century France* (Cambridge, Mass., Harvard University Press, 1995).
3 Many authors chose to cover this war not only chronologically but on a daily basis. The minutiae of these books reflects an antiquarian obsession with details. From a more practical point of view, the rewarding of unusual acts of courage in the defeat could only be accomplished through a careful examination of the smallest incidents. Baron A. du Casse, *La Guerre au jour le jour, 1870–1871* (J. Dumaine, 1875).

This feeling of unease is aggravated by the emphasis recent authors have put on this year. Daniel Pick has located the rise of a 'modernity of war' around the hypothetical 'watershed' of the 1870 wars.[4] Others, like Allan Mitchell, have invested this particular war with teleological meanings and argued that French politics, church, army and education consequently used the German model to reform themselves.[5] In both Mitchell's and Pick's narratives, the war came as a moment of truth.

The concept of war as an agent of change in history has been long contested by proponents of the *longue durée*, while the general public still regards a sequence of battles, generals and victories as the most entertaining form of history. The old sabre-rattling historiography and the cult of heroes still structure most people's education and understanding of the past: without these war-landmarks, history seems to them to flow in a continuous and monotonous manner.[6] Without a war and a sense of impending doom, the eternal Edwardian summer, the country-house lifestyle, and even the Victoriana of urban life would certainly lose some of their popular appeal. This impression certainly applies, with different terms, to the Franco-Prussian war and Commune. The over-attention paid to wars compensates for the amnesia of peace. As Raphael Samuel reminds us, academic constructs of the world constitute only a fraction of historical consciousness and do not hold the moral high ground either.[7] There may well be a deeper meaning in this obsession about war and violent conflicts.

If one sets aside the battle glory and the narratives of heroic masculinity, there is still much to be studied in wars. The study of war as an intense but short-lived reorganisation of social and individual relationships is still in its infancy. To write again the history of this *année terrible* can still be done without adding to the exegesis of the French defeat and of the siege of Paris.[8] In this book, however, the way the war was lost or won matters less than how medicine, society and politics

---

4 D. Pick, *War Machine: The Rationalisation of Slaughter in the Modern Age* (New Haven, Yale University Press, 1993), pp. 88–114.
5 A. Mitchell, *Victors and Vanquished: The German Influence on Army and Church in France after 1870* (Chapel Hill, University of North Carolina Press, 1984); *The Divided Path: The German Influence on Social Reform in France after 1870* (Chapel Hill, University of North Carolina Press, 1991) and *The German Influence in France after 1870: The Formation of the French Republic* (Chapel Hill, University of North Carolina Press, 1979) describe more subtle changes and more difference than convergence between France and Germany. E. P. Dreyfus-Brisac, *L'Université de Bonn et l'enseignement supérieur en Allemagne* (Hachette, 1879) and *L'Enseignement en France et à l'étranger* (A. Colin, 1880).
6 Even recent educational material provides for this market: P. Stroch, *Bataille de Froeschwiller* (Association des Oeuvres Scolaires, 1989); R. Sabatier, *Bataille de Wissembourg* (Association des Oeuvres Scolaires, 1989).
7 R. Samuel, *Theatres of Memory: Past and Present in Contemporary Culture* (Verso, 1992), pp. 5–39.
8 See, for instance, A. Horne, *The Fall of Paris: The Siege and the Commune 1870–1* (Reprint Society, 2nd edn, 1967).

combined and were reorganised. The dynamic of *Defeated Flesh: Welfare, Warfare and the Making of Modern France* springs from the apparent contradiction in terms. In studying the relationship between medicine, society and war, this original contradiction becomes increasingly semantic and the various elements of my subtitle do work together in the context of 1870–71. In other words, this apparent contradiction will be resolved. War is fundamentally a redefined social and political order and not chaos; it is rich with historical meanings for the contemporaries and the historian. In the effort of redefinition and reorganisation called 'mobilisation' (i.e. to make mobile or readily available for the purpose of war), medicine and welfare institutions played the dominant role in a hypothetical 'civilian sphere'. Donations to hospitals could match and complement war loans, the conversion of manors and luxury hotels symbolically minimised social differences. The Breton peasant shot at Le Bourget could go to, and often die in, the theatre of the Comédie Française or the Grand-Hôtel nursed by the actress Sarah Bernhardt or upper-class ladies.

While the rationale of mobilisation appears to harmonise a class society and erase differences, the volatility and mobility of the war situation also present unique opportunities for reform or innovation under duress.[9] Under the pressures brought about by the 1870 war, French society in the last years of the Second Empire was offered paradoxical opportunities and potential for revolutionary change. The loss of the war against the German coalition and the civil war of the Commune soon obliterated these opportunities and, indeed, enabled a social and political restoration in 1871.[10] The sense of defeat is a more existential concern, a truth harder to approach for the historian and an elusive form of despair. It matters, however, because it became a mode of representation and a trope of story-telling. This book attempts to deal with both history and memory, the national and the individual.[11] The history of medicine and of the body are here instruments to uncover another layer of human suffering. During 1870–71 the French, and more particularly the Parisians, experienced the Red Cross,[12]

---

9 B. Jenkins, *Nationalism in France: Class and Nation since 1789* (Routledge, 1990).
10 G. Bourgin, 'Une Entente franco-allemande : Bismarck, Thiers, Jules Favre et la répression de la Commune de Paris (mai 1871)', *International Review of Social History*, 1 (1956) 41–53.
11 See P. Nora (ed.), *Realms of Memory: The Construction of the French Past* (3 vols, New York, Columbia University Press, 1996–98) and R. Samuel, *Island Stories: Unravelling Britain* (Verso, 1998).
12 More precisely the Société internationale de secours aux blessés des armées de terre et de mer, the term 'Red Cross' seems to appear at a later date in Dutch and British writings c. 1871–82 to avoid the contraction Société internationale which had been confused by the French military with the Socialist Internationale during the bloody week of May 1871. Dr J. Naundorff, *Onder het Rodde Kruis* (Amsterdam, 1871) and M. S. Hudig, *In the Ambulance van het Roode Kruis* (Rotterdam, 1871); H. Templer, *A Labour of Love under the Red Cross during the Late War* (Guernsey, LeLièvre and London, Simpkin, Marshall and Co., 1872).

international humanitarianism,[13] mass mobilisation, the use of ersatz food, rationing, hunger, a major smallpox epidemic, the restoration of municipal and civic liberties, the shelling of civilians, civilian involvement in the running of war hospitals, and many tentative social reforms.[14] The recent debates on 'total war' are thus relevant at many levels.[15] Parisian society approached the model of total warfare even if the rest of France did not follow. The defeat reached deeper meanings than any before 1870. Survivors' lives were scarred and their writings and memories conveyed their mental and physical pain.

Their history has not yet been written, and it is the ambition of this book to analyse not only how the war was lived but also how it was narrated and remembered, and how acts of remembrance shaped the aftermath of the conflict. The material used to write this history has been left largely untapped by previous historians. There are some good reasons for this: many archives are incomplete and fragmentary, many precious documents were burnt in May 1871, and the archivists themselves have often only saved the more interesting documents by using them as the protective wrapper around a file. The uneven quality of secondary sources was partially compensated by their abundance. Their complexity and the wealth of emotion and personal involvement they contain are the main topic of the first part of this introductory chapter. A rough sketch of the organisation of the book and an explanation of the structure of my argument form the last section of this chapter. This sketching could not be entertained without the knowledge of how stories of the war came to be told, of how my narrative will complement what so many have written over the 128 years during which the French have reflected, meditated, remembered and also 'remembered to forget'.[16]

Meanings attributed to the war

The Franco-Prussian war, as it is commonly but inaccurately known, started in July 1870 and was objectively lost by the French imperial army by early September and

13 The definition of humanitarianism was and is a contested concept and not a moral category. G. Best, *Humanity in Warfare: The Modern History of the International Law of Armed Conflict* (Methuen, 1983). For opposing views see Pierre Boissier, *Histoire du Comité international de la Croix Rouge de Solférino à Tsoushima* (Geneva, Institut Henry Dunant, 1978); A. Destexhe, *L'Humanitaire impossible ou deux siècles d'ambiguïté* (Armand Colin, 1993); Isabelle Vichniac, *Croix Rouge: les stratèges de la bonne conscience* (Alain Moreau, 1988); or J. F. Hutchinson, *Champions of Charity: War and the Rise of the Red Cross* (Oxford, Westview Press, 1996). Also earlier historians: L. de Cazenove, *La Guerre et l'humanité au XIXe siècle* (Armand de Vresse, 1869, 2nd edn 1875).

14 1870 was the first war in which both parties had been signatories of the Geneva Convention and for which international and national organisations were set up. G. Moynier and L. Appia, *La Guerre et la charité* (Geneva, Cherbuliez, 1867).

15 S. Förster, and J. Nagler (eds), *On the Road to Total War: The American Civil War and the German Wars of Unification, 1861–1871* (Cambridge University Press, 1997), pp. 8–16.

16 B. Anderson, *Imagined Communities* (Verso, 2nd edn, 1991), pp. 187–206.

only stretched to January 1871 through a dramatic and improvised war effort. With over 7,000 books published on the subject before 1900, we could follow Marshal Leboeuf's boastful claim that his army was ready for war 'to the last gaiter button' and retrospectively count them before,[17] during, and after the war.[18] There is perhaps no other war that has received so much attention in proportion to its duration. Until 1914, any title containing the 'fateful dates: 1870–71' was sure to sell. This success should not hide the fact that many titles sold to different groups and narrated a whole series of different 1870–71 wars. Different meanings were attributed to the same events according to political and religious beliefs and, above all, whether they were inscribed within the sequential narrative of the war itself or that of the secular conflict of the two nations.

The bulk of the general literature tried to combine the two perspectives: a battle became a scene, an anecdote that varied in symbolic importance. It could either be a strategically insignificant skirmish in the suburbs of besieged Paris, a scene composed of individual bravery, a primitive struggle for territory, or a metaphor for the conflict between the two nations.[19] The authors usually mixed the genres, and combined the plight of the few, the defeated heroism of the mass, the anecdote, the wide panoramas and a moral narrative. During and after the war several painters contributed to this attribution of meanings and it becomes difficult to discern who came first: the painter and his panoramic warscape, or the historians who seemed to abide by a similar set of aesthetic and sentimental conventions. Critics noted that most paintings of the war were relatively small for the military genre, and that, even within the very large paintings of Detaille, the circular panoramas, the giant paintings, there was no order, no direction but mostly a crowd of individuals transfixed in the act of war.[20] Those paintings were not battle scenes resembling paintings of the Napoleonic legend. French painters on the whole chose to emphasise a fragmentary scale of events.[21] Nationalistic art critics deplored that

---

17 T. J. Adriance, *The Last Gaiter Button: A Study of the Mobilisation and Concentration of the French Army in the War of 1870* (Westport, Greenwood Press, 1987).

18 A literature of details relating to almost every unit or fortress can be gathered: C. Dolivet, *Histoire de la Garde Nationale et des bataillons mobilisés du IXe arrondissement* (l'auteur, 1872), pp. 92, 121, 152; Dr Abbaie, *Les Prussiens à l'Isle-Adam et à Parmain du 16 au 30 septembre 1870* (Masquier et Cie, 1871); C. Blanchaud, *Étapes du 71e mobiles* (Limoges, Ducourtieux, 1873); L. D. Coudray, *Défense de Châteaudun* (Châteaudun, Pouiller Vaudecraine, 1871) etc.

19 For instance the adventures and debated role of Sergeant Hoff: L. Louis-Lande, *Récits d'un soldat* (H. Lecène et H. Oudin, 1886).

20 See E. Montrorien, *Les Peintres militaires* (A. Laurette, 1881). Within less than ten years a whole artistic genre had grown in France. *Le Siège de Paris, exposition de peinture des épisodes civils et militaires de la défense* (Rueil, Galerie Durand, February 1871); A. P. Martial, *Les Femmes de Paris pendant le siège* (Codart, 1871); D. Thomas (ed.), *Battle Art: Images of War* (Oxford, Phaidon, 1977).

21 An anonymous book sums up the paradox of war descriptions in its title: *Grands cadres, petits tableaux, 1870–1871* (Coulommiers, Brodard, 1877).

> French painters of the young school do not claim to be part of either the *épopée*, the legend or the official convention. They make war in painting as they saw it, as they lived it perhaps ... They are the reporters of a thousand and one incidents of the campaign, they are chroniclers of the slaughter [*tuerie*] rather than historians.[22]

Montrosier contrasted the task of the chronicler who registers events to that of the historian who can make sense of the slaughter and find a deeper meaning in this loss of human life. The only meaning that could be found by historians and artists was in the incidents of the war and was summed up by the word heroism. The suicidal charge of 'Reichshoffen' or the sacrifice of the Margueritte squadrons at Sedan, when the heavy brigades rushed towards an early grave, could only be justified as splendid, albeit sterile, acts of gallantry.

In this register the desperate defence of Bazeilles and Balan[23] near Sedan by the army and the population of the village in flames was a glorious incident redeeming the defeat, a last stand *pour l'honneur*.[24] In a repeat of previous glorious military defeats, like Camerone for the Foreign Legion, the marines defended the road to Sedan from a humble bourgeois home in the small village of Balan until their last cartridge.[25] This futile self-sacrifice, which could not in itself compensate for the Sedan disaster, became a cliché of academic paintings and a military day of remembrance, so that while the Germans celebrated Sedan day, the French marines still have Bazeilles day celebrations.[26] In similar vein, contemporary French historians structured the narratives of the war in a manner which reversed the order of the conflict. From being the aggressor the French became the victims; instead of being losers they became moral victors. The historiography of the war also transformed geographic locations into landmarks of collective memory. Sedan the town and Sedan the defeat became irretrievably associated. The perception of the national territory, of history in space, involved this controversial political assimilation: Sedan, Metz, Alsace-Lorraine, Bazeilles ...

A simple survey of a handful of towns or villages where some killing happened turns into a survey of the failures of the imperial regime and of the French army. Unlike Dunkirk for the English reader, they do not imply an understanding of the rationale of the conflict and a positive collective experience. They simply mapped a geography of resentment and loss.

22 E. Montrosier, 'La Peinture militaire en 1878', *L'Art*, xiv, (1878) 32. Those disturbing paintings were forbidden in the Universal Exhibition of 1878 for diplomatic reasons.
23 Abbé Fouquet, *Balan pendant la guerre de 1870* (Charleville, Imprimerie Anciaux, 1891).
24 Bazeilles takes an important part in any account of Sedan. G. Bastard, *La Défense de Bazeilles* (Ollendorff, 1884); Abbé Fouquet, *Bazeilles pendant la guerre* (Balan-Sedan, Imprimerie du Patronage, 1895).
25 G. Hooper, *The Campaign of Sedan: The Downfall of the Second Empire, August–September 1870* (George Bell and Sons, 1897), pp. 298, 305–7, 311, 316–17, 324.
26 There is also at least one play on the same topic: A. F. Martin, *Les Dernières Cartouches* (Bordeaux, de Lanefranque, 1875).

Figure 1 A. de Neuville, *The House of the Last Cartridge at Balan*, 1873

The origins of the conflict seemed lost in a mist of contradictory interpretations: a diplomatic error, a trap carefully planned by Bismarck, a necessary conflict between two rising continental economic powers, revenge for previous wars, and so forth.[27] The meanings of the war ranged from Jaurès's analysis of the contradictions of the imperial policies to bitter regrets that the 1868 Niel reform to imitate the German *Landwehr* had failed to be implemented properly.[28] The historiography is sharply divided about these issues and the choice of one or the other option usually betrays a fundamental political orientation. This confusion about the causes of the war also left more scope for interpretative licence. The lack of clarity made possible illuminating but contradictory narratives of the war which sought to make sense of the events and the sequence in which they took place. Conspiracy theories mixed with either republican or religious exaltation provided explanations for everything. Those authors found in the anecdotes the proof that the whole picture did not reflect individual efforts. The sum of individual merits was well above the final collective result. Witnesses especially stressed the importance of individual experience and the validity of their subjective and narrow

---

27 E. Ollivier, *The Franco-Prussian War and its Hidden Causes* (Isaac Pitman and Sons, 1913), pp. 13–14; J. Rubio, 'La Vacance du trône d'Espagne (1868–1870) et l'équilibre européen, une révision du problème des candidatures', in P. Levillain and R. Riemenschneider (eds), *La Guerre de 1870–71 et ses conséquences* (Bonn, Bouvier Verlag, 1990), pp. 33–85.

28 J. Casevitz, *Une Loi manquée: la loi Niel 1866–1868* (Presses Universitaires de France, 1959); J. Dumont de Montroy, *Napoléon III et la réorganisation de l'armée de 1866 à 1870* (l'auteur, 1996).

view: 'The war in its brutal reality, such as a doctor sees it, the war as it is.'[29] No meta-narrative gained prominence during the war or even after the war, no imaginary narrative, no structuring form of story-telling.[30] The complexity of the situation on the fast-moving front and on static siege lines around key towns and fortresses meant that such meta-narrative was impossible.[31]

Armies waxed and waned in weeks. The Republic was proclaimed in Paris, the government ruled there while Gambetta had dictatorial powers over the rest of the territory.[32] At the heart of the turmoil, besieged Parisians lived on dreams, imaginary answers and expectations, an unhealthy diet which fed the historiography.

The central locus of most war narratives, however, (and this book is no exception) was the siege of Paris and the plight of the Parisians. The sieges of Paris from September 1870 to January 1871 and, against the Commune, from March to May 1871 became the foci of media coverage as well as the centre of French global strategy. Sources from Paris or about Paris all have a major point in common: the importance of time in their story. Time was food, and the struggle for survival at the expense of local rats, dogs, cats and any comestibles provides the rhythm for most narratives.[33] War memoirs recall the move from bread to biscuit, from biscuit to the crumbly plaster and straw adulterated bread of January, from horse meat to rat, from meat to ill-defined substances. Victor Hugo noted, 'It is not even horsemeat that we are eating. *Maybe* is it dog flesh? *Maybe* is it rat? I now suffer from stomach ache. We are eating the unknown.'[34]

It is tempting to make a parallel between this literature of details and a Proustian understandings of human memory,[35] and to see in this mass of recorded experience the *fin-de-siècle* shift noted by Pierre Nora from the historical to the psychological.[36]

In terms of material culture, the memorabilia of the war included a multitude of objects at odds with the artefacts of organised civic memory one expects from a post-war act of remembering, such as the building of war memorials or draping in

29 E. H. Beaunis, *Impressions de campagne, siège de Strasbourg, campagne de la Loire, campagne de l'Est* (Felix Alcan and Berger Levrault et Cie, 1887), p. vi.
30 L. S. Kramer, 'Literature and historical imagination', in Lynn Hunt (ed.), *The New Cultural History* (Berkeley, University of California Press, 1989), pp. 97–130.
31 Even the best synthesis avoids a large number of difficult issues. M. Howard, *The Franco-Prussian War: The German Invasion of France, 1870–1871* (New York, Dorset Press, [1961] 1990).
32 J. P. T. Bury, *Gambetta and the National Defence: A Republican Dictatorship in France* (Longmans, 1936). Baron C. von der Goltz, *Gambetta et ses armées* (Sandoz and Fischbacher, 1877).
33 E. de Goncourt, *Paris under Siege from the Goncourt Journal* (Ithaca, Cornell University Press, 1969), pp. 89–90; T. Astrie, *Le Siège de Paris en 1870 et 1871* (Le Bailly, 1871).
34 V. Hugo, *Carnets intimes, 1870–1871*, ed. H. Guillemin (Gallimard, 7th edn, 1953), p. 87.
35 Je comprenais trop que ce que la sensation des dalles inégales, la raideur des serviettes, le goût de la madeleine avaient réveillé en moi, n'avait aucun rapport avec ce que je cherchais souvent à me rappeler de Venise, de Balbec, de Combray à l'aide d'une mémoire uniforme', Marcel Proust, *Le Temps retrouvé* (Gallimard, folio, 1984), p. 226.
36 Nora, *Realms of Memory*, p. 11.

Figure 2 Souvenir of the siege of Paris, c. summer 1871

black the statue of Strasburg in Paris.[37] An entrepreneur sold, for example, souvenirs made of a little piece of bread adulterated with straw and plaster under a little crown of dry flowers and framed with two portraits of the emperors, a short chronology and an eloquent legend: 'four hours waiting in −10°C for a 200 g piece of this bread!' and a dismal list of enormously inflated food prices. War became food; food sustained the war effort.[38] There was none of the Napoleonic glory in this, the crown above the fragment of mummified bread was more a funeral wreath than a shrine. The meaning of the war now encompassed mundane details of life, and through this it becomes legitimate to study war and memory together. The overwhelming conflict seemed to imply the fabric of life, creating a post-war situation that would never be free from war memories, a continuum of existence, a negation of Proust's *mémoire uniforme*. Like the madeleine recalling happier days, the bread encompassing cold and hunger stayed to recall the detail of life, the broken narrative of everyday war. Sarcey stated that 'There is not one of us who has not kept a fragment of it as a sample and memento of the siege.'[39]

The nature of everyday war,[40] the discourse, experience and meanings of war which Foucault tentatively questioned in his aborted research, are the central

37 M. Agulhon, *Marianne au combat, l'imagerie et la symbolique Républicaine de 1789 à 1880* (Flammarion, 1979) and 'Esquisse pour une archéologie de la république : l'allégorie civique féminine', *Annales*, 28 (1973) 5–34. On remembrance see G. Mosse, *Fallen Soldiers: Reshaping the Memory of the World Wars* (Oxford University Press, 1990), pp. 70–106; A. Guldin, *Les Monuments des soldats de l'armée de Bourbaki décédés en Suisse en 1871* (St Gall, Merkur, 1898).
38 A. Legoyt, 'L'Alimentation et les prix pendant le siège de Paris', *Journal des économistes*, 66 (1871) 331–47.
39 F. Sarcey, *Le Siège de Paris, impressions et souvenirs* (Lachaud, 1871), p. 259.
40 M. Howard, *The Causes of Wars and Other Essays* (Temple Smith, 1983).

but elusive problem of this literature.⁴¹ The normality of the social state of war, its centrality in society and, as an experience, in individual lives, made for disturbed writings. The realisation that war and society are not antinomies brought home the knowledge that barbarity, violence and death still served a purpose in the civilised nineteenth century.

At an existential level this state of war represented more than a sequence of news, it became an intrusive narrative into which each and everyone was dragged and had to attempt to make sense of it. Edmont de Goncourt noted in his diary how the constant shelling gave him migraines. He was badly fed by his own standards, suffered from sleep deprivation and his perturbed senses shaped his understanding of war.⁴² His New Year's Eve entry in his diary illustrates this point: 'Saturday, December 31, 1870. Horsemeat, a meat that brings bad dreams and nightmares. Since I began living on it I had a series of sleepless nights.' In a later war, Marcel Proust himself could not stand the overwhelming intrusiveness of war in his cork-sealed bedroom.⁴³

Post-war reminiscences over emphasised seasons, and seem to expand the natural measure of time and invest it with new brutality. The wilderness and the cold of a harsh winter brought bourgeois authors to perceive their plight as a personal regression to primitive life.⁴⁴ This regression was paralleled by the political regression to chaotic democracy.⁴⁵ On the one hand we find the slow pace of hard times which affected most people, and on the other there is this breathtaking expectation of the next political or military event. The great *sortie en masse,* the tidal wave of the Parisians rushing out to break the German siege, never took place. It remained the strategy of most of those who did not have access to military information.⁴⁶ The great battle outside Paris, the large column of advancing armies, the ghosts of 1792, or even 1793, raising the nation against the invader did not give rise to victorious armies.⁴⁷ The other alternative of a great apocalyptic assault of German troops never took place. All messianic hopes placed on technological weapons or universal conscription proved to be an endless series of

41 M. Foucault, *Résumé des cours* (Julliard, 1989), pp. 85–94.
42 Goncourt, *Paris Under Siege,* pp. 155, 174, 184, 188–90.
43 W. Sanson, *Proust* (London, Thames & Hudson, 1973), pp. 91–3.
44 H. Cochin, 'Impressions d'un bourgeois de Paris pendant le siège et la Commune', *Revue des Deux Mondes* (1/08/1916) 526–55, (15/08/1916) 846–742.
45 E. Cresson, *Cent jours à la Préfecture de Police, 2 novembre 1870–11 février 1871* (H. Plon, Nourrit et Cie, 1901).
46 'Le siège de Paris, l'opinion publique et les opérations militaires', *Revue Bleue* (16/02/1901) 201–13.
47 R. D. Challener, *The French Theory of the Nation in Arms, 1866–1939* (New York, Garland, 1965). E. Hublot, *Valmy ou la défense de la nation par les armes* (Fondation pour les Études de la Défense Nationale, 1987).

delusions and disappointments.[48] At every level we find this constant mobilisation of hopes in an event that would reverse the fate of the war. There was no definition of what an event could be; it appeared like a trope in a tentative epic narrative. The measure of the war effort was quantitative rather than qualitative, and the epic dimension of the revolutionary revival was supposed to flow from this accumulation. Hospitals crammed in far too many beds, the soldiers inside Paris outnumbered the Germans two or three to one, hundreds of obsolete guns were made or mended in Paris. The troops paraded constantly, engaged in skirmishes or disastrously disorganised battles.

This *temps suspendu* of the war curiously contrasted with the momentum attributed to the conflict. Everything could have happened, everything *should* have happened, but very little did. In spite of this tiresome siege, the fermentation of Parisian society narrated at street level seemed to justify the imagery of a boiling cauldron of social and moral unrest.[49] The war people lived was not military but social, not national but individual.

Many post-war accounts were also informed by the events of the Paris Commune and retrospectively sought in the multitude of anecdotes the source of the revolutionary movement.[50] Paradoxically, it seems to most recent historians that this time of latency, this growing individual and collective frustration at a non-eventful siege (or over-eventful siege) and a similarly unexplained surrender, was probably the origin of the uprising itself.[51]

This momentum of insignificant events became the stuff of many narratives that read, perhaps unwittingly, like diaries.[52] Like diaries they contain the experienced and the mediated experiences. They mix introspection and historical perceptions, political analysis and dietary concerns.[53] They often reveal more than

---

48 M. Crosland, 'Science and the Franco-Prussian war', *Social Study of Science*, 6 (1976) 185–214.
49 L. Michel, *La Commune, histoire et souvenirs* (2 vols, Maspéro, 1970), vol. 1, pp. 77–90. On the extraordinary flowering of publications and street literature: F. Maillard, *Les Publications de la rue* (Auguste Aubry, 1874) and *Affiches, professions de foi, documents officiels, clubs et comités pendant la Commune* (E. Dentu, 1871).
50 Many texts about the Commune also echoed reactions against the 1848 Revolution. F. Lidsky, *Les Écrivains contre la Commune* (François Maspéro, [1970] 1982), p. 22.
51 A. Dalotel, A. Faure and J. C. Freiermuth, *Aux origines de la Commune : le mouvement des réunions publiques à Paris 1868–1870* (François Maspéro, 1980); J. Dautry and L. Scheler, *Le Comité central républicain des vingts arrondissements de Paris (Septembre 1870–Mai 1871)* (Les Éditions Sociales, 1960), pp. 9–12; M. P. Johnson, *The Paradise of Association: Political Culture and Popular Organization in the Paris Commune of 1871* (Ann Arbor, University of Michigan Press, 1996).
52 J. Janicot, *Trois Mois d'ambulance aux armées de la Loire et de l'Est* (Saint-Etienne, Freydier, 1871); L. Gallet, 'Guerre et Commune. Impressions d'un hospitalier', *Nouvelle Revue*, 105 (1897) 297–321, 551–75, 717–42.
53 This beside specific cookbooks issued during the conflict such as *La Cuisinière assiégée, par une femme de ménage* (Laporte, 1871).

was intended and add sexual and political images in an attempt to explain personal trauma.[54] This trauma reached different levels in different individuals. For some the tragedy of losing friends or family dominated over the more generalised but often deeply internalised loss of confidence, and loss of trust in oneself, in the nation and in even the most sacred institution. The suicide of the philosopher Prévost-Paradol (1829–70), the author of *La France nouvelle* (1868), on the day he learned of the outbreak of the war, perhaps epitomised this inability to cope with the personal guilt, the violence and absurdity of war.[55] Later, Rossel, a Protestant officer infatuated with his duties and military ideals, was crushed by the war.[56] To rebuild his ego, to recover his manhood and his honour, Rossel chose to serve the Commune, even though its politics were totally opposed to his social instincts.[57]

The time spent suffering in a manner almost passive and powerless (powerlessness and impotence are synonymous in French) unleashed an enormous social hatred of 'traitors'.[58] They could be bourgeois for the Communards or socialist traitors for the Versaillais. The orgy of violence and action that took place during the *semaine sanglante* of May 1871 illustrated the cultivation of hatred against one's own shortcomings in the previous collective humiliation.[59] The localisation of this violence is also particularly interesting. In Paris an unknown number of spies and traitors, German immigrants and even Alsatians ended in the river, were beaten up, or murdered.[60] In the 'village of cannibals' studied by Alain Corbin, the villagers chose the royalist notables as scapegoats, and killed and roasted a young man like one roasted meat after the killing of a pig. In Lyons, Commandant

---

54 S. Bernhardt, *Ma double vie* (2 vols, Édition Des Femmes, 1980), vol. 1.
55 M. Mohert, *Les Intellectuels devant la défaite, 1870* (Carréa, 1942), p. 73; P. Guiral, *Prévost-Paradol, 1829–1870, penseé et action d'un libéral sous le Second Empire* (Presses Universitaires de France, 1955).
56 J. Amigues, a notorious Bonapartist, published his papers under the title *Louis Nathaniel Rossel, papiers postumes* (Lachaud, 6th edn, 1871); also *Mémoires et correspondence de Louis Rossel*, preface by Victor Margueritte with a biography by Isabella Rossel (Stock, 1908); E. Thomas, *Rossel, 1844–1871* (Gallimard, 1967).
57 The resurgence of duels and manly behaviour after 1870 was arguably linked to the war R. A. Nye, *Masculinity and Male Codes of Honor in Modern France* (New York, Oxford University Press, 1993).
58 Rossel's letter to Gambetta, end of February 1871, 'your young fame reassured me and [went] against the impotence of your decrepit entourage'. *Mémoires et correspondance*, p. 283.
59 See P. Gay, *The Cultivation of Hatred: The Bourgeois Experience, Victoria to Freud* (Harper Collins, 1994). While I do not wish to follow the whole of Gay's argument over the cultural embeddedness of hatred in nineteenth-century society, the violence of May 1871 went further in terms of systematic cruelty than in any previous instance of political repression in France excepted the wars of religion.
60 See for a later but still hysterical account J. Bruno, *Les Reptiles prussien ou les crimes des espions* (Simon et Cie, 1888).

Arnaud was shot by his own men; elsewhere a baker was identified as a spy and shot.[61] These extreme incidents reflected the same social and national tension.[62]

Using reports to the departmental authorities, Stéphane Audoin-Rouzeau has shown convincingly that perceptions of the conflict fluctuated widely. Some 60 per cent of the national territory was never occupied. Those who had not lived the war themselves could not join in, and it is perhaps the purpose of such a large literature, of those framed fragments of life, to compensate retrospectively for the fragmentation of provincial responses towards the 'national' war.[63] These narratives mixing idiosyncratically religion, civic messianism, catastrophism and pessimism attempted in vain to create a unifying view of the war. Narratives following later world conflicts have had an easier task due to the sheer length of the conflicts and to universal conscription. There are, however, many similarities with the multitude of narratives following 1939–45 in France that tended to overcome wartime divisions to establish a new fundamental national myth around the Resistance. The oblivion into which collaboration fell is not dissimilar to that surrounding the imperial government.[64]

The fall of the Second Empire was analysed as a *débâcle*. This word is at the heart of many narratives, whether individual or collective. The word *débâcle* itself had been coined before the end of the war to describe the state of French society, after the war it became virtually synonymous with the conflict. It is also of course the title of Émile Zola's seminal contribution to the historiography.[65] The word literally describes the breaking up of the ice on a river in the spring. The motion involved – the drifting apart of the elements which when united constituted the whole – encapsulated the general disjointed perception of the defeat. French society appeared to be in a state of decomposition. Even the remarkable efforts of the revolutionary republic were, *a posteriori*, dwarfed by the reactionary republic of Adolphe Thiers. The parliamentary enquiry launched in 1871 thus sought to stress the shortcomings of the revolutionary government and was gathering information using remarkably

---

61 ADR, 2 R P 84, jugement du 1er conseil de guerre permanent de la 8ème division, *Le Courier du Centre* (Limoges) (04/11/1870 and 28/12/1870).
62 Hautefaye and Lyons massacres made a deep impression on urban elite. See D. Bingham, *Recollections of Paris* (2 vols, London, Chapman and Hall, 1896), vol. 1, p. 181. A. Corbin, *The Village of Cannibals: Rage and Murder in France, 1870* (Cambridge, Mass., Harvard, 1992), pp. 61–86. The villagers who murdered the local notables in Hautefaye were arrested by the imperial government in August 1870 and sentenced to death by the republican court in December 1870. On the other hand, the crimes committed in Paris before and during the siege, the killing of 'German spies', their drowning in the River Seine etc. were rarely punished. On the 'barbaric behaviour of the French' see the German point of view: E. Koslwitz (ed.), *Les Français avant, pendant et après la guerre de 1870–1871* (Leipzig and Paris, Werter, 1897), p. 137.
63 S. Audoin-Rouzeau, *1870, la France dans la Guerre* (Armand Colin, 1989).
64 Mohert, *Les Intellectuels*, pp. 13–17.
65 J. Claretie, *La Débâcle (4 septembre 1870)* (Librairie Centrale, 1870).

leading questionnaires.[66] Retrospective imagination, particularly after it became obvious that France was losing ground economically and demographically, construed the defeat as the result of a national inferiority and the war as the clearest expression of a European modernity that France was no longer leading.[67]

There had been a number of calls for reform of education and university,[68] military service[69] and medicine, calls to promote anti-alcoholism,[70] the fight against diseases of the race like syphilis and madness, well before the war. A social Darwinist[71] reading of the conflict increased their relevance. Alcohol, syphilis, corruption, nepotism, military routine and the mediocrity of education became fundamental explanations for the national defeat.[72] In this respect the defeat proved useful to pamphleteers and social campaigners.[73] They presented *their* war either as the starting point of *their* campaign (even if it pre-existed the war) or as the validation of their apocalyptic predictions. From Gobineau to Zola, the issue of degeneration pervaded the most pessimistic reinvention of the conflict.[74] In Gobineau's work, degeneration was a race against time in individual and national developments.[75] The whole decline could be understood as a regression, a defeat of man by time, the treason of the blood. The momentum of the conflict was explained by more global dynamics involving an ineluctable fall. Seen in detail, it revealed the 'mechanics' and 'symptoms' of decay, according to whether one used a technological or biological set of metaphors.

Gobineau summed up his views in *L'État de la France*: 'For a country to disintegrate like this, the disease must wreak its work from within; the wounds inflicted by the foreign assailant produce cuts, but never this purulent liquefaction of the marrow and the blood.'[76] Perhaps paradoxically in that context, Gobineau reinterpreted the war in the light of his racial theories and political predictions only when the war was actually finished. It took him several months in 1870–71 to lose his unusual optimism. The days of the war when Gobineau forced himself to

66 ADHV, 1 m 158, Examen des actes du gouvernement de la Défense Nationale (23/01/1872).
67 E. Andréoli, *Le Gouvernement du 4 Septembre et la Commune de Paris* (Bocquet, 1871).
68 K. Auspitz, *The Radical Bourgeoisie: The 'Ligue de l'Enseignement' and the Origins of the Third Republic, 1866–1885* (Cambridge University Press, 1982).
69 E. Guillon, *Le Nouveau soldat du service obligatoire* (n.p., 1873).
70 P. E. Prestwich, *Drink and the Politics of Social Reform: Antialcoholism in France since 1870* (Palo Alto, Cal., Society for the Promotion of Science and Scholarship, 1988).
71 Darwinism only slowly permeated the French scientific milieu, which was particularly slow to accept Darwinian ideas relevant to their concern about heredity. Y. Conry, *L'Introduction du darwinisme en France au XIXème siècle* (J. Vrin, 1974), p. 27; É. Gautier, *Le Darwinisme social* (Deveaux, 1880); M. de Bonnal, *Une Agonie, roman darwinien* (Angoulême, Luzol, 1877).
72 L. Dramard, *Transformisme et socialisme* (Bureaux du Prolétaire, 1882), p. 20.
73 J. de Blonay, *1870 : une révolution chirurgicale* (Geneva, Delta, 1975).
74 J. Andrieu, *Notes pouvant servir à l'histoire de la Commune de Paris en 1871* (Payot, 1971), p. 31.
75 R. Harris, *Murders and Madness: Medicine, Law and Society in the Fin-de-Siècle* (Oxford, Clarendon Press, 1989), pp. 51–64.
76 M. D. Biddis (ed.), *Gobineau, Selected Political Writings* (Jonathan Cape, 1970), pp. 204–5.

believe in the chances of the French army were unique in his life, and at odds with his former and later writings.[77] This pattern of war-induced altered consciousness could be found in many other writers.

To illustrate similar fears, albeit later in *La Débâcle*, Zola chose to narrate the conflicting paths of the simple, brutal, earnest peasant, Jean, and of the overeducated, refined and degenerate bourgeois weakling, Maurice, throughout the war and the Commune.[78] The former ends up with Versailles while the latter, partly by choice, partly by chance, ends up with the Commune. To give authority to his metaphorical analysis of French social races, Zola inscribed it at the two levels of the anecdote and of the national meta-narrative.[79] He visited the battlefields himself, following twenty-two years later in the footsteps of the marching army. He went to Sedan, annotated those details which validated contemporary texts, but he also judged and condemned the society under the Second Empire and the deeply rooted weaknesses of the French. He tried to sum up in a novel what contemporaries had attempted so often: the joint narrative of national history and personal stories.[80] In the last few pages the dying degenerate whispers his final advice: 'My dear Jean, you are the simple and solid one ... Go, go! take your pick, take your trowel! Go and plough the field, and rebuild the house!'[81]

Mixing of genres was attempted by writers from many diverse sections of society. Professional historians, journalists, medical practitioners, civil servants, 'ladies', soldiers and foreign visitors created a huge bibliography segmented in specialised sub-bibliographies. This diversity echoes the fragmented perception of the conflict. Each narrative is as valid as another, and in the time of political latency that followed the war, each account or prophecy could be validated one way or another.[82] The prophesied moral reconstruction of France or its social reorganisation could even mitigate the effects of the defeat.[83] The *revanche* grew less

77 M. D. Biddiss, *Father of Racist Ideology: The Social and Political Thought of Count Gobineau* (Weidenfeld and Nicolson, 1970), pp. 210–11; J. Boisset, *Gobineau, biographie, mythes et réalité* (Berg International, 1993).
78 P. Citti, *Contre la décadence, histoire d'l'imagination française dans le roman, 1890–1914* (Presses Universitaires de France, 1987).
79 D. Pick, *Faces of Degeneration: A European Disorder* (Cambridge University Press, 1989), pp. 74–86. Émile Zola, *La Débâcle* (La Pléiade, [1892] 1965), p. 322. 'The Degeneration of his race, which explained how France, virtuous with the grandfathers, could be beaten in the time of their grandsons, weighted down on his heart like a hereditary disease growing steadily worse and leading to inevitable destruction when the hour came.'
80 *La Débâcle* was not the only novel in which medicine played a fundamental part. A. Assolant, *Le Docteur Judassohn* (Dentu, 1873).
81 Zola, *La Débâcle*, p. 907.
82 B. Taithe and T. Thornton (eds), *Prophecy: The Power of Inspired Language in History* (Stroud, Sutton Publishing, 1997), pp. 1–14.
83 A. Chalanet, *Les Bienfaits de la guerre et les leçons de la défaite* (Lyons, Méra, 1871). This particularly optimistic but provocative pamphlet stressed before the end of the war that it had beneficial effects in mending the body politics against the common enemy in renewing the need for religion. This essay was reprinted in Lyons conservative press: *Le Salut Public* (24/01/1871).

on this ground than on glorified anecdotes. With time 'patriots' grew to dislike 'big narratives' of war, and preferred the glorious anecdotes:

> People congratulate Zola for moving masses and composing large frescoes.[84] I am myself weary of the synthesis that an artist, twenty years later in his study, makes from doctors', surgeons', and intendents' memoirs. All of them trailed behind the armies, remained out of battlefields and saw only the corpses ...[85]

Anecdotal evidence extended the relevance of personal experience to include the nation as a whole. From life experiences, the war and defeat became so-called landmarks. Their metaphorical and rhetorical importance grew and was not questioned until recently. *Annalist* or economist historians who take a longer-term perspective on historical periods, stress the fact that the war had a relatively small impact on the structures and vitality of French society.[86] The French economy was quite able to sustain six months of war, to pay 5,000 million francs to the victors and to lose Alsace-Lorraine.[87] French institutions showed very little will to reform from within, and behind the reformist intellectual discourse, little change affected public health services, the police, the universities, Parliament or even the army (excepting the high-command) until ten or twenty years later.[88] It became legitimate in the French historiography to disregard the war while often keeping it as a convenient, if almost meaningless boundary for textbooks.[89]

The provincial experience in 1871 seems to justify this attitude. From Brittany to Provence, the war did not quite acquire the agonising temporality created by siege conditions, and tourists had to buy those little framed boxes containing a sample of the adulterated bread of January to comprehend fully what Parisians had been through. Only twenty years later and most importantly at school did the war become the traumatic experience of defeated nationalism.[90]

---

84 N. Schor, *Zola's Crowds* (Baltimore, Johns Hopkins University Press, 1978); D. Baguley 'Le Récit de guerre: narration et focalisation dans *La Débâcle*', *Littérature*, 50:2 (1983) 82–90.

85 J. and J. Tharaud intr. Paul Déroulède, *Pages françaises* (Bloud, 1909), p. xi.

86 Levillain and Riemenschneider, *La Guerre de 1870–1871*.

87 F. Crouzet, 'Essai de construction d'un indice annuel de la production industrielle française au XIXe siècle', *Annales*, 22 (1970) 56–99; C. Heywood, *The Development of French Economy, 1750–1914* (Cambridge University Press, 1995).

88 Hospital reform for instance was associated with secularisation, and the religious debates which polarised French politics after 1870 slowed any real institutional innovation: H. Alpy, *Le Coût de la laïcisation des hôpitaux de Paris* (Le Sage, 1892).

89 The war became less an event in itself than the cause of the fall of the Second Empire. Napoléon III's death might have had the same consequence. Economically the war has been compared with prolonged spell of bad weather for French agriculture. F. Braudel and E. Labrousse, *Histoire économique et sociale de la France* (4 vols, Presses Universitaires de France, 2nd edn, 1993), vol. 3, p. 987.

90 H. Contamine, *La Revanche 1871–1914* (Berger Levrault 1957); A. Dupuy, *Sedan et l'enseignement de la Revanche* (Institut National de Recherche et de Documentation Pédagogique, 1975); S. Audoin-Rouzeau, 'Guerre et brutalité (1870–1914), le cas français', European Review of History/*Revue européenne d'histoire*, 0 (1993) 95–110, at pp. 104–5; C. O. Carbonell, 'Les Historiens français chroniqueurs de la guerre Franco-Allemande et de la Commune', *Bulletin de la société d'histoire moderne*, 13 (1975) 37–56.

The bulk of the literature and the uneasy mix of political/personal stories/history attempted to achieve an epic narrative that could compare with the Napoleonic ones or those of the 1790s revolutionary era.[91] In this, chroniclers of the war failed. They perceived the past as a literary genre they were unable to replicate.[92] They merely expressed a collective distress and often a way of coming to terms with the war.[93] The war was translated into a series of texts codifying individual experiences into an increasingly simplified story.[94] Each book, each account, gathered another layer of detail without ever adding to the meaning of this intense and absurd period of their lives. The accumulation repressed painful memories[95] rather than liberating fresh views.[96] Thirty years later the importance of the war became assumed for individuals and society alike, and the witnesses of those 'important' days could turn back with barely hidden nostalgia to the days when their lives mixed with what they thought of as 'history'.[97] By 1910 the survivors frequently gathered in a cult of remembrance, religion and nationalism.

Figure 3 is a very symbolic picture of 1910, in which a general gives the Légion d'honneur to Canon Faller, the priest who founded the war museum and memorial of Mars-la-Tour in 1870.[98] Faller, like many other priests, maintained and fostered a cult of memory, but this cult was not always focused towards *revanche*. In Alsace, German officers laid commemorative wreaths on the monuments to the first French victim of the war.[99] By 1910 war veterans had historicised their experience and made sense of it in terms of individual sacrifice to the making of the nation.

91 R. Tombs, 'L'année terrible 1870–1871', *Historical Journal*, 35:3 (1992) 713–24. This tendency led to fictional accounts of the war and Dick de Lonlay's work for children, [Hardonin] *Français et Allemands, histoire anecdotique de la guerre de 1870–1871* (6 vols, Garnier Frères, 1887–91); there was also a sub-genre in Britain, E. E. Green, *Ringed by Fire: A Story of the Franco-Prussian War* (Thomas Nelson and Sons, [1904] 1914); G. A. Henty, *Single Works, the Young Francs Tireurs* (F. V. White, 1872); *A Woman of the Commune* (F. V. White, 1895).
92 Poets also tried to achieve similar results: J. Aguilé, *Lettres d'un conscrit pendant la guerre, poésies* (Sillé le Guillaume, Besnardeau, 1875).
93 A. Lüdtke, 'Coming to terms with the past', *Journal of Modern History*, 65:3 (1993) 542–72.
94 P. Aurousseau, *Les Chiens des dieux, le siège de Paris et la Commune* (Saurat, 1986).
95 It is perhaps not insignificant that studies of inhibition became central in French science over the thirty years following the war. R. Smith, *Inhibition: History and Meaning in the Sciences of Mind and Brain* (Free Association Books, 1992), pp. 149–52.
96 A Freudian analysis of war could be attempted in other circumstances: Pick, *War Machine*, pp. 210–70.
97 In fact such accounts carried on being published well into the twentieth century: Un Artilleur de la Batterie du Pas-de-Calais, *Histoire d'une batterie de volontaires du Pas-de-Calais, Armée du Nord* (Lille, A. Noël, 1921); V. Boucabeille, *Jours de marche : journal de guerre d'un soldat de 1870* (Épigones, 1992); H. Cavaniol, *L'Invasion de 1870–1871 dans la Haute-Marne* (Montreuil, Delbos, [1973] 1989); L. Lapert, *La Guerre de 1870–1871 à Yvelot et ses environs* (Yvelot, Imprimerie Nouvelle, 1971); L. Leseigneur, *Les Prussiens à Barentin pendant la guerre de 1870–1871* (Res Universis, 1992).
98 É. Bader, *Mars-la-Tour et son monument national* (Mars-la-Tour, Ritter-Roscop, 1893).
99 *L'Illustration* (30/07/1910), 68.

Figure 3 The ceremony to honour Canon Faller

The cult of memory shaped a multitude of sacred *lieux de mémoire* which help focus the national experience. A strictly Weberian hypothesis leaves little room for this important national communion in the intellectual making of the Frenchman.

Defeated flesh

In writing this book my intentions were to associate with the surgeons, the non-combatant participants and all the people who followed the armies, who did not participate in the rituals and the excitement of battles but picked up the bodies, reflected on their role and prepared the aftermath of the wars.[100] Following Zola's steps, in a sense, is particularly relevant for a defeat when the traces of heroism and carnage leave a peculiarly sour taste and when the cuts go much deeper in the body politic than originally anticipated. I also wanted to stress the processes which led to the concept of a 'home front' with which the twentieth century has

---

[100] J. Weille, *Souvenirs de la campagne de 1870–1871 par un médecin militaire* (Reims, Molet Droin, 1896).

been so sadly familiar. Our general perception of war in the nineteenth century tends to be blinded by the colourful attires of Napoleonic and even Victorian armies, and we tend to believe that separate civilian/military spheres existed in the golden age of a military-led warfare. This set of images has largely been shattered by the recent scholarship on the French revolutionary armies, the dynamics of conscription, Clauswitzian total war, and even the making of the formidable war machine which ground its way to the twentieth-century wars of attrition.[101] Much of my story may have been narrated, but not about 1870–71.

The historiography which celebrates the Parisians at war rarely attributes any political meaning to their struggles and the forms their political aspirations may have taken beyond the three attempted insurrections of October 1870, January and March 1871. By looking not only at the insurrectional forces but also at the diverging and contradictory projects uttered by civilian and military doctors, moderate politicians and administrators, one gets a much wider picture of what the war became in French history. The politics of health, of care, of food, of education and religion show that through the many short-lived political projects attempted during the wars a picture of an alternative French history emerged, a picture of so many disappointed hopes that it enlightens further the developments of the much-maligned Third Republic.

During the wars and the siege the state, local democracy, centralisation, health care and humanitarianism were all essentially contested concepts at the heart of ideas of citizenship dating from 1789. In other words the key lessons of the great revolution were renegotiated and embedded afresh through the revolutionary episodes of 1870 and 1871. Following François Furet's sweeping assessment of a century of revolutions, 1870–71 were the revolutions to end all revolutions in France less because of the purge of May 1871 than because this year recast revolutionary ideas and saw the final failure of revolutionary myths and alternatives. The defeat in itself was a lesson in broken illusions: the war *à outrance* was the first political ideal to go; decentralisation, administrative democracy, anti-militarism, state provisions for health and a thorough reform of care and medicine followed. The first experience of power for many of the men who later led and shaped the Third Republic – Jules Ferry, Gambetta, Georges Clemenceau to name but a few – was traumatic and immensely formative in a restrictive manner. The first five chapters in this book deal with various aspects of this experience.

Following on from this chapter, Chapter 2 is mostly a brief introduction to the diplomatic, military and political historiographical debates which surround the Franco-Prussian war and the Commune. This reference chapter will not deal with the detail of the war itself, and Michael Howard's study of the war, complemented

---

101 See R. Aron, *Penser la guerre, Clausewitz* (2 vols, Gallimard, 1976), vol. 2, p. 31; M. Handel, *Masters of War: Sun Tzu, Clausewitz and Janini* (Frank Cass, 1992); P. Paret, *Clausewitz and the State, the Man, his Theories and his Times* (Princeton University Press, [1976] 1985).

since with a few other important works, will remain necessary reading for those interested in all things military.[102] Instead, my chapter focuses on a handful of major historiographical debates: on the origins of the war, the causes of the defeat, and the origin and consequences of the Commune. The relevance of the history of the 1870 war to modern readers is not in providing a flawed comparison with the defeat of 1940, but in helping us understand modern attitudes towards war, humanity and the state.

Following chapters dwell largely on the history written by medical men, which fittingly integrated individual sufferings and national overviews.[103] Many of them were bourgeois thrown into the conflict as semi-military ambulance staff or as volunteers of the Service de Santé. Their writings illustrate the complex and paradoxical relationship between war and civilian social practices, in this instance, medicine. While few challenged the notion that war is a terrible situation, the nature of their writing, mixing anecdotes[104] and casebooks, showed a universal belief that wars offer useful clinical and surgical experience.[105] The surgeon's trademark on this type of writing is perhaps more obvious, but the belief in the 'goodness of war' for medicine is at the heart of most analyses.[106] At a time of social and political upheaval, the expectations rising from the fall of a system of government before the emergence of another, stirred the deeply divided French medical world of 1870 and uncovered layers of political dissent rarely touched on by political historians and which ought to enrich our perception of the democratic culture of the Second Empire.

Chapter 3 'The politics of social practice', demonstrates the richness of political debates dividing Parisian professions before and after the war. It also sketches the situation of Paris at the time of the siege, while paying close attention to the welfare institutions of Paris during the war. The Assistance Publique, dreaded and indispensable institution of social control, played a particularly important role in the making of a giant hospital/fortress torn between civilian revolutionary aspirations and war priorities. This chapter shows how theories of decentralisation and municipal government sketched out in Sudhir Hazareesingh's work came to be

---

102 C. Troquet, *La Banlieue Est pendant le siège de Paris* (Vincennes, l'auteur, 1980).
103 For instance Dr Girard, *Contribution à l'histoire médico-chirurgicale du siège de Paris* (n.p., 1872); T. Auger, *Le Siège de Paris* (Parent, 1871).
104 C. Amanieu, *Récits anecdotiques* (Sauvaître, 1888).
105 Beaunis, *Impressions de campagnes*, pp. 1–15.
106 R. Cooter, 'The goodness of war', *Canadian Bulletin of Medical History*, 7 (1990) 145–59. For positivist appraisals of the war see: J. Rochard, *Histoire de la chirurgie Française au dix-neuvième siècle* (J. B. Baillière et Fils, 1875), pp. 857–76. E. Delorme, *Traité de chirurgie de guerre* (2 vols, Felix Alcan, 1888–93), vol. 2, p. 355; C. A. Gordon, *The Siege of Paris: A Medical and Chirurgical Study* (Baillière, Tindall and Cox, 1872); P. Brouardel, 'Pathogénie de quelques unes des maladies qui ont régné pendant les blocus de Metz et de Paris', *Revue Scientifique*, 49 (1/06/1872) 1165–8; P. Astruc, 'La Guerre de 1870 et la médecine', *Progrès Médical*, 80 (1960), 219–26, 236–46, 256–9, 275–81, 295–300.

tested in the heat of the war and how reformism found its own limits in democratic practices.[107]

Chapter 4 deals with the tensions created by mass mobilisation and militarisation in Paris. The war came at a crucial stage in the redevelopment of both French army strategies and medical practices. With the failings of the imperial army, the military Service de Santé had to integrate new political priorities and look at the French people in a different way. In a manner comparable with the Boer war recruitment panics in Britain, this disciplining gaze directed at a changing and heterogeneous crowd produced an agonising discourse of decline and an analysis of national unfitness. Malingering and other disciplinary categories added to a more global evaluation of French inadequacies. The medical staff's anxiety at fighting diseases in a corrupt and alien urban environment is also perceptible in the manner in which they attempted to organise and structure a disciplinary medical environment.

The following three chapters contribute to a political analysis of care in warfare. Chapter 5 thus investigates the politics of food, rationing and home care in besieged Paris. The provision of sufficient food to the right people involved the creation of a multitude of agencies rationing and distributing food, controlling the origins and the quality of food, and even creating ersatz food. The medical evidence and the scientific options were discussed in the academies but also in the daily press and in public debates.[108] Food rationing and requisitions touched a raw nerve and contested property rights enshrined in the bourgeois legal codes. In practice, the rationing of food gave renewed powers to municipal *arrondissements* in Paris and became one of their main priorities and a major source of legitimacy in the war context. Food was only one key issue of the conflict. Policing, housing, unemployment, all fell into the hands of the civic administration. Parisian urban administration had always been under the close scrutiny of the state, but in besieged Paris the reverse seems to have been true and Parisian municipalities concentrated in their hands effective power if not the legitimate jurisdictions.[109] Through the debates on food and care, the state itself came to be contested and eventually confronted by municipal democracy. The Commune of Paris may in this context appear to be the continuation of wartime social order.

Chapter 6, on the Commune's policies, analyses these continuities between war order and revolutionary order. The Commune had to deal with the politics of care and social order with more urgency than the Versailles government. The

---

107 S. Hazareesingh, *From Subject to Citizen: The Second Empire and the Emergence of Modern French Democracy* (Princeton University Press, 1998).
108 G. Grimaud de Caux, *L'Académie des Sciences pendant le siège de Paris* (Didier et Cie, 1871); E. Saint-Edme, *La Science pendant le siège de Paris* (E. Dentu, 1871).
109 E. N. Suleiman, *Private Power and Centralization in France: The Notaires and the State* (Princeton University Press, 1987), pp. 16–17.

power-base of the Commune, its legitimacy even, were closely linked to its ability to deliver or maintain welfare and symbolic measures introduced during the siege, such as the moratorium on rent and loan debts, enforced secularisation or pension rights. The Commune did not simply inherit a complex situation and very unwieldy administration from the National Defence government, it also attempted to create and legislate according to a mixture of historical precedent and ideological dogma. The Commune's dealings with health provisions, medical practitioners and medical training illustrate some of the fundamental contradictions of Communard politics. In becoming an interventionist power in medical issues, the Commune of Paris responded to some radical medical aspirations but failed to enlist much support from this traditionally radical fraction of the bourgeoisie.

A key issue of this chapter on the Commune is to explore precisely the role of medical men and, more generally, the role of professions in the modern French state. By systematically betraying the Commune, medical men not only followed their social instinct, they also asserted their role as unpaid servants of the state in the meritocratic republican order. The Commune's bloody end enabled Thiers's government to revert to the *status quo ante* and arguably even attempt a restoration of the pre-1851 political and social order. In all social areas, however, the war and the civil war had raised most of the issues which the Third Republic later tackled in an often very similar manner.

Continuing on the issue of the state and its role, Chapter 7 questions the role of humanitarian politics and the early days of the Red Cross. The involvement of national and international societies for the help to the wounded and the sick played an important role during the war and in many ways singularly complicated the task of mobilising society in the war effort. For the many governments and societies involved in the conflict, the international missions played the useful part of surrogate diplomacy but also enabled the collection of information on modern warfare. Within France the Red Cross channelled money and people towards new forms of warfare involvement. The divisions and contradictions in the Red Cross movement reflected not only the social fabric of French medicine but also the inherent contradictions of humanitarianism at war.[110] This chapter concludes the part of this book devoted to the politics of care in war by pointing out the discrepancies between the rise of internationalist idealism and the integration of humanitarianism in war as an auxiliary of combating armies.

The last three chapters analyse the defeat rather than the war. Scrutinising medical practices and discourses during and after the conflict, they focus on sets of metaphorical representations produced from a reflection on the causes of the defeat and on the embodiment of defeat. To show how political issues and medical

---

110 For the Quaker view of humanitarianism: W. K. Sessions, *They Chose the Star* (York, Ebor Press, [1944] 1991).

metaphors interconnect and permeate each other's semantic field, I have chosen three essentially medical debates which were also explicitly political: amputations, alcoholism and syphilis. The first issue is debated in Chapter 8 which discusses representations of France not only as Marianne wounded but also as an amputated hero. By contrast with this heroic imagery, the sordid haggles on pension rights, the fact that the defeat had to remain the unspoken issue at the back of 'one's mind', created a situation in which people were oblivious of war veterans and cripples. One had to wait until 1912 for a medal to be coined for war veterans, and until the 1930s to see it distributed to the remaining few.[111]

The political language did not simply borrow from the medical register a series of medical metaphors to describe the loss of Alsace-Lorraine; the reverse was also true. The controversy on conservative surgery, the most contested practice of the war,[112] involved a number of radical choices on the risk, rationality and purpose of a long and difficult treatment which did not often involve antisepsis.[113] The political and surgical choices of medical men and their post-war involvement in politics overlapped and led to mixed practices and discourse. As Jack Ellis remarks, the French tradition of *médecine préservatrice* dating from the early age of the clinic 'had enormous political implications, for in extending diagnosis from the bodily to the social organism, doctors sought to make all institutions the legitimate objects of medical inquiry'.[114] By 1870 the medical language pervaded many forms of social and political representation.

The penultimate chapter deals similarly with the links between alcohol, syphilis and the defeat. By looking at two constituting elements of the medical phantasms of French *fin de siècle,* any analysis may either state that French *fin de siècle* did start in 1870 or deny that it did. Alcohol constructed as a social scourge serves as a counterfactual to check the evidence provided by the debates on syphilis. Drunkenness and defeat did become closely associated during and immediately after the war, but it was drunkenness as an agent of disorder subverting discipline, not as a major cause of racial inferiority. On the other hand syphilis had the potential to affect the race. While civilian administrations neglected the police regulation of prostitution, army surgeons dealt, with some trepidation, with a large contingent of unfit conscripts. Post-war regulationism was simultaneously

---

111 AdCR 1 m 286, *Médailles commémoratives de la guerre de 1870*; ADHV 2 r 115–6.
112 E. Lantier, *Conservation des membres blessés par armes à feu perfectionnées* (Asselin, 1872) and *L'École antiseptique conservatrice* (Auclaire, 1889). Lantier claimed to have used antisepsic surgery.
113 J. D. Ellis, *The Physician Legislators of France: Medicine and Politics in the Early Third Republic, 1870–1914* (Cambridge University Press, 1990), p. 6.
114 Ellis, *The Physician Legislators of France*. Jack Ellis shows how medical men became a consistently large group in Parliament in the years following the 1870 war. The war experience was often the beginning of a long career: Clemenceau and Combe benefited from the power vacuum of 1870–71.

attacked on political grounds and defended much more vigorously and anxiously on medical ones. In Alfred Fournier's post-war analysis of the dangers of syphilis, combined with psychiatric analyses of the defeat and Commune, venereal disease and particularly heredo-syphilis took on a more sinister role as causative agents of decadence. The *fin de siècle* began in this medicalised introspection of the defeat. The two other banes tuberculosis and alcoholism did so more indirectly, and this is my caveat to previous analyses of this conflict: one ought to distinguish very clearly between representations and meanings attributed twenty years later to the war and those originating from the war experience itself.

The overall ambition of this book is to read the 1870 conflict through the lenses of medicine, humanity and social debates in order to reverse the common assumption that it is war that shapes all. War as narrative is indeed a complicated text which includes many bloody pages and much rosy reconstruction. By looking at the diversity of opportunities and choices available in 1870, I would hope to demonstrate that if 1870 was indeed a watershed it was not the product of fate but of choice, informed and ideological, and debate, explicit and implicit, which shaped modern France.

2 The Franco-Prussian war, revolution and Commune: an overview

Over the last thirty years the Franco-Prussian war has received relatively little critical historical attention. Since Michael Howard's masterly survey, however, a certain amount of work on aspects of the military and political history of the war have changed some parameters of historical research without altering fundamentally his account.[1] Stéphane Audoin-Rouzeau, writing against the grain of *longue durée*, described in more depth than anyone previously the general understanding of the war across France.[2] More traditional summaries by Allan Mitchell, François Roth and William Serman have added to the detail or have improved on some aspects of the war without changing the overall picture. The latter two authors made no apologies for writing a relatively unproblematic account of momentous days.

As Chapter 1 indicated, a war about which thousands of books, pamphlets and articles were published for forty years,[3] and from which two regenerated nationalist mythologies[4] sprang, cannot possibly be defined as belonging unproblematically to narrative history.[5] This chapter is not yet another chronological account,[6] but an attempt at addressing some of the most important historiographical issues raised by this conflict.[7]

The three major areas for debate concern the origins of the war, the cause of the French defeat, and eventually the origins of the Commune. In this chapter as in

---

1 M. Howard, *The Franco-Prussian War: The German Invasion of France, 1870–71* (New York, Dorset Press, [1961] 1990).
2 S. Audoin-Rouzeau, *1870, la France dans la guerre* (Armand Colin, 1989), pp. 16–17.
3 B. Palat, *Bibliographie générale de la guerre de 1870–1871* (Berger Levrault, 1896). This bibliography lists around 6,800 publications for the first 26 years alone. Another 1,000 were published between 1894 and 1920.
4 C.-O. Carbonell, 'Les Historiens français chroniqueurs de la guerre franco-allemande et de la Commune, naissance du nationalisme historiographique, 1871–1875', *Bulletin de la Société d'histoire moderne*, 13 (1974) 37–56; A. Dupuy, *Sedan et l'enseignement de la revanche* (Institut National de Recherche et de Documentation Pédagogique, 1975); H. Contamine, *La Revanche, 1871–1914* (Berger Levrault, 1957); H. Guillemin, *Nationalistes et nationaux (1870–1940)* (Gallimard, idée, 1974), pp. 9–54.
5 M. Jeisman, *Das Vaterland der Feinde* (Stuttgart, Klett-Cotta, 1992), pp. 161–295.
6 G. Sée, *Aujourd'hui Paris, ou les 133 jours du siège, 1870–1871* (Versailles, Les Sept Vents, 1988); Baron A. du Casse, *La Guerre au jour le jour, 1870–1871* (J. Dumaine, 1875); A. Bataille and E. de Barins, *Nouveau mémorial* (Pick de l'Isère, Librairie Nationale, 1880).
7 R. Tombs, 'L'Année terrible, 1870–1871', *Historical Journal*, 35:3 (1992) 713–24. Tombs adds some interesting figures to the bibliographical countdown given in note 6, stressing that the flood of publications turned into a trickle after 1936: 69 between 1936 and 1959, 48 between 1960 and 1984, p. 713.

the rest of the book, it seems impossible to dissociate the Commune from the war in spite of the existence of two separate historiographical traditions.[8] The overall objective of this chapter is to freshen the reader's memory and to provide the backdrop of the rest of the study.

The origin debates

The origins of the war remained confused to those who lived through the early days of the conflict.[9] The apparent causes of the crisis of July 1870 centred on the Hohenzollern candidacy to the then vacant throne of Spain.[10] Historians and contemporaries have nevertheless traced the origins of the war to the 1864 war and earlier French involvement in the politics of nationalities in Europe.[11] In a sense the real origin of the war might well be the 1851 coup which established a more flamboyant style of government for the Prince-President Louis Napoleon Bonaparte.[12] Of all the portfolios of the new dictatorship, the foreign office was the most closely controlled and also often bypassed by the dictator's secret diplomacy. One has to look back to Napoleon I to find diplomacy which reflected so clearly the idiosyncrasies of the French ruler.[13] Napoleon III's diplomacy[14] was notoriously secretive, mixed the most cynical and idealistic intentions, and lacked a clear long-term agenda.[15] The mixed signals that a two-track diplomacy gave to the world made French policies confusing and threatening.

An official French foreign office enquiry in the early twentieth century traced the diplomatic origins of the 1870 war to the Austro-Prussian victory over Denmark. In this they were careful to distinguish diplomatic origins from historical origins. Their understanding of the latter went as far back as the succession of

---

8 H. Guillemin, *Les Origines de la Commune* (3 vols, Gallimard, 1973) defined the war as the premises of the Commune. One could easily reverse the analysis and read the Commune as the postscript of the war. Also see recent examples of separate treatment, F. Roth, *La Guerre de 1870* (Fayard, 1990); W. Serman, *La Commune de Paris : 1871* (Fayard, 1986); S. Edwards, *The Paris Commune 1871* (Eyre and Spottiswoode, 1971).

9 The imperial government had to fund an expensive campaign of explanations in the first few days of July 1870.

10 E. Ollivier, *The Franco-Prussian War and its Hidden Causes* (Isaac Pitman and Sons, 1913); Howard, *The Franco-Prussian War,* pp. 48–56; L. Steefel, *The Hohenzollern Candidacy and the Origins of the Franco-German War of 1870* (Cambridge, Mass., Harvard University Press, 1962).

11 See J. Jaurès, *La Guerre franco-allemande de 1870–71* (Flammarion, [1908] 1971), pp. 45–188.

12 M. de Maupas, *Mémoires sur le Second Empire* (2 vols, E. Dentu, 1884), vol. 1, pp. 603–18.

13 J. F. McMillan, *Napoleon III* (Longman, 1991); W. H. C. Smith, *Second Empire and Commune* (Longman, 1985); T. Zeldin, *The Political System of Napoleon III* (Macmillan, 1958).

14 W. E. Echard, *Foreign Policy of the Second Empire: A Bibliography* (New York, Greenwood Press, 1988), and *Napoleon III and the Concert of Europe* (Indianapolis, Indiana University Press, 1983).

15 Service Historique du Grand État-Major Prussien, *La Guerre franco-allemande de 1870–71* (J. Dumaine, 1872), pp. 3–12.

Charlemagne!¹⁶ The choice of 1864 as the origin of the war was mainly justified by the series of mistakes and hesitations characterising French policy towards Prussia. The general pattern of this conflict was that while it created a rush of diplomatic activity across Europe, it remained, like the later Franco-Prussian war, a localised conflict.¹⁷ The French and British position was to deny any responsibility towards Denmark despite a long-forgotten 1720 convention which made the two countries guarantors of Danish borders. The Franco-British effort was simply to ensure that the conflict did not turn into a major European war undermining further the fragile European equilibrium.¹⁸

A similarly hesitant and eventually passive policy prevailed during the Prusso-Austrian war of 1866, which saw the surprisingly rapid defeat of the Austrian empire and the terminal demise of its influence on German states. On both occasions the French administration arguably missed the opportunity to maintain its influence on German internal politics.¹⁹ The reasons for this passivity were complex. By 1864 and even more so in 1866, the Second Empire had lost some of its original momentum. The Mexican campaign, which maintained artificially alive the straw empire of Maximilian, turned into an unbearable long-term involvement which did not pay the financial dividends originally anticipated.²⁰ The less speculative wars in Italy or Crimea had also been costly. Napoleon III had also some grounds to question whether the French armies could be spread so thinly as to intervene in Europe while defending a diversity of interests ranging from the Papal territories to Beirut, Algeria, Mexico and Indo-China. The colonial adventures, while mostly successful in Algeria, had gone disastrously wrong in Mexico. They had also revealed alarming signs of military inefficiency, high casualties and low morale. In neither 1864 nor 1866 was the French army able to mobilise quickly enough to fight in Germany while maintaining itself in so many distant locations.²¹

Napoleon III was also sufficiently versed in all things military to realise that French successes owed a lot to chance. Military historians have clearly

16 P. Deluns-Montaud, A. Aulard, E. Bourgeois and J. Reinach (eds), *Les Origines diplomatiques de la guerre de 1870–1871* (10 vols, Gustave Ficker, 1910–15), pp. vii–xiii. Other authors went further back to the Germanic invasions of Gaul: General Ambert, *Gaulois et Germains, récits militaires* (4 vols, Blond et Barral, 1884–85).
17 E. B. Washburne, *Recollections of a Minister to France, 1869–77* (2 vols, Sampson Low, Marston, Searle and Rivington, 1887), vol. 1.
18 R. Millman, *British Foreign Policy and the Coming of the Franco-Prussian War* (Oxford, Clarendon Press, 1965).
19 G. Rothan, *Les Origines de la guerre de 1870, la politique française en 1866* (Calmann-Lévy, 1879) and *Souvenirs diplomatiques, l'affaire du Luxembourg* (Calmann-Lévy, 1882).
20 P. Gaulot, *L'Expédition du Mexique* (P. Ollendorff, 1889–90); N. N. Barker, *The French Experience in Mexico, 1821–1861* (Chapel Hill, University of North Carolina Press, 1979); J. F. Lecaillon, *Napoléon III et le Mexique* (L'Harmattan, 1994).
21 R. Holmes, *The Road to Sedan* (Royal Historical Society, 1984), pp. 14–26.

demonstrated that the victories of Solferino or Sebastopol had been Pyrrhic victories, often the fruit of fortuitous circumstances rather than revealing military superiority. In 1864 and 1866 the Prussian-led victories took most French analysts by surprise. Napoleon III had the wits but not the strength to cash in on his indecisiveness. In 1866, for instance, Napoleon attempted to become the arbiter of Europe at no cost whatever, but failed to mobilise his armies to stop the Prussian campaign. Instead his convoluted diplomatic exchanges and his last-minute compensation claim were cut short by the sudden victory of Sadowa and the termination of the war.[22] French expansionism seemed to loom again over the future of Europe.[23]

1866 was clearly, if retrospectively, understood as a key date in French history.[24] French media resented the government's lack of initiative and the humiliation of the compensation claims, and pointed out the dangers of Prussian superiority in Germany.[25] One of the real problems of this shambolic diplomacy was that the French government had alienated most of its potential allies. In his most ambitious days Napoleon III had intended to become the broker of a new European order and had called for a European congress since 1863. This call remained unanswered. In Italy the survival of the Papal state depended on French support and alienated the Italian aspirations.

Internally, the liberalisation of the Empire, in itself a major historical debate, created tensions amongst the ageing governmental elite.[26] Morny, the Emperor's half-brother, had died in 1865.[27] Eugène Rouher and Persigny,[28] the strong men of the regime, and the Empress Eugénie herself opposed any liberal reforms. Napoleon nevertheless granted increased rights to Parliament from 1860 onwards. In 1867 the regime seemed to move towards parliamentarianism. In 1869–70 Emile Ollivier[29] and Prévost-Paradol joined the government and thus signalled the acceptance of the Empire by members of the moderate parliamentary opposition.[30] By 1870, ministers were individually accountable to a chamber elected

22 C. de Grumwald, *Bismarck* (Albin Michel, 1949), pp. 238–82; A. Sorel, *Histoire diplomatique de la guerre franco-allemande* (2 vols, H. Plon, 1875). The correspondent of *The Times*, *Letters on International Relations before and during the War of 1870* (2 vols, Tinsley Bros., 1871), vol. 1, pp. 432–8.
23 A. Armengaud, 'L'Opinion publique en France et la crise nationale allemande en 1866' (unpublished thesis, Université de Dijon, 1962); E. A. Pottinger, *Napoleon III and the German Crisis, 1865–1866* (Cambridge, Mass., Harvard University Press, 1966).
24 J. V. A. de Broglie, *Mémoires du duc de Broglie* (2 vols, Calmann-Lévy, 1938), vol. 1, pp. 326–7.
25 L. M. Case, *French Opinion on War and Diplomacy* (Harrisburg, Pennsylvania University Press, 1954).
26 A. Plessis, *The Rise and Fall of the Second Empire 1852–1870* (Cambridge University Press, 1985); T. Zeldin, *Emile Ollivier and the Liberal Empire* (Oxford, Clarendon Press, 1963).
27 F. Loliée, *Le Duc de Morny* (John Long, 1910), pp. 304–20.
28 R. Schnerb, *Rouher et le Second Empire* (Armand Colin, 1949), pp. 221–58.
29 Zeldin, *Emile Ollivier*, pp. 120–52.
30 P. Guiral, *Prévost-Paradol, 1829–1870, pensée et action d'un libéral sous le Second Empire* (Presses Universitaires de France, 1955).

through universal male suffrage, and the freedom of the press,[31] of strike action and limited trade unions had been established. In many ways France had become one of the most liberal countries of Europe. This shift from a very authoritarian regime to a quite liberal one in 1870 remains difficult to understand fully. So much depends on the personality of Napoleon III himself and so little is known of him that a lot must be left for conjecture.[32] In terms of evidence, we know that Napoleon's health and power of concentration declined sharply in the last five years of his personal regime.[33] By 1870 he was suffering considerably from bladder stone and was probably unfit to rule.[34] Beyond biographical anecdotes, this liberalisation of the regime was risky but probably good politics. Even though the regime had lost its majority in most towns, it remained nevertheless very popular in the country and France was still over 70 per cent rural. The call to the moderate Orleanist bourgeoisie of 1870 could well have been successful and would have enabled a renewal of the elite and a widened support for the Ollivier government preparing the ground for Napoleon IV. The plebiscite of 8 May 1870 supporting the reforms had been a great success, giving 67.5 per cent support to the eighteen-year-old regime. The internal reform of the Second Empire showed the strain of a period of difficult transition marked with social tensions and numerous strikes, but most of these could have been solved without the adventure of a war. In July 1870, however, there were surprisingly few people ready to oppose the war. Adolphe Thiers stood almost alone in opposing the conflict.[35]

Immediate causes of the war

In approaching a German prince for the Spanish throne, the Spanish dictator Prim revived the spectre of a continental encirclement and made possible if not probable a war on two fronts against France. As often in the diplomatic *Kriegspiel*, the nature of the danger was its potential implications rather than anything Spain could add militarily to Prussia. The kingdom of Spain had been in deep chaos since 1868 and diplomats across Europe had tried pushing one or another candidate for the throne. The King of Prussia, head of the Hohenzollern dynasty, had agreed reluctantly to his nephew's candidature. Bismarck had also pushed for this

31 I. Collins, *The Government and the Newspaper Press in France, 1814–1881* (Oxford University Press, 1959); N. Isser, *The Second Empire and the Press* (The Hague, Martinus Nijhoff, 1974); R. J. Goldstein, 'Censorship of caricature in France, 1815–1914', *French History*, 3:1 (1989) 71–107.
32 J. M. Thompson, *Louis Napoléon and the Second Empire* (Basil Blackwell, 1965).
33 R. Williams, *The Mortal Napoleon III* (Princeton University Press, 1971).
34 L. Girard, *Napoléon III* (Fayard, 1986), p. 450. Girard asserts that by June 1870, Napoléon III and Eugénie had agreed to abdicate in 1874, on the imperial prince's eighteenth birthday. K. John, *The Imperial Prince* (Putnam, 1939).
35 M. E. Connol, 'French public opinion on war with Prussia in 1870', *American Historical Review*, 31:4 (1926) 679–700.

Spanish adventure, and to the French the whole scheme looked increasingly like an unfriendly intrigue.[36] Under much French and British pressure, Leopold von Hohenzollern renounced the Spanish throne without any official intervention from the King of Prussia. At that stage of the incident the French government had won at a low cost for itself a discreet diplomatic success.

The Ollivier government had understood the matter to be a diplomatic provocation, however, and not simply a dynastic matter. The French government sought Prussian assurances that no such candidature would occur again. As the head of the dynasty King Willhelm endorsed the renunciation, but as the King of Prussia he would not make any commitments for the future. The meeting in Ems between a badly briefed ambassador Benedetti and the King bore the mark of this confusion.[37] The King, impatient with French demands, refused to answer them. Without any provocation from Bismarck the French were already on the way to war. Bismarck intervened, however, and the Ems telegram made war almost ineluctable. In diplomatic language this humiliation meant war. What it meant for the provincial Frenchman is still rather unclear. Audoin-Rouzeau signals that for most Frenchmen, otherwise occupied, the war came as a surprise and was seen as the result of a very short crisis.[38] Any analysis of the causes implied an understanding of diplomatic history and of geostrategy.[39] Many debates have arisen in France after the defeat to apportion the responsibility of this war and the subsequent defeat. The French confusion over the role of the King of Prussia in the Spanish crisis had been compounded by Bismarck's provocation and his claims to a genial masterplan.[40] The French government could not allow itself to be surrounded by enemies; it could not take the Ems telegram as it stood. It had, in fact, only the choice of losing face, thereby bringing down the government and possibly even the regime, or going to war.

The war and defeat

As military historians remind us, the causes of defeats are usually complex and combine several factors. While the early historiography greatly emphasised the military genius of Von Moltke,[41] the general superiority of German strategy, high

---

36 J. Rubio, 'La Vacance du trône d'Espagne (1868–1870) et l'équilibre européen, une révision du problème des candidatures', in P. Levillain and R. Riemenschneider (eds) *La Guerre de 1870/71 et ses conséquences* (Bonn, Bouvier Verlag, 1990), pp. 33–85.

37 É. Bavoux, *Les Causes de la guerre. Solution à la crise actuelle* (Sauton, 1871); V. Benedetti, *Ma Mission en Prusse* (Plon, 1871).

38 Audoin-Rouzeau, *1870, la France dans la guerre*, pp. 19–36.

39 J. Claretie, *Paris assiégé, tableaux et souvenirs* (Alphonse Lemerre, 1871), pp. 25–6.

40 J. Bainville, *Bismarck et la France* (Nouvelle Librairie Nationale, 1911).

41 D. Hughes, *Moltke and the Art of War* (Noveto, Periodic Press, 1993); H. Karl von Moltke, *La Correspondance militaire du Maréchal de Moltke, guerre de 1870–71* (5 vols, Henri Charles Lavauzelle, 1899–1901).

command and equipment (notably their breech-loaded Krupp guns),[42] the more recent historiography scrutinises the minutiae of both armies and points to more structural deficiencies.[43] From this detailed investigation even the Prussian army's golden aura comes out a little tarnished.

The divisions between the various French armies – colonial, guardsmen, metropolitan regiments – were important. The most recent war experience had been earned fighting guerrillas either in Mexico or in North Africa. Officers were often promoted in these small wars and emphasised the values most useful in this context: courage, a talent for improvisation and initiative. All these positive values could in turn become negative against a more organised opponent and be read as carelessness, improvidence, disobedience and self-sacrificing stupidity. One of the most popular French officers in 1870, Marshall Bazaine, had thus made it to the top from the ranks and showed great political awareness more than a masterly control of a large French army.

The French army was officially a conscript army, but the practice of selective conscription based on a lottery and on a long period of service meant that the rich could buy a substitute and contribute to the creation of an older professional army which lacked reserves and resources to renew itself. Marshall Niel's military reforms of 1868 building on the Prussian *Landwehr*, a trained reserve territorial army, had yet to bear their fruit in 1870. Niel's successor, Leboeuf, had not obtained the credits necessary for the full-scale implementation of the reform and was reluctant to waste money in a scheme few professional officers trusted and many parliamentarians rejected as wasteful and undemocratic.[44] The Garde Mobile, a territorial reserve composed of those who avoided the real military service, only existed on paper in 1870 for the most part. In many ways the French army was in the middle of important reforms in July 1870, but remained closer to the army of 1854 than to any new model army. On the other hand the argument that the French were less well equipped than the Prussians seems quite fallacious. The French war rifle, the Chassepot, was probably much superior to the Prussian needle gun, the Dreyse. Napoleon had also funded privately some secret military developments like a breech-loaded bullet gun, the mitrailleuse. The French muzzle-loaded artillery was certainly inferior to the Krupp guns but could not be dismissed off-hand and the difference between the two artilleries does not explain the crushing defeats of

---

42 Général de Woyde (sic), *Causes des succès et des revers dans la guerre de 1870* (3 vols, R. Chapelot, 1899–1900).
43 Holmes, *Road to Sedan*, pp. 73–86, and L. Sukstorf, *Die Problematik der Logistik im deutschen Heer während des deutsch-französischen Krieges 1870/71* (Frankfurt am Main, Peter Lang, 1994), pp. 139–227.
44 C. Moussy, *Tableau des finances de la France, années 1869 et 1869 à 1874, avec la situation de la France à l'époque de la guerre 1870–71* (Lessertisseux, 1874).

August 1870.⁴⁵ With a million modern rifles, a regular army reckoned at nearly 500,000 men with a nominal reserve of 420,000, the French stood a reasonable chance on paper in July 1870.

As Michael Howard noted, the French anticipation of a rapid offensive depended on the ability to mobilise and concentrate troops efficiently. These two phases of war preparation were confused in the French plans: mobilised soldiers arrived in disorder at the camps where the concentration took place. Regiments went to the camps and waited there for the mobilised soldiers to arrive. The soldiers had to travel to the depot, be equipped and then be sent to their regiments, which had often moved in the meanwhile. The railway system was also disorganised and not fully under military control.⁴⁶ Supposedly time-saving measures were bungled and left enough time for the Germans to mobilise and concentrate their troops in an orderly manner.⁴⁷

Without the advantage of surprise the offensive chances of the French were slim and the French command started the war with resolutely defensive plans. A skirmish attack on Saarbrücken, hailed as a great victory, was thus the only 'battle' fought on German ground. In spite of the great amount of media coverage this little incident received, the French high command, a loose structure around Marshal MacMahon and the Emperor, had already renounced any significant offensive plan. On 4 August, a few days after the bombing of Saarbrücken, the French suffered their first defeat on French soil at Wissembourg. From this battle one defeat followed another. The French army split in two and lost any cohesion, half the army retreating with Marshal Bazaine towards Metz while the rest retreated with MacMahon and the Emperor. On 10 August the siege of Strasburg began. The Palikao conservative government in Paris decided on mass mobilisation of all men aged 25 to 35 the same day. By 20 August General Trochu arrived in Paris to prepare the potential siege and secure the government. On 21 August the siege of Metz, where Bazaine's army had retreated, began. The Emperor stayed with MacMahon and his army, which slowly moved north in the direction of Sedan. Isolated, exhausted, encircled in Sedan, the French were defeated. Sedan demonstrated the superiority of German artillery and good tactics. On 2 September, Napoleon surrendered to Willhelm in a futile chivalric gesture which did nothing to stop the

---

45 L. Rousset, *Histoire générale de la guerre franco-allemande 1870–1871* (7 vols, La Librairie Illustrée, 1895–96), vol. 6, pp. 315–16.

46 A *commission des chemins de fer* had been planned in the Niel military reform but neglected after the death of the minister. The full account can be found in two quite different accounts: A. A. Ernouf, *Histoire des chemins de fer français pendant la guerre franco-prussienne* (Librairie Générale, 1874) and F. Jacqmin, *Les Chemins de fer pendant la guerre de 1870–1871* (Hachette, 1872). Jacqmin blamed the French army for its technical inefficiency and its systematic use of trains (p. 186) while Ernouf accuses the French government of incompetence and cowardice (pp. 279–84). Also A. P. Delambre, *Étude sur les chemins de fer au point de vue militaire* (Amyot, 1874).

47 J. V. Lemoyne, *La Mobilisation* (Berger Levrault, 1872).

war. It took another two days for the news to travel to Paris, and for the imperial regime to be toppled without violence on 4 September.

The month of August had been exhausting militarily for both armies and had cost more to the German armies than the rest of the war would. The fortified positions of the east and the experienced soldiers had been difficult to break. Nonetheless, by 4 September the war was objectively over. The French had no professional army left to fight, most of the officers were either in captivity or in Metz, the fortresses of the east were unable to survive longer than a few months, and, considering the great mobility of the German armies, using the famous Uhlans to cover disproportionately large areas, it was only a matter of days before Paris became besieged within its 1846 fortifications.[48]

A few days after the revolution, the new power was already challenged by the Commune in Lyons, which claimed to have the same legitimacy and possibly even equal sovereignty with the government of Paris.[49] The south of France also showed some federalist inclinations and the *ligue du Midi* became the expression of a left-wing undermining the Paris government.[50]

The new Republic and the National Defence government composed of Parisian representatives under the direction of General Trochu had to act promptly.[51] The republican option was the only one which could gather public support within Paris,[52] which was a link with the pre-imperial past and which bore the promises of a victorious war against invading nations.[53] Nonetheless, as contemporary observers noted, there was an undoubted political risk for the republicans, still a minority in France, in any armistice or in a war short of a victory.[54] The army in Paris numbered around 100,000 *mobiles*, 200,000 *gardes nationaux sédentaires*, untrained and unequipped, and around 100,000 policemen, *gendarmes* and fully trained soldiers. It was protected by a network of strong forts around the perimeter of the city and by an extensive wall. Paris had some food stored, perhaps enough for two months, and the morale after the revolution was high. The revolutionary legend of the improvised armies of 1792 made it possible for the unelected government to claim the historical legacy of 1789[55] and

---

48 Therefore outdated for siege warfare. E. Terrot, *Paris et ses fortifications* (Germer Baillière, 1880).
49 J. Guetton, *Six mois de drapeau rouge à Lyon* (P. N. Josserand, 1871).
50 A. V. Roche, *Provençal Regionalism: A Study of the Movement in the Revue Félibréenne, Le Feu and Other Reviews of Southern France* (Evanston, Northwestern University Press, 1954), p. 62; L. M. Greenberg, *Sisters of Liberty: Marseille, Lyon, Paris and the Reaction to a Centralized State, 1868–1871* (Cambridge, Mass., Harvard University Press, 1971), p. 48.
51 P. A. Bertocci, *Jules Simon* (Columbia, University of Missouri Press, 1978).
52 J. Chastenet, *L'Enfance de la Troisième, 1870–1877* (Hachette, 1952), p. 16.
53 P. M. Pilbeam, *Republicanism in Nineteenth-Century France, 1814–1871* (Macmillan, 1995).
54 L. Dupont, *Tours et Bordeaux, souvenirs de la république à outrance* (Dentu, 1871), p. 307.
55 F. Furet, *La Gauche et la révolution au milieu du dix-neuvième siècle* (Hachette, 1986) and *La Révolution 1770–1880* (2 vols, Hachette, 1988).

hope for another Valmy victory.[56] The example of 1792 also revived the memory of revolutionary institutions such as the Commune of Paris.[57] This enthusiasm for war was not universally shared in the provinces, however. In Laon, for instance, the civilian populations, fearing German reprisals and massacres, convinced the commanding officer to abandon the city rather than defend it.[58] The rumour of the massacre of the village of Bazeilles and of pillaging after some Alsatian battles had spread across France, and the sight of a few Uhlans was often enough for a village or even a town to surrender without fighting.[59] Conversely the Germans had suffered from some instances of guerrilla warfare by *francs-tireurs* (registered but irregular troops) and had become very wary of civilians bearing arms against them.[60]

To spread the revolutionary message to the more cautious provinces, the traditional ground of Bonapartism, the government decided to stay in Paris but to send a delegation to Tours, sheltered to the west from the invading armies and benefiting from a good network of communication with the south and west of France.[61] The decision to stay in Paris was logical in many ways: the government members were for the most part representatives of the capital; moreover the 4 September riot was the only form of legitimacy it had. This decision posed a number of problems, however, and had a number of strategic implications: the war was now centred on Paris. If Paris fell the government fell too, like Napoleon III at Sedan. Moreover, radical public opinion, more prevalent in Paris, Marseilles and Lyons, was on the whole not representative of France. The 4 September revolutionaries were aware of this discrepancy and of the need to appease army officers. Their government was thus a moderate coalition led by a devout Catholic career officer with notorious Orleanist sympathies. Such a timid government was bound

---

56 R. D. Challener, *French Theory of the Nation in Arms, 1866–1939* (New York, Columbia University Press, 1965); E. Hublot, *Valmy ou la défense de la nation par les armes* (Fondation pour les Études de la Défense Nationale, 1987); J. Favre, *Le Gouvernement de la Défense Nationale du 30 juin au 31 octobre 1870* (Plon, 1871), pp. 92–6; J.-P. Penin, *Valmy, première victoire de la nation* (Groucher, 1989).
57 Claretie, *Paris assiégé*, pp. 79–84.
58 G. Dupont, *L'Explosion de la citadelle de Laon* (Caen, Le Blanc Hardel, 1877).
59 P. A. Conte, *Le Ulhan et le raid* (E. Dentu, 1871).
60 The registration of *francs-tireurs* was always reluctant and politically motivated. They imposed themselves on the French government but were never fully recognised by the Germans. AN, F9/1348; VdP, VD6/1529. I. P. Troinin, 'Questions of guerilla warfare in the laws of war', *American Journal of International Law*, 11 (1946) 534–62. Capitaine Sansas, *Première compagnie des francs-tireurs de Tours* (Tours, Grassien, 1873); ADHV, 2 R 177, reports on the Cies de francs-tireurs 'les Amis de Paris' and the 'Francs-Tireurs de la Haute-Vienne'; L. Armagnac, *Étapes d'un franc-tireur parisien de Paris à Sedan* (Hachette, 1889).
61 *Rapport sur les actes de la délégation du gouvernement de la Défense Nationale à Tours et à Bordeaux* (Versailles, Le Cerf, 1876); *Bulletin officiel du ministère de l'intérieur, délégation de Tours et de Bordeaux* (Poitiers, A. Dupré, 1871). For a very negative assessment see Dupont, *Tours et Bordeaux*.

to be viewed with equal suspicion by the more radical political fringes of Paris and provincial conservatives.

The clubs of Paris found an echo in the Garde Nationale republican traditions and democratic practices. Thanks to the re-establishment of the election of Garde Nationale officers, extended to the Garde Mobile on 17 September, the Paris army became very closely aligned to the movements of public opinion. The committees of surveillance established very early on during the siege showed how the National Defence government remained hostage to Parisian public opinion.[62]

As soon as the siege of Paris began (19 September), all military efforts were focused on the liberation of the capital. For armchair strategists and the numerous tacticians who trained on the maps of the war until 1914,[63] the solution was elsewhere and the French stood a better chance of achieving a draw by outflanking the German armies and cutting them off from their distant bases, thus severing their stretched supply lines.[64] The political obsession with Paris meant that, in spite of Bourbaki's belated effort at threatening German bases in the midst of winter, French strategy could not ignore the plight of the capital city.[65] Help had to come from the provinces and, combined with the large Parisian army, spearhead the counter-offensive against Germany. After 20 September the *guerre à outrance* was declared. *Guerre à outrance* has subtle meanings that go beyond the literal meaning of 'war to the last'. *Outrance* is normally used in a pejorative manner, meaning excess, which contradicts bourgeois values and provincial notions of decency.

Even in the choice of words, the National Defence government made provocative gestures to a large part of the population. Gambetta, who fled Paris in a balloon and joined the Tours delegation, was not the sort of leader a lot of the provincial notables dreamed of. After 9 October, the republican dictator had virtually unlimited powers to reorganise provincial armies and provide them with the

---

62 J. Dantry and L. Scheler, *Le Comité central des vingts arrondissements de Paris, septembre 1870 – mai 1871, d'après les papiers inédits de Constant Martin et les sources imprimées* (Éditions Sociales, 1960).
63 The study of the war was an integral part of *école de guerre* and specialised schools training in its most minute details, see for instance ASSAT, box 62/18, 'Une Étude du siège de Belfort', école du train de Versailles, 1911. A. von Boguslawski, *Tactical Deductions from the War of 1870–1871* (Tyndall and Co., 1872); idem, *Considérations générales sur la manière de diriger les troupes* (C. Tanera, 1873); idem, *Physionomie du combat d'infanterie pendant la guerre de 1870–1871* (C. Tanera, 1872); H. Brackenbury, *Les Maréchaux de France* (Lachaud, 1872); T. Fix, *Souvenirs d'un officier d'état-major* (2 vols, F. Juven, 1898); J. L. Lewal, *Études de guerre* (Jean Dumaine, 1873) and *La Réforme de l'armée* (Jean Dumaine, 1871).
64 Rousset, *Histoire générale de la guerre*, vol. 6, pp. 325–32.
65 L. d'Eichthal, *Le Général Bourbaki* (Plon, 1885). Bourbaki's mission was primarily to relieve the Belfort garrison and threaten the Prussian lines in Alsace.

necessary equipment.[66] He had only made his name in the Delescluze trial following a subscription to erect a statue of anti-Bonapartist deputy Baudin, killed in 1851.[67] His military and administrative experience was limited in the extreme, and neither Gambetta nor Freycinet had ever served in any capacity.[68] Both Gambetta and Freycinet compensated for their lack of experience with extraordinary activity, inventiveness and enthusiasm.[69] Under Gambetta's high command the French managed to create several armies totalling up to 600,000 men from very little available organised troops. The main effort was in creating the Armées de la Loire to the south of Paris. After some initial victories they were eventually blocked near Orléans and never managed to break the siege of Paris. The Armée du Nord initially led by Bourbaki and then Faidherbe was smaller and its only role was to limit the Germans northern expansion.[70] To the south-east, controlling the Rhone valley and Lyons, the Garibaldi army of international volunteers coming to the rescue of the French Republic played a more controversial role in the defence of Dijon and the subsequent battle near Beaunes in Burgundy.[71]

Two wars were fought, each of which had a different chronology and very different parameters: a siege war and a war of movement. The siege war started with the siege of Strasburg (10 August – 28 September), carried on with the siege of Metz (21 August – 28 October), that of Paris (19 September – 28 January 1871) and at the signing of the armistice, Belfort, besieged since November, was still

---

66 J. P. T. Bury, *Gambetta and the National Defence: A Republican Dictatorship in France* (Longmans, 1936), p. 273. The theme of a 'republican dictator' originally had mostly negative connotations: H. R. Blandeau, *La Dictature de Gambetta* (Amyot, 1871); E. Béraud, *Gambetta dictateur* (Poitiers, H. Oudin, 1881), p. 5; for a defence of Gambetta's action: A. Glais-Bizoin, *Dictature de cinq mois* (Dentu, 1873).
67 J. P. T. Bury, *Gambetta and the Making of the Third Republic* (Longman, 1973), p. 4.
68 E. Andréoli, *Le Gouvernement du 4 septembre et la Commune* (A. Bocquet, 1871); A. Wachter, *La Guerre de 1870–71, histoire politique et militaire* (E. Lachaud, 1873), pp. 545–7.
69 Baron von der Goltz, *Gambetta et ses armées* (Sandoz and Fischbacher, 1877), pp. 12, 26, 342. This German author stressed the quality of the work done. Also Col. Lonsdale Hale, *The 'People's War' in France 1870–1871* (Hugh Rees, 1904), pp. 1–32. Recent French authors such as Roth, *Guerre de 1870*, pp. 411–51, give a more pessimistic account of his action.
70 General Faidherbe, *Campagne de l'armée du Nord* (E. Dentu, 1871); *Note supplémentaire adressée à la commission d'enquête du 4 septembre sur les opérations de l'armée du Nord* (E. Leroux, 1873); SHAT Lf 1–9, correspondence of the Army of the North.
71 R. Middleton, *Garibaldi, ses opérations à l'armée des Vosges* (Garnier Frères, 1872), pp. 249–77. L. P. de Ségur, *Les Marchés de la guerre à Lyon et à l'armée de Garibaldi* (H. Plon, 1873). Those two texts attacked Garibaldian troops for their lack of discipline and for the unscrupulous requisitions they made. This denunciation of Garibaldi does not undermine the originality of a foreign volunteer movement in a war like this one, nor their relative effectiveness at defending Dijon and then Lyons. R. Garibaldi, *Souvenirs de la campagne de France 1870–71* (Nice, La Semaine Niçoise, 1899), pp. 118–19; P. A. Darmoy, *Les Trois Batailles de Dijon* (Librairie Militaire Dubois, 1894), pp. 370–3; SHAT Lg 1, correspondence of the Vosges Army.

standing.[72] Besides these fortresses, a significant number of smaller places slowed down the German invasion.[73] Strasburg played a very important role in stopping a large army quite early in the war,[74] and also in being the first predominantly civilian city to be bombarded into submission.[75]

The siege of Metz played a much more damaging political role. In Metz Marshall Bazaine, perhaps wishing to play a political role after the defeat, surrendered the largest remaining French army without a real fight.[76] This intrigue-prone character was subsequently tried and sentenced to death, only to escape soon after his sentence had been reduced.[77] The news of his surrender, which reached Paris on 30 October, undermined considerably the republican regime and determined the insurrection of 31 October, during which north Parisian *gardes nationaux* attempted to proclaim the Commune.[78] The loss of Metz also enabled large German armies to move west to cover Paris against the attacks of the Loire armies.

The armies besieging Paris were able to benefit from the French disorganisation to settle down and entrench themselves. At the end of November their position was strengthened by the arrival of long-range breech-loaded guns. The French military position in Paris was paradoxical as the mass of troops at the disposal of Trochu, the general commanding the city and chief of government, would have made it a formidable army were it not for its variable quality. The forts were staffed with soldiers, marines and trained *mobiles*. The walls were divided into nine sectors and were staffed with *mobiles* and *gardes nationaux*. Taking into account the number of soldiers, their increasingly large artillery and the quality of the fortifications, the siege situation was solid for the French but did not really allow for any counter-offensive.[79] Trochu made some efforts in that direction: for instance, he reorganised the army on 6 November and attempted to turn more of the reserve Garde Nationale into operative units. Another reform on 14 December created thirty regiments.[80] Historians are divided about the worth of the troops within Paris. Early defeats had created the signs of panic and lack of discipline,

---

72 Belfort acquired great symbolic importance which explains why it was never assimilated to Alsace again or the presence of the square Denfert-Rochereau adorned with the Belfort Lion in Paris. L. Belin, *Le Siège de Belfort* (Paris and Nancy, Berger Levrault, 1871).
73 *Rapports du conseil d'enquête sur les capitulations des places fortes* (Librairie Centrale, 1872).
74 H. E. Beaunis, *Impressions de campagne, 1870–1871, siège de Strasbourg, campagne de la Loire, campagne de l'Est* (Félix Alcan and Berger Levrault et Cie, 1887).
75 G. Fischbach, *Guerre de 1870. Le Siège et le bombardement de Strasbourg* (Cherbuliez, 1871); J. Flach, *Strasbourg après le bombardement* (Strasburg, Imprimerie de Fischbach, 1873).
76 E. Bapst, *Le Siège de Metz en 1870* (Lahure, 1926), pp. 364–415.
77 *Extrait des causes célèbres de tous les peuples, le maréchal Bazaine, relation complète* (Lebrun, 1874), vols 7 and 8, esp. vol. 8, pp. 155–71, 173.
78 M. Dommanget, *Hommes et choses de la Commune* (Marseille, Éditions des amis de la coopérative des amis de l'école émancipée, n.d., 1936?), pp. 2–11.
79 A. A. Ducrot, *La Défense de Paris (1870–1871)* (4 vols, E. Dentu, 1875).
80 SHAT, Li 56, historical account of the second army (6/11/1870 to 20/02/1871).

but later attacks on the Marne (28 November – 3 December) and at le Bourget in January exemplified the lack of preparation and the limited skill of French tacticians and gave credence to those who accused the commanding officers of not trying hard enough. The cold of January, malnutrition and diseases certainly weakened French soldiers, but the low morale of officers and generals added to their miseries. In fact officers' views on the situation were probably at an all time low precisely when the Prussian army officers feared them most. The diary of the Prussian Crown Prince illustrates how weary of the siege the besiegers were by December and January.[81] The signs of a diplomatic reversal of fortune were also on the wall: the shelling of Paris in January was a sign of impatience and undermined the German cause abroad.[82] As the two forces dug themselves into almost total immobility and a war of shelling and short-lived raids, there was another war happening outside.

Reconstructing the path of the army in the war of movement is rather difficult but the general pattern is one of organisation, defeat and reorganisation. The armies organised by Gambetta lacked experience and equipment. There are a number of examples of shoes with cardboard soles and of unusable weapons, but many incidents were later blown out of proportion. During the conflict, the Tours delegation managed large sums to equip the mass of conscripts and volunteers who joined the new republican armies. The war effort was by no means limited to the republicans. As Claretie noted in his diary, the Bretons *mobiles* in Paris, many of them unable to understand or speak French, symbolised the anti-revolutionary areas of France, the France of counter-revolutionary Chouans and devout Catholicism.[83] The *zouaves pontificaux*, previously used to defend the Pope's territories, represented the most ultramontane trend in Catholicism and followed Chouan names like Cathelieau or Charette with their 'Sacred Heart of Jesus' flag.[84] Trochu himself was Breton and Catholic.[85] In many areas, the emphatic calls to war issued by Freycinet and Gambetta echoed not only Danton but also Bonaparte. The ability to organise armies came from the creation of instruction camps, the use of depots, separate mobilisation and concentration of troops, and a good dosage of patriotism.

81 A. R. Allinson (ed.), *The War Diary of the Emperor Frederick III, 1870–1871* (Westport, Greenwood Press, 1971), p. 240.
82 H. de Sarrepont, *Le Bombardement de Paris par les Prussiens en janvier 1871* (Firmin Didot Frères, 1872).
83 Claretie, *Paris assiégé*, pp. 190–3. On Catholics in Brittany see C. Ford, *Creating the Nation in Provincial France: Religion and Political Identity* (Princeton University Press, 1993).
84 Colonel D'Albiousse, *Le Drapeau du Sacré-Coeur* (Rennes, Hauvespre, 1873); Abbé J. S. Allard, *Les Zouaves pontificaux* (Hugny, 1880); H. Arsac, *Les Mercenaires ou les zouaves pontificaux en France* (Reims, Imprimerie Coopérative, 1873); R. A. Jones, 'Anxiety, identity and the displacement of violence during the année terrible', *French Historical Studies*, 21:1 (1998) 55–76.
85 Although Catholic, Trochu did not carry with him the full weight of the Catholic political majority. L. Veuillot, *Paris pendant les deux sièges* (2 vols, Librairie de Victor Palmé, 1871), vol. 1, pp. 280–1.

The defeats were often balanced by small victories, if not in the open field, at least in a war of ambush and in the growing unease of the occupying armies. The initial victory over Orléans was followed by a series of defeats and Chanzy then did his best to avoid direct confrontations with von der Thann's armies.[86] In the south, the fight for Dijon eventually ended in stalemate, a result achieved by Garibaldian troops. In fairness the south had never been a real objective of the Prussian armies and General Werder only intended to cover the flank of the invading armies. Lyons was never occupied.[87] The armies of the north lost a number of smaller battles and Normandy was largely occupied, but Amiens remained contested and the German advance halted. A look at a map on 7 November, when the French refused the conditions for an armistice which would have resulted in the loss of Alsace-Lorraine, reveals the situation: the German armies were present in twenty-two departments, their front was nearly 850km long but only 80km wide. Besides, ten fortresses were still held in their rearguard. From a less Paris-centred point of view than that of the 4 September government, this meant that between two-thirds and three-quarters of the territory were free from the invasion. The war could still, if not be won by the French, at least end in a stalemate. The two conflicts, however, the mobile and the immobile, had different political weight. At the end of January the government in Paris had claimed once again, 'Suffer and die if needed, but win we must! *Vive la République!*', before losing again a vain battle on the outskirts of Paris.[88] As a consequence, Paris had been shaken by another attempted coup on 22 January. With the Parisian population freezing and starving, the option of surrendering became increasingly tempting. The armistice of the 28th ended the siege war at least temporarily but excluded from its terms the east of France. The government attempted to leave the door open to a potential victory. In fact Bourbaki's army was defeated and had to retreat in the snow to Switzerland in early February.

A requirement of the armistice was to re-establish a legitimate government empowered to carry on the war or negotiate peace. In reality the intention behind the armistice was to find a rapid peace settlement. Then as now there were two fundamentally opposed schools of historical analysis: one arguing that the war was lost virtually from the start, and one which argued with Gambetta that it was not. The analysis made after the armistice about the possibilities of resuming the conflict put in evidence the onerous and enormous war effort made in so few

---

86 M. de la Combe, *Souvenirs de l'invasion, l'occupation d'Orléans* (Orléans, Douniol, 1871); L.-J. Charpignon, *Souvenirs de l'occupation* (Orléans, Herluison, 1872); A. E. Chanzy, *L'Armée de la Loire* (Gautier, 1895); SHAT, Le 19, Chanzy reports, more sceptical: R. M., *Mémoires sur l'armée de Chanzy* (E. Dentu, 1871).
87 L. Marchant (trans.) *La Bourgogne pendant la guerre et l'occupation allemande (1870–1871)* (Dijon, Marchand & Maniere-loquin, 1875), pp. 231–3.
88 P. Chasteau (ed.), *Recueil des dépêches françaises officielles* (3 vols, A. Lacroix, 1871), vol. 2, p. 60.

months and the unwillingness of the political elite to fight this war. The danger identified by people like Thiers and the old Orleanist right, and verified in two unsuccessful attempts of October and January, was that a more radical revolution might come out of the war and lead to a repetition of the excess of 1793 and the Terror.

They had good reasons to be worried. The government, a prisoner in Paris of a situation of its own making, was under constant threat from the organised extreme left. The situation in the provinces had been largely defused by Gambetta's negotiation but the crisis in Paris was more intractable.

Politics and the Commune

The historiographical debates about the Commune of Paris have aged singularly over the last twenty-five years and the decline of the Communist historical school has reduced much of the relevance of those controversies.[89] To summarise them in few words, the Commune has been diversely understood either as the first 'modern', socialist, revolutionary movement, inspired if not led by members of the Internationale; as the last artisan-led French revolution; or more syncretically, as a composite of the above two.[90] The work of Jacques Rougerie convincingly makes the latter point clear.[91] The Commune of Paris had old roots which linked it with the June days of 1848, the riots of 1832 and the episodes of the French Revolution, especially those of the year 1793.[92] It also had more immediate causes in the perceived deficiencies and duplicity of the government, which launched murderous battles a week before it negotiated peace on the terms rejected a couple of months before. Combining political naiveté with inefficiency, the French government negotiated an opt-out clause for the disarmament of the Garde Nationale in Paris after the surrender. The defeat was badly received by the Parisian population, who had endured terrible sufferings and whose lot did not improve overnight at the end of the war. Moreover the hastily organised election of 8 February 1871 returned a true blue *chambre introuvable,* decidedly reactionary and pacifist. The outcome of this election was obvious from the opening

---

[89] H. Lefebvre, *La Proclamation de la Commune* (Gallimard, 1971); V. I. Lénine, *La Commune de Paris* (François Maspéro, 1971).

[90] E. Schulkind (ed.), *The Paris Commune of 1871: The Point of View of the Left* (Jonathan Cape, 1972) and 'Socialist women in the 1871 Paris Commune', *Past and Present,* 106 (1985) 124–63.

[91] J. Rougerie, *La Commune: 1871* (Presses Universitaires de France, 1988); *Procès des Communards* (Julliard, 1964); Serman, *La Commune de Paris (1871)* confirm his theory. The Commune did contain a number of socialists, anarchists etc. but the overall balance of its action does not enable a clear labelling.

[92] A. Dalotel, A. Faure and J.-C. Freiermuth also made the point that a specific urban revolutionary culture was maturing in the last ten years of the Second Empire. *Aux origines de la Commune : le mouvement des réunions publiques à Paris, 1868–1870* (François Maspero, 1980).

eight days later when the new Assemblée Nationale sat in the theatre of Bordeaux. All the Parisian representatives were isolated; the Alsacian deputies resigned; Garibaldi, elected in several constituencies, was not allowed to sit; Victor Hugo resigned; Gambetta, exhausted, withdrew from political life. The leadership of 4 September was either set aside or compromised in the peace negotiation. The more moderate members of the emergency government joined forces with Adolphe Thiers.[93]

Adolphe Thiers, previously Orleanist Prime Minister and the strong man of the centre-right opposition to the Empire, became *chef de l'éxécutif*, a title which bundled the roles of head of state and government. His major political project was to restore at least the reactionary republic of 1849, and perhaps even the Orléans dynasty.[94] The early acts of his government – the dissolution of the Garde Nationale, the end of the moratorium on rents and debts, the dismantling of the Loire and Northern armies – were at best clumsy, if not provocative. The armistice conditions also included a German parade and a symbolic occupation of a small part of Paris. This demonstration of power contributed to an increase in the unrest in Paris. The last straw leading to a general breaking up between the elected government and Paris came with the attempt at evacuating the Parisian guns from Montmartre. Those had been made during the siege and had become a symbol of municipal pride and of Parisian independence. At dawn on 18 March 1871, the soldiers sent to take them away were swiftly surrounded and chose to lift their rifle butts in the air as symbols of mutiny. Two generals, Lecomte who had led them and Clément Thomas who was passing by, were shot. Thomas was well known for his part in the massacres of June 1848.[95]

The government subsequently chose to withdraw from Paris and decided on a controlled civil war, rejecting off-hand the many conciliatory attempts at a negotiation.[96] The provincial communalist movements which Jeanne Gaillard and Louis Greenberg have rescued from oblivion since 1971, and which often preexisted the Paris Commune, did not present the same armed resistance and were rapidly repressed.[97]

93 Bertocci, *Jules Simon*, pp. 151–80.
94 F. M. Atkinson (ed.), *Memoirs of M. Thiers, 1870–1873* (George Allen, 1915), p. 117; J. P. T. Bury and R. P. Tombs, *Thiers 1797–1877* (Allen & Unwin, 1986), pp. 192–210; G. Bouniols (ed.), *Thiers au pouvoir, texte de ses lettres, annoté et commenté* (Delagrave, 1921), pp. 97–100; M. d'Aiguy, *Quel gouvernement la France se donnera-t-elle?* (Lyons and Paris, Félix Girard, 1871).
95 M. Delpit, *Rapport fait au nom de la commission d'enquête ... [sur] les causes de l'insurrection du 18 mars* (3 vols, Versailles, Le Cerf, 1872), vol. 1, pp. 407–9, vol. 2 (déposition de M. Choppin), pp. 105–23.
96 P. G. Nord, 'The party of conciliation and the Paris Commune', *French Historical Studies*, 15:1 (1987) 1–35; C. Yriarte, *Les Prussiens à Paris et le 18 Mars* (Henri Plon, 1871), pp. 144–5.
97 J. Gaillard, *Communes de Province, Commune de Paris 1870–1871* (Flammarion, 1971); Greenberg, *Sisters of Liberty*; M. César, *La Commune de Narbonne* (Perpignan, Presses Universitaires de Perpignan, 1996); J. Girault, *La Commune et Bordeaux (1870–1871)* (Éditions Sociales, 1971).

As Charles Rihs has noted a long time ago,[98] the Commune movement was deeply divided between factions:[99] Proudhonists, international socialists, and a conglomerate of Blanquists and Jacobin revolutionaries.[100] The dominant faction by all accounts was the Jacobin–Blanquist group, whose ideology was woolliest and whose action was paralysed by the lack of serious revolutionary leadership.[101] Their 'natural' leader and theoretician, Auguste Blanqui, was held in prison by the Versailles government.[102]

As will be seen later in this book, the *arrondissement* structure of Paris also made for fractionated policies negotiated at the local level, so that the federalist tendency of the Commune was manifested first within itself.[103] In spite of legitimate if poorly attended elections, the Commune was never recognised by any authorities, either German or foreign. Another paradox was that while the Commune pleaded originally the *guerre à outrance*, it later negotiated the neutrality of the German armies still besieging Paris. The political structure constantly shifted and was never really stable over the mere seventy-six days of the insurrection.

As Robert Tombs remarked, the war against Paris was led with a lot of care and caution by Thiers's government.[104] Contacts between regular army and Communards were rightly deemed dangerous and the war of extermination led by the reconstituted French army staffed mainly by ex-prisoners of war was both very violent and marked by a terrorism aimed at the Communards as well as at the rank of the army itself.[105] The military structure of the Commune, in spite of the desperate efforts of a handful regular officers like Rossel, could not match the regular army in the open or even in urban warfare.[106] When the regular army felt confident enough to invade Paris, the multiple units of *francs-tireurs* groups, female militias

---

98   C. Rihs, *La Commune de Paris, 1871* (Seuil, reprint, 1973). Rihs made perhaps more sense from the confusion of the Commune than was perceptible in 1871.

99   B. Noël, *Dictionnaire de la Commune* (Fernand Hozon, 1971).

100 One of the dominant leaders of the Jacobin faction, fed on historical traditions and readings of Robespierre and Saint Just, was Charles Delescluze (1809–71). M. Dessol, *Un Révolutionnaire jacobin: Charles Delescluze* (Marcel Rivière et Cie, 1952).

101 P. H. Hutton, *The Cult of the Revolutionary Tradition,1864–1893: The Blanquists in French Politics, 1864–1893* (Berkeley, University of California Press, 1981), pp. 59–99. Hutton points out the diversity and confusion of political attitudes within the Blanquist movement itself, and rightly questions the validity of 'party' labels when discussing the Paris Commune. Blanquists were probably more inspired by the Hébert faction of the French Revolution than by the more mainstream Jacobin tradition.

102 M. Dommanget, *Auguste Banqui au début de la Troisième République (1871–1880)* (Moraton, 1973).

103 R. Tombs, 'Prudent rebels: the second arrondissement during the Paris Commune of 1871', *French History*, 5:4 (1991) 393–413.

104 R. Tombs, *The War Against Paris, 1871* (Cambridge University Press, 1981), pp. 94–108.

105 G. Bourgin, 'Une Entente franco-allemande : Bismarck, Thiers, Jules Favre et la répression de la Commune de Paris', *International Review of Social History*, 1 (1956) 41–53.

106 P. Kessel (ed.), *Gustave Paul Cluseret, la Commune et la question militaire* (Union Générale d'Éditions, 1971).

and Garde Nationale brigades were quickly reduced to a handful of strongholds which they defended until the last days of May. In the course of the invasion of Paris, the army committed a number of unparalleled atrocities. On the Commune side, a number of hostages, including the Archbishop of Paris, were suddenly executed. A large portion of the middle-class population were horrified by these excesses but supported governmental action.[107] Communard arson, dense shelling and the hazards of street warfare led to a number of fires which devastated the Tuileries Palace, the rue de Rivoli, the Chancellerie, the Préfecture de Police, the Hôtel de Ville and other important buildings. These fires led to the myth of the *pétroleuses*,[108] an incendiary militia of sexually ambiguous women who were blamed for planning and spreading the disaster throughout the city.[109] The Bloody Week led to another of those impossible historical calculations of massacre victims. Historians differ on the numbers of victims; estimates vary between 10,000 and 35,000.[110] The lower estimate now seems far too moderate. It perhaps matters less that the French killed so many of their own nationals, than the fact that Thiers agreed to or even intended this purge to be the one that would cure Paris of revolution by literally exterminating the class held responsible for previous agitation.[111] Robert Tombs makes the point that this systematic repression signalled the emergence of an age of rationalised political violence.[112] In this cynical massacre, Thiers was most successful: the Third Republic which eventually emerged from this crisis long bore the infamous mark of the 1870 defeat and the 1871 victory but never had to face similar insurrections again.[113]

Conclusion

One of the most important aspects of this briefly sketched chronology is the emotional roller-coaster into which, after an initial crushing defeat, the Republic dragged if not the whole of France at least most of Paris. So much hope was invested in the Republic and its offspring, the Commune, that the double defeat

---

107 H. Cochin, 'Impressions d'un bourgeois de Paris pendant le siège et la Commune, *Revue des Deux Mondes* (15/08/1916) 846–74.
108 É. Thomas, *Les Pétroleuses* (Gallimard, 1963); and *Louise Michel ou la vélléda de l'anarchie* (Gallimard, 1971); G. Gullickson, *Unruly Women of Paris: Images of the Commune* (Ithaca, Cornell University Press, 1996).
109 P. Lidsky, *Les Écrivains contre la Commune* (François Maspéro, 1982); P. Cogny, 'Le Discours de Zola sur la Commune: étude d'un problème de réception', *Cahiers Naturalistes*, 54 (1980) 17–24.
110 Tombs, *War Against Paris*, pp. 190–4. One has to add 5,000 deported prisoners sent to New Caledonia. S. Clair (ed.), L. Redon, *Les Galères de la République* (Presses du CNRS, Singulier Pluriel, 1990).
111 P. Farmer, *France Reviews its Revolutionary Origins: Social Politics and Historical Opinions in the Third Republic* (New York, Octagon Book, [1944] 1973).
112 Tombs, 'L'Année terrible, 1870–1871', p. 723.
113 Bury and Tombs, *Thiers, 1797–1877*, pp. 206–11.

of 1870–71 at the end of a double war proved a difficult experience to live through.

Another point worth stressing is the revolutionary nature of 1870. The fall of the Empire did imply a considerable weakening of the state and a renegotiation of many established social and political institutions. Many of the social and medical issues dealt with in this book were made more acute by the shortcomings of the state. Its contested legitimacy, its insularity during the siege and its peculiar relationship with Parisian politics made it more susceptible to address differently the needs and the condition of the people. In terms of war history, historians often conclude by presenting the bill, the magical numbers which enable a final moral judgement on the futility of war, and incidentally a factual index of who really won.[114] The temptation to join them is great and I hope I will be forgiven for doing so. Statistics, as we will see later in this book, were notoriously poor for France, but official records give us the following improbably precise 'score': French casualties 470,521 (not including the Commune war), 131,100 of whom dead or missing; German casualties 172,617; 45,000 of whom died.[115] The 1870 wars had been among the bloodiest in French history in proportion to their duration. There is a bitter paradox in the fact that the prestige of the French army which contributed so much to the stability of the Third Republic found its bloody legitimacy in a single military victory against the Parisians.[116] In some respects the repression of May 1871 signals the end of the whole political experience of 1870–71. The Third Republic which grew from the 1870s lacked a revolutionary legitimacy, the glory of a military victory and in fact turned its back on these dated values. The parliamentary settlements and compromises which shaped it ultimately rejected the dangerous practice of revolutionary traditions. For one year in 1870–71 these traditions came to life again and shaped a unique social and political experience.

---

114 Claretie, *Paris assiégé*, pp. 254–5.
115 J. C. Chenu (ed.), *Rapport au conseil de la Société française de secours aux blessés des armées de terre et de mer* (Jean Dumaine, 1874), p. lxxi.
116 J.-C. Jauffret, *Parlement, gouvernement, commandement : l'armée de métier sous la Troisième République, 1871–1914* (2 vols, Vincennes, SHAT, 1987), vol. 1, pp. 182–202. This epuration left a bitter taste and led to internal pressure in favour of the creation of a policing 'Gendarmerie Mobile', better trained for this task.

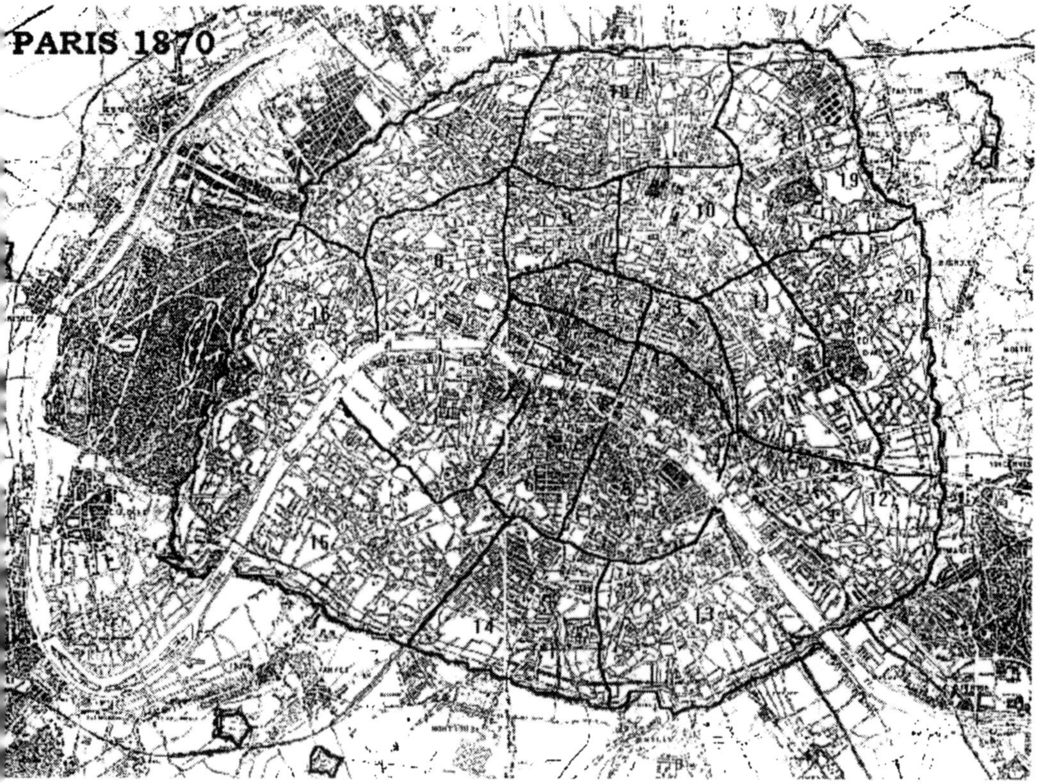

Figure 4 Paris in 1870–71

Figure 5 Paris region in 1870

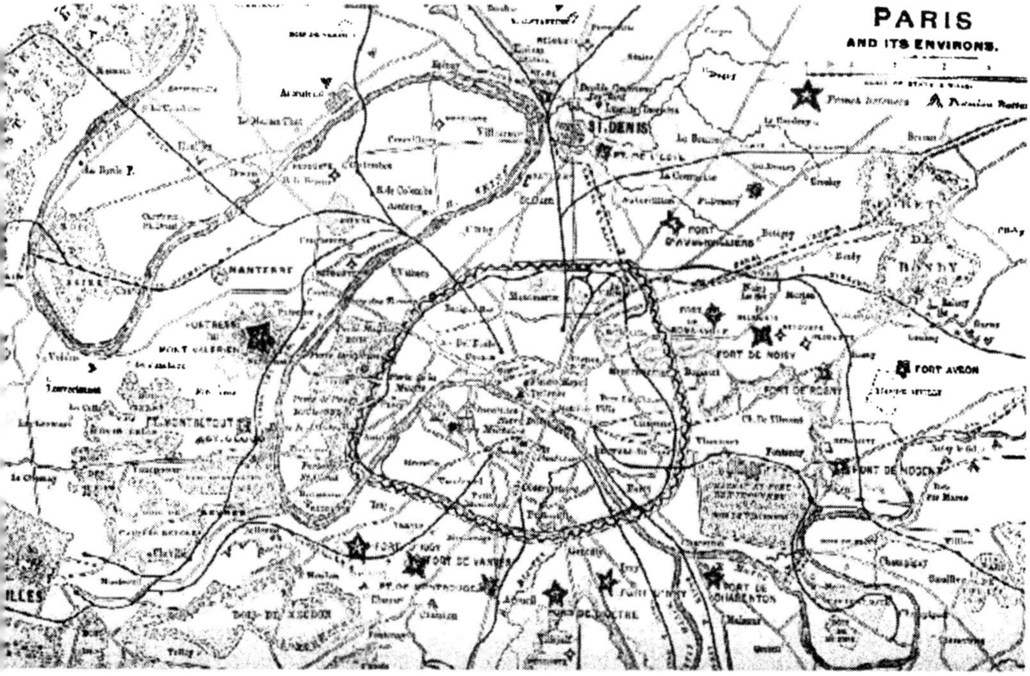

3 The politics of social practice: medicine, war and revolution in Paris

Historians tend naturally to consider the final result of armed conflicts as a statement of national superiority in a multitude of contexts, in some instances so casually that their comments resemble those of sports commentators. Aloof in their dealings with past sufferings, they can treat the real life *Kriegs* like a *Kriegspiel*, a boardgame whose winner receives an all-round *satisfecit* while the loser's defeat comes to be explained by multi-layered causes. For 1870 this cold dissection started early after the six-week defeat of the French Empire. A London play inspired by Wilkie Collins's novel *The New Magdalene* thus melodramatically staged the French defeat through a medical anecdote: a British middle-class lady, left for dead by a French surgeon, is revived by a German specialist who dismisses his French counterpart's science as quackery.[1] This crude characterisation of the German victory could also be found implicitly in the reports published in *The Lancet* during the war.

Historians keen on periodisation consider the 1870 war as a reminder that the French clinical tradition was declining while underfunded French laboratories could not compete with German ones.[2] Allan Mitchell's imposing and masterly three-volume analysis of the German influence on France after 1870 makes the same fundamental assumption that the war signified the depth of French decline in all areas, including medicine.[3] In this analysis of 1870, the defeat was therefore more symptomatic than determinant, while the duration of the war itself lost some of its intensity as a period of change and opportunity. Even though this chapter intends to look more closely at these few months and to avoid any teleological projections, there is some truth in this clear-cut scientific polarity France–Germany.

---

1 *The New Magdalene*, was first staged at the Olympic Theatre in May 1873 and staged again in April 1884; Wilkie Collins's *The New Magdalene* (Stroud, Alan Sutton, 1992).
2 The grand narrative of the rise of German laboratory-based medicine is obviously much more complex. T. Lenoir and R. L. Kermer's articles in A. Cunningham and P. Williams (eds), *The Laboratory Revolution in Medicine* (Cambridge University Press, 1992); also P. Weindling's 'Scientific elites and laboratory organisation in *fin-de-siècle* Paris and Berlin', in the same volume, pp. 170–88, at 170–1; R. Durand-Fardel, *L'Internat en médecine et en chirurgie des hôpitaux et hospices civils de Paris* (Steinheil, 1904), p. 107; J. L. Biret, M. Bui and F. Greffe, 'Les Laboratoires dans les hôpitaux de l'Assistance Publique au dix-neuvième siècle', *Histoire et Nature*, 26–27 (1985) 77–84.
3 A. Mitchell, *The Divided Path: The German Influence on Social Reform in France after 1870* (Chapel Hill, University of North Carolina Press, 1991), pp. 132–3.

In spite of the work of Claude Bernard in 1865,[4] or even the conciliatory attempts made by Charcot, French clinicians and established medical authorities only reluctantly accepted laboratory-based medicine.[5] An internalist account of this conflict would show that political disputes on the attribution of funds, together with a more fundamental debate on the scientific status of the medical 'art', largely explained this stalemate. As George Weisz has shown, most French centres of learning and excellence were showing their age, their unwillingness to expand on their precarious funding, and the symptoms of a routine-prone administration.[6] A post-war contrast between the technically superior Krupp gun and the ancient-looking French muzzle-loaded guns made the contrast all the more striking. On the other hand the whole historiography has taken too literally the claims published over the following fifty years that this conflict enabled scientific developments, that it was a war won by innovation, efficiency and progress.[7]

This chapter intends to put the 1870 war in its medical context and to approach not only its impact but also the political conflicts to which it gave rise. As Ann La Berge noted, there is scarcely any secondary study of the French medical world under the Second Empire and this chapter cannot fill this gap and will only sketch some key issues.[8] From a general portrayal of the political and scientific debates that agitated the French medical establishment in 1870, we will move on to a description of the medical situation as it presented itself to contemporaries of the siege. The smallpox epidemic, the high mortality rates of hospital surgery and the chaotic functioning of what became a giant hospital offered the dismal and yet sadly familiar picture of a whole city at war. This social practice of medicine and the politics of health care shaped a distinctive civilian sphere in the midst of war and defined in relation to the war effort.

---

4   C. Bernard, *Introduction à l'étude de la médecine expérimentale* (Flammarion, [1865] 1984); G. Canguilhem, *Le Normal et le pathologique* (Presses Universitaires de France, 1991), pp. 32–51; M. Grmek, *Claude Bernard et la méthode expérimentale* (Payot, 1991).
5   J. M. Charcot, *La Médecine empirique et la médecine scientifique* (Delahaye, 1867), pp. 16, 22–3. It is worth contrasting Charcot's opinion of German science in 1867, 'la science n'est d'aucun pays', criticising Virchow's nationalist militancy with his own fiercely nationalistic views after the war; H. G. Schlumberger, 'Rudolph Virchow and the Franco-Prussian war', *Annals of Medical History*, 4 (1942) 253–67; H. W. Paul, *The Sorcerer's Apprentice* (Gainesville, University of Florida Press, 1972) and *From Knowledge to Power: The Rise of the Science Empire in France, 1860–1939* (Cambridge University Press, 1985); M. Bonduelle, T. Gelfand and C. G. Goetz, *Charcot* (Michalon, 1996), pp. 86–8.
6   G. Weisz, *The Emergence of Modern Universities in France, 1863–1914* (Princeton University Press, 1983), pp. 18–89.
7   J. de Blonay, *1870 : une révolution chirurgicale, les origines et le développement de la chirurgie civile et militaire moderne* (Geneva, Delta, 1975). Blonay took on board every whiggish account published until 1914. M. Crosland, 'Science and the Franco-Prussian war', *Social Study of Science*, 6 (1976) 185–214. On military epidemiology see M. Osborne, 'French military epidemiology and the limits of the laboratory', in Cunningham and Williams (eds), *The Laboratory*, pp. 189–208.
8   A. F. La Berge, *Mission and Method: The Early-Nineteenth-Century French Public Health Movement* (Cambridge University Press, 1992), p. xiii.

During the siege, doctors played an important political part in supporting war morale among civilians. This chapter also argues that it allowed a number of possibilities and long-awaited prospects to many medical men and volunteer female nurses. The focus of this chapter is exclusively civilian, dealing with war measures taken by the civilian administration, and most of the next chapter will deal with military medicine, despite the blurring of such clear-cut distinctions in times of war. Chapter 7 is specifically devoted to the issue of humanitarianism and to the rise and purpose of the Red Cross movement.

The first section of this chapter deals with the politics of medicine and the structure of the medical world in 1870, the second section sketches the extent of the physical emergency in besieged Paris in 1870, while the third section deals with the revolutionary reforms attempted by the Jules Ferry for the National Defence government. The ultimate failure of a reformist agenda in 1870 illustrates the limits of republican decentralisation and the resilience of hierarchies and elite solidarity.

French medicine in 1870

French medicine in 1870 was in a state of political crisis denounced by many. Parisian medicine, while still powerfully attracting a cosmopolitan crowd of students to its clinical lessons, did not enjoy the scientific prominence and the international cultural hegemony of the first half of the century. French medicine appeared to be in relative decline, the Academy was ageing and years of collusion with an authoritarian regime had brought its toll of resentment and opposition.

The structure of French medicine by 1870 could be simplified thus: Paris dominated, with some minor and declining competition from Montpellier[9] or Strasburg.[10] The teaching of medicine in Paris worked through a complex and incredibly dynamic association of teaching hospitals and the medical faculty.[11] Since the French Revolution, French doctors had mimicked the hierarchical structures of French science and established a professional structure which acted as a guarantor of their scientific status.[12] Over the whole structure presided the Academy of Medicine. Academicians had an official status and the Academy served both as a talkshop, a pool of expertise and a symbol of professional

---

9 L. Dulieu, *La Médecine à Montpellier* (5 vols, Avignon, Aubanel; Montpellier, Quickprint, 1990–95), vols 4 and 5.

10 Osborne, 'French military epidemiology', p. 190; O. Faure, *Histoire sociale de la médecine* (Anthropos, 1994), pp. 81–3.

11 G. Weisz, 'Reform and conflict in French medical education, 1870–1914', in R. Fox and G. Weisz (eds), *The Organisation of Science and Technology in France, 1800–1914* (Cambridge University Press, 1982), pp. 62–3, 66. Weisz estimates that 62 per cent of French medical students studied in Paris immediately before the war, p. 66.

12 M. Crosland, *Science Under Control: The French Academy of Sciences, 1795–1914* (Cambridge University Press, 1992), pp. 399–405.

aspirations. As George Weisz has shown, the Academy was increasingly staffed with members of the medical faculty of the University of Paris and the most successful if not the best medical men of the Parisian elite.[13] The faculty even more than the Academy was the target of many medical radicals by 1870. Faculty and hospital appointments were notoriously nepotistic and increasingly the result of political interference.[14] Since 20 April 1853 the imperial government had taken a prominent part in naming hospital practitioners and lecturers.[15] On the other hand, the higher chamber, the Senate, counted a number of doctors and scientists appointed by the Emperor, such as Nélaton or even, late in the Empire, Pasteur.[16]

In this area as in many others, the heavy hand of government was resented. After years of dictatorship the thawing of the regime did not encourage the expected renewal of support. If anything, criticism became more virulent and opposition more open in the declining years of the authoritarian Empire, in the early *débâcle* preceding the defeat of 1870.[17] To express more freely very radical views, journals like *L'Opinion médicale* went as far as paying the fiscal stamp and duty attached to political newspapers.[18] For that price the editor, Félix Roubaud, could afford to criticise openly the imperial regime and to warn of the decline of French influence abroad:[19]

> Do we have to be silent when facing a regime which has disorganised our education and has allowed our intellectual level to drop so low that foreign students forget the path that leads to France and go instead to Würsburg [*sic*], Vienna or Berlin?[20]

More internalist *La Lancette française* also stated:

> our faculty of medicine complains of the lack of medical respect among doctors. It grumbles about students' irreverence. It only harvests what it planted. For the last twenty years, what has happened to the right to recruit its own members? It refused Claude Bernard at the *agrégation*, it rejected the applications of Chassaignac, Vidal.... Who is responsible for appointing so many professors who cannot get an audience?[21]

---

13 G. Weisz, *The Medical Mandarins: The French Academy of Medicine in the Nineteenth and Early-Twentieth Centuries* (Oxford University Press, 1995), pp. 50–1, 237–80.
14 R. Gilpin, *France in the Age of the Scientific State* (Princeton University Press, 1968), p. 92.
15 A. Des Cilleuls, *Histoire de l'administration parisienne au dix-neuvième siècle* (2 vols, H. Champion, 1900), vol. 2, pp. 352–3.
16 J. Léonard, *La Médecine entre les pouvoirs et les savoirs* (Aubier Montaigne, 1981), pp. 227–9.
17 Claretie summed up the republican and true liberal views in *La Débâcle*: 'Order, this social order we all expect, order is not a cultivated plant in a hot greenhouse, under the vigilant eye of a well armed guard, it is a wild flower growing in the meadows, which needs an atmosphere of freedom to blossom' (Librairie Centrale, 1870), p. 9.
18 *La France médicale* (4/06/1870).
19 This decline was slow, gradual but qualitatively important: J. H. Warner, 'Remembering Paris: memory and the American disciple of French medicine in the nineteenth century', *Bulletin of the History of Medicine*, 65 (1991) 301–25.
20 Leader in *Opinion médicale et scientifique* (1/01/1870).
21 *La Lancette française* (26/04/1870) article by E. Le Sourd.

This critique of the faculty grew increasingly strident in spring 1870. *La France médicale*, a radical and relatively marginal journal, announced in June 1870 the union of all radical forces to fight a war against the faculty, the Academy and the establishment. The radicals opposed their alternative to all forms of established medicine.[22] They offered their teaching (*enseignement libre*) to replace the redundant and dated faculty teaching and to introduce students to the latest developments and fringe therapeutics.[23] Their assembly, the Conférence Médicale, aimed to replace the moribund Academy of Medicine.[24] Apart from the Conférence Médicale, most of these alternative medical institutions had a long history, and the novelty thus was to propose to substitute them for the established institutions. This medical radicalism was deeply ingrained in republican political beliefs and had been cultivated in the opposition over thirty years.[25] The Conférence Médicale, was a revival of democratic forums of the 1840s. In spite of this self-referencing idealism, few had kept the idealism of François-Vincent Raspail and even those fighting in favour of greater equality in medicine did not advocate a return to an unregulated market of medicine or a move towards state-owned medicine.[26] For being idealistic this opposition was nevertheless very vocal and forceful. In 1869 medical students provoked some unrest within the faculty and were controversially expelled.

Between 2 and 6 April, Professor Tardieu, a lecturer in forensic medicine who had been a witness for the defence of Pierre Bonaparte, the murderer of the republican journalist Victor Noir, was shouted down by students: 'to the Senate, down with the scab! Down with the government! Vive Rochefort!'[27] On 14 July 1870 radical students in medicine joined forces with some workers to demonstrate noisily on Bastille day.[28]

These incidents, the theoretical nature of the syllabus, the age of the lecturers and the arbitrariness of their appointment had shifted the locus of real medical knowledge to the hospitals.[29] Parisian hospitals housed a number of *services* where the training was increasingly specialised. On the whole, however, French doctors

22 On the making of the French medical press see Léonard, *La Médecine*, pp. 195–9.
23 Weisz, 'Reform and conflict', pp. 62–3; J. Goldstein, *Console and Classify: The French Psychiatric Profession in the Nineteenth Century* (Cambridge University Press, 1987), pp. 346–8; *Le Mouvement médical* (10/07/1870).
24 *La France médicale* (22/06/1870).
25 J.-C. Caron, 'L'Impossible réforme des études médicales, projets et controverses dans la France des notables (1815–1848)', in *Sources 31/32, Maladies, Médecines et Sociétés* (2 vols, L'Harmattan, 1993), vol. 2, pp. 206–17.
26 J. Poirier and C. Langlois (eds), *Raspail et la vulgarisation médicale* (Vrin 1988) especially F. Denier, 'Démocratie politique et démocratie culturelle chez Raspail de la Révolution de 1830 à la Révolution de 1848', pp. 27–59; B. Béguet, *La Science pour tous* (Arts et Métiers, 1990).
27 *Le Gaulois* (4, 5, 6/04/1870); Léonard, *La Médecine*, p. 225.
28 *Le Gaulois* (14/07/1870).
29 E. Ackerknecht, *Medicine at the Paris Hospital, 1794–1848* (Baltimore, Johns Hopkins Press, 1967); W. Coleman, *Death is a Social Disease: Public Health and Political Economy in Early-Industrial France* (Madison, University of Wisconsin Press, 1982).

were not really specialised and either deplored specialised medicine[30] or, on the contrary, denounced it as something specifically Germanic and fragmented.[31] Among the hospital specialists were earlier figureheads such as Philippe Ricord, the President of the Academy in 1868, who had long been the most popular teacher and yet never managed to obtain a full position in the faculty.[32] Students therefore individually tailored their own education, attending fee-paying preparatory schools.

To add to the complexity of French medicine, intermediate forms of qualification – *officiers de santé* trained summarily in local schools, *externes* who only attended lectures in hospitals, and the elite *internes* who had been trained in hospitals – threatened the cohesion or even the real existence of a single medical professional identity.[33] In terms of knowledge, theories and praxis, even the French clinical backyard resounded with the polyphony or even cacophony of conflicting medical discourses.[34] After medical students took their doctorates the struggle was still not over.[35]

The structuring of the French medical world owed a great deal more to the social composition and political domination of a few than to revolutionary French meritocratic ideals.[36] Hospital appointments which guaranteed higher private incomes were extremely difficult to obtain. The physicians and surgeons who did obtain these posts could then use them to promote themselves. Borsa and Michel have argued that they also played an important role in the fund-raising activities of hospitals and that, if they benefited from their hospital status to raise their private fees, they reciprocated by propagating the renown of their institutions.[37] For the average practitioner the fees remained modest and difficult to earn.

The Parisian medical market often appeared to observers as overcrowded and extravagantly over-provided for in comparison with the French provinces.[38]

---

30 *L'Abeille médicale* (15/08/1870). On specialisation see G. Weisz, 'The development of medical specialisation in nineteenth-century Paris', in A. F. La Berge and M. Feingold (eds), *French Medical Culture in the Nineteenth Century* (Amsterdam, Rodopi, 1994).
31 L. Fiaux, *L'Enseignement de la médecine en Allemagne* (Baillière, 1877), pp. 55, 75.
32 C. Eginer, *Philippe Ricord, 1800–1889, sa vie, son oeuvre* (Le François, 1939), p. 36. Ricord became the Emperor's private surgeon in 1869.
33 Durand-Fardel, *L'Internat en médecine*; Léonard, *La Médecine*, pp. 48–52, 84–8.
34 This notion of polyphony is used by R. Porter and L. Hall to describe the production of sexual knowledge in the nineteenth century. *The Facts of Life: The Creation of Sexual Knowledge in Britain, 1850–1950* (New Haven, Yale University Press, 1995), pp. 133–4.
35 This 'glut' is not unique to France but we need an authoritative account matching A. Digby's *Making a Medical Living: Doctors and Patients in the English Market for Medicine, 1920–1911* (Cambridge University Press, 1994), pp. 136–48.
36 M. Ramsey, *Professional and Popular Medicine in France, 1770–1830: The Social World of Medical Practice* (Cambridge University Press, 1988).
37 S. Borsa and C. R. Michel, *La Vie quotidienne des hôpitaux en France au dix-neuvième siècle* (Hachette, 1985), p. 135.
38 P. Brouardel, *La Profession médicale au commencement du vingtième siècle* (Baillière et Fils, 1903), pp. 12, 44.

Most books published by faculty members in 1870 stressed the Malthusian crisis of French (Parisian) medicine and called for yet more elitism and strict control. There was a real contrast between elitists and idealists like Dr Combes who campaigned for greater social and intellectual status, writing that if 'for egoist reasons, society refuses doctors the ranks they deserve in the social hierarchy', society should then admit the moral authority of high-class doctors, and protect the junior members of the profession scraping a living in impoverished neighbourhoods.[39] The medical world was also divided in two groups: those who belonged to the Association générale des médecins de France under the imperial patronage and those who opposed any contacts with the government.[40] This crowd numbered a great number of ambitious young Turks or disappointed opponents to the Empire who saw the war as an opportunity for change.

With almost 12,000 beds, or something like one bed for every 208 inhabitants, Paris had a unique caring capacity.[41] Hospitals could easily be adapted to face high numbers of war casualties, but this meant a number of changes. It notably meant the end of the traditional care for the terminally ill, the insane and the poor Parisians too ill to stay at home. In August the Assistance Publique, foreseeing a siege, ordered a large proportion of the chronically insane to be taken by train to the provinces and to its properties across France from Normandy to Languedoc. The terminally ill, vagrants and a number of prostitutes[42] suffering from syphilis and depending on the police services were also deported.[43] The deaf and dumb school was evacuated to Bordeaux to make more room for the war casualties.[44] The old and senile patients in the hands of the Assistance Publique were gradually put into the care of charitable associations and religious orders while their institutions (the Petits Ménages at Issy and the Incurables at Ivry) were converted into military hospitals.[45] The Assistance Publique's financial situation was sound and disposable in case of emergency.

Of all the fortified places that were besieged during the war, Paris certainly had the best capacity to cope with epidemics and sieges. It had a relatively modern

---

39 E. Combes, *De l'État actuel de la médecine et des médecins en France* (A. Delahaye, 1869), p. xii. Combes's only concrete proposition was to close yet again the gates to the 'flood' of new medical recruits. G. Sussman, 'The glut of doctors in mid-nineteenth-century France', *Comparative Studies in Society and History*, 19 (1977) 287–304; E. B. Ackerman, *Health Care in the Parisian Countryside, 1800–1914* (New Brunswick, N.J., Rutgers University Press, 1990), pp. 32–59.

40 *L'Union médicale* (22/10/1870) 559; Léonard, *La Médecine*, pp. 190–2.

41 P. Darmon, *La Vie quotidienne du médecin parisien en 1900* (Hachette, 1988), p. 83. These figures stand for 1900 but would not have been significantly lower in 1870.

42 AAP, 542 Foss 78. Issy sent away 1,372 men and women, Bicêtre 618 patients.

43 C. J. Lecour, *La Campagne contre la Préfecture de Paris* (Asselin et Cie, 1881), p. 20 and *La Prostitution à Paris et à Londres, 1789–1877* (Asselin et Cie, 1877), p. 296.

44 *GMP*, 25 (1870) 493.

45 A. Benoist de la Grandière, *Compte rendu chirurgical de l'ambulance des soeurs de Saint Joseph de Cluny* (Baillière, 1871), p. 6; AAP, 542 Foss 78.

infrastructure, a great number of hospitals in varying states of disrepair and the highest concentration of qualified physicians and surgeons in France. Ideologically the concepts of public health and centralised action were also more deeply rooted in Paris than in most other French urban centres.[46] These factors meant that medicine played a more important part in the longer siege of Paris than in that of other besieged cities like Strasburg, Metz,[47] Belfort, or of unthreatened large cities like Lyons.[48]

Health in Paris in 1870

It seems almost impossible to sum up the rich historiography relating to the social history of Paris and the Parisians.[49] Paris was very largely populated with poor inhabitants who lived either in garrets or 'income-generating lodgings' (*immeubles de rendements*).[50] Paupers represented 10 per cent of the population of the poorest XX, XIII and XIV *arrondissements* within the city walls. Many of the poorer neighbourhoods were shanty towns built on the wasteland surrounding the walls and were pulled down during the clearing works in preparation for the siege.[51] In spite of the attentions paid by the imperial regime, the situation of Parisians does not seem to have been much improved and the slum clearance schemes of Baron Haussmann probably had the perverse effect of most slum-clearing schemes in making the nearby slums even more crowded. On the whole Paris remained a city of high morbidity and mortality rates. Cholera visited Paris during the pandemics of 1849 and 1865–66 and remained residual in 1870, typhoid[52] and typhus were almost endemic, while smallpox epidemics struck Paris at regular intervals.[53] In 1870 the latter three diseases were the ones which dominated the mortality returns before the war and in the first months of the war.

---

46 La Berge, *Mission and Method*, pp. 113–27.
47 E. Grellois, *Histoire médicale du blocus de Metz* (J. B. Baillière, 1872).
48 A. Desgranges, *Ambulances sédentaires de Lyon pendant la guerre de 1870–1871* (Lyons, Bellon, 1872).
49 J. Gaillard, *Paris la ville, 1852–1870* (Lille, H. Champion, 1976) is perhaps one of the better works on Paris; in a more popular and accessible format also see A. Fierro, *Histoire et dictionnaire de Paris* (Bouquins, Robert Laffont, 1996); L. R. Berlanstein, *The Working People of Paris, 1871–1914* (Baltimore, Johns Hopkins University Press, 1984).
50 O. du Mesnil, *L'Hygiène à Paris, l'habitat du pauvre* (J. B. Baillière et Fils, 1890), p. 30; R. Marjolin, *Causes et effets des logements insalubres* (Masson, 1881); Société française des habitations à bon marché, founded in 1889 (reconnue d'utilité publique 1890), produced important literature on housing which stretched back to the period before the 1870 war.
51 Gaillard, *Paris la ville*, p. 119.
52 The use of the River Seine to provide drinking water was the cause of a small-scale persistence of the disease. Typhus and typhoid were often confused and linked to one another. G. Viguier, 'Rappel historique sur l'épidémiologie des infections typho-paratyphiques' (Thèse de doctorat en médecine, Université de Paris, 1960), pp. 2–10.
53 P. Darmon, *La Longue Traque de la Variole* (Librairie Perrin, 1986), pp. 358–85.

The war did not change the pathology of the city, but it worsened its manifestations. During the siege typhus and typhoid seemed to kill more patients than in peacetime. More than the relative increase in morbidity, this increase in mortality worried doctors as it underlined the declining physical stamina of the Parisian population. Typhoid in particular killed over 40 per cent of the sufferers.[54] Medical advice to the public played down the importance of typhus and typhoid epidemics, while it advised the public to rush to the vaccination centres to be re-vaccinated against smallpox and to eat acidic fruits to avoid scurvy.[55] Typhus made a spectacular come-back in the last weeks of January and prompted Nélaton to use the venereal hospital of Midi to isolate 5,000 patients affected by the epidemic.[56]

It was the smallpox epidemic, however, which raised the most urgent political issues in the spring of 1870.[57] The Conférence médicale organised at the call of Marchal (de Calvi) met to discuss more openly the efficiency of 'cow pox vaccine', to unionise radical doctors and to reform the medical world by bypassing the Academy.[58] The smallpox epidemic 'was the occasion for the medical world [*corps médical*] to assert its autonomy and power. From this meeting should result a new institution, a new jurisdiction which would legislate on all the major scientific and professional questions.'[59] In his most exalted pages, Marchal (de Calvi) appealed to every medical practitioner and called for renewed professional democratic corporatism and revolutionary meritocratic traditions to justify his new movement. What the smallpox had started the war would end, however, as military priorities postponed any reform *sine die*. The 1870 smallpox epidemic took a particularly heavy toll among a largely unprotected population. The legislation on vaccination was old and largely permissive. The 1803, 1809 and 1811 Napoleonic decrees meant that, the regular army excepted,[60] most of the French rural population was either not vaccinated or had been vaccinated once only by arm to arm vaccination.[61] The early enthusiasm for vaccination had seriously flagged between the 1820s and 1870s.[62] The Second Empire had renewed some of the provisions of the First and the army had been consistently vaccinated since the 31 December 1857 directive, but this

---

54 *GMP*, 26 (1871), p. 10.
55 E. Onimus, *Conseils hygiéniques aux habitants de Paris pendant le siège* (Charles de Mourgues Frères, 1870), pp. 27–30. A. L. Delpech, *Le Scorbut pendant le siège de Paris* (J. B. Baillière, 1871); and Dr Leven, *Une Épidémie de scorbut observée à l'hôpital militaire d'Ivry* (Delahaye, 1872).
56 Dr A. Tardieu, *Huitième ambulance de campagne de la Société de secours aux blessés* (Delahaye, 1872), p. 80. The study of typhus is still limited, see for instance J. Robins, *The Miasma: Epidemic and Panic in Nineteenth-Century Ireland* (Dublin, Institute of Public Administration, 1995), pp. 48–61.
57 M. Delpech, *Rapport sur les épidémies pour les années 1870, 1871, 1872* (G. Masson, 1875).
58 *La Lancette française* (10/05 and 23/06/1870).
59 *La Tribune médicale* (29/05, 3/06 and 17/07/1870).
60 C. Saumade, 'Histoire des vaccinations dans les armées françaises' (Thèse de doctorat d'état en médecine, Bordeaux II, 1979), pp. 20–6.
61 Léonard, *La Médecine*, pp. 62–3.
62 La Berge, *Mission and Method*, pp. 101–9.

regulation did not apply to the mass of volunteers who formed the bulk of the republican armies[63] and who largely contributed to the spread of the epidemic throughout France,[64] Germany, Switzerland, Belgium and, eventually, the rest of Europe.[65] In Paris, the Academy had among its prerogatives to organise vaccinations with the help of the Assistance Publique dispensaries and hospitals. The arrival of the conscripted Breton *gardes mobiles* who had never been vaccinated in the midst of a major epidemic turned the problem into a crisis and the army medical services estimated that 40 per cent of the troops could contract the disease.[66] The argument for mass vaccination won the day and easily overruled the reservations of radicals like Marchal (de Calvi). Only a few geriatric members of the Academy of Science opposed vaccination and they were not heeded.[67]

Vaccination on the left arm had to be applied to all, but even though Baron Larrey, the head of the army medical services, was a member of the Academy and was fully aware of the crisis, he could not contribute financially to the huge vaccination programme. The major issue was to obtain good vaccine serum from several sources.[68] Human lymph had become fairly rare and the Assistance Publique had to raise the rates, paying 15 francs per vaccine child, 5 francs to the midwives and 3 francs for the mothers bringing their offspring to the vaccination centres.[69] In the autumn the Assistance Publique published the Academy's report to convince both parents and patients that vaccination was truly innocuous.[70] While not reaching the level of scepticism found in Britain at the same epoch, the news that syphilis could be passed on through vaccination[71] had had a significant impact.[72] In spite of

63 Ministère de Guerre, *Aperçu statistique sur l'évolution de la morbidité et de la mortalité générales dans l'armée* (Imprimerie Nationale, 1932), plate 35. The morbidity rate of smallpox in 1868 was at 5.56 per thousand, the vaccination and revaccination efforts of the war and immediate aftermath brought it down to 0.4 per thousand in 1872.
64 T. Gallard, *Malades et blessés de l'armée de la Loire* (J. B. Baillière et Fils, 1871), p. 20; Darmon, *La Longue Traque de la variole*, pp. 362–3. Darmon estimates the number of casualties of smallpox in France at c.200,000 for the years 1870–71.
65 There is clear evidence that the conflict spread it to most neighbouring countries of France. T. Saucerotte, *Lunéville pendant la guerre et le rapatriement* (Gazette médicale de Paris, 1872); ASSAT, box 64/26, p. 8.
66 ASSAT, box 62/13 Note sur la revaccination dans l'armée (October 1870?); O. Faure, *Les Français et leur médecine au XIXe siècle* (Belin, 1993), pp. 260–1.
67 G. Grimaud de Caux, *De septembre 1870 à février 1871 : L'Académie des Sciences pendant le siège de Paris* (Didier et Cie, 1871), p. 155; Crosland, *Science Under Control*, pp. 328–30.
68 ASSAT, box 62/13, Lettre à Monsieur l'intendant Général, 7/11/1870.
69 AAP, 542 Foss 96, rule of 10/11/1870. One could get vaccinated every day of the week at the central dispensary and at four hospitals at a time according to a roll.
70 AAP, 542 Foss 2, *Minutes des séances du Conseil Général des Hospices*, 8/10/1870, Broca noted that there was a real popular belief that vaccination only took place in the spring.
71 Académie de Médecine, *Mémoires sur la transmission de la syphilis par la vaccination et la vaccination animale* (J. B. Baillière, 1865).
72 Parisian children had to be vaccinated to go to school since 1865. VdP, VD6/1347/3; fonctionnement du service de vaccination, 1871–76.

technical difficulties and expenses, vaccine cows were then perceived to be a viable investment.[73] The government eventually devoted the ridiculously small sum of 3,000 francs to provide enough animal serum by mid-October, well into the epidemic.[74] This was an innovation, for the Academy had always been very reluctant to spend its limited budget on vaccine cows. The results were nevertheless very disappointing. Overall the Academy's vaccination campaign proved insufficient in spite of prodigious individual efforts; for instance, the academician Depaul vaccinated alone over 15,000 men in six weeks, an extraordinary number. Even figures like these remained a drop in the ocean and could not protect the 400,000-strong Parisian army.[75] To add to the problems of vaccination, a number of patients who had been vaccinated in childhood fell ill and these observations confirmed the necessity to re-vaccinate.[76] This multiplied the number of patients at risk and put the task well beyond the Academy's efforts.[77]

The Assistance Publique and the city municipality then used well-tried incentives to find some private medical support by issuing *jetons*, tokens entitling the vaccinators to a fee. Doctors and midwives who co-operated with the scheme were paid one silver token for 16.17 vaccinations [*sic*]. This scheme guaranteed around 32,000 vaccinations per year in time of peace at that leisurely rate.[78] In time of war, emergency measures were required and all cases of smallpox had to be notified, isolated and sent to a limited number of army hospitals.[79] The Bicêtre asylum had been converted into an isolation hospital for about 1,500 patients by mid-October,[80] to which was added the veterinary school of Maison d'Alfort.[81]

While smallpox had had a considerable political impact before the war, its relative importance declined during the war despite its contribution to the high mortality rates. From January to November 1870 it killed 8,027 people, more than the 1865 cholera epidemic, but it principally affected the provincial troops and the suburban refugees, and that was an important electoral consideration.[82] Over the

73 *BAIM*, 35 (1870) 735, 739–40; ASSAT, box 62/1, Conseil de Santé, letter to the minister, 3/10/1870.
74 *BAIM*, 35, (1870) 752.
75 *BAIM*, 35 (1870) 813.
76 *GMP*, 25 (1870) 506.
77 VdP, VD6 2450/3, Conseil d'hygiène publique et de salubrité du département de la Seine, *Rapport addressé à Monsieur le Préfet de Police sur les faits de l'épidémie variolique observée à Paris*, Delpech rapporteur, November 1870?
78 AAP, 542 Foss 96, Attributions des jetons de vaccination pour l'année 1869.
79 ASSAT, box 62/13, File containing the letter from the mayor of the VII *arrondissement* and the notification forms.
80 H. Larrey, *Discours prononcé par Monsieur le baron Larrey le 14 juin 1880* (Librairie des Publications Législatives, 1880), p. 56; ASSAT, box 63/2, Léon Colin au baron Larrey sur l'asile de Bicêtre, 7/04/1879.
81 ASSAT, box 64/31, Rapport médical sur le service de santé de l'annexe militaire de l'école vétérinaire pendant l'hiver de 1870–1871 par le Médecin Principal de seconde classe Dufour.
82 *GMP*, 25 (1870) 588.

Table 1 Mortality in Parisian hospitals and hospices

Date	No. of deaths	Date	No. of deaths
1869		1870	
19/09–30/09	386	19/09–30/09	609
October	987	October	1,827
November	1,176	November	2019
December	1,099	December	2,936
1870		1871	
January	1,243	January	4,026
1/02–19/02	910	1/02–19/02	2,309
Total	5,801	Total	13,726

Source: AAP. 542 Foss 124, a study of mortality rates.

Table 2 Breakdown of the mortality by disease declared in Paris (comparing 1869–70 and 1870–71 and excluding all suburban areas)

Cause of death	Sept 1869–Feb 1870	Sept 1870–Feb 1871	Observations
Smallpox	634	7,320	
Scarlet fever	135	222	
Measles	238	433	
Typhoid	567	3,689	Numerous cases of 'typhus like typhoid' (sic)
Erysipelas	158	219	
Bronchitis	1,318	5,221	
Pneumonia	1,686	4,300	
Diarrhea	263	2,216	
Dysentery	60	813	
Cholera	28	32	
Pharyngitis	100	227	
Croup	219	258	
Puerperal fever	158	224	
Various (sic)	15,056	33,874	
War diseases (sic)		775	Municipal statistics categorised war wounds separately from 20 January 1871
Scurvy		1	Most victims of scurvy died outside Paris in Ivry and were not accounted for
Shelling		89	

Source: AAP, 542 Foss 124, a study of mortality rates.

following two months smallpox killed another 2,436 people, showing a slow but steady increase.[83] If one compares 1869–70 to 1870–71, the rather unreliable statistics show a tenfold increase in the mortality. This was only partly the result of the war; the epidemic had started in November 1869 and reached its peak during the siege. Before the siege, smallpox mortality rates virtually doubled from month to month and showed no sign of remission. A 1,154 per cent rise of mortality from 634 to 7,320, however, was in itself startling.[84] The overall mortality rates for all diseases during the siege of Paris showed a more moderate threefold increase from 20,616 to 59,913. If one takes into account the normal cycle of an epidemic and the added hardship of the war, the smallpox rates seem slightly less alarming. Moreover the rates of morbidity were not commensurate and confirm the contemporaries' view that the level of morbidity rose less than the level of mortality for each disease. In other words, more people died of their illness than in peacetime. Table 1, established from the official mortality returns, shows how fast growing the global mortality was throughout 1870 and 1871.

A greater number of recorded deaths were attributed to lung diseases, bronchitis and pneumonia in the winter months, reflecting the harsh weather and the absence of any heating. The average temperatures during the day in December and January inside Paris were -0.7 and -0.8°C respectively, with extremes of -11°C. Outside the walls the temperatures were considerably lower.[85] What medicine could do against this type of morbidity is dubious. The statistics established in 1872 show the massive decline in the survival rate of patients afflicted with respiratory disorders. While a patient with tuberculosis had a 50 per cent chance of leaving the hospital alive if not cured in 1872, in 1871 a similarly afflicted patient had a 75 per cent chance of dying in hospital.[86] Someone with pneumonia also saw the normal odds of two in three reduce to one in three.[87] The Parisian hospitals were barely heated and lit, and in many respects the limitations of preventative medicine exposed above in the case of smallpox also applied to every other affliction.

The Parisian school of clinical medicine in 1870 was perhaps at its peak in terms of diagnosis and pathological science, but very poor in any other respects. The great wards of Parisian hospitals still functioned uniformly and indiscriminately. The isolated patients could still be treated by martyrdom-seeking nuns without much protection. Smallpox thus decimated a largely unvaccinated nursing population, which contributed to the spread of the disease. Table 3 shows the high rates of mortality for each major medical affliction. It also illustrates well the medium-term

83 *GMP*, 26 (1871) 9.
84 H. Sueur, *Étude sur la mortalité à Paris pendant le siège* (Sandoz et Fischbacher, 1872).
85 Benoist de la Grandière, *L'Ambulance des soeurs de Saint-Joseph de Cluny*, p. 15.
86 D. S. Barnes, *The Making of a Social Disease: Tuberculosis in Nineteenth-Century France* (Berkeley, University of California Press, 1995), pp. 33–73. According to Barnes, TB had a rather confused ethiology before 1870.
87 AAP, 542 Foss 125, Secrétariat général de la statistique, rapport, 1872.

Table 3 Mortality and discharges in Parisian hospitals

	November 1870	December 1870	January 1871	February 1871	March 1871	April 1871	May 1871	June 1871	July 1871
Mortality	*1,401*	*2,176*	*2,750*	*2,621*	*1,903*	*1,363*	*1,482*	*1,114*	*707*
Typhoid	159	179	223	221	216	141	93	96	118
	80	*184*	*289*	*267*	*174*	*63*	*36*	*26*	*13*
Smallpox	706	742	768	543	258	85	81	86	33
	289	*267*	*239*	*126*	*58*	*18*	*13*	*5*	*7*
Bronchitis			899	767					
			186	*171*					
Pneumonia			198	234					
			310	*308*					
Pleurisy			65	96					
			22	*38*					
TB			174	206					
			505	*555*					
Gunshot	28	386	118	230	34	56	215	622	214
wounds	*16*	*212*	*146*	*40*	*15*	*101*	*417*	*231*	*30*
	22	**92**	**59**	**67**	**37**	**32**	**47**	**130**	**38**
Battles near Paris		Champigny	Buzenval				Bloody Week		
Dysentery	94	95	93	62	49	17	23	38	41
	21	*33*	*25*	*76*	*46*	*20*	*6*	*4*	*6*
Diarrhea	83	109	104	137	133	85	54	55	86
	43	*43*	*78*	*81*	*94*	*62*	*24*	*20*	*26*
Scurvy	3	2	4	9	57	51	30	26	16
				13	*23*	*6*	*11*	*3*	

Note: First lines of numbers show patients discharged from hospitals and following lines (*in italics*) those who died in hospital during the month. Numbers for gunshot wounds are minimal estimates with the third line (**in bold**) representing infections.

effects of the siege. The medical situation ignored the armistice, and the medical crisis which probably peaked at the end of January and early February had perceptible consequences for the following eight or nine months in Parisian hospitals.

The issue of war surgery will be further discussed in Chapters 4 and 8, but its poor results reflected the appalling figures of established civilian hospitals. Parisian mortality rates after operations were extremely high in comparison with London ones. Dr Berkeley-Hill and Dr James Simpson pointed out that after a study of 6,000 cases Parisian hospitals seemed to have a mortality rate approaching 60 per cent for major operations, while British hospitals of over 300 beds only peaked at 40 per cent and less when the hospital was smaller.[88] Chenu's overall

88 M. Berkeley-Hill, *Treatment of the Sick and Wounded: Illustrated by Observations Made at the Seat of War* (James Walton, 1870), p. 10.

Table 4 **Mortality after major war surgery in 1870–71**

Operations	Operated	Dead	Mortality (%)
Amputated arms	2,026	1,420	70.09
Desarticulated arms and elbows	559	377	67.44
Amputated forearms	227	149	65.64
Amputated fingers	1,010	72	7.13
Amputated thighs	3,794	3,452	90.99
Desarticulated legs	151	129	85.43
Amputated legs	3,704	3,050	82.34
Amputated feet	148	107	72.30
Amputated metatarsus	117	89	76.07
Amputated toes	462	96	20.77
Double amputations	143	112	78.32
Total	12,341	9,053	73.36

figures for the operations that took place in the military context during the war, shown in Table 4, tell a sad tale.

Chenu's record did not clearly discriminate between the Parisian experience and the provincial one, but all the indications seem to prove that Parisian rates were even worse.[89] There are also a number of discrepancies between the number of pensionable (amputated) survivors and the number of cases Chenu reported, which seem to indicate that Chenu took a rather pessimistic view of war rates.[90] Even if his results are moderated by 10 or 15 per cent, rates averaging at 65 per cent on young and fit patients would be poor by the hospital standards of peacetime.

These figures raised a number of key questions on Parisian hospital practice, but doctors often deflected them successfully by questioning the racial quality of the French. The defeat was embodied in their patients' flesh. 'In any case of operation, statistics prove that the success rates obtained on the Anglo-Saxon race are well over what can be obtained here.'[91] Some of the key hospitals like the Hôtel-Dieu were ancient and their planned replacement was being built against all the hopes of hospital planners.[92] The inward-looking French medicine had yet to

[89] J. C. Chenu, *Aperçu historique, statistique et clinique sur le service des ambulances et des hôpitaux pendant la guerre de 1870–1871* (2 vols, Jean Dumaine and Hachette and Masson, 1874), vol. 1, p. 493.

[90] Le Comte de Riencourt, *Les Blessés oubliés, les pensions militaires pour blessures et infirmités* (Abbeville, Paillart, 1882), p. v. Riencourt in 1882 estimated at 6,250 the number of forgotten cases. The first five classes out of six of pensionable wounds implied the loss of a limb, but many were not operated upon by French doctors and would not qualify in Chenu's statistics; many more had lost eyes or ears which were not accounted for in Chenu's account. pp. 7–8.

[91] *BAIM*, 36 (1871) 83.

[92] C. Tollet, *Les Hôpitaux modernes au dix-neuvième siècle* (l'auteur, 1894), p. 17; P. Valley-Radot, *Un Siècle d'histoire hospitalière de Louis-Philippe à nos jours, 1837–1949* (Dupont, 1948).

adopt more generally Listerian theories and practices. The propagation of Listerian ideas certainly benefited from the input of British aid in the French Red Cross. In the northern ambulances (in the sense of temporary hospitals), organised and supplied partly by the British, each ambulance carried the means of antiseptic action.[93] While Listerian spraying was debated, the efficacy of antiseptics was often recognised if not put to use.

The Academy debated the best means to use phenic acid and took comfort in the fact that this fundamental medical product was a by-product of gas production and would not go amiss in the war.[94] This was a considerable gain as many other drugs and medication, distributed by private and public pharmacies went in rapid short supply.[95] One should not emphasise too much the drug shortages.[96] One of the great advantages of medicine in 1870 in terms of medication was that it did not rely on complex compounds and that the most important medical issues it addressed were linked to procedure rather than drugs. Surgical techniques were central to all discussions and experimentation of the war: for instance, pneumatic occlusion, the use of a pump which sucked the pus from a wound and excluded any contact with the vitiated air of the hospital.[97] This fear of any contamination from the vitiated air outside reflected the current non-dogmatic belief in a mix of germ and miasma theories to explain contamination and high hospital mortality rates.

Revolution and medicine

Hygienic concepts are highly political and relate closely to ideals of order and bourgeois respectability. This paradigm of the social history of medicine has been long established and this study can only add to a familiar story.[98] It is still striking how far public health remained limited to the *appearance* of cleanliness and order, and how hygiene had much more credence as a moral and policing concept than as

---

93 A. Houzé de l'Aulnoit, *Historique et mode de fonctionnement des caisses de secours des bataillons de mobiles et mobilisés de l'armée du Nord* (Lille, L. Danel, 1871), pp. 24–9. Per bataillon, 200 opium pills, 100 g of Laudanum, 1 litre of chloroform, 150 g of Ether, 2 litres of alcohol, 300 g of iron perchlorate, 150 g of phenic acid, 50 g of chlorine, 120 g of Collodion, 30 g of iodine.
94 *BAIM*, 35 (1870) 721.
95 M. Ferré, *Rapport sur les services des ambulances municipales du troisième arrondissement* (Rigal, 1872), p. 10.
96 C. Moison, *Le Service pharmaceutique pendant la guerre franco-allemande 1870–1871* (Cahors, Coueslant, 1965).
97 Dr A. Cousin, *Histoire chirurgicale de l'ambulance des ponts et chaussées* (Malteste, 1872), p. 2.
98 All history of public health refers to this straightforward axiom. M. Ramsey, 'Public health in France', in D. Porter (ed.), *The History of Public Health and the Modern State* (Amsterdam, Rodopi, 1994), pp. 45–118; La Berge, *Mission and Method*, pp. 15–17; this is also the basis of L. Murard and P. Zylberman's fierce attacks on the Third Republic. 'L'Autre guerre, 1914–1918 : la santé publique sous l'oeil de l'Amérique', *Revue Historique*, 276 (1986) 367–98; *L'Hygiène dans la République* (Fayard, 1996).

a clinical one. One of the great guarantors of public hygiene in Paris was in fact the second division of the Préfecture de Police. During the siege the sanitary police had been one of the victims of the political downsizing of the Préfecture.[99] The practice of hygiene policing, like that of general policing, was thus in real decline during the siege but it was not contested in the same terms. In many instances the word hygiene intervened to reform a political and social situation or to qualify a general description of the besieged Parisian people. The medical statistics and accounts of the physical fitness of the population were scrutinised by the press and at every level of government. The mortality rates published weekly in the few remaining medical journals and repeated in the dailies provided a grim reminder of the reality of war while it also mixed civilian and military figures into one. They did not simply provide a factual index of public health, they also gave a rhythm to the war, a collective identity in suffering, above class and political divides. As Catherine Kudlick has shown, such statistical tables had played a similarly important role during the previous cholera epidemics in 1832 and 1849.[100] During the war they were generally consistent and credible.

These monthly figures were very rough and often lacked any comparative perspective to be intelligible to non-initiated readers, yet the figures remained as a reminder of impending doom. The medical information which trickled down to the reader during the war served a collective purpose and fed directly into a martyr/redemptive narrative of the war. In other terms statistical accounts from the war proved very deficient. Even the few medical authors who cared to produce statistical returns changed perceptibly their nosology or used idiosyncratic names for the same diseases. Some doctors actually openly questioned the validity of French summary statistical evidence.[101] Medical descriptions remained vague and almost impossible to compare within the same book![102] The army itself had not included in its epidemiological and statistical returns any of the most important diseases: measles and scarlet fever were only reported from 1874, syphilis and malaria from 1875, meningitis in 1885, mumps, diphtheria and tuberculosis in 1888, influenza in 1889, and dysentery and rheumatism entered the medical returns when the nosology was overhauled in 1901.[103] In 1870–71, therefore, many of the medical statistics were based on amalgamated diseases (venereal diseases), under-reported or using misplaced categories (various diseases, pulmonary diseases, cold etc). The debates that have taken place on tuberculosis

---

99 E. Cresson, *Cent Jours à la Préfecture de Police, 2 novembre 1870 – 11 février 1871* (H. Plon, Nourrit et Cie, 1901), pp. 60–1.
100 C. J. Kudlick, *Cholera in Post-Revolutionary Paris : A Cultural History* (Berkeley, University of California Press, 1996), pp. 135–7.
101 E. Delorme, *Traité de chirurgie de guerre* (2 vols, Félix Alcan, 1888–93), vol. 2, p. 347.
102 L. Fiaux, *L'Hygiène militaire, esquisses historiques et médicales* (Victor Rozier, 1871), pp. 67–9.
103 Ministère de la Guerre, *Aperçu statistique*, pp. 41, 45, 50, 58, 66, 72, 95, 80, 85, 89, 103.

in *fin-de-siècle* France could also take place over every single disease reported in 1870.[104] From this confusion nevertheless emerged a distinctive picture of medicine as the instrument of clarification and rational understanding of the crisis. The role played by medical accounts to make sense of the 'feverish state' of Paris during the siege certainly explains how medical discourses later permeated in most accounts of the period and structured social sciences and even literature. This prominence given to medicine renewed many unsatisfied ambitions.

The 4 September revolution with its more explicit references to the 1789–99 period also reminded historically aware medical men of the great changes that had taken place seventy-eight years before, when medicine was in a deeper state of crisis from which emerged the great renewal of French clinical medicine.[105] The radical medical press welcomed the return of liberty and stated that medicine was by nature the most republican art and science:

> as a science, [medicine] had, through public hygiene, which is first and foremost in its area of competence, the closest relations with social economy. When [the revolution] will organise the new state of things and will care about the people's well-being, the law makers and administrators will need the advice of hygienist and physician. His studies have made him more open to liberal tendencies.... He is therefore called to join the general movement.... Medicine must also be introspective and see whether, in its own organisation there is nothing to amend. Official quackery has competed shamelessly with street quackery.[106]

Among the many institutions that needed reform urgently, none had more political undertones than the Assistance Publique of Paris, which had provided the poor with a basic safety net since the revolution and which remained free to the poorest in spite of budgetary restrictions.[107] Maxime du Camp, the notorious reactionary author and friend of Flaubert, called it 'the honey cake: it does not feed Cerberus, it appeases it'.[108] In the same page he also predicted that: 'the day the Assistance Publique would disappear, the pavements would be crowded by the crippled, epidemic diseases would take over the city, infanticide would strangle illegitimate new-born babies and the mob would riot and break into the bakeries'.

To many of his contemporaries the Assistance Publique played a unique role in social control. It also regulated an important section of the medical world of

104 See the debate on French statistics after the publication of A. Mitchell, 'An inexact science: the statistics of tuberculosis in late nineteenth-century France', *Social History of Medicine*, 3:3 (1990) 387–404.
105 D. M. Vess, *Medical Revolution in France: 1789–1796* (Gainesville, Florida State University Press, 1975), pp. 54–114; Faure, *Histoire sociale de la médecine*, pp. 62–7; L. Brockliss and C. Jones, *The Medical World of Early Modern France* (Oxford, Clarendon Press, 1997), pp. 802–18.
106 *GMP*, 25 (1870) 483.
107 Gaillard, *Paris la ville*, p. 320. Survival rather than comfort was the norm; R. Fuchs, *Poor and Pregnant in Paris: Strategies for Survival in the Nineteenth Century* (New Brunswick, Rutgers University Press, 1992); A. Pain, *Des divers modes de l'Assistance Publique* (Baillière, 1865).
108 M. du Camp, *La Charité privée à Paris* (Hachette, 1885), p. 2.

Paris. The Assistance Publique was in charge not only of some hospital appointments but also of the staffing of the wards, the finances and the distribution of relief. Under the Second Empire the Assistance remained under the tight grip of the imperial government and under the patronage of the Empress herself. The government seized the hospitals' endowments and repaid them with the more precarious *rentes d'état*, while simultaneously expropriating the Assistance Publique from many of its properties to make room for Haussmann's grand rebuilding of Paris.[109] Under an authoritarian regime the Assistance Publique proved to be a docile servant of the state. Autocratic managers like Husson, 'the khediv of the Assistance Publique'[110] put into early retirement on 27 September 1870, extended the dictatorial practices to the administration.[111] The apathy of its administration even in cases of emergency provided the radical medical press with opportunities to proclaim the primacy of medical control over social priorities. *L'Abeille médicale* thus proclaimed that 'one should make the same social reform of the Assistance Publique as our forefathers have done with the clergy and the property of the church'.[112]

In the first month of the new Republic the Assistance Publique, closely associated to Haussmann's administration, was put under serious pressure not only from the medical press but also from the streets of Paris. Eugène Razoua,[113] one of the most important leaders of the extreme left and later of the Commune of Paris, led his 61st Battalion of the Garde Nationale in arms to the Hôtel de Ville to demand 'the abolition of the current Assistance Publique'.[114] Under this firm political pressure, the head of staff of the Assistance Publique, Armand Husson,[115] was replaced by Möring, an administrator whose political opinions were more to the left.[116] Jules Ferry,[117] acting Prefect of the Seine, then undertook to reform the Assistance Publique, changing its name and role, to make it both more democratic and more accountable to the new municipality of Paris.[118] Among the major points of Ferry's reform were an enlargement of the Assistance Publique services to the

---

109 Des Cilleuls, *Histoire de l'administration parisienne*, vol. 3, p. 355.
110 *Le Mouvement médical* (14/08/1870).
111 *GMP*, 25 (1870) 530; *L'Union médicale* 10 (29/09/1870) 453.
112 *L'Abeille médicale* (15/08/1870).
113 Razoua (1830–78) led the 61 until the attempted coup of the 31 October and his sacking by the government. He is representative of the socialist left wing which had a lot of influence on the troops of the north of Paris. APdP, Ea 103 21 and Ba 1237.
114 Des Cilleuls, *Histoire de l'administration parisienne sous la troisième république* (Picard Fils and Cie, 1910), p. 168.
115 Des Cilleuls, *Histoire de l'administration parisienne*, vol. 3, p. 354.
116 A. Morillon, *L'Approvisionement de Paris en temps de guerre* (Didier, 1888), p. 72.
117 Jules Ferry became Prefect of the Seine in May 1871 for a few weeks. The 1870–71 period made him unpopular in Paris. J.-M. Gaillard, *Jules Ferry* (Faillard, 1989); L. Fiaux, *Jules Ferry, un malfaiteur public* (Librairie Internationale, 1886).
118 AAP, 542 Foss 1.

whole of the Seine department, the devolution of charitable help and income support in kind and money to the *arrondissement* municipalities, and the creation of a general council of hospices for his own selection of potentially republican medical luminaries.[119] Among the medical figures Ferry had chosen for this committee, which had to manage the Assistance through the crisis and create permanent democratic institution for after the war, were Léon LeFort, Paul Broca and a number of moderate republicans.[120] To structure his committee and his reforms, Ferry had respected the hospital medical hierarchies in the misguided hope of obtaining their support. As the non-medical members tended not to attend regularly, the medical representatives took over the management of this *assemblée constituante* of the hospices.

Over the following few months the relations between Ferry, Möring and the committee became increasingly tense.[121] The executive side of this revolutionary management, Möring and Ferry, had to cope with real emergencies and a fundamental reorganisation of a key instrument of power. Ferry was originally rather vague and seemed to believe that a meritocratic and elected internal democracy could guarantee the independence of the Assistance Publique while firmly anchoring it to republican traditions: 'I wish to avoid the dangers of personal government, which, in this case like in every other, has proven fatal[ly wrong], and the danger of collective administration, which has rightly been accused in 1849[122] of lacking resolution and energy.'[123]

The medical members of the committee looked with increased suspicion upon Ferry, who after 31 October had both mandates of Mayor of Paris and of Prefect of the Seine. His initiatives seemed to threaten their right to pontificate like a second Academy of Medicine and to influence the lives of millions of Parisians. They also felt uneasy with the republican government and feared that any decision taken during the war might be repealed and backfire on them if they validated it.

By choosing high-ranking medical 'experts', Ferry had committed a major mistake and had put one of the most important reforms of the Parisian administration in the hands of people who were least likely to undermine their own positions. One of the key issues to arise, beyond that of the legitimacy of any committee, was the devolution of real power over hospital appointments. The medical members of the committee wanted this power for themselves, while Ferry wanted to keep a controlling veto on administrative and medical appointments. In the middle of the war, Broca published a small pamphlet on this fairly obscure but professionally

119 AAP, 542 Foss 3, *Procès verbal du conseil général des hospices.*
120 F. Schiller, *Paul Broca, explorateur du cerveau* (Éditions Odile Jacob, 1990), pp. 78–9.
121 AAP, 542 Foss 2, 23/11/1870.
122 The law of 10 January 1849 had created a strong administration in the hands of the Prefects of Police and of the Seine department. A. Fleury, *De l'Assistance Publique à Paris* (Rousseau, 1901), p. 10.
123 AAP, 542 Foss 3, 15/10/1870.

vital issue.[124] From mid-November onwards Ferry found himself facing a resolutely antagonistic medical committee. After the disastrous elections of February 1871, Jules Ferry's last priority was to save the Assistance Publique from the new government's interventions. His strategy at that stage was to link this administration to the republican Parisian municipality and to create a self-governing internal democracy. His 18 February decree, the last one he was entitled to issue, called for all the professional groups of the Assistance Publique to elect representatives to the committee. It meant a noticeable reduction in the number of doctors on the committee; it also meant hastily organised elections. Within forty-eight hours all the employees of the administration had voted except the physicians and surgeons. Broca and Verneuil then proceeded to obtain the support of Thiers and of members of the old administration to undermine Ferry's position.[125] In a fierce debate in March the medical members of the committee clearly denounced Ferry's ambitions, calling his government '*gouvernement de la défense*', consciously avoiding the word '*nationale*'. The meeting turned sour and Ferry left, unable to break the medical veto which considered that 'the reaction does not seem to us as frightening as it is to Monsieur le préfet. Were it to triumph, its success could only be ephemeral. In any case, the existence of the Conseil des Hospices seems assured forever.'[126]

This political assessment was to be proven somewhat optimistic when, a few months later, Thiers's edict of 15 June re-established the hated hierarchy and gave Husson[127] increased powers at the Préfecture.[128] In a nutshell the debates on the autonomy and internal democracy of the Assistance Publique were a real test of Ferry's decentralist views. His practice while in power was to allow some freedom while keeping a decisive role for the Prefect. As he foresaw a period of opposition he then attempted to decentralise further, only to be opposed by corporatist interests. This episode, like all other incidents of the war, had longer-term consequences. Möring eventually returned to his functions with the return of Jules Ferry's administration, but Ferry never attempted again to reform or democratise the medical and health services of Paris, letting instead the Paris Conseil Municipal take the reality of power from this administration.[129]

Beyond the internal debates of the Assistance Publique, the wider medical world was also in turmoil. The revolutionary discourses reached deep in a long history of political and social frustration, yet the revolutionary tradition referred

---

124 *Rapport au conseil général des hospices du département de la Seine sur l'exercice du droit de représentation* (Charles Mourgues Frères, 1870).
125 AAP 542 Foss 3, 1/03/1871, p. 2.
126 AAP 542 Foss 3, 1/03/1871, p. 6.
127 AAP 542 Foss 10, Réorganisation de la préfecture de la Seine.
128 Fleury, *De l'Assistance Publique*, p. 13.
129 Des Cilleuls, *Histoire de l'administration parisienne*, p. 171.

less to the years of intolerance and crisis and more to the hazy memories of the *good* revolutions of 1789 and 1848. In Jules Ferry's words of February 1870 to the Conseil des Hospices, one had to return to 'the systems which took place in 1848 when the ideas which so rightly triumph today were first voiced and developed but could not prevail'.[130] After the Second Empire stalemate, the spectre of 1848 politics revived and asked again some of the most fundamental questions as to the rationale of the medical hierarchy and the cohesion of the medical profession. The radical press, led by *L'Opinion médicale*, *La France médicale* and *La Gazette médicale de Paris*, thus attempted to redefine yet again the role of medical men in society and their progressive role in French politics and society. The elected medical staff of the Garde Nationale met on 5 November, a few days after the attempted coup against the Republic. They discussed a programme in five points which summarise many political issues dividing French medicine:

1. Equality between all doctors, the real basis of confraternity.
2. Independence and autonomy [*sic*] of the [medical] corps of the national guard.
3. As little organisation and regulation as possible.
4. An extended [freedom] to private initiative.
5. Freedom for wounded or ill guards to be treated at home or in the ambulance they would choose.'[131]

The young Turks, elected by the soldiers they cared for, claimed a popular legitimacy and intended to turn their war effort to professional and political advantage. After the first few months of the conflict, the only radical medical journal which continued to be printed throughout the war made it clear that the lower ranks of the medical world had reformist ambitions which were to renew pre-war aspirations and address both the content of the medical curriculum and the power structure of the medical world. The *Gazette médicale de Paris* radicalised further and professed a return to the revolutionary free trade of the 1790s; it wished the abolition of large power-producing hospitals and the replacement of faculty-based teaching with apprenticeship at the bedside.[132] While a backlog of frustration and jealousy did influence the more strongly expressed articles, there was also the realisation that the clinical tradition of Parisian hospital medicine was alienating doctors from their patients and that it did not serve best the poorer patients and therefore limited the size of the market.

While none of these much-expected measures showed any signs of materialising, the *Gazette* noted sharply that the newly created Commission d'Hygiène et de Salubrité informing the government 'included men who were called, under the

---

130 AAP, 542 Foss 1, 3/10/1870.
131 *GMP*, 25 (1870) 563.
132 *GMP*, 25 (1870) 572.

ancien régime, princes of science; one would also find a prince of administration. We simply note the facts, later we will discuss the principles.'[133] If they had been in any doubts as to the unwillingness of members of the establishment to renegotiate their status and relinquish their power and habits of nepotism after their obstructionism at the Assistance Publique, these were to be swiftly dispelled. The academicians and the more conservative mandarins had the support of a significant fraction of the press to influence government. The *Union médicale* led by Amédée Latour, a conservative journal established after the 1845 medical congress, promoted established medical men's efforts with the support of the conservative daily press.[134] In October the dominant Red Cross organisation (see Chapter 7) launched a campaign against the smaller private ambulances in competition.[135] The same month the same narrow elite attempted to exclude the majority of the medical men of Paris from the ranks of the privileged few allowed to operate on wounded soldiers. The Commission d'Hygiène et de Salubrité published an announcement:

> aware that this information will be undoubtedly useful to private ambulances which could require urgent surgical help, we believe that we must publish the following list, including a number [66] of civilian surgeons especially competent in matters of operations ...[136]

Later in the siege this lobbying bore its fruits and it became clear that faculty reforms were to be limited to the 9 November franchise which confirmed previous appointments and simply gave back the autonomy lost under the Empire.[137] Radicals seemed on their way to a complete defeat. Any status obtained during the war relied on the unlikely survival of emergency institutions.

Doctors of the Garde Nationale units, for instance, had been elected for the most part. This election process had been re-established in an effort to democratise the armed forces and perhaps find in the republican war effort some new talents who could compare to the great revolutionary heroes. Medical radicals stressed the fact that elected doctors were free from the universal charge of nepotism and only made it through their patients' vote of confidence.[138] This legitimacy had to hold in the balance against the army's disapproval of elected officers. Moreover the radicals were a heterogeneous crowd and the medical status of some of these elected surgeons was sometimes dubious or no more than the second rate *officiers*

---

133 *GMP*, 25 (1870) 509.
134 Léonard, *La Médecine*, p. 195.
135 *GMP*, 25 (1870) 562.
136 *GMP*, 25 (1870) 544.
137 *L'Union médicale* (12/11/1870).
138 *GMP*, 25 (1870) 522.

de santé.¹³⁹ The revolutionary regime tried to implement democratic reforms while relying on established administrations and systems of control. Even when radical views were voiced within these institutions they never managed to become predominant and to alter the shape of administrative mechanics.¹⁴⁰ The radical press could only find a bitter pleasure in quoting the *mea culpa* of the Academy of Science and in sarcastic views on what would come out of any attempts to revitalise French science and medicine. By the end of the siege it did not attempt to undermine in a significant way the legitimacy of the hierarchy any more.¹⁴¹ In the spring of 1871, the 'princes of science' seemed to have truly won against the proletariat of medicine. Pasteur's pamphlet *Some reflections on science in France: why France did not find superior men at this time of danger*,¹⁴² calling for a new better-funded French science, only poured salt on the wounds of the radicals.¹⁴³ To have been so close and yet so far from achieving reforms became an added element of the defeat. The old disputes of 1848 ended the same way.

Post-war scientific priorities led by military concerns built on the existing hierarchies and reinforced them.¹⁴⁴ They also reinforced the trust invested in individual merit hiding rampant nepotism, the French *Sonderweg* in science noted by many historians of science since. The other paradox was that, as Robert Fox noted many years ago, scientists used science to achieve a higher social status and employ their talent in other spheres.¹⁴⁵ The cult of Pasteur and the renewed emphasis on a handful of individuals hides the chronic underfunding of medical and scientific institutions and the lack of openings to collective work.¹⁴⁶ The moral order restoration of 1871, following a Commune that few medical men were to follow, was also a full restoration of the social order of pre-1870 with a greater awareness of scientific and medical shortcomings but little if any impetus to change.¹⁴⁷

Husson, Baron Haussmann's friend and servant, came out of his early retirement and found a post in the republican Préfecture de la Seine as the General

---

139 Vess, *Medical Revolution*.
140 AAP, 542 Foss 3, 11/03/1871. Léon LeFort, champion of medical rights, thus tried to establish a medically controlled Assistance Publique defiant of both city and army.
141 *La France médicale* (15/03/1871).
142 *GMP*, 26 (1871) 522; A. Bopierre, *Pourquoi la France n'a pas trouvé d'hommes supérieurs au moment du péril? Réponse à M. Pasteur, de l'Institut* (Masson, 1871).
143 B. Latour, *The Pasteurization of France* (Cambridge, Mass., Harvard University Press 1988), p. 10.
144 J.-F. Picard, 'L'Organisation de la science en France depuis 1870, un tour des recherches actuelles', *French Historical Studies* 17:1 (1991) 249–68, p. 258; Paul, *From Knowledge to Power*, ch. 1.
145 R. Fox, 'Scientific enterprise and the patronage of research in France, 1800–1870' in G. L. E. Turner (ed.), *The Patronage of Science in the Nineteenth Century* (Leyden, Noordhoff International Publishing, 1976), pp. 9–38.
146 J.-F. Picard, *La République des savants* (Flammarion, 1990), pp. 20–3.
147 R. R. Locke, *French Legitimists and the Politics of Moral Order in the Early Third Republic* (Princeton University Press, 1974).

Secretary. The imperial administration and elite carried on unabated until retirement.[148] The most reactionary medical journals also tried to call for a revival in French medicine which would express definitively the superiority of unspecialised clinical medicine over German theories and methods. The backlash against all things German and the competition with 'Teutonic medicine' does not indicate the sort of servile imitation postulated in Allan Mitchell's work. If anything the war led to a more dogmatic national medicine. Following Elisabeth Crawford's analysis of nationalism and internationalism, one cannot underestimate the fundamental role of a rhetoric of the nation in any reform movement coming after the 1870 war.[149] In many instances, the nostalgic calls for a national science contrast with the rhetoric of internationalism and progress professed before and in the early days of the conflict:

> Before the invasion of the Krupp guns and the Dreyse rifles, French medical science suffered the invasion of German medical science, a deplorable invasion to which our schools, Academies, the press opened their arms with a shameful overzealousness [*empressement*]. ... Almost alone then, *L'Union médicale* resisted this fad. ... We could never see any progress in that arrogant and rude so-called science which forecasted the implacable and ferocious politics which we are now suffering from. ... *L'Union Médicale* wants France to take again the lead of medicine that it once enjoyed without contest, that our schools become again the rendezvous of the youth of the world.[150]

148 *Le Mouvement médical* (13/08/1871).
149 E. Crawford, *Nationalism and Internationalism in Science, 1880–1939* (Cambridge University Press, 1992), pp. 28–46.
150 *L'Union médicale*, 25 (07/01/1871).

4 Militarisation and war effort: Paris, the 'giant hospital'

On 14 June 1880 Baron Hippolyte Larrey (1808–95), the son of the man Napoleon I had called 'the most virtuous man I have ever known', the so-called 'great Larrey',[1] acted as one of the last direct links with the imperial legend and delivered his most important speech in the French Chamber of Deputies.[2] Larrey, himself a 'virtuous' man, represented simultaneously the old guard of imperial France and the medical elite of his time.[3] After his retirement from the military medical services, Larrey was elected in 1877 to the provincial constituency of Bagnères-de-Bigorre, from where his father originated. Larrey was a Bonapartist at heart, but his speeches mostly illustrated his professional loyalties and defended either the rights of pensioners or the need for comprehensive military reform.[4] The very long June speech of 1880 supported the independence of the army medical corps. A real *tour de force* that lasted several hours, this speech retraced his father's career and his own campaigns. It weaved together the glorious days of the Napoleonic victories and the infamous conditions of the wounded and sick at war. Largely building up on the tropes developed by Henry Dunant in his *Souvenirs de Solferino*, Baron Larrey mixed sentimental imagery with forceful sanitarian and organisational discourses to develop his political programme for military medicine. The 1870 war in this speech took a paradoxical role: it was altogether the focus of a major national crisis, a sanitarian disaster and the evidence of what an

---

1 The myth of the 'great' Dominique Larrey, pioneer, soldier and doctor, heroic and romantic figure, replaced that of Ambroise Paré among army surgeons across the world. P. Triare, *Dominique Larrey et les campagnes de la Révolution et de l'Empire, 1766–1842* (Tours, Alfred Mame et Fils, 1902); A. Soubiran, *Le Baron Larrey, chirurgien de Napoléon* (Fayard, 1966); J. H. Porter, *On Some Forms of Contemporeanous Conveyances for the Sick and Wounded in Peace and War* (Harrison and Sons, 1878), p. 3.

2 L. J. B. Berenger-Féraud, *Le Baron Hippolyte Larrey (1808–1895)* (Fayard Frères, 1899), pp. 91–100; *Discours prononcés le 18 octobre 1895 aux funérailles du baron Hippolyte Larrey* (Librairies-Imprimeries Réunies, 1895). Larrey was very attached to the Empire and retired immediately after the end of the Commune war in 1871. J. Rieux and J. Hassendorfer, *Centenaire de l'école d'application du service de santé militaire (1850–1950)* (Paris and Limoges, Charles Lavauzelle and Cie, 1951), p. 61.

3 Hippolyte Larrey's grave read simply 'worthy of his father', who was himself described above 'as the most virtuous man I have ever known' by Napoleon. This indirect link to the Emperor in lieu of an identity is one of the ironies of Larrey's life. See F. Brown, *Père Lachaise: Elysium and Real Estate* (New York, Viking Press, 1973), p. 25; P. Reclus, *Éloge du baron Hippolyte Larrey* (Masson, 1898).

4 E. Bloesinger, *Quelques grandes figures de la chirurgie* (2 vols, J. B. Baillière et Fils, 1947), vol. 1, pp. 196–8.

independent military medicine could achieve when self-governed and organised. Larrey argued that only an autonomous medical corps could make rapid practical scientific applications. In his more optimistic pages, he did not hesitate to claim that 'it is to military medicine that one should attribute today some of the best research on hygiene, it is also from military surgery that some of the greatest advances in the practice of the art come'.[5]

This crucial speech quoted a number of documents since lost or which only survived in draft form.[6] These letters to Trochu, the government or the military hierarchy all point to the equivocal position of military medicine in 1870 France. The war weakened the hierarchies and enabled French military surgeons and physicians to voice their grievances about their status in the forces. The 1880 speech was in many ways the culmination of a campaign started in 1870. While he stood as the incarnation of responsible management and heroic imperial traditions, Larrey singularly failed to narrate the minutia of his own powerlessness, for instance the fact that he had to organise his services on a tourist map produced for the 1867 Universal Exhibition, fully illustrated with small sketches of the most important Parisian sites, but neither covering the peripheral *arrondissements* properly nor on the right scale.[7]

This chapter follows some of principal themes of Larrey's story. It discusses the position of army medicine before and during the 1870 war, and the forms of knowledge that military practice developed within French medicine. If applied to French society, this specific way of thinking about health, hygiene and fitness was not without disturbing consequences.

After the defeats of the summer of 1870 and the structural collapse of the army, the republican forces gathered more volunteers and conscripts than ever since the Great Army of Napoleon I. The problems created by this army of an unknown quantity of poorly equipped conscripts were also on an scale unprecedented since the Revolution. The French only partially mobilised and it may be excessive to describe the 1870 war as a total war in the twentieth-century sense,[8] but the reality in Paris at least approached the original Clausewitzian concept.[9]

5 Baron H. Larrey, *Discours prononcé par Monsieur le baron Larrey le 14 juin 1880 su sujet du projet de loi sur l'administration de l'armée* (Librairie de Publications Législatives, 1880) p. 11. Dujardin-Beaumetz in his '*éloge funèbre*' of Larrey put a great deal of emphasis on the impact of this speech: *Discours prononcés le 18 octobre 1895*, p. 7.
6 The Larrey papers are stacked in the archive boxes of the ASSAT, box 62 particularly.
7 ASSAT, box 63/3.
8 S. Förster and J. Nagler (eds), *On the Road to Total War: The American Civil War and the German Wars of Unification, 1861–1871* (Cambridge University Press, 1997), pp. 8–16.
9 D. Pick, *War Machine: The Rationalisation of Slaughter in the Modern Age* (New Haven, Yale University Press, 1993) pp. 113–14; R. Aron, *Penser la guerre, Clausewitz* (2 vols, Gallimard, 1976), vol. 2: *L'Age planétaire*, p. 31; C. Bassford, *Clausewitz in English* (Oxford University Press, 1994).

The central argument of this chapter and that of Chapters 5 and 7 is that militarisation did indeed take place over the period and involved a multiplicity of governmental and non-governmental agencies. The contested concept of 'militarisation' presumes a reorientation of both military and governmental control and initiative in order to mobilise national manpower for the purposes of fighting the war and for industrial war production.[10] As a result, civilian activities become redirected to military aims, such that any distinction between civilian and military spheres becomes meaningless. Seen from this perspective, while Gambetta's call to arms might have seemed to his contemporaries to be an almost nostalgic look backwards to the French revolutionary wars, it might also be announcing the complete involvement of societies in total wars. Thus in 1870 the French fought a 'people's war', organised around Gambetta's call for universal conscription and for *guerre à outrance,* or war to the last. These two aspects are recognisable features of total warfare: mass mobilisation would have united the whole nation in the war effort; while *guerre à outrance* stated uncompromising war aims of unconditional victory. To an extent, this interpretation has been challenged by historians who argue, first, that war to the last ceased to be an option in January 1871, and secondly, that mass mobilisation failed to be enthusiastically endorsed in much of France.[11] I will suggest, however, that those who argue this latter point have taken too narrow a view of the war effort, have focused too much on volunteering and other obvious signs of patriotism, and have failed to take account of other forms of mobilisation.

German observers, aware of these theoretical issues, pointed out that Gambetta's objective had been 'to turn a whole people into an army'.[12] Later English commentators made the same point and described a great deal of the republican campaigns as a 'people's war'.[13] The recruits' (un-)fitness, their (lack of) discipline, their malingering, their abuse of alcohol,[14] their weakness under the knife even, raised a number of issues which could then be applied to the whole

---

10 See for instance K. Grieves, *The Politics of Manpower, 1914–18* (Manchester University Press, 1988); J. Winter, 'Military fitness and civilian health in Britain during World War One', *Journal of Contemporary History,* 15 (1980) 211–44.
11 T. J. Adriance, *The Last Gaiter Button: A Study of the Mobilisation and Concentration of the French Army in the War of 1870* (Westport, Greenwood Press, 1987); F. Roth, *La Guerre de 1870* (Fayard, 1990); S. Audoin-Rouzeau, *1870, la France dans la guerre* (Armand Colin, 1989); idem, 'French public opinion in 1870–1 and the emergence of total war', in Förster and Nagler (eds), *On the Road to Total War,* pp. 393–412; compare with J.-J. Becker, *The Great War and the French People* (Oxford, Berg, 1985).
12 Baron von der Goltz, *Gambetta et ses armée* (Sandoz and Fischbacher, 1877), p. 12.
13 H. M. Hazier, *The Franco-Prussian War: Its Causes, Incidents and Consequences* (2 vols, William Mackenzie, 1873); Lonsdale Hale, *The 'People's War' in France, 1870–1871* (Hugh Rees Ltd, 1904), pp. 2–4.
14 ASSAT, box 62/1, Le Médecin en chef à Monsieur le Contre-Amiral du Quilio, 8/11/1870.

nation.[15] Militarisation means that there is no such thing as a military defeat any more.

Army medicine thus had to negotiate with civilian mobilisation and forms of civic enthusiasm which were culturally alien to this inward-looking and rather specialised profession.[16] While a later chapter discusses in more depth the impulse behind the Red Cross movement in 1870, this chapter will expose how Paris turned into a 'giant hospital',[17] where houses, hotels, theatres even turned into ambulances[18] and improvised hospitals, while makeshift quarters were set up in parks.[19] General Trochu even asked the governmental Commission d'Hygiène et de Salubrité[20] to convert the walls of Paris into a belt of ambulances and hospitals.[21] The relationships between army medicine, army Intendance (Commissariat) and voluntary organisations were complicated and equivocal.[22] While Chapter 8 is more specifically devoted to the issue of conservative surgery, this chapter will illustrate how the giant hospital grew and was structured around principles of circulation, distribution and movement, and also how, when it stopped growing, it started to rot. The great fears of military surgeons and physicians, who, like the rest of the army, were poorly trained and unequipped to face a siege war, materialised. Rot, hospital rot and human decay took place at the alarming rate they had themselves anticipated.[23] The moral universe of military hygiene could not really exist in the confined and unsanitary boundaries of a besieged walled city. Luxurious drapes in converted hotels or bourgeois homes held the putrid air and made it stagnate, openings let in more putrid air from other wards, soiled sheets and inexperienced nurses carried deadly poisons.[24] This narrative will run its course and end with the slow dismantling of the giant hospital which lived out its final days in makeshift wards, soldiers cleaning up schools and buildings and accountants fighting over unpaid bills after all nationalistic fevers had cooled down.

15 *BAIM*, 35 (1870) 961–74, 988.
16 SHAT, Lu 1, Order of 01/09/1870 on the use of civilian doctors.
17 G. H. Boyland, *Six Months under the Red Cross with the French Army* (Cincinnati, Robert Clarke and Co., 1873), p. 232.
18 The word *ambulance* in 1870 had the double meaning of wagon or carriage designed to transport wounded patients, and that of an improvised hospital usually of more than six beds.
19 Baron Larrey coined the phrase *immense hôpital*, *Discours*, p. 59.
20 VdP, VD6 772/1, Fonctionnement du Comité Central des Ambulances, 23 September 1870; ASSAT, box 63/3 Rapport sur les ambulances de rempart; O. Du Mesnil, 'L'Hygiène pendant le siège de Paris', *Annales d'Hygiènes*, 35 (1871) 413–28.
21 *GMP*, 25 (1870) 522.
22 L. J. Bégin, *Études sur le service de santé militaire en France* (V. Rozier, [1849] 1860); R. Vaultier, 'La Médecine militaire en 1870', *La Presse médicale*, 65 (1957) 2203–7.
23 For a discussion of the specific etiology of 'hospital rot' see A. Trémeau de Rochebrune, *Essai de statistique médicale* (Savy, 1871), p. 36.
24 C. A. Gordon, *Le Siège de Paris au point de vue de l'hygiène et de la chirurgie* (J. B. Baillière, 1871), pp. 13, 17.

Military medicine

In the mythology of triumphant French medicine, epic stories based around the exploits of the 'Great Larrey', Percy and their colleagues of the revolutionary and Napoleonic wars shrouded the heroic military medicine with fragments of the imperial legend.[25] The Academy of Medicine still has its walls adorned with giant paintings relating to the exploits of imperial surgeons.[26] Since the end of Napoleonic wars, however, the position of French military medicine had consistently been challenged from within and without. The army had two centres of medical training: one in Strasburg for the early years and one in Paris at the Val-de-Grâce for the final years. Controversial medical figures like Broussais had made the Val-de-Grâce one of the most illustrious teaching institutions. The Strasburg school served a basic purpose and initiated doctors to the specific forms of medical knowledge they had to acquire.

While on paper the training seemed adequate, the army consistently under-recruited and many vacancies in regiments could not be filled due to a definite lack of volunteers.[27] In the early days of the war, 1,295 posts had to be filled hastily through a call to volunteers which produced 2,000 applicants.[28] The low status of military medical men, their fairly dangerous lifestyle and relatively low income did not attract vocations comparable to the enthusiasm for civilian medicine. One of the army medical officers' grievances was that their wages were so low that they could not capitalise enough to be able to settle in a decent private practice on their retirement.[29] Moreover, the life of the army medical man, vegetating in some obscure garrison town in France or Algeria, lacked any appeal and did not favour profitable marriages. Beyond the work done at the Val-de-Grâce, military medicine produced a handful of contributors to the few specialised journals. The type of medicine they practised specialised them early into disciplinarian forms of epidemiology concerned mostly with venereal diseases, fatigue and simulated ailments.

The status of military medicine within the army was also a subject of incessant dispute between the medical staff and their hierarchical superiors. After a few decades of relative independence, military medicine depended on the Intendance, the commissariat that also dealt with food and equipment services and which

---

25 Soubiran, *Le Barron Larrey*; C. Laurent, *Histoire de la vie et des ouvrages de P.F. Percy* (Versailles, Daumont, 1827).
26 G. Weisz, *The Medical Mandarins: The French Academy of Medicine in the Nineteenth and Early-Twentieth Centuries* (Oxford University Press, 1995).
27 SHAT, Lu 1, *Rapport sur le fonctionnement du Service de santé militaire*, October ? 1870.
28 M. Lévy, *Notes sur les hôpitaux-baraques du Luxembourg et du Jardin des Plantes* (J. B. Baillière et Fils, 1871), p. 5.
29 P. Maublanc, *Nouveau mode de recrutement de la médecine et de la pharmacie militaire* (J. Dumaine, 1871), p. 3.

poorly provided for its various needs. This umbilical link to the least glorious corps of the French army was felt to be not only ignominious but also a constraint. This situation was not the result of an accident of history. The army had effectively grown to fear the notorious independence of spirit of army medical officers.[30] After the 1848 revolution many medical officers were displaced or sacked,[31] Marchal (de Calvi), a radical figure still agitating by 1870, among them.[32] The creation of the schools of Strasburg and Val-de-Grâce had precisely the purpose of creating an *esprit de corps* separated from civilian politics.[33] After the repression of 1851, the army had awarded a supposed equivalence between military ranks and medical ones which did not alleviate the surgeons' lack of authority. Even with an equivalent rank to that of a captain, a medical man could not give orders or be obeyed by a private. In regiments, army medical officers disposed of the musicians to officiate under them as stretcher-bearers and to cope with the high levels of casualty. The medical officer serving in a regiment only had his bag and the odd mule-load of equipment to face the basic needs of a large unit.[34] To compensate for this minimal organisation, there were a number of attempts at *premiers secour* (first aid). Soldiers in some provincial armies, like the Armée du Nord, also kept a small bottle of chloride (*chlorure de fer*), a band of fabric and a little square of cloth to dress superficial wounds.[35] This basic equipment served as a reminder that they were left to themselves or to the enemy's services.[36]

Such an absence of logistical support posed many problems for the wounded themselves obviously, but it also undermined the cohesion of the squad. The excuse of taking a friend to cover enabled one or two men to retreat discreetly. Volunteers for moves like these abounded and this 'humanitarian' desertion undermined the morale of those who stayed. When a number of small units of stretcher-bearers emerged during the war, its members were often perceived as traitors.[37] The left radical clubs constantly denounced stretcher-bearers and the

30 Rieux and Hassendorfer, *Centenaire de l'école d'application*, p. 47.
31 J. L. Rouis, *Histoire de l'école impériale du Service de santé militaire de Strasbourg* (Berger Levrault, 1898), p. 185. ASSAT, box 66/3.
32 C. J. Marchal (de Calvi), *Lettres à l'Académie de Médecine à propos du procédé dit de syphilisation* (Plon Frères, 1852), p. 4, and *La Guerre de 1870, formule du Communalisme* (Pau, Imprimerie Véronèse, 1871).
33 Rieux and Hassendorfer, *Centenaire de l'école d'application*, pp. 48–54.
34 A. Flamarion, *Le Livret du docteur* (Le Chevalier, 1872), p. 25.
35 F. Quesnoy, *Campagne de 1870* (Furne Jouvet et Cie, 1872), p. 48.
36 P. Déroulède, *Pages françaises* (Bloud, 1909), pp. 39–42; *1870, feuilles de route, des bois de Verrières à la forteresse de Breslau*, (F. Juven, 31st edn, 1907), pp. 208–11. The army provided this basic equipment to a number of soldiers, but in many instances, like in Déroulède's case, parents provided these widely available first aid materials. Proposals in that direction originated from civilians: F. Broussière, *Lettre à Monsieur le Major Général de l'armée du Rhin relative au pansement des blessés sur le champ de bataille* (Marseille, Imprimerie Commerciale Doucet, 1870).
37 A. Chassagne, *Contre le Prussien: I Hier…, II aujourd'hui, … III demain* (Paris and Limoges, Henri Charles Lavauzelle, 1896), p. 65.

government eventually mobilised them on 31 December 1870.[38] Within besieged Paris, the municipality reinforced an already large mobile network of *ambulances volantes* with all the omnibuses and cabs available.[39] Larrey's wish to create a proper stretcher-bearers corps from unarmed *gardes nationaux* remained unanswered by their commander, General Clément Thomas.[40] In all the wars of the 1860s, or even in 1870 on the open battlefields, French medical officers operated on the most serious cases on the spot or bandaged summarily the most superficial ones before moving them along to a network of trains.[41] Following the French strategy based on mobility, the army believed in rapid transportation on the back of donkeys and in carriages away from the battlefield, and, often away from their concern, to let the wounded fall into the hands of civilian hospitals.

The record of French military medicine during the Second Empire was bleak: the Crimea had been disastrous, particularly towards the end; Italy had led to Dunant's denunciation. Because all European wars had ended in French victories, Chenu's laborious accounts of the problems of organisation and the causes of high mortality rates, while always well reviewed, failed to impress durably either public opinion or key members of the administration. Chenu, backed by Larrey, attempted several times to bring the issue onto the political agenda. Maxime du Camp, Marchal (de Calvi), G. Dubois and Montanier all reviewed his work in journals as diverse as the *Tribune médicale, Le Journal des débats,* the very governmental *Moniteur universel* and *L'Opinion nationale.*[42] Left-wing and right-wing newspapers admitted his views to their columns and many explicitly endorsed his conclusions.[43] The wars in Mexico or in North Africa had also exposed the French troops to a series of epidemiological disasters which remained to a large extent inextricably linked to the geography and were too specifically colonial to inspire any measurable reform. In these respects, perhaps, 1870 provided the first opportunity for a real reflection on the role of military medicine and, for army medical men at least, a necessary breakthrough.

There are problems in this narrative of progress, and while one cannot deny that the administration of war medicine by the *intendants* had been often

---

38 L. de Cazenove, *Compte rendu des travaux du comité sectionnaire Lyonnais de la Société Française de secours aux blessés et malades des armées de terre et de mer* (Lyon, Imprimerie de Bellan, 1872), p. 11.
39 J. de Marthold, *Mémorandum du siège de Paris, 1870–1871* (Charovay Frères, 1884), p. 206. This requisition came late in the siege, around 10/12/1870.
40 Larrey, *Discours,* p. 55.
41 ASSAT, box 62/7, Circulaire du Ministère de la Guerre (Bordeaux) sur la réorganisation des résaux d'évacuation, 12/01/1871.
42 *The Lancet,* 2 (24/12/1870) 897.
43 J. C. Chenu, *De la mortalité dans l'armée et des moyens d'économiser la vie humaine* (Hachette, 1870), pp. 130–4.

disastrous for the patients,[44] it is perhaps more debatable to put military medicine at the heart of any strategic thinking.[45] The *intendants* maintained that military medical men had hegemonic views over their administration and attempted to distract from the real matter of organising and equipping more fresh troops. They also rejected the assimilation of human lives with a capital implied in one of Chenu's works (Chenu talked of *économiser la vie humaine*) in favour of the more common and more widely held glorious tropes of a discourse of sacrifice and heroism.[46] They also reflected, often implicitly, on the well-known axiom of modern warfare: 'wounded soldiers are more of a hindrance [to the work of the army] than dead ones'.[47] In another instance, Intendance officers were reported to have stated: 'you keep soldiers for too long with too much medical attention, you keep the lazier ones and the deserters. One cannot be so weak in the army! One needs to know when to sacrifice 10,000 men to save 300,000.'[48]

If this insensitive sabre-rattling played into the hands of the reformers, it remains unclear, on the other hand, that a simple devolution of powers to the medical staff would have necessarily meant an improvement in efficiency, however accurately such an ideal could be measured. It remains also debatable that the evidence brought forward during the 1870 war had anything like the weight to carry a reform. Baron Larrey's speech came a little prematurely and the final objective of autonomy did not come through until 1882.[49] The Intendance came out of the war completely discredited for having sent the equipment to the wrong places and, in other instances, having dispatched the ammunitions away from the army while showing a blind bureaucratic attachment to forms and orders.[50] However, Chenu and Larrey's attempts to capitalise on this discredit were not always successful.[51] Larrey's remarks that, on the one hand, the Intendance had left doctors inactive and, on the other, it had used them too hastily to staff the regiments contradicted each other within a few paragraphs.[52] Chenu's discourse on administrative blunders contrasted with his own largely administrative role in the Red Cross and with his support of an unqualified administrative

---

44 Each profession has its corporatist account, however, which helps balance the picture a little: P.-J. Linon, *Officiers d'administration du Service de santé* (ERMM, 1983).
45 Many witnesses have quoted a multitude of instances of administrative chaos, a feeling archival sources confirm. É. Gavoy, *Étude de faits de guerre* (Paris and Limoges, Henri Charles Lavauzelle, 1894), p. 16; AAP, 542 Foss 80, Rapport de l'hôpital Necker, 14/07/1871, p. 5.
46 L. Chapplain, *De l'Intendance du corps médical militaire et de la mortalité dans l'armée* (Librairie Jean Dumaine, 1872), p. 83.
47 J. E. Rochard, *Histoire de la chirurgie française* (J. B. Baillière et Fils, 1875), p. 856.
48 H. Monod, *Rapport du comité évangélique* (Sandoz and Fichbacher, 1875), p. 41.
49 Rieux and Hassendorfer, *Centenaire de l'école d'application*, pp. 62–5. 1882 saw the creation of a *service de santé* and 1889 the real autonomy of this new service.
50 R. de Belleval, *Les Souvenirs de guerre d'un intendant militaire* (Calmann-Lévy, 1886).
51 Quesnoy, *Campagne de 1870*, pp. 10–11.
52 Larrey, *Discours*, pp. 52–4.

staff and command.⁵³ His association with aristocratic sponsors and his endorsement of social hierarchies cast a shadow on his reputation.⁵⁴ The Intendance also tried to work out the lessons of the conflict and attempted to reform itself before it had to cope with any governmental dictate. The reports published in 1875 thus claimed, rather too late, to implement whatever lessons came from the American Civil War.

The medical services showed their shortcomings almost immediately at the outbreak of the war. Many regiments did not dispose of the required number of medical officers. Few in the army knew anything about the Geneva Convention and were either ready or willing to abide by its terms.⁵⁵ All the defeats turned into substantial sanitary disasters, especially in Sedan,⁵⁶ while the large number of besieged fortresses and cities soon presented new problems.⁵⁷ Largest among all of them was Paris, which also withheld one of the longest sieges of the war.

Larrey, who had been with the Emperor's army, managed to escape from the trap of Sedan, and to return to Paris by 15 September 1870. There he found a chaotic situation which only gradually took the shape of a giant hospital. This chaos reflected not only the inoperativeness of an improvised government but also a great shift of emphasis to a Paris *libre*, a revolutionary city once again leading the world, which co-existed uneasily with a giant hospital able to endure the siege, to suffer patiently and not die.

Larrey found in Paris a military organisation deeply divided and uneasy with the troops they had to command to a victory most did not believe in. There were great differences between the various volunteers and mobilised units: the *gardes nationaux*, the bourgeois forces which had been the support and downfall of so many regimes in the nineteenth century, had been reinforced with a new militia from the working-class corners; the *gardes mobiles*, relatively better equipped and better trained, were largely provincial troops, many of them Breton and unable or unwilling to communicate in French;⁵⁸ while a smaller number of semi-professional soldiers, many from the marines (*troupes de marine*), were serving in the forts around Paris. The Garde Nationale was the largest body and its size was all

---

53 E. Delorme, *Traité de chirurgie* (2 vols, Félix Alcan, 1888–93), vol. 1, p. 348; M.-R. Brice and Capitaine Bottet, *Le Corps de santé militaire en France* (Berger Levrault and Cie, 1907), pp. 373–403.
54 G. Wyrouboff, 'Les Ambulances de la Société française de secours aux blessés pendant la guerre de 1870–71', *Philosophie positive*, 6 (1875) 379–403, p. 386.
55 C. Lüder, *La Convention de Genève au point de vue historique, critique et dogmatique* (Erlangen, Besold, 1876), p. 227. See Chapter 7.
56 ASSAT, box 64/11–14 bis.
57 ASSAT, box 64/23, G. Coignon, *État sanitaire de Bitche pendant le siège*; F. Poncet, *Le Siège de Strasbourg (1870)* (Montpellier, Boehm et Fils, 1873); É. Bancel, *Relation médico-chirurgicale du siège de Toul* (Nancy, Berger Levrault, 1872).
58 Regional differences created problems for their lodgers and for the normal service. VdP, VD6/1454/4, letter to the mayor of the sixth *arrondissement*.

but impressive. Since 14 September 1870 all men between the ages of twenty-one and sixty had had to register with their local Garde Nationale forces.[59] In fact the army had such a loose grasp over this force that it had to attempt several reorganisations in the course of the war to turn some of them into proper fighting units, differentiating between the *mobilisé* (the marching units) and the sedentary ones who simply staffed the walls of Paris. In spite of this effort the Parisian army retained a deeply parochial identity and the Garde Nationale had its deepest roots in the urban neighbourhoods and solidarity networks. Soldiers resented having to serve with people 'from streets absolutely foreign' to their own.[60] This evidence reinforces Gould's central argument on the 'neighbourliness' of 1870–71 politics, with the caveat that such neighbourhoods were fixed because of the war and dependence on *arrondissement* provisions.[61] This large republican army (including the *gardes mobiles*) also enjoyed revived revolutionary privileges[62] and could elect its non-commissioned officers[63] and medical officers.[64] These elections were seen as the symbol of the new Republic or a return to the revolutionary chaos by the left and the right respectively.

Larrey took part in the reorganisation of Paris into nine sections that divided the city into segments cutting through the very political outer rings (*faubourgs*)/ centre division and uniting under one command the red neighbourhoods with bourgeois ones. He instituted a military hierarchy of medical officers in chief for each section, who then reported to him as to the functioning of the hospital administration.[65] The army medical service brought its priorities to the management of the conglomerate of private ambulances and hospitals of Paris. As seen in Chapter 7, these priorities could be widely different from those of civilian medical men.

They also brought into this enthusiastic but wasteful administration a sense of hierarchy which was alien and often unappealing to civilian doctors. Among the more specific forms of containment, the army still believed fervently in practices of quarantine and isolation. With smallpox devastating the *moblots* (Breton soldiers' ranks), two hospitals were defined as more strictly designated to contain the disease:

59 J. P. T. Bury, *Gambetta and the National Defence: A Republican Dictatorship in France* (Longmans, 1936) p. 143.
60 VdP, VD6/1567/1, VIIème arrondissement, assistance aux gardes nécessiteux, letter of 14 December 1870.
61 R. V. Gould, *Insurgent Identities: Class, Community and Protest in Paris from 1848 to the Commune* (Chicago University Press, 1996) pp. 165–85.
62 G. Carrot, 'La Garde nationale, une institution de la nation' (Thèse de doctorat du troisième cycle, Université de Nice, 1979), p. 224. A. de Grandeffe, *Mobiles et volontaires de la Seine* (Dentu, 1871), p. 66.
63 M. Bazan, *Les Conscrits* (Berger Levrault, 1981), p. 19; G. Wright, 'Public opinion and conscription in France, 1866–1870', *Journal of Modern History*, 14:1 (1942) 26–45.
64 Delorme, *Traité de chirurgie militaire*, vol. 1, p. 352.
65 ASSAT, box 63/4–5.

Bicêtre and later the veterinary school of Maison d'Alfort.[66] In fact they probably contributed to the spread of disease as the thirty odd carriages which brought the sick soldiers usually carried other passengers on the way back.[67] Beyond quarantine and disciplinarian measures taken against the spread of syphilis (see Chapter 9), army medical men and civilians who had served in previous conflicts, like Léon LeFort, attempted to impose drastic methods of malinger hunting.

To seek those who actively conspired to deceive medical officers by cheating had been the subject of a series of Val-de-Grâce lectures in the 1869 academic year. In this series of lectures, Edmond Boisseau tried to define malingering and simulated diseases as a forensic nosological category.[68] As Roger Cooter reminds us, the history of malingering might well be a history without an object since malingering remains entirely defined by only one side of this tense relationship between a doctor and a patient.[69] What malingering reveals is more the military doctor's obsession with the control of the supposedly passive body of subordinate patients. What was malingering then may be later deemed a psychological form of damage. Military doctors paid very little attention to the mental health of soldiers. Civilian statisticians working for the Parisian hospitals could not see any direct link between the war and cases of insanity.[70] The number of psychiatric cases reported remained small and always related to some direct impact on the brain tissues. The most obvious manifestations of this were forms of ataxia, paralysis, loss of memory or speech impediment, usually followed or preceded by strokes.[71] On the other hand, some medical authors later designated war itself as the manifestation of 'social ataxia', the expression of a lack of muscular co-ordination, a collective crisis of epilepsy.[72]

In spite of a greater awareness of the dangers of malingering, its extent should not be exaggerated. Stéphane Audoin-Rouseau, in his study of army morale, does not bring forward instances of self-mutilation in the early days of the war and one can find little or no evidence of real self-mutilation during the siege of Paris.[73] While extreme forms of malingering may not have been practised as much as in the Napoleonic wars,[74] softer options were available. Mocked illnesses or minor

66 Monod, *Rapport du comité évangélique*, p. 55.
67 Larrey, *Discours*, p. 56.
68 E. Boisseau, *Des Maladies simulées et des moyens de les reconnaître* (J. B. Baillière et Fils, 1870).
69 R. Cooter, 'Malingering', as yet unpublished paper, version 6.3.96, p. 3.
70 AAP, 542 Foss 125, Secrétariat Général de la Statistique, rapport, 1872, p. 1.
71 A. Benoist de la Grandière, *Compte rendu chirurgical de l'Ambulance des soeurs de Saint-Joseph de Cluny* (Baillière, 1871), pp. 56–65.
72 H. E. Beaunis, *Impressions de campagne, 1870–1871, siège de Strasbourg, campagne de la Loire, campagne de l'Est* (Félix Alcan and Berger Levrault et Cie, 1887), p. 2.
73 Audoin-Rouzeau, *1870*, pp. 37–73.
74 A. Forrest, *Conscripts and Deserters: The Army and French Society during the Revolution and Empire* (Oxford University Press, 1989).

injuries justifying an extended stay in the homely comfort of private ambulances were routinely denounced by army medical inspectors but seemed a relatively minor problem. On over ten days of inspection of the third military sector, while temperatures were already falling below freezing point and at a time when skirmishes became more violent, Dr Vauthier could identify only thirty-two cases of imaginary, chronic or minor ailments, justifying a sanction and a return to a regiment.[75] Far from avoiding military service, soldiers volunteered to benefit from a range of interesting benefits in kind. Serving in the Garde Nationale guaranteed an income in days of very slack employment. Many middle-class young men actually volunteered to serve in the central offices. Through active patronage the staff of the ministry soon grew from 13,000 men to 41,000, few of whom were, according to the rules, short-sighted, with a limp or under the minimum size.[76]

What troubled Larrey and his colleagues was perhaps less that civilian doctors lacked the training to identify sophisticated forms of simulated ailments, than that they might be too soft with convalescent patients who seemed to fail to return to the combating units at the rate one was entitled to expect.[77] 'They treat [the soldiers] like normal patients ... and distribute exemptions and hospital tickets in large numbers.'[78]

Closer examination of the evidence seems to show that, on the contrary, many civilian practitioners actually made a point of imitating their military counterparts and of seeking out the malingerers among their patients. Many of the accounts of malingering cases were silenced for decades after the war. When they emerged, they were often linked to some other narrative of the causes of the defeat or were so long after the events that they seemed to matter less.[79] These righteously indignant accounts tend to be quite technical and resemble detective fiction. Sarah Bernhardt, an example of a patriotic actress turned nurse, thus relates in her autobiography how a soldier seemed to suffer from dysentery every time his wounds looked about to heal. The doctor in charge of the ambulance asked the actress, perhaps one best qualified to judge simulators, to spy on the patient. Bernhardt found that the soldier was chipping his copper bed. The ingenious bed-chemist then mixed the metal dust with some salt and water to oxide it and ingested the poison to avoid front-line service.[80] She denounced him immediately and had him removed from 'her'

75 ASSAT, box 63/4, 'Maladies simulées ou affections trop légères pour necessiter un séjour dans les ambulances', 3e secteur, inspection du 26/11/1870 – 8/12/1870.
76 L. Fiaux, *L'Hygiène militaire, esquisses historiques et médicales à propos d'un bataillon de la garde mobile de l'armée de Paris* (Victor Rozier, 1871), p. 25.
77 ASSAT, box 62/6, Notes sur un dépôt de convalescents, 22/11/1870.
78 ASSAT, box 64/30, Rapport du Dr Ricque, rapport sur le service médical du corps des gardes nationaux mobilisés et sur les ambulances de la ligne de Vierzon à Chateauroux, p. 3.
79 Official histories like the historical account produced by the army in 1908 kept all details on malingering or desertions in separate files 'not to be published'. SHAT, Lu 117–18.
80 S. Bernhardt, *Ma Double vie* (2vols, Des Femmes, 1980), vol 1, p. 245.

ambulance. To add credence to the armies' claims, many smaller and private ambulance keepers were less astute or willing to track malingerers and were less than cooperative in returning more or less healthy soldiers to their task.

Their notions of health and convalescence proved very flexible and based on bourgeois understanding of 'perfect health' (*parfaite santé*). The early concerns voiced in August 1870 remained valid for the duration of the war: 'You [the managers of private ambulances] must watch constantly and remind them of their duties to the country, and prevent the abuses that may arise from an excess of well-being, forgivable in their intentions, but in effect disastrous ...'.[81] Civilian concepts implied a long-nursed recovery period that contrasted with the often strictly limited and bureaucratically controlled[82] recovery time allowed to soldiers which rarely exceeded two weeks.[83] The urban world proved to be a difficult space to discipline. The city did not convert easily into a giant barracks. Some soldiers saw in the giant hospital the ultimate refuge from the horrors of the battlefield, and the giant hospital was large enough and complicated enough to provide them with hiding places.

The 'giant hospital'

The giant hospital was the product of the conjunction of a series of voluntary actions showing willingness to support the war effort and a growing centralising effort to control this effort and bring all the ambulances and dispensaries under a central administration. In the first days of the war the various humanitarian agencies, latent since the signature of the Geneva Convention, came into existence with some good fortune. Some of these voluntary ambulances were attached to the specific services of one or several doctors in charge. These ambulances often benefited from local backing, often based around the practice of well-established practitioners and supported by deeply rooted neighbourhood solidarity.[84] The instance of the Palais-Royal ambulance is a case in point. The Palais-Royal doctors 'constituted themselves in a medical commission' that covered fourteen private ambulances and the larger one bearing the name of the neighbourhood (as its name indicates, it was located within the Palais-Royal walls). Founded on 12 September, the ambulance gathered around 17,661 francs and only spent 12,162, thus making a considerable disposable surplus, like most philanthropic organisations of 1870.[85] The popularity of these voluntary institutions created in a political and regulatory

---

81 A. Mony, *Notes d'ambulance, août 1870–février 1871* (Plon, Nourrit and Cie, 1907), p. 53.
82 AAP, 542 Foss 111.
83 A. Bucher de Chauvigné and M. Collet, *Rapport sur le service de l'évacuation des militaires blessés et malades* (Lefebvre, 1875), p. 5.
84 In some *arrondissements* medically led *conseils de familles* were established to support ambulance work. VdP, VD6/791/6, 1er arrondissement.
85 A. Josat, *L'Ambulance municipale du Palais-Royal* (Henri Plon, 1871), p. 9.

vacuum led to a number of charges as to the intentions behind this calculating philanthropic impulse. In a later chapter the debates surrounding the Red Cross will be dealt with in more depth; suffice it to say at this stage that this enthusiasm was unbridled and to a certain extent beyond the reach of central administrators.

Larrey's attempts at dealing with the issue had to be very sensitive and protracted. The *intendant général* reminded the military administration that private ambulance services were necessary and closely linked to public enthusiasm. The press denounced early attempts of the imperial government to subordinate civilian efforts to the *intendant général*.[86] All military efforts to regulate them and to put them under governmental control only came to fruition by December, too late to alter the organisation of health care in Paris. Without the authority to rule over the giant hospital, the military medical administration tried to organise and negotiate as best it could with civilian enthusiasts. The nine military sectors created by Trochu for the defence of the capital[87] had become sanitary sectors and created an army-controlled hierarchy. In each of these sectors one large hospital, a main pharmacy and one inspector organised the procedures and ruled over the food supply.[88] Civilian counter-attempts to organise sanitary action on an *arrondissement* basis or to control the sanitary sectors[89] were promptly resisted by the Intendance and the army.[90] The army slowly structured the giant hospital along the lines of an ever-tighter rationing of goods.[91] In a letter to the *intendant général*, Larrey sketched out the limited authority he wanted to see his men acquire: the power to direct the sick to an ambulance of their choice, to 'wisely limit the number of admissions to those [ambulances] which were in a poor sanitary state, to evacuate to private ambulances the convalescent sick or wounded soldiers'.[92]

Larrey's wishes were only reluctantly granted. He made sure that he did not seem to be attacking the private medical initiative but only tried to regulate better the flow of wounded soldiers from October 1870.[93] This rationing was partly necessary and partly a measure to reclassify some ambulances at the expense of the municipalities. The Comédie-Française thus became a municipal ambulance checked every day by a sergeant from the Val-de-Grâce hospital and Larrey's

86 *GMP*, 25 (1870) 435.
87 SHAT, Li 3.
88 Marthold, *Mémorandum*, pp. 36–7; ASSAT, box 63/4–5, Note to the intendant général, 09/1871; M. Barberet, 'Rapport sur le service des ambulances pendant le siège de Paris dans le cinquième secteur', 28/06/1871, p. 2
89 AAP, 542 Foss 2, *Minutes des séances du Conseil Général des Hospices*, 29/10/1870.
90 M. Ferré, *Rapport sur les services des ambulances municipales du troisième arrondissement pendant le siège de Paris, 1870–71* (Rigal, 1872), p. 8.
91 *GMP*, 25 (1870) 531.
92 Larrey, *Discours*, p. 61; SHAT, Lu 119.
93 ASSAT, box 63/4, Ambulances défectueuses, 12/01/1871, 3e secteur M. Barberet, 'Rapport sur le service des ambulances pendant le siège de Paris dans le cinquième secteur', pp. 13–14; Decree of 20/10/1870.

administration.[94] Wounded soldiers were the most closely monitored desirable goods. The shortfall of wounded soldiers compared with the astonishingly large number of available beds gave each wounded hero an aura of desirability that eluded their sick or frozen counterparts.[95]

The soldiers' broken bodies were real objects of desire. They could be welcomed, passive and tied up in their bandages in the warmth of a bourgeois household, by women suddenly empowered through nursing skills,[96] while the sick presented more obvious threats to the integrity of the family and might bring in the seeds of destruction.[97] Medical officers themselves could, almost in the same breath, denounce this greed for wounded and bruised flesh and make sure that they only brought home to be treated the healthier and tragic body of a freshly wounded soldier. Beyond the many forms of self-interest that justified this attention to wounded heroes, many used these broken bodies to involve themselves in the national conflict and went as far as paying the expenses of burials.[98] The need to justify the existence of an ambulance by the number of soldiers it contained enabled the army to attempt to extract lists of names and precise returns of casualties.

The discipline to which professional soldiers were accustomed was neither automatically acquired nor recognised by their civilian counterparts. The 'glory-economy' of wounded soldiers also pushed many ambulances to keep their patients for as long as possible. In other instances, the female medical staff of a large ambulance/hospital were entitled to lodge recovering patients of whom they had grown fond.[99] Caring had become a way of appropriating. Military observers noticed that 'it became difficult to prevent the doctors or ambulance directors from monopolising the wounded [found on the battlefield] and taking them to their own establishments'.[100] The superficial links between army medicine and civilian or *gardes* medicine did not tie the latter to the military hierarchy. During a siege of non-events, of '*lamentable monotonie*',[101] unfulfilled expectations and latent disillusion, the medical work accomplished in ambulances served a useful political purpose. They distracted the Parisian people from the realities of war. Descriptions

---

94 Bernhardt, *Ma Double vie*, p. 241.
95 While there were around 26,675 beds for a notional army of 475,000 (i.e. just above 5 per cent of the forces), only a fraction of these 475,000 men went to battle. C. A. Gordon, *Lessons on Hygiene and Surgery from the Franco-Prussian War* (J. B. Baillière, Tyndall and Co., 1873), p. 43.
96 *GMP*, 25 (1870) 531; M. Bailin, *The Sickroom in Victorian Fiction: The Art of Being Ill* (Cambridge University Press, 1994), pp. 28–9.
97 AAP, 542 Foss 2, *Minutes des séances du Conseil Général des Hospices*, 29/10/1870, letter from Intendant Général Wolff to Brillon; *GMP*, 25 (1870) 531.
98 J. P. Bonnefont, *Ambulances internationales et privées* (Bureau de l'*Union Médicale*, 1871), p. 2.
99 Josat, *L'Ambulance municipale*, p. 23.
100 ASSAT, box 63/4, M. Barberet, 'Rapport sur le service des ambulances pendant le siège de Paris dans le cinquième secteur', 28/06/1871, p. 14
101 T. Saucerotte, *Lunéville pendant la guerre et le rapatriement* (Gazette *médicale de Paris*, 1872), p. 8.

of ambulance work would narrate the detail of small miracles of charity or the unexpected conversions of actresses or ladies into angel-like nurses.[102]

The minister of education's directive went in the same direction and stated that 'every school must become an ambulance, every school teacher a nurse, every school mistress a sister of charity'.[103] However futile or misplaced this enthusiasm seemed to sceptical observers, even vanity ambulances served a purpose. The Comédie-Française ambulance was a relief from the unadulterated sanitary disasters of the better-established ambulances like the Grand-Hôtel.[104] The former provided a model of radical conversion from the frivolous to the holy and came to take a great symbolic importance for the later views of the siege.[105] A good example of this shift can be found in the generally hostile writings of Archibald Forbes, *The Times* reporter: 'The sins for which Paris had used to be famous, seemed all to belong to the past. She had been half-starved, half-beaten into morality, or it might have been ... that other than physical influence had led her to wash and be clean.'[106]

The most famous representation of the Comédie-Française ambulance still adorns the great staircase of the faculty of medicine of Paris leading to the library and museum (see Figure 6). This major painting identifies each character on whom the light falls like a faint halo; they shine in the forefront of a long corridor of mirroring images. The nurses support the fainting soldiers, bleeding amputees, and patients and nurses are bathing in a deeply religious atmosphere, flesh and blood among the statues of the great men of French literature. The bed scene repeats itself almost endlessly in the picture, as it did throughout Paris. The mobilisation of Paris into a healing machine as well as into a war machine had to use such artistic tropes to achieve this unprecedented effort. Militarisation can work not only through heroic imagery but can also reach deeper in society through sentimental narratives. The 1870 war effort thus left its imprint at so many levels in popular and national consciousness, in child stories, novels, paintings, representations of femininity, that it modified in depth cultural representations of Frenchness. Military narratives cannot account for this and only pervasive organisations such as the giant hospital, the Red Cross and other forms of social organisation can explain the depth of the war trauma.

A great step towards a rationalisation of the giant hospital was justified purely in hygiene terms. Jules Ferry,[107] who presided over the ambulance

---

102 This conversion took place in Paris and did not involve a move to the front. See M. H. Darrow, 'French volunteer nursing and the myth of war experience in World War One', *American Historical Review*, 91:1 (1986) 80–106.
103 *L'Union médicale*, 10 (27/08/1870), 295.
104 Léon LeFort, *Oeuvres*, ed. Félix Lejars (2 vols, Félix Alcan, 1896), vol. 2, pp. 356–63.
105 *GMP*, 25 (1870) 509.
106 A. Forbes, *My Experiences of the War between France and Germany* (2 vols, Hurst and Blackett, 1871), vol. 2, p. 401.
107 J.-M. Gaillard, *Jules Ferry* (Fayard, 1989).

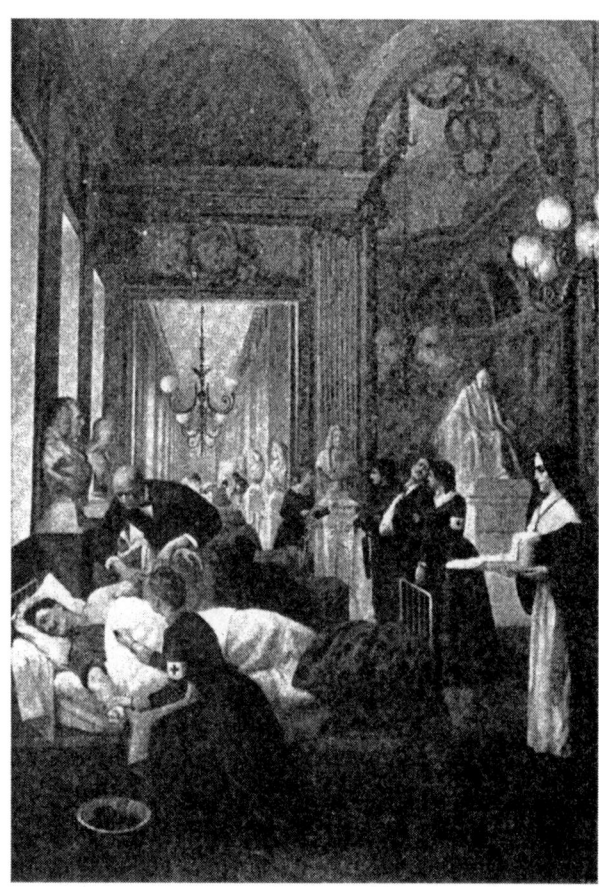

Figure 6 A. Brouillet, *The Ambulance of the Comédie Française, c.* 1885

commission created on 20 October, did not greet Larrey's hegemonic interference with too much glee. Through the military hierarchy, the government kept warning him:

> The only right he has got over the private ambulances is to refuse them the authorisation to treat soldiers, this right I recognise as entirely his. To go beyond this would impede private initiative and would, according to me, block the huge and happy war effort which has led to these patriotic institutions which can only live when free ...[108]

Created at Larrey's initiative, the commission soon took on itself to add another layer of administrative control over the Intendance, Larrey himself and the Parisian network of ambulances.[109] In its composition, the Commission

108 ASSAT, box, 62/1, Note à Monsieur le médecin en chef [Larrey], Murno, Intendant Militaire de la 1ère division, 7/01/1871.
109 ASSAT, box 63/4, Dr Perut, 'Du fonctionement des ambulances pendant le siège de Paris, ambulances du neuvième secteur', 1/03/1871, pp. 5–7.

supérieure des ambulances represented the range of institutions and fields of expertise found in Paris. Ferry presided over the *intendant général* Wolf, Baron Larrey, Chenu of the Red Cross, Broca from the Assistance Publique, two professors from the medical faculty and two hospital doctors and a couple of token priests. This representativeness did much to ensure its inefficiency and little to establish its legitimacy. In the privacy of their own organisations these wise men did not hide their mutual contempt for each other. Within this commission, they slowly tackled their politically sensitive work. Their unwillingness or incompetence explains why it took them over a month to enact the first serious reform.[110] The 20 November reform limited itself to tracking down the soldiers/patients and keeping them on the books.[111]

It was only gradually that private ambulances came to recognise the supremacy of the great hospitals, while the largest among them still continued to treat many important cases.[112] Through this commission's work, however, Larrey's grip slowly tightened up after 14 December, when food became so scarce that private or international ambulances had to turn to the state for their survival.[113] After this turning point ambulances were listed by *arrondissement*, inspected and classified in function of their size.[114] The largest ones could still carry on with major surgery, the medium-sized ones could have wounded and sick patients, while the smaller ones catered for minor injuries and ailments.[115] In spite of the measures taken at the end of November by the commission, the slick democratic machinery never really functioned as planned.[116] In practice Larrey controlled the work of this inspection and established the official list of authorised and monitored ambulances. The 31 December 1870 reform institutionalised the Red Cross, centralised all civilian war efforts in this organisation, and directly linked and subordinated the whole to the army.[117] The original impetus to assemble the giant hospital had come mostly from civilians and respected the integrity of both the great charitable teaching institutions and their methods. After Larrey's intervention,[118] towards the end of the conflict and during the Commune war, the numbers of private ambulances declined and were increasingly excluded from the flow of

110 *GMP*, 25 (1870) 562.
111 J. C. Chenu, *Rapport au conseil de la Société française de secours aux blessés des armées de terre et de mer* (J. Dumaine, 1874), p. 17.
112 Bonnefont, *Ambulances*, p. 4.
113 ASSAT, box 63/4, Perut, 'Du Fonctionement des ambulances', p. 8.
114 ASSAT, box 63/1, handbook produced by the Commission supérieure des Ambulances for the Gouvernement de la Défense Nationale.
115 AAP, 542 Foss 80, Rapport de l'Hôtel-Dieu, 27/04/1871 and 14/12/70.
116 ASSAT, box 63/3, Circulaire Jules Ferry, 20/11/1870.
117 *Recueil de décrets, statuts, règlements et instructions concernant la . . . la Croix Rouge française* (Croix Rouge Française, 1936), p. 36.
118 ASSAT, box 65/3, *Circulaire à messieurs les médecins des ambulances*, 25/01/1871.

patients.[119] What remained of this badly integrated network of hospitals, ambulances and pharmacies became increasingly shaped around the ideals of military medicine. This increased sanitarian and bureaucratic control found municipal counterpowers which stressed that they did not wish to be 'constrained by any control which I would not call useless but which seem to diminish private initiative'. Even last minute resistance still slowed down this militarisation and stole Larrey's victory.[120]

Discipline and space

The role of war medicine in a militarisation of thoughts is perhaps to extend the militarised universal physiological implications of medicine to the whole population. In other words, military medicine, saturated with notions of discipline and efficiency, could then, by extension, apply to the whole population and measure the chasm between ideals of combative fitness and urban reality.[121] If one takes on board again the disciplining gaze described in Foucault's work,[122] there is perhaps no purer expression of this gaze than in the army. It is however a pre-normed gaze which judges rather than sees.[123] Even more than a normative analysis of the nature of humanity, this essentially negative appreciation of the civilian war effort acquired a discursive dimension and informed all narratives of the defeat. In this vision of the world, all the failures of the giant hospital, its inability to maintain discipline and order, its heavy casualty rates and the highly symbolic prevalence of 'hospital rot', gangrene and septicaemia, could be attributed to the human material treated in them and to the civilian superstructure that the army had to respect.

In the forts which the navy officers wished to command like as many ships, soldiers suffered from the plague of the sailors lost at sea: scurvy.[124] Rot was creeping in through the wasteland between the forts and the walls of the city. The metaphor of the ship carried with it the logic of quarantine and *cordon sanitaire*.[125]

---

119 Larrey, *Discours*, p. 64.
120 ASSAT, box 63/5, *Ambulances municipales du XVII arrondissement*, report to Baron Larrey by Dr Angelot, December 1870.
121 For a comparative perspective, Winter, 'Military fitness and civilian health in Britain during World War One'.
122 Particularly the two key works on the theory of a development of a medical 'gaze' in *Discipline and Punish* (Penguin, 1979) and the earlier *Birth of the Clinic* (Tavistock, 1973).
123 This point is accentuated by a defeat but is a central element of all war manpower management after 1870. Grieves, *The Politics of Manpower, 1914–18*.
124 E. Ducaine, 'Le Siège de Paris au point de vue de l'hygiène et de la chirurgie', *Revue scientifique*, 20 (11/11/1871) 468–71, 469; Gordon, *Le Siège de Paris*, p. 8; *La Lancette française* (26/11/1870).
125 The Saint Nazaire epidemic of yellow fever so well described by William Coleman, for instance, was still fresh memory. *Yellow Fever in the North* (Madison, University of Wisconsin Press, 1987), pp. 59–138.

Only disciplinary measures, invisible but real walls between the corrupt civilian world and the military, could now save the army from this threat and in some respects shape this amorphous mass into a proper army.[126]

The American ambulance in Paris brought in the American Civil War experience in terms of hospitals for citizen-soldiers.[127] It contained a number of square tents, heated from the ground, and large enough to accommodate around twenty patients. These tents were mobile and cheap enough to be pulled down at will at the first sign of hospital rot.[128] Thomas Evans had bought the whole American exhibit of the Universal Exhibition of 1867 and put it to use, completing it with more purchases from the start of the conflict.[129] In 1870 the French first applied the American model during the siege of Metz.[130] The American model largely reconstructed the experience of mobility, the moral universe not of the ward but of a war of movement in the open fields where illness was the enemy and could be eluded physically.[131] This way of thinking was well rooted in French military medicine. In Italy, Larrey had dispersed the wounded soldiers to save them from hospital infections.[132] In the provinces this policy was facilitated by the railway network and enabled a distribution of wounded soldiers along the lines,[133] in station ambulances from Rennes to Libourne, Bordeaux to Angers.[134] Within besieged Paris, the rigidity of 'civilian medicine' and the Assistance Publique's structural imperfections made them impervious to reforms.

126 D. Armstrong, 'Public health spaces and the fabrication of identity', *Sociology*, 27:3 (1993) 393–410. I am indebted to Janice Wilcock for this reference. Also see the geographer F. Driver, 'Bodies in space: Foucault's account of disciplinary power', in C. Jones and R. Porter (eds), *Reassessing Foucault: Power, Medicine, and the Body* (Routledge, 1994), pp. 113–31; C. Rosenberg, *Explaining Epidemics and Other Studies in the History of Medicine* (Cambridge University Press, 1992), pp. 90–108.
127 LeFort, *Oeuvres*, vol. 2, pp. 32–3.
128 A. Doyon, *Notes et souvenirs d'un chirurgien d'ambulance* (Lyons, Vingtrinier, 1872), pp. 53–4; ASSAT, box 63/3, V. C. Joly, *L'Ambulance américaine*, roneotype, 12/1870.
129 T. W. Evans, *Memoirs of Dr Thomas W. Evans*, ed. E. A. Crane (2 vols, London, Fisher Unwin, 1905), vol. 1, p. 215. The ambulance was officially created on 25 July 1870; ASSAT, box 63/4, M. Barberet, 'Rapport sur le service des ambulances pendant le siège de Paris dans le cinquième secteur', 28/06/1871, p. 11.
130 William MacCormac, *Notes and Recollections of an Ambulance Surgeon* (J. A. Churchill, 1871), p. 5. The Metz hospital reproduced the Lincoln General hospital; B.-J. Stanhope, *The Evolution of Preventive Medicine in the United States Army* (Washington, D.C., Office of the Surgeon General of the US Army, 1968).
131 ASSAT, box 63/3 *L'Ambulance américaine* report of Dr Joly, December 1873.
132 Chenu, *De la mortalité*, p. 50.
133 J. H. Plumridge, *Hospital Ships and Ambulance Trains* (Seeley, Service and Co., 1975), p. 86. Adapted wagons modified to accommodate stretchers had been exhibited at the 1867 exhibition by the Austrian Baron Mundy.
134 P. Casimir, *Les Pages douloureuses de la guerre* (Niort, L. Favre, 1872), p. 101. The evacuation of the Niort hospital took place on 25 December 1870. Some unfortunate soldiers reached the terminus or the Spanish border.

Table 5 Soldiers admitted in the major civilian hospitals of Paris (Hôtel-Dieu, Pitié, Charité, St Antoine, Necker, Cochin, Beaujon, Lariboisière, St Louis)

Major battles	Dates	Wounded	Fevers	Total
Châtillon	19/09–22/09	64	91	155
Chevilly	30/09–03/10	56	163	219
Bagneux	13/10–16/10	36	459	495
Malmaison	21/10–24/10	29	452	481
Bourget	29/10–02/12	61	654	715
Champigny	29/11–04/12	2,380	518	2,898
Drancy	21/12–24/12	808	986	1,794
Montretout	19/01–22/01	773	1,368	2,141
Total		4,207	4,691	8,898

Source: AAP, Foss 112.

Table 6 Soldiers admitted in the major military hospitals of Paris (Val-de-Grâce, St Martin, Gros Caillou, Vincennes, asile de Vincennes (Maison d'Alfort missing))

Major battles	Dates	Wounded	Fevers	Total
Châtillon	19/09–22/09	234	782	1,016
Chevilly	30/09–03/10	289	547	836
Bagneux	13/10–16/10	82	418	500
Malmaison	21/10–24/10	58	368	426
Bourget	29/10–02/12	62	497	559
Champigny	29/11–04/12	932	957	1,889
Drancy	21/12–24/12	144	442	586
Montretout	19/01–22/01	69	394	463
Total		1,870	4,405	6,275

Source: AAP, Foss 112.

This unwillingness to reform on military terms did not signify that civilian practitioners and hospital managers dragged their feet to help. The Assistance Publique had agreed, albeit reluctantly, to a considerable war effort. The following tables show its importance in relation to what the military could deliver with their establishments. Tables 5, 6 and 7 give a minimal estimate of the number of hospitalised casualties over the period after each major Parisian battle. Table 8 is more complex and contains the figures for both the numbers of patients coming in, out and dying in hospitals and the total number of beds at the army's disposal in the Assistance Publique's hospitals. With 10,621 beds, the great civilian hospital administration became the most important provider of hospital space.

More is not always better, however. The figures shown in Table 8 illustrate that beyond a few new hospitals created in the Magasins Réunis and the Hôtel du

Table 7 **Entries to the Bicêtre military hospital, 1870–71**

Month	Entries	Discharged	Deaths
October	1,306	521	81
November	2,370	2,118	288
December	1,948	1,097	296
January	1,627	1,483	394
February	719	1,005	192
March	147	463	47
April	10	26	7
May	49	149	9
Total	8,176	6,862	1,314

Source: AAP, Foss 112.

Louvre relatively late in the war, most of the new bed space was created within the confines of existing hospitals, using sheds, barracks, or simply cramming more beds into the same old wards. Critics were prompt to compare the model American system and the Grand-Hôtel to show a variation in mortality rates between 13 per cent and 80 per cent.[135] This comparison was unfair on two accounts: one was the specialisation of the Grand-Hôtel in the most desperate cases, the other was the general unsuitability of the hotel. This latter point was precisely what army surgeons disliked about civilian hospitals.

'A hospital that remains on the same spot for any length of time accumulates putrid matter, concentrates and *capitalises* miasma.'[136] Tent hospitals, however cold, were ventilated and flexible, and in many other respects organised in a military order. In the ambulance of the Chemin de Fer du Nord, a lower ceiling of tent fabric was used to attempt to create an artificial flow of air and introduce a mobile element in a rigidly structured environment.[137] Michel Lévy's barrack hospital built in the Luxembourg gardens in September 1870 had the same purpose and role and was cheap to build and destroy.[138] Like those of Longchamps, built at the end of the war, these barracks reinstated a purely military and rational, simplified ground plan, economical and movable. Lévy's views certainly reflected the geometrically arranged mass-barrack hospitals built in America during the Civil War and integrated recent hygienist views and disciplinary concerns.[139]

---

135 H. van Holsbeck, *Souvenirs de la guerre franco-allemande* (Brussels, Muquardt, 1872), p. 19.
136 Doyon, *Notes et souvenirs d'un chirurgien d'ambulance*, p. 55.
137 *GMP*, 26 (1872) 24.
138 Lévy, *Notes sur les hôpitaux baraques*, p. 20. For a biography of Michel Lévy (1809–72) see Bloesinger, *Quelques grandes figures de la chirurgie*, vol. 1, pp. 303–23.
139 C. Tollet, *Les Hôpitaux modernes au dix-neuvième siècle, descriptions des principaux hôpitaux français et étrangers* (l'auteur, 1894), p. 206.

Table 8 The civilian war effort in Paris: number of soldiers treated in civilian hospitals

Hospital	Soldiers: In/out/dead normal wards surgical wards	Communards: In/out/dead normal wards surgical wards	Beds allocated to the army	Extra beds in normal wards	Extra beds in surgery wards	Total of extra beds
Hôtel-Dieu	1045/642/292 317/203/91	16/15/1 153/75/44	416	227	60	287
Pitié	781/645/96 205/157/38	49/26/17	44	81	44	125
Charité	542/422/47 129/50/32	47/22/3 152/58/55	100	66		66
Charité annexe	1276/1086/190 125/114/11	9/6/3 102/85/17	267	1,315	92	1,407
St Antoine	1747/1189/273 534/326/179	3/2/1 289/133/98	453	409	120	529
Necker	139/115/24 125/100/25	193/76/117	5	30	5	35
Cochin	147/120/27 120/110/10	2/2 77/58/19	121	38	121	159
Beaujon	600/455/112 459/300/133	24/18/5 293/145/124	407	82	68	150
Lariboisière	490/273/68 235/176/42	132/30/29 97/67/42	159	102	57	159
St Louis	1275/1166/109 348/390/58	1/1 295/207/88	102	50	102	152
Midi	441/432/6 81/68/13		194	10		10
Lourcine			10		10	10
Enfants malades	39/18/21 169/107/7 64/45/22	2/2 54/44/10	88	12	88	100
St Eugénie	127/113/14 46/39/7	51/42/9	64	44	64	108
Maison d'accouche-ments	1/1 2/2		3	45	3	48
Cliniques			66		66	66
Maison de Santé	82/43/20 66/48/7 48/32/8	17/11/2 11/3/2	40			
Enfants Assistés	109/98/11	4/4	42	196	42	238
Salpêtrière			275	848	268	1,116
Ménages	893/799/86 258/237/24	6/6 135/97/34	436		90	90
Laroche-Foucauld	386/344/42		130			
St Périne	70/58/3 46/28/15	6/16 25/21/620	18		38 20	38 20
La Recon-naissance	54/49/5 144/101/43	8/5/3	109	200	109	309
Bicêtre			160 1,415		160	160 1,415
Les Incurables	117/64/12 71/32/17	75/103/13 362/50/46		80 1,920	80	80 1,920
Nourrices			28	106	28	134
Ste Anne			30		30	30
Magasins Réunis	417/392/25 188/177/11	64/56/8	600	300	600	900
Hôtel du Louvre	106/98/8 134/126/8		400		400	400
Vieillesse Hommes		2/2 16/4/1				
Vieillesse Femmes	601/395/88	97/4/37				
Chardon Lagache	34/28/ 11/7/3	13/9/4				
Total	1,1032/8,744/1,466 4,412/3176/919	327/225/55 2,555/1,279/784	8,032	7,496	2,765	10,261

Source: AAP, Foss 112.

Civilian doctors did not share this enthusiasm for mobility and precariousness: 'the worst houses are still preferable to tents.' Cottage hospitals distributing the practice across the city and sheltered in safe buildings represented a more familiar image of what the national war was about for civilians: a citizens' war fought on the walls by 'citizen-soldiers and not soldier-citizens'[140] living and treated at home.[141] For the French army, fundamentally attached to the war of movement inherited from the earlier colonial wars and the Napoleonic legend, the siege conditions were unbearable and did not entice them to get the best of their troops.[142] The contrast between the tentative offensives during the Paris siege and the more impressive results obtained from similar troops by commanders like Chanzy in the open fields illustrates this point.[143]

The link between hygiene, discipline and efficiency was already at the heart of military thought, and the sanitarian chaos of Paris mixing with the lack of discipline revolted and frightened army officers.[144] Within the closed and vitiated moral universe of the city, a number of initiatives came to re-establish the flow, the discipline and flexibility of a 'real' war experience. One of the unsuccessful plans was to create an ambulance on a hulk on the River Seine.[145] Rochard promoted the fact that the flow of water would carry with it all human impurities and the wind would blow away the vitiated air. The water would isolate soldiers from the corrupt Parisian soil and populace.[146] Larrey and Wolf supported this project and endorsed the hygienic principles of this hulk ambulance in 1871.[147] This endorsement came too late and the end of the war made the project redundant in every respect. This theory found a limited use, however. The Seine carried the wounded and the 1867 exhibition *bateaux mouches* found another purpose to their frivolous existence.

The disciplinarian aspects of these measures could also be measured in medical terms and by then the two aspects had become virtually interchangeable. These militaristic tropes pervaded the language of government and this quarantine

---

140 VdP, VD6/1333/1, daily reports to the maire de Paris, mairie du Vème, 19/10/1870. There were a number of protests at the 'militarisation' of the Garde Nationale into *bataillons de marche* abiding to normal military law.
141 Dr S. Pietrowski, *La Guerre et la Société de secours* (E. Dentu, 1870), p. 39; ASSAT, box 62/6, Dépôts de convalescences, letter from the 5th sector.
142 W. Serman, *Les Officiers français dans la nation, 1848–1914* (Aubier, 1982), p. 28.
143 Von der Goltz, *Gambetta et ses armées*, pp. 26–41.
144 R. Tombs, *The War Against Paris, 1871* (Cambridge University Press, 1981), p. 23. Later guides aimed at army officers stressed this link between hygiene, well-being, physical development and discipline. See G. E. Schneider and M. Troussaint, *Pages d'hygiène militaire pour les officiers* (Paris and Limoges, Charles Lavauzelle, 1906 reprinted until 1914).
145 F. Rochard, *Projet d'une ambulance sur la Seine* (Imprimerie Renou, 1871); ASSAT, box 63/6, project of an ambulance on the River Seine with notes by Larrey.
146 *GMP*, 26 (1871) 32; Van Holsbeck, *Souvenirs de la guerre*, p. 21.
147 Tollet, *Les Hôpitaux modernes*, p. 198.

obsession reached its peak under Adolphe Thiers and during the war against the Commune of Paris. As Robert Tombs has already pointed out, Thiers personally monitored the war against Paris from Versailles.[148] Thiers's and the *état-major*'s main concern was to avoid any socialist 'contamination' and cross-fertilisation from the Communards. Thiers also had some pretensions in military administration and, since his multi-volume history of the First Empire, did not hide his servile imitation of Napoleon I.[149] He was directly involved in the minutiae of military planning and organisation between March and May 1871. The siege took so much time precisely because the army was not trusted to carry on the reconquest of Paris. Thiers had similar concerns for the wounded and sick soldiers. He particularly dreaded the emollient civilian influence on the warriors.

To prevent these different types of contamination Thiers disposed of a suitable tool as all his armies enjoyed a complete medical service.[150] In that respect at least, the Versailles regime enjoyed better facilities and staff than the Empire had at the beginning of the previous conflict. Versailles troops did not require the dreaded civilian collaboration. Larrey and Thiers acknowledged the Red Cross's fidelity but did not call the head of the Red Cross services to them until the Commune expelled them.[151] In the words of the Red Cross officials themselves, they became 'auxiliaries of the army' and lost any claims to an independent management. The Intendance largely used the civilian funds as its own and organised 1,200 beds at the expense of the society. The army organised thus a battery of hospitals, arranged in a half circle around Paris, in the towns of the vicinity.[152] The giant hospital was surrounded by another. The soldiers invading Paris could then be treated outside Paris and avoid the contagion and vice of the capital city. In practice and despite Larrey's best advice, Thiers insisted on very solid barrack hospitals, recreating a rigid discipline but lacking the mobility of the tent-hospital. In this latter case the army discipline was at the expense of medical theories: the air soon vitiated and hospital rot slowly infiltrated the barracks. When the hospital construct stopped growing, it started to rot and decline from within.

Larrey then restructured this network of hospitals and applied his vision of military and hygienic order. Small tent hospitals combined with converted buildings and seemed to have had lesser mortality rates.[153]

---

148 Tombs, *The War against Paris*, pp. 129–30.
149 Général du Barail, *Mes Souvenirs, 1864–1879* (Plon, 1896), p. 272.
150 SHAT, Lu 1, Report of the 6th direction, 3rd bureau on the state of army ambulance services, 10/02/1871.
151 *Compte rendu des opérations du conseil d'administration siégeant à Versailles* (SSBATM, 1871), p. 3.
152 *Compte rendu des opérations du conseil d'administration siégeant à Versailles*, p. 10.
153 J. Grange, *Rapport à monsieur le président de la SSBATM sur l'ambulance de Bougival, projet d'ambulance permanente de perfectionnement* (Chaix, 1872), p. 20; AAP, 542 Foss 80, Report de l'hospice Brézin, annexe de Ville D'Avray, July? 1871.

Socialism represented the other fierce kind of rot likely to set. The problem did not arise in any considerable manner in the early days of the siege as the Versailles troops rarely took prisoners. During the assault, however, the army medical officers re-invested a number of Communard ambulances, and converted willingly into prison wardens as they sent most wounded Communards to a makeshift ambulance in the Palace of Versailles.[154]

Post-war

After the end of the civil war, the 'giant hospital' started to be dismantled slowly; it took several months before the many civilian spaces appropriated during the war returned to their legitimate owners. This slow pace of return to civil order reflects the fact that Paris was to rebuild after the Commune. The government retained Paris under intense military pressure in a permanent *état d'urgence*. The great fires of May 1871 had destroyed most of the rue de Rivoli, the Hôtel de Ville, many buildings on the left bank and perhaps appropriately the chancellery of the Légion d'honneur. The high mortality rates caused by the deprivations of the siege did not stop immediately after the war and smallpox remained impervious to political settlements.

It was only towards the end of 1871 and for the most part in 1872 that the army abandoned some of its large *annexes* devoted to venereal and infectious diseases or sick Communards.[155] This move accelerated when the legitimate owners of buildings and sites started claiming retroactively the rent they were owed by the military administration.[156] Disinfecting work, claims for compensation, pension rights, and, as I will discuss later, claims for promotions and military decorations replaced the heroic scenes of the war.[157] Generous donors suddenly attempted to claim back the value of their pointless patriotic gifts.[158] Demobilised soldiers not wounded seriously enough to claim a pension had to turn to their networks, mutual societies[159] or families to return to civilian life.[160] This slow work of demobilisation, when it took place in the bitter memory of a defeat and a Pyrrhic victory over part

154 AAP, 542 Foss 116, 30/05/1871, order from Général de Cissey.
155 ASSAT, box 65 bis/1–8, Lettre à Monsieur le Ministre de la Guerre, Direction Général du Matériel, Évacuation de l'asile du Vesinet, 9/10/1871. Fermeture de l'ambulance de Clichy (transfer de l'ambulance de Courcelles), 21/06/1872. Rapport fait au Ministre au sujet du service hospitalier de la place de Paris, 13/09/1871. A Monsieur l'Intendant Général de la première région, 3/06/1872 [on the closure of the venereal wards of Clichy and Gros Caillou].
156 ASSAT, box 65 bis/1, Ambulance de Courcelles, 20/03/1872.
157 ASSAT, box 62/17, Propositions pour la légion d'honneur.
158 Dr Pomard, *La Quatrième ambulance de la Société nationale de secours aux blessés* (Aubonel Frères, 1915), p. 34.
159 A. Houzé de l'Aulnoit, *Historique et mode de fonctionnement des caisses de secours*, (Lille, L. Danel, 1871) p. 8.
160 J. Bernet, *La Mutualité et la guerre de 1870* (Étampes, Société Régionale d'Imprimerie et de Publicité, 1962), pp. 4–9; O. Faure, *Les Français et leur médecine au dix-neuvième siècle* (Belin, 1993), pp. 121–30, 140–3.

of the population, proved too unpleasant for many military medical officers. Larrey resigned when the conflict ended and watched from without as his colleagues attempted to break away from the Intendance.

While they had planted the seeds of the discursive medical analysis of the defeat, Larrey, Lévy and other prominent medical officers took a distant part in the post-war debates on the causes of the defeat.[161] Civilian-trained doctors on the other hand used the war as a fundamental narrative in their life-stories and wrote abundantly about the details of their wars. They also took it to heart to apply some of the lessons of military medicine to the civilian context. The engineer C. Tollet saw in the war's insalubrious 'giant hospital' the demonstration of his principles and the best means of bringing home the message of sanitary reform: 'through a more or less long stay in barracks and military hospitals, all the families of the nation had been reached.'[162]

Léon LeFort and many others drew some bitter conclusions about the state of France and French medicine. If defeat enables self-examination which can perhaps have salutary consequences, civil war offers no such possibilities and had to become half-remembered and half-forgotten.[163] Perhaps more fundamentally, the giant hospital provided the backdrop for many ideological debates: the rise of politics revolved around notions of care, socialism and humanitarianism. More deeply entrenched in the experience of 1870–71, the languages of defeat produced in and around this rotting and immense hospital worked their way towards the *fin de siècle*.[164] The medical narratives about alcohol,[165] venereal disease, tuberculosis[166] and even amputation[167] contributed strongly towards this metaphorical vocabulary which Susan Sontag and Elaine Showalter have described.[168] As Ruth Harris and Robert Nye have rightly pointed out, these ideas were not new but the

161 Rieux and Hassendorfer, *Centenaire de l'école d'application*, p. 62.
162 Tollet, *Les Hôpitaux modernes*, p. 158.
163 Serman, *Les Officiers français*, p. 56 on how even army officers refused to fight.
164 J. P. T. Bury, *Gambetta and the Making of the Third Republic* (Longman, 1973), p. 25; C. Digeon, *La Crise allemande de la pensée française* (Presses Universitaires de France, 1959), pp. 4–8.
165 T. Gallard, *Leçon de clinique médicale* (J. B. Baillière et Fils, 1872), pp. 7–9; P. C. H. Brouardel, *La Profession médicale au commencement du vingtième siècle* (J. B. Baillière et Fils, 1903), p. 210. Brouardel triumphantly announced that medicine was now leading the struggle for the protection of children since the Roussel law of 1874, the struggle against alcoholism (public drunkenness law of 1873), the fight for public morality and for public health. J. Léonard, *La France médicale au dix-neuvième siècle* (Archives, Gallimard/Julliard, 1978), pp. 172–210; M. L. Hildreth, *Doctors, Bureaucrats and Public Health in France 1888–1902* (New York, Garland Publishing, 1987), pp. 36–106.
166 P. Guillaume, *Du désespoir au salut : les tuberculeux aux XIXe et XXe siècle* (Aubier, 1986), pp. 112–15; D. S. Barnes, *The Making of a Social Disease: Tuberculosis in Nineteenth-Century France* (Berkeley, University of Califirnia Press, 1995).
167 J. Harsin, 'Syphilis, wives and physicians: medical ethics and the family in late-nineteenth century France', *French Historical Studies*, 16:1 (1989) 72–95.
168 E. Showalter, *Sexual Anarchy: Gender and Culture at the Fin-de-Siècle* (New York, Viking, 1990); S. Sontag, *Illness as Metaphor* (New York, Viking, 1979); W. Greenslade, *Degeneration, Culture and the Novel* (Cambridge University Press, 1994), pp. 15–31.

political and social context of the immediate aftermath of 1870 recast them as central to medical and social debates.[169] At the armistice, Dr Chauffard addressed the Academy of Medicine in these terms:

> Gentlemen, in spite of the sadness and anxiety of this hour, the academy cannot have more legitimate purpose than to study the great banes which undermine the prosperity of our race, its physical development, its ability to expand and resist. After the discussion on tuberculosis came the debates on infantile mortality. These debates ... tuberculosis, infantile mortality, alcoholism, are the most active causes of destruction, and weakening of our people, especially the working and urban people.... Therefore it is not simple chance ... that such questions arise in this academy.... It is our fate [*la force des choses*] that wants it, it is the consciousness of public dangers.[170]

In this rhetorical orison pronounced at the very end of the war, many of the key issues of the post-war sanitarian and epidemiological debates were raised. While Jacques Léonard rightly minimised the direct 'impact' of the war on policies, its rhetorical importance should not be underestimated, and rhetoric which shapes political thinking *does* matter.[171] As an *ordre du jour* army despatch produced in January 1871 by *francs-tireurs* units put it, the war was 'a war between races'.[172] Even though the war did not produce any new theory of hereditarianism,[173] it provided the most powerful demonstration of the validity of such theories.[174] It took the war to hear the premises of social Darwinist analyses[175] in French intellectual circles.[176] As shown in Daniel Pick's work, concepts of degeneracy ferment in the experience of defeat and loss and, when allied with social and gender fears, they make for a powerful brew.[177]

---

169 R. Harris, *Murders and Madness: Medicine, Law and Society in the Fin-de-Siècle* (Oxford, Clarendon Press, 1989), p. 51; R. Nye, *Masculinity and Male Codes of Honour in Modern France* (New York, Oxford University Press, 1993), pp. 72–97.

170 *BAIM*, 36 (1870) 56; W. H. Schneider, *Quality and Quantity* (Cambridge University Press, 1989), pp. 20–7.

171 Léonard, *La Médecine*, p. 161.^

172 ASSAT, box 62, Ordre du jour, colonne du général Lipowski, 4ème bataillon des francs-tireurs. This type of semi-official army dispatches reflected the grass-root feelings more certainly than the more measured ones produced by headquarters.

173 D. B. Paul, *Controlling Human Heredity* (Atlantic Highlands, N.J., Humanities Press International, 1995).

174 I. Dowbiggin, 'Degeneration and hereditarianism in French mental medicine 1840–90: psychiatric theory as ideological adaptation', in W. Bynum, R. Porter and M. Shepherd (eds), *The Anatomy of Madness* (2 vols, Cambridge University Press, 1985).

175 É. Gautier, *Le Darwinisme social* (Derveaux, 1880), pp. 80–4. Social darwinism tended to be better received in left-wing circles.

176 Y. Conry, *L'Introduction du darwinisme en France au XIXième siècle* (J. Vrin, 1974), p. 27.

177 Pick, *War Machine*, pp. 88–114; R. A. Nye, *Crime, Madness and Politics in Modern France: The Medical Concept of National Decline* (Princeton University Press, 1984), pp. 132–8; J. Pierret, *L'Imaginaire décadent (1880–1900)* (Presses Universitaires de France, 1977), p. 19.

5 The politics of care and order

> During the siege, Paris lacked any responsible authority, *état de siège, état de guerre*, empty words, no effects. Military power, political power, administrative power, all struggled against each other, neutralised each other and produced an unspeakable chaos.[1]

Maxime du Camp's verdict on the siege of Paris has often been accepted by historians more concerned by political issues than social ones.[2] Du Camp's snappy conclusions are superficially valid but they undervalue dramatically the problems posed by such extraordinary circumstances. There was undoubtedly a power-vacuum that the municipal authorities filled using the paternalist welfare network established by previous governments in Paris. In some respects the municipalities recovered rights recognised to the most modest French *commune*, in others,[3] local government took over responsibilities that overlapped with the state's own. The politics of parochialism[4] worked through the constant interaction between the municipalities of Paris and the government and contributed to vital new democratic practices for the city of Paris. The Communard political project grew from this confusion between local and national jurisdictions.

These disputes around the carving up of jurisdictions and 'real' powers revolved around what I would term the 'politics of care' of Paris. The ability to care conditioned the survival potential of the 4 September revolution. While military actions were constantly reported in time and while the chances of a successful rescue action combined with the enigmatic 'Trochu plan' seemed increasingly remote, the ability to manage the complete blockade of one of the world's largest cities became the universal yardstick by which to measure the government's suitability to govern.[5]

This chapter deals with hunger and appetite as political issues. Bourgeois appetite and working-class hunger saturate most accounts of the siege of Paris.

---

1 M. du Camp, *Les Convulsions de Paris* (4 vols, Hachette, 1878), *Les Prisons avant la Commune*, vol. 1, p. 4.
2 A. Horne, *The Fall of Paris: The Siege and the Commune 1870–1* (Reprint Society, 2nd edn, 1967).
3 B. Leclère and V. Wright, *Les Préfets du Second Empire* (FNSP, 1973), pp. 41, 113.
4 Parochialism only recently became a historical topic worthy of sympathetic investigation. T. W. Margadant, *Urban Rivalries in the French Revolution* (Princeton University Press, 1992), and for a literal exploration of the '*esprit de clocher*', A. Corbin, *Les Cloches de la terre* (Albin Michel, 1994).
5 P. Ch. Joubert and A. de Vresse, *De la défense de Paris pendant le siège au point de vue de l'alimentation* (Arnauld de Vresse, 1871), p. 7.

They structure the siege situation as a political and social regression that fits roughly with Stephen Mennell's and Piero Camporesi's views on the centrality of hunger and appetite in the western civilisation process.[6] They also illustrate what Bourdieu's analysis of habitus and 'tastes of necessity and luxury' reveals of class distinction.[7] The loss of necessities of life and luxuries struck at the heart of all Parisians' view of civilisation. While to us the idea of the state intervening to provide basic necessities might appear 'progressive' or even a step towards a Utopian welfare state, to the contemporaries these efforts were the signs of a social and political regression, a step towards a republic of beggars and a land of hunger. The political gains were thus on the margins and focused on the ability to free and feed, to help and not pauperise.

The basic narrative of the siege misery relates to the political reorganisation of Paris. The management of hunger addressed sensitive issues of class inequality and key legal debates on bourgeois property rights. Feeding oneself became the daily concern of everyone, from the richest to the poorest. The poor starved, the rich either had difficulties in digesting horse meat or generally suffered from their impoverished diet. To cope with this situation, the revolutionary government created political powers in the *arrondissements* which managed each of the twenty *arrondissements* of Paris like a separate city. The tourist in modern Paris can only find traces of this war obsession with food in the few *boucheries chevalines* created during and after the war.[8] Deeper, and beyond the nutritional debates agitating Academies and cooks, the important question addressed the relationship between state and citizens, or even the definition of both state and citizenship. To feed the people implicitly meant to assess the people in function of their rights but also of their importance and value to the state. Readers may find the idea of food ration and war requisitions as, if not normal, at least tolerable constraints imposed by exceptional situations. Indeed the continuation of war rationing in France or England until well after the Second World War may suggest to some with a long memory that this type of situation would be justified in cases of economic emergency.[9] The concept was still recent in 1870 and the practice seemed debatable or

---

6 S. Mennell, 'On the civilizing of appetite', *Theory, Culture and Society*, 4 (1987) 373–403; P. Camporesi, *The Land of Hunger* (Cambridge, Polity Press, 1996), pp. 52–133.

7 P. Bourdieu, *La Distinction, critique sociale du jugement* (Les Éditions de Minuit, 1979), pp. 198–9.

8 *Boucheries chevalines* or *hippophagique* had been introduced on a small scale in 1867. A. Morillon, *L'Approvisionnement de Paris en temps de guerre, souvenirs et prévisions* (Perrin, 1888), p. 184.

9 The politics of food for the First World War are well known and show much reluctance to get involved in the vicious circle of rationing and providing for the civilian population. L. M. Barnett, *British Food Policy during the First World War* (Boston, Allen and Unwin, 1985); R. Wall and J. Winter (eds), *The Upheaval of War Family, Work and Welfare in Europe, 1914–1918* (Cambridge University Press, 1988); M. Teich, 'Science and food during the Great War: Britain and Germany', in A. Cunningham and H. Kamminga (eds), *The Science and Culture of Nutrition, 1840–1940* (Amsterdam, Rodopi, 1995), pp. 213–34.

even undemocratic. When property rights are enshrined in the constitution and valued as second only to life, requisitions cannot be so coolly ordered.

The politics of food and care are multifaceted. The first section of this chapter deals with the Parisian political structures created to face the crisis. The second and third sections deal with the politics of food as seen from the municipalities' and customers' points of view. The fourth is on the politics of care and synthesises the key political implications of the siege for the notions of state and citizenship.

To free Paris

Nineteenth-century readers, twenty or thirty years after the events, could still feel the enormity of the situation. To starve for over 133 days one of the ten largest cities in the world, which, a few years earlier, had been host to a Universal Exhibition displaying the symbols of economic and technological progress, was beyond belief. Some of the most important historical narratives of contemporary history were shattered. The age of telegraphic communications, trains and imported grain contrasted painfully with the return to an age of hunger, scarcely lit streets and freezing houses. After a few weeks the glittering shops and restaurants reverted to petrol lamps and the streets plunged into incremental darkness as the city settled down for a very cold winter. By 8 December the boulevards alone were lit; streets, public places and homes sunk into obscurity and cold.[10] Contemporaries could not tackle war in its most physical expression of hunger, cold, wounds, sickness and death. This reluctance to confront reality was also a problem for the revolutionary government of 1870.

Between the bloodless revolution of 4 September and the beginning of the siege, there were only two weeks spent busily reorganising the highest spheres of government and the commanding structure of the army.[11] General Trochu had symbolically been chosen to lead the government in spite of his conservative or even royalist opinions. Trochu had the advantage of having forecast the defeat and his insightful writings on the state of the French army now seemed prophetic. Three years earlier they had made him unpopular with the court, and thus, albeit by simple association, a virtual opponent to the regime. Other ministerial appointments were also based on fortuitous circumstances and enthusiasm rather than merit. Few knew into what political adventure the heady days of September were to lead them and they had little time to savour their new powers before the Germans arrived within sight of Paris.

To add to the complexity of the situation the planners could only guess at the size of the Parisian population. The only figures available were those established

---

10 J. de Marthold, *Mémorandum du siège de Paris 1870–1871* (Charovay Frères, 1884), p. 203.
11 J. Chastenet, *L'Enfance de la Troisième, 1870–1871* (Hachette, 1952).

by the municipal statistics and the general statistics of France that had given an exact figure of 1,879,264 for 1869 and growing at the rate of around 26,000 people a year.[12] This estimate excluded all the neighbouring towns and villages *extra-muros*.[13] After the exodus of wealthy and foreseeing Parisians and the forcible eviction of permanent hospital inmates and prostitutes,[14] the Parisian population *intra-muros* should have been between 1,600,000 and 1,800,000 strong. To this number the government had to add the suburban refugees in Paris to increase it to anything between 1,800,000 and 2,000,000. The government used the 2,000,000 figure to plan the food supply.[15] However, another electoral census on 20 October gave a higher figure of 2,116,600 with the addition of 260,000 regular soldiers.[16] This higher figure of 2,376,600 seems very high and does not take into account the difficulties of collecting food-related information. Another census in January gave a population of 2,219,877 inhabitants. This means a 10–15 per cent variation on the estimates used to plan food supplies, i.e. two or three weeks worth of food.[17]

In a well-informed city where rumours could turn into panics, planning could also have adverse political consequences, and to plan for a long siege would implicitly fuel fears and create a rush for food that could then have dramatic political consequences. Not to plan a long siege would, on the other hand, risk endangering the fighting capability of the city. This dilemma justifies the slow implementation of ever-more restrictive rules on rationing and nutrition during the siege. This political incursion in the Parisians' kitchens meant a much finer and detailed level of government. As the state administration had quite enough military problems to keep the short-staffed administrations busy, the bulk of the responsibility was devolved to the *arrondissements'* mayors.[18] While before the war they simply acted as public registry offices, *arrondissements'* municipalities became real administrative and autonomous entities. The government had originally planned one municipal council for the whole city but the state of emergency justified a cancellation of the 22 September elections. Gambetta then emulated the previous authoritarian regimes and nominated mayors for the twenty *arrondissements*.

12 T. Loua, *Atlas statistique de la Population de Paris* (Dejey, 1873).
13 C. Ély, *Paris, étude démographique et médicale* (Masson, 1872), p. 4.
14 The Assistance Publique's tendency over the previous thirty years had already been to resettle out of Paris the needy and invalids; J. Gaillard, *Paris la ville 1852–1870* (Lille, H. Champion, 1976), pp. 318–19.
15 Morillon, *L'Approvisionnement de Paris*, p. 104.
16 *GMP*, 25 (1870) 588.
17 *L'Union médicale*, 25 (4/02/1870).
18 J. Bréjean and J. Humblot, *Les Mairies de Paris* (Chaix, 1907), pp. 2–10. *Maires d'arrondissements* were nominated by the central power and seconded by three to five civil servants *adjoints* who were really civil servants. Later reforms of the government of Paris were enacted in 1871 when the Conseil Municipal elected in July started sitting on 4 August. A. Fierro, *Histoire et dictionnaire de Paris* (Bouquins Robert Laffont, 1996) pp. 329–30.

These mayors, though unelected, had a legitimacy of sorts often attached to their earlier career. They were all republicans, some of them Freemasons, and well-known opponents to the imperial regime. Among the twenty mayors nominated on 5 September to be in charge of one *arrondissement* of Paris, there were a number of former members of Parliament, some of them dating from the Second Republic: Greppo (IV), Corbon (XV) and an ex-member of the February 1848 government, Carnot (VIII). Among the other professional interests represented one can find two barristers (one of whom was *avocat à la cour de cassation*, I, VI), two medical doctors: Clemenceau (XVIII) and Ribeaucourt (VII), two *hommes de lettres* politicians Ranc (IX) and Favre (XVII), one historian Henri Martin (XVI), one engineer (XIII), one paternalistic employer Richard (XIX), a teacher (XI), five businessmen (I, III, X, XII, XX), an *ex-adjoint au maire* (V) and one journalist (XIV).[19]

Few of these people had ever exercised power or had had any civic responsibilities at this level but they were all fiercely republican. In this respect they reflected far more faithfully Parisian political inclinations than previous nominees. Among all the cities of France, Paris had been most consistent in electing known opponents to the regime as deputies. Parisians also voted 'no' to the May 1870 plebiscite which sanctioned the liberal reforms of the liberal Empire. By recreating municipal authorities the government intended to renew a political bond with the Parisian people. In the old Arago's words, 'Yes it was in the *arrondissements* that the life of the city was, and when it appeared elsewhere, it referred back to these centres of republican action'.[20]

To flesh out these municipalities Jules Ferry gave them the control of the Bureaux de Bienfaisance of the Assistance Publique, which were in charge of distributing benefits to registered paupers. His intentions were 'to give back to the municipality its real political and moral role and its legitimate influence on the portion of the population that requires most of its solicitude and devotion'.[21]

In contrast to these new powers, the Parisian administration was on the whole reluctant to obey newly imposed authorities who ignored some of the most established routines of administrative management. The republicans rightly felt uneasy using the tools of their oppression and attempted in vain to abolish some of them.[22] The most dangerous of these civil servants belonged to the police. The police had always been a very serviceable instrument of autocratic power.[23] Prefect Piétri was one of the closest friends and associates of the Emperor and eventually followed the imperial family in their English exile. The republican

19 Marthold, *Mémorandum*, p. 35; *La Guerre illustrée* (10/09/1870) 114.
20 E. Arago, *L'Hôtel de Ville au 4 Septembre et pendant le siège* (J. Hetzel, 1871), pp. 328–9.
21 AAP, 542 Foss 2, Minutes du Conseil Général des Hospices, 3/10/1870.
22 E. Cresson, *Cent jours à la Préfecture de Police, 2 novembre 1870–11 février 1871* (H. Plon, Nourrit et Cie, 1901), pp. 12–25.
23 É. de Kératry, *Le 4 Septembre et le gouvernement de la Défense Nationale* (A. Lacroix and Verboechoven et Cie, 1872), pp. 16–18.

government attempted to weaken the Bonapartist party further by merging the police into the army. The sedentary *gardes nationaux* replaced policemen in peacekeeping missions.

More widesweeping reforms of the police and other services in fact proved difficult if not impossible to enact.[24] The new authorities found that they could rule but not administer. The new mayors had to act independently from established services and sometimes illegally. Bypassing administrative routines had its advantages and the mayors created small decision-making units that were directly accountable to the administered and were often very proactive in dealing with local issues. Between September and November, nevertheless, the mayors found a solid political base which eluded the more distant government. After the attempted revolutionary coup of October, the elections of 5 November mostly reinstated the governmental candidates. Perversely some of this electoral triumph was due to the radical views of earlier nominees and the elections were seen as a triumph for the left. The mayors of the I, II, III, VI, VIII, XII, XIII, XV, XVI and XVII *arrondissements* were re-elected. One of the reasons for this rapid political success was undoubtedly the distance between the mayors and the government. Many of the September nominees were more radical than the government, like Bonvalet in the III *arrondissement*. The September reform had given a large amount of power to untested municipalities who could then become the tools of radical policies. Clemenceau, elected mayor of the XVIII, had made himself popular by creating a food charity in his *arrondissement* within the first days of the siege and before any of his colleagues.[25] In late September the measure was still largely symbolic but it became a central part of Parisian politics which will be discussed later.

When there was a conflict between the government or the administration and the mayors it always benefited the latter. Clemenceau thus obtained his re-election in the XVIII *arrondissement* after staging his resignation.[26] Mottu, the anticlerical radical who had been sacked from the XI *arrondissement*, was triumphantly re-elected.[27] Of the eight remaining *arrondissements,* only predictably radical *arrondissements* really chose a red alternative to the government candidates with the likes of Ranvier and his *adjoints* Millière and Flourens, all involved in the recent insurrection, and Delescluze (XX and XIX).

All was not given away and the other leg on which the government rested was the army. On 8 September the army sectors already discussed in Chapter 4 superimposed a strict military grid of command over the townships. To moderate

---

24 B. F. Martin, *Crime and Criminal Justice Under the Third Republic: The Shame of Marianne* (Baton Rouge, Louisiana State University Press, 1990), pp. 39–124.
25 *GMP*, 25 (1870) 529.
26 J. D. Ellis, *The Early Life of Georges Clémenceau, 1841–1893* (Lawrence, Regent Press of Kansas, 1980), p. 44.
27 Gaillard, *Paris la ville*, p. 287.

this military domination some military institutions conversely took on unexpected civilian aspects. For instance, the *conseils de revision* that arbitrated on the conscripts' fitness or availability for active military service[28] were selected among judges and elected among local solicitors.[29] Volunteers and conscripts were registered by the mayors and equipped at the municipality's expenses.

The three layers of government – the municipalities, the army and the government – overlapped and co-operated but the boundaries remained blurred and were constantly re-negotiated. Trochu led both the army and the government. On the other hand, the government organised the army. Gambetta took many strategic decisions and largely led the army; the army was also largely composed of volunteers who looked back to their municipality for guidance, etc. To sustain any government or municipality, food had to become the absolute priority. Because it was a shared priority, the top-down view that has been taken usually by the few historians who have condescended to deal with the practical aspects of feeding Paris is misjudged.

In terms of global planning, the revolutionary government had few options and simply followed the previous administration. The situation at the end of August was relatively good and the government had started storing reserves of food to feed the population for about two months.[30] A large herd of cattle and sheep grazed in and around Paris. Urban dairies would provide some milk while the central stores near the Canal St-Martin, or *greniers d'abondance,* were almost full of wheat. In order to purchase more food Paris and the government had to break very strict accounting and budgetary rules and find the products in the provinces. The privately owned railways did not help significantly and by and large the bulk of provincial and central administration only reluctantly obeyed orders. To reorganise the key areas of government was in itself an immense task for people who had only a distant understanding of their administration; to make the most of it was impossible.

The members of the government made every effort to find a middle ground on which their revolution would stand and endure after the war. The interests of the bourgeoisie distracted them from testing radical proposals. In spite of Michel Lévy and Edmond Dupouy's advice, the government did not create a ministry of public hygiene able or willing to centralise all the key health decisions in one office.[31] Such a ministry would have undermined the Academy of Medicine for instance and the government used academicians to staff its commissions. The Commission d'Hygiène et de Salubrité had a consultative role and used established channels to

---

28 Active military service meant that the *gardes* would fight in the field.
29 J. Fabre, *La Justice à Paris pendant le siège et la Commune 1870–1871* (Marchal et Godde, 1919), p. 37.
30 Morillon, *L'Approvisionnement de Paris*, pp. 5–6.
31 *La Tribune médicale* (11/09/1870).

transmit what amounted to scanty advice or concern to the military, the Assistance Publique and municipal authorities on the quality and availability of food and health care.[32]

To feed Paris

The earliest concern of the administration and of the Academies of Science and Medicine was not about solid nutrients but about water.[33] Five years after the last cholera epidemic such a concern was legitimate. It was also consistent with a long tradition of public health and hygiene thinking.[34] Under pouring autumn rains, however, Paris standing on a shallow bed of limestone by the Seine had a good chance of finding fresh water supplies even if the Germans decided to cut off drinking water supplies from outside. This anxiety on the quantity but also the quality of the water enabled the Société Chimique to raise its public profile. The alarmist advice of the commission led to the boring of new wells as early as 27 September (rue de Trévise). The chemical analysis of water was then used to reassure Parisians as to the purity of their supply in spite of its high lime content and cloudy aspect.[35] Chemical analyses and medical diagnoses took an important place in the general debate, not least when chemical preparations entered the food-chain. The debates of the Academy of Science especially became the antechamber of a fantastic cuisine of ersatz and replacement foodstuffs.

Over the duration of the siege they recommended beef and horse black pudding as proposed by M. Riche and some Parisian industrialists. They advised converting the remains of all animals into meat replacement gelatine, to turn mutton and horse fat into 'Parisian butter',[36] to rehydrate the dried albumin used in textile printing to compensate for the lack of eggs, to turn beer-making products into bread, to make tapioca popular, to eat wheat like rice in the 'ancient Roman way',[37] to mix sugars and gelatine into appetising jams and marmalades, and to convert candle fat into purified cooking fat.[38] The more geriatric members of the Academy of Science related their experience in previous wars at great length and supported the use of

---

32 VdP, VD6/1538/3, Services médicaux et pharmaceutiques 15/09/1870.
33 G. Grimaud de Caux, *De septembre 1870 à février 1871: L'Académie des Sciences pendant le siège de Paris* (Didier et Cie, 1871), p. 21; M. Crosland, *Science Under Control: The French Academy of Sciences, 1795–1914* (Cambridge University Press, 1992), pp. 328–30.
34 A. F. La Berge, *Mission and Method: The Early-Nineteenth-Century French Public Health Movement* (Cambridge University Press, 1992), pp. 190–4.
35 VdP, VD6 1551/3, Visites des puits par la société chimique. On water analysis and chemical debates on water see C. Hamlin, *A Science of Impurity: Water Analysis in Nineteenth-Century Britain* (Bristol, Adam Hilger, 1990), pp. 178–240.
36 Grimaud de Caux, *L'Académie des Sciences*, p. 53.
37 Grimaud de Caux, *L'Académie des Sciences*, p. 28.
38 M. Payen, 'L'Académie des Sciences pendant le siège et la Commune', *Revue scientifique*, 2 (8/07/1871) 37–47.

nutritious garlic soup.[39] Daring businessmen, experts in food adulteration rather than ersatz techniques, found their age-old practices legitimated and immediately followed the academicians' advice and sold beetroot as redcurrant jelly, pumpkin jam as apricot jam.[40] The famous *pâtissier* Pons started retailing one of the most novel ersatz foods of the war, *osseine*, invented by Frémy and made from bone extracts to be used as a meat replacement in soups, pâtés and cakes.[41]

Academic urges to use horse meat met with more ridicule than admiration; the naive concerns about the edibility of horse meat were soon very dated. Medical journalists ironically commented:

> Your promenades around town sharpen your appetite, [*aiguisent l'appétit*] especially on a windy day, they enabled you to find new strength in a banquet which will become the experimental demonstration of hippophagia and its advantages. This heroic feast, the menu and impressions of which were reported in the press, was a glorious event for the guests and most edifying for the public![42]

This bitter caricature touched on the great class divide between unfulfilled appetites and hunger, between lifestyle and life.[43] The central governmental Commission d'Hygiène et de Salubrité provided similarly inane advice. Dr Onimus's pamphlet thus advised 14 m^3 of air per person, to ventilate and to spray phenic acid in proletarian houses. It promised 1 kg of bread per Parisian for the length of the siege and provided some basic dietary information. Following Étienne-Jules Marey's imagery, Onimus compared the human body with a furnace. His classification divided carbon-based food from albumin-based foods meant to help mend the machinery.[44] Onimus then proceeded to explain the losses individuals incurred each day and the best ways to compensate for them. It justified the rationing in terms of basic survival needs while keeping the composition of the ration open and introducing a diversity of alternatives. Beyond these contradictory and sometimes difficult notions, Onimus repeated the academic advice on ersatz

---

39 *GMP*, 25 (1870) 559.
40 Joubert and de Vresse, *De la défense de Paris*, p. 19
41 Grimaud de Caux, *L'Académie des Sciences*, pp. 56, 71, 93. Bone gelatine had been experimented upon in the 1830s. Debates between Frémy and Dumas at the end of November on the real nutritive value of osseine reflected the one which had taken place forty years earlier between Chevrul and Magendie; E. Saint-Edme, *La Science pendant le siège de Paris* (E. Dentu, 1871), p. 195. Some 20,113 kg of gelatine were sold in the last week of the meat rationing in February 1871. VdP, VD6/1586/3, *Histoire du fonctionnement des services ordinaires et extraordinaires du huitième arrondissement durant le siège*, 1874, p. 58.
42 *GMP*, 25 (1870) 541.
43 Mennell, 'On the civilizing of appetite', 373–403; F. Papillon, 'Hygiène et alimentation de Paris pendant le siège de 1870', *Revue des Deux Mondes* (1/10/1870) 575–84.
44 A. Rabinbach, *The Human Motor: Energy, Fatigue and The Origin of Modernity* (New York, Basic Books, 1990), pp. 90–7.

food and milk. It is unclear what comfort, if any, the reader would obtain from this worthy publication in October 1870.[45]

The earliest indication that food might become scarce came after the government decided to fix the price of bread, still the basic and most symbolic food of the Parisians.[46] On 23 September the first measure affecting bread fixed the price at 10 centimes for 215 g, 15 for 325 g and 20 for 435 g. The franc was worth approximately ninepence h'appeny of the time. Ten centimes would thus make approximately a pennyworth of bread. The allocation of each guardsman was at around 1,50 francs and 75 centimes a day for their legitimate or common-law wives. This allocation represented a militarised unemployment benefit.[47] By comparison a recent estimate put the average Parisian daily wages between 1870 and 1875 at 5 francs for a man and 3 for a woman.[48] For those who stayed at home and only had a minor defensive role, these new prices made life quite difficult by limiting the family's daily purchases to around 1½ kg of bread at a time when the daily individual intake approached 1 kg. This earlier measure which re-established a maximum price for bread could be seen as the re-enactment of the law of Maximum of the revolutionary period.

As in 1793 it meant to stop the inflation of the price of bread. The Maximum laws refer obviously to the conflict between factions – Hébert, the Commune and the Montagne – that ended in the gradual elimination of all the parties involved. The government of 1870 did not share its forefathers' cynical intentions to see the Parisian administration fail and become unpopular in decentralising the 'subsistence' issues to the municipality. Yet this decentralisation had the same paradoxical effect as seventy-seven years before and it reinforced *arrondissements*' municipal powers.[49] It also addressed the grievances of the small-shop-keepers who largely depended for their supplies on a handful of large capitalist retailers.[50] Similar revolutionary measures of food requisition started at a government level

---

45 E. Onimus, *Conseils hygiéniques aux habitant de Paris pendant le siège* (Charles de Mourgues Frères, 1870), pp. 11–23; A. Riche, *Conseils sur la manière de se nourrir dans les circonstances présentes* (Germer Baillière, 1870).

46 The symbolic value of bread in France is something which needs more work and which could build on the work of Roland Barthes and Michel de Certeau. R. Barthes, 'Pour une psycho-sociologie de l'alimentation contemporaine', in J. J. Hémardinquer (ed.), *Pour une histoire de l'alimentation* (Armand Colin, 1970), pp. 307–15; M. de Certeau, L. Giard and P. Mayol, *L'Invention du quotidien* (2 vols, Gallimard, 1994); J.-P. Aron, *Le Mangeur du XIXe siècle* (Payot, 2nd edn, 1989).

47 Morillon, *L'Approvisionnement de Paris*, p. 117.

48 S. Rials, *Nouvelle histoire de Paris : de Trochu à Thiers, 1870–1875* (Hachette, 1985), p. 31.

49 I. Fourneron, 'La Décentralisation de l'administration des subsistances. Pache et la Commune de Paris, février–septembre 1793', *Annales historiques de la Révolution Française*, 306 (1996), 649–74, pp. 658, 669.

50 E. Furlough, *Consumer Cooperation in France: The Politics of Consumption, 1834–1930* (Ithaca, Cornell University Press, 1991), pp. 30–1; P. Nord, *Paris Shopkeepers and the Politics of Resentment* (Princeton University Press, 1986).

Table 9 The Assistance Publique's bread production, 1870–72

Month	Quantities 1870 (kg)	Daily average	Quantities 1871 (kg)	Daily average	Quantities 1872 (kg)	Daily average
January	415,792	13,412	*707,971*	*22,837*	314,148	11,424
February	386,521	13,904	*574,199*	*20,506*	346,116	11,935
March	413,294	13,332	*620,063*	*20,002*	291,648	9,408
April	392,283	13,076	*538,693*	*17,956*	288,361	9,621
May	416,713	13,442	*330,617*	*10,663*	297,581	9,599
June	419,465	13,982	265,636	8,854	288,806	9,626
July	428,491	13,822	258,324	8,333		
August	549,041	17,711	250,521	8,081		
September	*631,418*	*21,180*	249,095	8,303		
October	*704,570*	*22,728*	275,158	8,876		
November	*719,360*	*23,978*	275,159	9,171		
December	*797,794*	*25,735*	341,007	11,000		

Source: AAP, 542 Foss 84, Boulangerie Centrale, fourniture de pain.

by 29 September[51] and referred to the revolutionary laws of 19 Brumaire An 3 (1795).[52] All wheat reserves became the property of the state.

By that stage the state had to prepare the measures to grind the wheat and produce the flour. The idle steam engines of the Gare de l'Est were converted into industrial mills.[53] There is something very symbolic, even though it was unintentional, in converting the station used for the traffic to Alsace-Lorraine into a war mill. The state also had to increase the supply of bread to direct dependants. Wounded soldiers in hospitals had to be provided for with quality food.[54] Table 9, which gives the volume of bread produced over the period by the central bakeries of the Assistance Publique, illustrates this burden. Bread-making had to double compared with a normal year.

The figures in italic cover the siege period. These figures illustrate among other things the effort made and how the second siege had less importance than the first over Parisian food supplies. It also shows that these large institutional demands had an impact on the Parisian market and necessarily affected the availability of bread disposable on the market. To optimise their grasp on this market the government had to take urgent measures in keeping with capitalist values.

These early measures mostly affected commercial interests and neglected privately held stores. Bakers by law had to keep thirty-five days worth of flour in their shops to prevent politically dangerous crises of subsistence.[55] The authorities

---

51 *Recueil officiel des actes du Gouvernement* (Librairie Administrative de Paul Dupont, 1871), p. 419.
52 VdP, VD6/1454/4, Réquisitions.
53 Marthold, *Mémorandum*, p. 110.
54 AAP, 542 Foss 84, Boulangerie Centrale, decree of 17/11/1870.
55 A. Husson, *Les Consommations de Paris* (Guillaumin and Cie, 1856), p. 91.

had taken into account these reserves of flour for their calculations but had neglected the speculative interest of the owners of food reserves. Private property remained an area difficult to approach.[56] As early as 28 September, the government attempted, apparently in vain, to stop *gardes nationaux* visiting illegally and requisitioning empty houses.[57] Some more politically sensitive properties were not systematically exploited until quite late in the siege. The clergy, for instance, only had to surrender all its reserves of grain and fuel for the national effort at the very end of the siege.[58] Only by 19 January did the state authorise what was often taking place already, and privately owned vacant properties were searched to find hidden preserves and reserves of wheat.[59]

On the left, the radical clubs constantly asked for immediate requisitions and emergency orders against *ancien régime* figures like the 'speculators' and 'profiteers' stockpiling to generate money from the common misery.[60] However politically expedient a few scapegoats would have been, the National Defence government could not maintain its centre-left stance and its broad coalition and simultaneously attack sacrosanct bourgeois property rights.

The government was already having a complicated task to explain the revolution as something other than a revolution, and any hasty measure fuelling bourgeois fears would have seriously undermined its fragile political stability. The regime owed a great deal of its relative stability to the concerted efforts of the army and the bourgeois *gardes nationaux*. This reliance on conservative forces grew after each insurrection. Even the Catholic Church led by the liberal Archbishop Darboy[61] supported the Republic and called for the re-establishment of the Liberty, Equality and Fraternity motto on churches.[62]

The government found itself relying on the same contradictory forces that its predecessor of June 1848 had had to rely on. As in 1848 the revolution lived on the myth of 1789–92 and attempted to balance precariously popularity and military discipline.[63] Food requisitioning moreover smacked of military dictatorship and Bonapartist management techniques. They nevertheless became increasingly necessary and municipalities pre-empted the government. By January 1871 the level of policing in this respect had reached its maximum potential and the

---

56 ASSAT, box 63/4, Service de santé [du quatrième secteur] pendant la durée du siège, p. 7.
57 *Recueil officiel des actes du Gouvernement*, p. 420.
58 AEP, 5b2 10, Letter of Mgr Darboy to the government, 29/12/1870.
59 Joubert and de Vresse, *De la défense de Paris*, p. 35.
60 A. Farge, *Fragile Lives: Violence, Power and Solidarity in Eighteenth-Century Paris* (Cambridge, Polity Press, 1993), pp. 258–62.
61 J. O. Boudon, 'Une Promotion épiscopale sous le second empire, l'abbé Darboy à l'assaut de Paris', *Revue d'histoire moderne et contemporaine*, 39:3 (1992) 465–82.
62 Marthold, *Mémorandum*, pp. 68–9.
63 C. Nicolet, *L'Idée républicaine en France, essai d'histoire critique* (Gallimard, 1982), pp. 159–62; P. Nord, *The Republican Moment: Struggles for Democracy in Nineteenth-Century France* (Cambridge, Mass., Harvard University Press, 1995).

Table 10 **The rationing legislation of 1870–71**

Dates	Taxation	Requisition	Rationing
29/09		Wheat	
01/10	Pork, butter		
08/10			Meat in VI *arrondissement*
19/10		Animal feed	
26/10			Meat (50g/day)
27/10			Refugees' bread
28/10			Lighting gas
12/11			Coke suppliers
14/11		Horned beasts	
21/11		Potatoes	
22/11			Charcoal
25/11		Petrol and oils	
26/11			Coke/coal/lignite
26/11			3 days rations: 125g rice 50g cheese/500g potatoes
28/11			*Meat every other day*
29/11		*Pork meat*	
30/11			*Army rations: 150g of meat per day*
08/12			*End of gas provisions*
10/12		*Horses, wood, fuel, coke etc.*	
11/12	*Flour cannot be sold*		
13/01			*Cards needed to buy bread*
16/01			*Bread at 400/500 g/head*
18/01			*Bread at 300 g/head*

Source: P. Ch. Joubert and Arnaud de Vresse, *De la défense de Paris pendant le siège au point de vue de l'alimentation* (Arnaud de Vresse, 1871), pp.11–40.

threshold of acceptability. Table 10 illustrates better than a long enumeration the progress of this coercive legislation.

Entries in italic indicate the weeks when the temperature varied between 0 and −8°C at midday. As this table shows, the government's action was incremental and only imposed requisitioning when the products had either virtually disappeared or were becoming very scarce. The municipal agents had to count discreetly the number of privately owned horses in October before any real requisitioning of equine meat could be carried out.[64] Similar prudence marked the slow enactment of rationing measures.

64 APdP, Ba 366/4, Recensement nominatif des chevaux et fourrages.

After the 31 October insurrection, the government buried most governmental plans to requisition food and more particularly to inspect private homes to find hidden food stores. Similarly the panic caused by only slightly premature rumours of bread rationing that took place around 11 December caused an immediate crisis and food shortage. The rationing was then delayed a few days and set at an unrealistically high level, soon lowered to 300 g per head, which often proved unobtainable. By that stage there was little military hope left and the government almost unanimously considered an armistice. The Red Poster called for free food distributions and this political dimension of the food crisis became a more direct threat after the second insurrection led by the Blanquists on 22 January 1871, which precipitated the peace talks with Bismarck.

A retrospective reading of the siege which ignores the helpless situation of the Parisian government would be grossly a-historical. Even if the government had been able to ration food from the beginning it remains doubtful that the siege could have lasted much longer than 132 or 136 days (starting dates for the siege vary a little). The most important problem Parisians faced by the end of January was perhaps less the lack of food (although the government expected the stocks to last for only another ten days) than the lack of fuel. As the tables of Chapter 3 have shown, people started dying more from pneumonia, lung diseases and simple cold than they did from any other infectious or contagious diseases. The army itself, although better fed, heated and equipped than most civilians, suffered a rising toll of front-line frost bite, frozen feet and hands leading to cases of gangrene and death.[65]

The limitations of state interventionism in the free market meant that while the short list of essentials became severely monitored, a number of other products were still available at extravagant prices. Victor Hugo in the comfort of his hotel saw his hotel and restaurant bills increase prodigiously over the duration of the siege.[66] Eggs, chicken, game, zoo meat, cats, rats and dogs were widely available to those who could afford them. Some of these products were probably less exotic than Parisians thought; cats had long transmuted into rabbits in local canteens and cheap restaurants.[67] With skinny rats worth between 30 and 60 centimes in November and nearly 3 francs in January (or two soldier's daily pay), few could afford this delicacy. Anecdotally a specific rat market adorned the Place de l'Hôtel-de-Ville where the government met. This symbolic scene did not escape the contemporary observers.[68] The Academy of Science, after deciding that well-cooked rats were perfectly edible, estimated their population at around 25 million

---

65 SHAT, Li 4, Registre de lettres confidentielles du général gouverneur de Paris, 24/12/1870.
66 Restaurants carried on producing parodic high cuisine during the siege. A. Berte, *Les Menus d'un restaurant de Paris* (Toulon, Tardy, 1872).
67 Saint-Edme, *La Science pendant le siège*, pp. 167–71.
68 F. Vincent, *Histoire des famines à Paris* (Librairie de Médicis, 1946), p. 123.

for Paris. Were the rat population exterminated the rat ration of each Parisian would only be around twelve rats.

Hunting more metaphorical rats, speculators and *accapareurs* (hoarders), the mayors of the most radical *arrondissements* used their *gardes nationaux* to enter empty houses to enforce the requisitioning of any comestibles or fuel left behind. The denunciation of speculators also started illegal but highly popular inspections. It did not eliminate the black market, however.[69] A number of riotous incidents took place during the siege and the *accapareurs* were molested and often survived only through rapid military action. The popular anger directed at those who exploited the famine dated from immemorial age and had been one of the more common causes of riots under the *ancien régime*. In France, however, food scarcity and food riots dated from the terrible agricultural crisis of 1846. Parisians had since suffered from the provision of exceedingly expensive bread during the Second Empire but the rise of wages had largely offset this inflationary curve.[70] Since then international commerce and the relative freedom of trade had enabled government to avoid what had become an 'archaic' form of unrest. The governmental coyness to deal with the *accapareurs* and prevaricators became the focus of extreme-left attacks in the press from 10 October when the daily press recovered its freedom of expression. The radical medical press joined in and the repulsion for any trader and shop-keeper grew to the point when fully armed *gardes nationaux* stood by authorised shops, partly to protect the trader and partly to check business practices.

This suspicion was not unfounded. The January announcement of the armistice provoked a sudden rush of hidden foods to the market stalls. Rabbits, cheese and preserved foods suddenly emerged and flooded the stalls of Les Halles. For a few swallowed insults, it seems from all available evidence that the small businesses of the metropolis did rather well during the siege and universally speculated on the un-rationed foods or black-market deals.[71]

Beyond the strictly political, food rationing also inferred the rough calculation of the value of individuals in the besieged city. The army therefore appropriated the lion's share of food supplies. Soldiers received 1 kg of bread, later reduced to 750 g and then 500 g, 150 g of meat, 100 g of rice, 50 g of biscuits and half a litre of wine.[72] All the wet fish from the ponds in the forests around Paris or even from the river went to wounded soldiers.[73] Fish flesh replaced red meat for the

---

69 A. Legoyt, 'L'Alimentation et les prix' pendant le siège de Paris', *Journal des économistes*, 66 (1871) 331–47, p. 336. Restaurants favoured an inflationary black market economy.
70 Vincent, *Histoire des famines*, pp. 117–28; J. Singer-Kerel, *Le Coût de la vie à Paris de 1840 à 1954* (Armand Colin, 1961).
71 H. Lizier, 'Le Marché noir à Paris pendant le siège', *Histoire locale de Beauce et du Perche*, Chartres, 34 (1971) 27–8.
72 ASSAT, box 62/1, Ministère de la guerre bureau des subsistances, 28/11/1870.
73 Joubert and de Vresse, *De la défense de Paris*, p. 13.

weakened constitution of recovering patients. A soldier's meat ration had perhaps greater nutritional importance in the eyes of military medical staff and was consistently put at well above three times that of the civilian ration. Soldiers also usually managed to obtain their food ration whilst civilians were often left outside the door when the butcher closed his shutters. Indeed in December and January while meat rations were decreasing for the civilian population, they were increased to 175 g and then 200 g for privates until the end of the siege.[74] During any military action outside Paris, front-line soldiers benefited from huge food rations by civilian standards: 750 g of bread, 250 g of meat, some rice or dried beans, salt, coffee and sugar. Soldiers principally suffered from the sharp qualitative decline in their food supply rather than from a quantitative decline. Their medical officers described the food as 'too warming, and tiring eventually even the best stomachs'.[75] For their families, on the other hand, those who could not qualify for emergency soup kitchens had to queue for over three hours, in the very cold winter morning, to obtain an ever smaller and rougher ration of bread.[76] To add to their misery, the rationing of fuel – wood, coal or charcoal meant – that it became increasingly difficult to cook anything or even to keep oneself warm.[77]

In spite of municipal *lingeries* providing basic elements of clothing,[78] many starving Parisians were poorly dressed for the severe weather.[79] The aggregate amount of suffering that the Parisian population went through during this extremely severe winter explains to a large extent their anger at the armistice when its sacrifices were not paid back in political or social change. Besides the assimilation of civilian war victims to military victims for pension rights or the adoption of war orphans by the nation, little had been gained.[80]

The politics of food

From relatively early in the siege the government knew that there was a real political danger in intervening too much in the food market. In January 1871 a Chinese

---

74 ASSAT, box 62/1, Ministère de la guerre bureau des subsistances, 20/12/1870, 15/01/1871, 24/01/1871. These increases were justified by a proportional decrease in rice, biscuits and bread. Meat rations were again increased in February and March 1871.
75 L. Fiaux, *L'Hygiène militaire, esquisses historiques et médicales à propos d'un bataillon de la garde mobile de l'armée de Paris* (Victor Rozier, 1871), p. 34.
76 VdP, VD6/1586/3, *Histoire du fonctionnement des services ordinaires et extraordinaires du huitième arrondissement durant le siège*, 1874, p. 75.
77 A commission in charge of rationing, the Commission de répartition des combustibles, started working from 10 December 1870 but dealt with the remnants of the fuel stocks. VdP, VD6/791/6, I arrondissement.
78 VdP, VD6/1586/3, *Histoire ... des services ... du huitième arrondissement durant le siège*, p. 128.
79 M. Ferré, *Rapport sur les services des ambulances municipales du troisième arrondissement pendant le siège de Paris, 1870–1871* (Rigal, 1872), p. 29.
80 Marthold, *Mémorandum*, p. 139.

whisper around town denounced the rationing of bread as a conspiracy against the poor.[81] By contrast the proactive municipalities, offering a wide range of policies from the non-interventionist right-wingers to the collectivist radicals, offered a refreshing alternative government. Many peripheral and radical *arrondissements* did not hesitate to create their own rationing and alimentation cards which only gradually became normalised throughout Paris.[82] The diary of Edmond de Goncourt, a rich bourgeois and eminent socialite, illustrates the attraction the communal model had on all Parisians during the siege.

The archival material remaining from the destruction of the Hôtel de Ville in May 1871 gives a fractured view of the local administration of Paris during the siege. What is obvious, however, is that those mayors who chose to re-create municipal powers in their respective *arrondissements* were free to do so.[83] They were also free to act on the vital issues of food supplies and charitable enterprises. There are therefore many communal models for the siege of Paris, just as there were several communes after the 18 March 1871 insurrection.[84] The main priority of many of the most densely populated and peripheral *arrondissements*, where the insurrectionist tradition was the liveliest, was to safeguard public order and to distribute food evenly across the population.

Of all foodstuffs meat was the most sensitive, partly because the nutritional qualities of meat had been flaunted around for many years and partly because the governmental dietary advice insisted on the necessity of eating meat products. Meat was associated with civilisation and the usually discreet debates of the Academy of Medicine made this point clear. When Dr Hardy asked how whole nations could actually live on rice alone, in contradiction to his colleague's views on this type of food, Dr Gubler answered: 'these peoples live or rather vegetate in deep idleness and are unable to perform any labour necessitating the use of muscular strength [*sic*]'.[85]

In spite of the dangers of Chinese indolence, rice was already an important part of the working-class diet in the winter months.[86] Beyond the recognised need for energy-rich food, the social value of meat increased as it became more obvious that all were not suffering the same blockade and that rich consumers might be able to bribe their butchers. The butchers' social status was in itself sensitive and placed them in permanent contact with the artisans and poor of Paris while they enjoyed

81 Joubert and de Vresse, *De la défense de Paris*, p. 31; G. Flourens, *Paris livré* (Lacroix and Cie, 1871), pp. 171–4.
82 M. E. Denormandie, *Le VIIIe arrondissement et son administration* (Garnier Frères, 1875), pp. 135–9.
83 Denormandie, *Le VIIIe arrondissement*, pp. x–xi.
84 R. Tombs, 'Prudent rebels: the second arrondissement during the Paris Commune of 1871', *French History*, 5:4 (1991) 393–413.
85 *BAIM*, 35 (1870) 762.
86 Legoyt, 'L'Alimentation et les prix', p. 331.

some wealth and a petit-bourgeois lifestyle. The image of such shop-keepers is illustrated in Émile Zola's *Ventre de Paris*, which stresses the relative wealth and the suspicion surrounding their commercial practices. Food adulteration in time of peace enabled them to offer their products cheaper and with a higher return than would otherwise have been the case; in time of war they were reminders of class inequality, exploitative practices and even betrayal.[87] Allegations that butchers added extra bones to the already meagre rations,[88] used hollow weights and sold some of the rationed food for their profit provoked a wave of popular anger and[89] dozens of denunciations.[90] Meat was the first foodstuff after milk to be rationed using ration cards issued in early October[91] and imposed from the 22 October.[92] Six days later, the rations fell to a mere 50 g per head, provided one could afford it.

Historians of food disagree on the amount of meat made available to workers in urban France,[93] but it seems probable that a large section of the Parisian proletariat had meat on a regular basis, even if only third-rate cuts ever reached the popular table.[94] The alternative to butcher's meat only took a limited place on the Parisian tables: apart from the various animals sacrificed for this craving for proteins, French versions of Justus von Liebig's meat extract were primarily reserved for the ambulances and the army.[95] The Academy of Science had moreover dismissed Liebig's claims about his products and their nutritional value. Scientists tried to improve the means of preserving meat, enabling the authorities to kill the animals when still fat, for they had nothing to eat either. Drying, ventilated cold, salting, 'carbon tins', and phenic acid were used to preserve meat with similarly poor results.[96] Consumers rejected the strong smell and flavour of such preserved meat.[97]

87 VdP, VD6/1586/3, *Histoire ... des services ... du huitième arrondissement*, p. 48. The addition of congealed blood, rice and fat to offals enabled retailers to double the volume of the product.
88 Joubert and de Vresse, *De la défense de Paris*, p. 11. Vresse, a royalist denunciator of the regime, accuses the butchers of mixing up to 50 per cent of bones in the meat they sold.
89 VdP, VD6/1591/5, Lettres de dénonciation à Monsieur Carnot, Maire du VIIIème; VD6/1796/1, Service de boucherie du Xe arrondissement; VD6/1414/3, boucheries municipales du VIe.
90 Legoyt, 'L'Alimentation et les prix', pp. 336, 340–1.
91 VdP, VD6/1586/3, *Histoire ... des services ... du huitième arrondissement*, p. 25.
92 Joubert and de Vresse, *De la défense de Paris*, p. 12.
93 G. Thuillier, 'Note sur les sources de l'histoire régionale de l'alimentation pour le France du XIXe siècle', in Hémardinquer (ed.), *Pour une histoire de l'alimentation*, pp. 216–18.
94 L. R. Berlanstein, *Working People of Paris, 1871–1914*, (Baltimore, Johns Hopkins University Press, 1984) pp. 46–55. Berlanstein argues that meat was one of the great dietary gains of the Second Empire. Armand Husson estimated the consumption of beef, mutton and pork at c. 60 kg per head a year, *Les Consommations de Paris*.
95 On Liebig's extract of meat see M. R. Finlay, 'Early marketing of the theory of nutrition', in Cunningham and Kamminga (eds), *Science and Culture of Nutrition*, pp. 48–74; 'Quackery and cookery: Justus von Liebig's extract of meat and the theory of nutrition in the Victorian age', *Bulletin of the History of Medicine*, 66 (1992) 404–18.
96 S. Thane, *The History of Food Preservation* (Pantheon Publishing, 1986), pp. 59–83.
97 Saint-Edme, *La Science pendant le siège*, pp. 201–16.

One of the earliest reforms by the central municipal government called all Parisian butchers to meet at the Freemasons' headquarters to form a union in each *arrondissement* to distribute food evenly.[98] When this measure failed, municipalities designated some of them as municipal butcheries dealing at imposed prices and under close supervision.[99] The situation was quite tense and the butchers of the more riotous northern *arrondissements* refused to co-operate with the new municipal authorities, protesting that all these controls were a yoke smacking of authoritarianism. Under the rationing scheme, the *arrondissement* would receive its food from the central administration and create sectors covered by one or several municipal butcheries.[100] This led to complaints that Belleville received less than the south and west, and that 100 kg bags only contained 80 kg of food when they were destined to the poor. However unfair these complaints were, they contributed to make Ferry *la famine* the most hated figure of the government.[101] The *arrondissement* then had to decide on its priorities and, like many Parisians, valued the sick and wounded soldiers more than the rest. The common meat intake was therefore taxed for the ambulances.[102] Popular anger then turned against the soldiers or whoever was in charge, the flow of denunciation grew, meat thieves were arrested and risked being lynched, while rationing rules varied enormously according to the radicalism of the *arrondissement*'s mayor.[103]

The meat rationing scandals comforted bourgeois observers in their dislike for other forms of food rationing. The Academic advice went in that direction. Dr Fauvel expressed a generally held view when he stated: 'Freedom is always much preferable to regulation in those matters.... Meat was never so poorly or so unfairly distributed than since the municipal administration has seized it for itself [*s'en est emparé*].' His report on the topic was supported by all the members sitting in the Academy of Medicine.[104] A few days later the government found some supporters who could draw on their long experience to justify rationing.[105] Throughout the siege the Academy retained an unusually political and tense atmosphere in its debates. Another set of data helps measure the extent of the difficulties. Hospitals had to buy their meat from the government at a preferential rate that still enables us to ascertain the quantitative decline of meat supply and the proportional increase in price (see Table 11).

---

98 VdP, VD6/1586/3, *Histoire ... des services ... du huitième arrondissement*, p. 15.
99 VdP, VD6/1333/1, Rapports journaliers au maire de Paris par la mairie du Ve, 27/09/1870.
100 VD6/1796/1, Service de boucherie du Xe arrondissement.
101 L. Fiaux, *Jules Ferry, un malfaiteur public* (Librairie Internationale, 1886), p. 42.
102 Ferré, *Ambulances municipales du troisième arrondissement*, p. 24.
103 VdP, VD6/1414/3, Boucheries municipales du VIe.
104 *BAIM*, 35 (1870) 764.
105 *BAIM*, 35 (1870) 769. On 25 October, Gaultier de Claubry (1792–1878) defended governmental policies and obtained a favourable reaction.

Table 11 **Comparative table of the meat available through the Central Butchery**

Month	1869–70 quantities (kg)	Average price (francs)	Value (francs)	1870–71 quantities (kg)	Average price (francs)	Value (francs)
September	123,641	1.25	154,551.25	119,326	1.76	209,013.76
October	123 465		154,331.21	117,018		205,951.68
November	120,800		151,000.00	86,723		152,632.42
December	127,963		159,953.75	74,026		130,285.76
January	139,474	1.26	175,737.24	62,269	1.45	90,290.05
February	116,556		146,860.56	65,430		94,873.50
March	129,012		162,555.12	99,180		143,811.00
April	122,086		153,828.36	98,800		143,280.00
May	132,121		166,472.46	84,978		123,218.00

Source: AAP, 542 Foss 83, Boucherie Centrale.

However useful as an index of central needs and prices, a table like this still hides the content of bones per kg and the number of people to feed. The hospital population more than doubled while the meat provisions halved by January 1871. After the end of the siege the free market soon recovered and large butchers were soon able to provide 3,000 kg of meat a day to the Assistance Publique.[106] The scars of this conflict of the haves and have-nots nevertheless prepared the ground for the Commune.

This struggle over meat was exacerbated in January by similar concerns about bread. The quality of bread had declined so badly that it often included sawdust and various inedible fragments. At that stage the government had been in control of the bread production process for several months and was directly accountable. The other problem the Parisian administrations faced was to know precisely who were the people they administered and to whom they had to supply rationed food and organised soup kitchens. Emergency food provisions started as early as 4 October, one month after the revolution.[107] As mentioned above, the Parisian population was a relatively unknown entity both quantitatively and qualitatively. In the most popular sections of the city the high turn-over of working-class tenants and the high number of sub-let rooms had always been a headache for security-conscious policemen. When the police lost many of its men and a great deal of its authority, the picture became even more blurred.

The conservative republican prefect Cresson who replaced the radical Edmond Adam, who himself followed de Kératry at the head of the police in November 1870,[108] attempted to stop the decline of the policing structure and

---

106 AAP, 542 Foss 83, Boucherie Centrale, a contract with Anzot and Marchand (April–June 1871), on the provision of 3,000 kg of meat per day at 1.8 francs per kg (without bones).
107 Joubert and de Vresse, *De la défense de Paris*, p. 11.
108 Fabre, *La Justice à Paris*, p. 62.

reclaimed some of his men from the army.[109] He then used his men to find out more about the population. Some Parisians had left the city before the siege; many others had joined the forces and thus received their subsistence from the well-funded army stores; some *banlieusards* (suburbans) had entered the walls as soon as the shelling ruined all the peripheral villages and enjoyed a precarious status with smaller rations. To add to the misery of the Parisian municipality, the distribution of food between the various *arrondissements*, based on recent electoral rolls, was rigid and did not allow for much movement between the various *arrondissements*.

The shelling of January 1871, which reached most of the south bank *arrondissements*, enticed many Parisians to seek refuge with friends or relatives north of the river if they could not hide in cellars.[110] These refugees presented a number of problems difficult to solve. Would they receive two rations a day if they returned to queue in their original neighbourhood, or, on the other hand, were they not in danger of starving?

The *arrondissements* started a visit scheme, which, as most of the evidence available points out, had a double purpose of identifying the needy and tracking down hidden resources and cheats. To care for the people meant to know the people and to police it more effectively. A system of social networks and home visits shows that, perhaps for the first time, the municipal administration tried to know systematically and in detail the social make-up of the *arrondissements*.[111] For instance, the investigations at the Cité-des-Fleurs, rue Caroline and Impasse Marboulet produced an in-depth analysis of the pauper population of Paris. Unlike previous administrations which relied on the poor to make themselves known, the municipality took the initiative to investigate their plight. The tenement survey of the 'Cité-des-Fleurs' produced an interesting sample of working-class Parisians (see Table 12).

This type of investigation was often limited and many refugees were not accounted for. Others were not in at the time of the census. Some 128 residents of the Cité were not properly accounted for during the inspection. In the siege context these investigations fitted in with the notion of targeted and calculated relief. Some products especially had to be rationed carefully. Milk, which always had been deemed a limited resource, was now rationed and limited to use for the sick and children in this order of priority. With 4,000 cows for the whole of Paris producing 40,000 litres a day for 39,957 children under the age of two, resources were barely adequate but did not provide for the sick and elderly.[112] Watering milk proved not to be an option since most available milk was already watered down by

109 Cresson, *Cent jours du siège à la Préfecture*, p. 11.
110 F. de Biotière, *Paris dans les caves, épisodes du siège de 1870–1871* (Saguier, 1872).
111 Denormandie, *Le VIIIe arrondissement*, p. 100.
112 Morillon, *L'Approvisionnement de Paris*, p. 8.

Table 12 **Social analysis of the inhabitants of La Cité-des-Fleurs**

Occupations	Number of households
Unskilled labourers and servants	71
'Propriétaires', petits bourgeois	35
Skilled labourers, artisans	32
Educated (architects, priests, doctors, artists, engineers)	10
Total	148 households, 395 people

Source: VdP, VD6/2307/1.
Recensement des bouches à nourrir pour le XVIIéme arrondissement.

the retailers to the point of turning blue.[113] Ersatz milk recommended by a special committee of the Academy of Medicine proved to be almost useless since it was based on beaten eggs, absolute rarities, and often reserved to the rich owners of pet chickens. This mixture was based on a nutritional breakdown of the components of milk which had been studied by Vernois and Becquerel in 1853.[114] Dubrunfaut offered a scientific alternative made of sugar, gelatine, carbonate of soda and olive oil or 'horse oil'. If this ersatz seems closer to a laxative than to food for the weaker stomachs, the commercial alternatives went further: gelatinous waters that contained only starch and soda, almond and dried albumin milks competed for a share in a desperate market.[115] The debate on ersatz milk reflected the doubts left in the early days of a science of nutrition which uneasily alternated experimental science and adulteration methods.[116]

To solve this thorny issue the academies advised mothers to breast-feed to enable the authorities to see the sick as the absolute priority for milk rations.[117] This advice was in keeping with a much more important debate on the women's duty to nurse their own children and feed them their milk, but the siege gave it new relevance.[118] Infant mortality[119] tripled from 1869 and made 19,016 victims over

113 *BAIM*, 35 (1870) 762.
114 V. A. Fildes, *Breasts, Bottles and Babies: A History of Infant Feeding* (Edinburgh University Press, 1985).
115 Saint-Edme, *La Science pendant le siège*, pp. 176–8.
116 *BAIM*, 35 (1870) 757–62.
117 The issue of breatfeeding is obviously wider. Cow milk was recognised as relatively unsuitable for infant dietary needs. On this topic see: T. B. Mepham, 'Humanizing milk', *Medical History*, 37:3 (1993) 225–49, p. 227.
118 G. D. Sussman, *Selling Mothers' Milk: The Wet-Nursing Business in France, 1715–1914* (Urbana, University of Illinois Press, 1982), pp. 127–8; D. Dwork, *War is Good for Babies and Other Young Children* (Tavistock, 1987), pp. 94–5; R. D. Dombrow, *Mothers and Medicine* (Madison, University of Wisconsin Press, 1987).
119 A. Husson, *Note sur la mortalité des enfants du premier age* (Librairie Administrative de Paul Dupont, 1870).

the duration of the siege.[120] This situation persisted after the siege. Cattle plague devastated the municipal herd, which was hastily slaughtered and sold as reduced-price meat by the Assistance Publique.[121] Natural milk was then replaced in hospitals by concentrated milk, deemed superior in every respect to the goods available in Paris in March 1871. The debate on milk shows the fragility of the subsistence economy of a major capital city in Europe at a time when transport had made retailing easier but when foodstuffs could not be kept for any length of time.[122] Tentatively Paris was surrounded with forbidden gardens and dangerous battlefields of potatoes and cabbages.

A famous picture printed by *La Guerre illustrée* summarised this issue by depicting a human corpse, shot in the head and rotting among the vegetables (Figure 7).[123] Death and food were again intimately tied together and the siege experience was one of hunger or even starvation and death. The central government had to extend its jurisdiction and its responsibility to feed and care for all. Few administrators felt confident with this role.

The politics of care

If requisitions and rationing remained difficult issues, soup kitchens were in a different league. Municipal authorities had a long experience of organised charities, either as sponsors, organisers or even as donors. When the war started to affect the economic climate, the imperial regime decided to provide cheap food through the *fourneaux économiques* (municipal canteens).[124] After the revolution the municipal soup kitchens and canteens could be invested with a secular and political mission. They entered into competition with religious soup kitchens,[125] which, like the municipal ones, were often attached to an ambulance and presented to the world a demonstration of the charitable war effort.[126] The organisation of soup kitchens was in the hands of unpaid and socially advantaged donors, but the materials used for the confection of fat soups and nutritious proletarian meals came from the municipal powers themselves. Soup kitchens demonstrated the willingness of municipal authorities to compete with and emulate private efforts rather than to

---

120 Morillon, *L'Approvisionnement de Paris*, p. 195.
121 A major epidemic of cattle plague devastated the French herds, E. Dubos, *La Peste bovine* (Beauvais, Père, 1874).
122 AAP, 542 Foss 83, Boucherie Centrale, livraisons aux hôpitaux pendant le siège et la Commune, 14/03/1871. Diseased meat sold for 90–120 francs per 100kg compared with the 150–210 francs safer meat would command.
123 D. Reid, *Paris Sewers and Sewermen: Realities and Representations* (Cambridge, Mass., Harvard University Press, 1991), pp. 60–70. This concern for urban food production led to the expansion of Genevillier sewage farms immediately after the war.
124 VdP, VD6 1481/5, Fourneaux économiques, enquête du Préfet de la Seine, 23/08/1870.
125 VdP, VD6/1586/3, *Histoire ... des services ... du huitième arrondissement*, p. 112.
126 J. d'Arsac, *Les Frères des écoles chrétiennes* (F. Curot, 1872), p. 228.

Figure 7 Lange & Verdeil, *Skeleton of a Marauder Shot Among the Cabbages*, 1871 – this picture published in an illustrated newspaper served as a warning to no-man's land thieves

supersede them. Only in December did the government see fit to allocate 500,000 francs to the creation of new soup kitchens.[127] To obtain this type of benefit, people had to register as paupers with the municipality in charge of the local Bureau de Bienfaisance since the reform of the Assistance Publique.

Bureaux de Bienfaisance had existed in their current form since 1816. They enjoyed a mixed private/public status supported by donations, fund-raising events, and subsidies from the Assistance Publique.[128] To benefit from home-relief, Parisians had to prove they had inhabited the city for three years and were unable to earn their living (*indigents*). Those in a slightly less precarious position received a smaller amount as *nécessiteux*.[129] During the war the requirements were simplified and municipal administrators made the most of their discretionary powers. The number of paupers in Paris increased fourfold in comparison with the year 1869. As the 'citizen mayor' of the fourteenth *arrondissement* noted in his project for a uniform welfare safety net,[130] *arrondissements* had to support a very uneven burden.[131] The following two tables illustrate this diversity. They show not

127 *Recueil officiel des actes du Gouvernement*, Decree of 3 December 1870, p. 552.
128 AAP, 542 Foss 1, Organisation du conseil général des hospices du département de la Seine, Minutes du Conseil Général, 2/10/1870.
129 A. Fleury, 'De l'Assistance Publique à Paris' (Thèse de doctorat, Faculté de droit, Rousseau, 1901), p. 140; Bréjean and Humblot, *Les Mairies de Paris*, pp. 162–3. The paltry sums given to paupers varied according to complex administrative rules.
130 AAP, 542 Foss 1, 14 October 1870, Organisation du conseil général des hospices du département de la Seine.
131 Morillon, *L'Approvisionnement de Paris*, p. 120

Table 13 **Soup kitchens in Paris**

Arrondissement	Number of soup kitchens	Number of paupers 30/09/1870	Number of paupers 30/01/1871
I	2	3,313	8,000
II	2	1,924	12,000
III	3	4,064	24,000
IV	4	7,560	19,000
V	4	12,278	15,000
VI	2	4,367	15,000
VII	2	3,932	10,800
VIII	2	2,783	8,000
IX	3	2,674	14,300
X	2	7,523	20,000
XI	3	10,932	30,000
XII	11	4,836	25,000
XIII	4	7,035	34,000
XIV	3	3,265	15,000
XV	3	3,641	24,000
XVI	6	2,025	12,000
XVII	3	3,059	19,454
XVIII	5	3,797	60,000
XIX	10	3,265	66,000
XX	7	4,322	20,000

Source: VdP, VD6/721/13, Recensement numérique de la population indigente de la ville.

only the variations in the numbers of paupers but also the willingness of each municipality to engage with the problem and to invest in their respective bureaux de Bienfaisance. Table 13 contrasts the number of kitchens and the number of registered paupers. Table 14, produced from Assistance Publique data, shows the type of help delivered locally by the municipal powers and the overall cost, as far as records enabled them to be compiled.

Two *arrondissements* with a pauper population roughly equal at the start of the siege thus behaved in radically different ways: the I *arrondissement* only created two soup kitchens and registered around 5,000 more paupers during the siege, while for the same period the radical XIX *arrondissement* created ten soup kitchens and registered another 63,000 paupers. In these two extreme examples some factors explain the discrepancies. The I *arrondissement* was wealthier and quite small geographically, so that a few kitchens could conveniently cater for much of the local population; its artisan population was also less likely to come forth for pauper relief. The XIX, a large *arrondissement,* was also among the poorest, probably under-reporting the numbers of paupers before the war and its less

Table 14 **The type of help delivered to paupers: analytical breakdown by** *arrondissement*

*	a	b	c	d	e	f	g	h	i	j	k
I	2	7			140,017	528,287			28,860 (a) 113,930 (b)		including 22,986 sold in a) and 89,922 in b)
II											
III	2	16		27,300		6,454,364			953,950 (b)	31,400	including 577,690 francs to bakers and 20,953 sold
IV		3					52,682			19,500	canteen directed by the Bureau de Bienfaisance
V	4	26				436,139	122,500		562,187 (b)	46,642	expenditure include 324,855 francs from the Comité d'assistance patriotique
VI		6				1,315,549			283,663		
VII		14					117,286		125,235	75,068	not including bread vouchers paid to the Assistance Publique
VIII	3	4	2,634	6,420	166,605	481,500					
IX											
X		10		23,000							
XI											
XII		12									Bureau de Bienfaisance not active
XIII		15		27,000		4,973,397	111,702				only bread
XIV	3	3	6,913	26,357	946,643	963,043	142,192	aucun	47,352 (a) 511,919 (b)	32,270	total expenditure 1,200,996 francs
XV		4				1,216,115	358,741		93,3724 (b)	60,000	
XVI	6		3,038		73,144				31,845 (a)	11,248	not including the bread, the Bureau de Bienfaisance took charge of civilians and the town soldiers' families
XVII		5							290,289 (b)		
XVIII	4	24				4,896,930	218,748		325,788 (b)		including cash support
XIX	5		64,000		4,011,149					67,000	Bureau de Bienfaisance only
XX		7	?	?	?	?	?	?	?	?	probably 2,950,000 total expenditure

* *Arrondissement*

Notes: a) number of soup kitchens; b) municipal canteens; c) using soup kitchens; d) using canteens; e) vouchers for **a**; f) vouchers for **b**; g) help to the military; h) help to refugees; i) money spent for **a** and **b**; j) number of beneficiaries; k) comments.

Source: AAP, 542 Foss 47, *Caisse de bureaux de bienfaisance.*

well-off population had to go cap in hand to beg for food. Furthermore the I and the XIX had very different leadership and political leanings. Charles Delescluze (1809–71), who later led the last days of the Commune, was the mayor of the XIX and strongly believed in a generous charitable state if not in socialism.

Table 14, compiled from accounting documents, simplifies greatly the type of relief available and perhaps magnifies the coverage of this municipal welfare. It also shows that the patronisingly named Bureau de Bienfaisance was not necessarily the tool of predilection for municipal welfare. The XII *arrondissement* did not make any use of it for instance. One could try to deal with poverty by other means than through politically dubious gratuities in kind.

Many other institutions such as municipal orphanages revived long-disused revolutionary laws.[132] Other imperial institutions were only spared for political purposes in spite of representing, as indeed the soup kitchens did, the most objectionable face of charity to 'real' republicans.[133] Empress Eugénie's Orphelinat des Jeunes Ouvrières, for instance, was preserved as a closure 'would provoke the most unfavourable reactions in the faubourg Saint Antoine where it is well known and appreciated'.[134] Secularists had problems fighting off the very successful public relations exercise coming from the various charitable religious orders.[135]

This paternalistic charitable activity answered real needs and carried on unabated. With the added proviso of the unemployment imposed by the war situation, there is no real evidence that old-style philanthropy was questioned by the more conservative *arrondissements*. Louis Asseline, the mayor of the XIV *arrondissement,* in an address to his employees gave the tone of moderate republican welfare provisions:

> You will undoubtedly find this idea that the state or the city owe a debt to poor citizens at so much a head per day ... I cannot but advise you to fight off this incredible pretension and to remind all families with which you will have dealing that the Republic has no other duty than to help those citizens who, from an unwanted circumstance (age, disease, industrial unemployment) are currently unable to provide for themselves.[136]

To maintain this fiction, food was rarely given free but usually charged at 5 centimes a ration. The more radical leaders of Paris challenged the phraseology but not the practice. They opposed the terms 'charity' as Christian and 'assistance'

---

132 AAP, 542 Foss 75, 26/11/1871 reviving the tutelle on foundlings. A. Dupoux, *Sur les pas de Monsieur Vincent* (Revue de L'Assistance Publique à Paris, 1958), pp. 293–330.
133 This questioning of *bureaux de bienfaisance* and other traditional municipal outlets does not date from the Commune as Allan Mitchell seems to argue: Mitchell, *The Divided Path: The German Influence on Social Reform in France after 1870* (Chapel Hill, University of North Carolina Press, 1991), p. 76.
134 AAP, 542 Foss 73, 9/10/1870.
135 F. Bournand, *Les Soeurs martyres* (Tours, A. Cattier, 1894).
136 VdP, VD6/791/6, Ier arrondissement, Adresse du Maire au conseil, October 1870?

as insulting, and offered 'national benefaction' as an alternative.[137] The alteration of linguistic categories did not affect the practice of old-style charity. Food distributions were always implemented in the hope of deeply rooting the moderate republic in the Parisian ground. Many mayors used food to develop their patronage network and negotiated a food-entitlement which rewarded active citizenship and war effort.[138] The citizens then depended on this food entitlement to eat and the mayors depended on their political support. Indeed some excelled at distributing subsistence rations, as for instance the municipal soup kitchens of the IX *arrondissement* which served 78,000 rations a day in November 1870.[139] While the soup kitchen scheme enabled the poorer to obtain a meal or even two if they were cunning enough,[140] they were socially unacceptable for the petite bourgeoisie and the underpaid salaried clerks. The Garde Nationale also had a crucial role. The Garde functioned as an electoral college of sorts constantly re-negotiating authority within its own ranks and contesting any external authority. The *gardes* often petitioned the government in the most urgent terms, renewing what they perceived to be an imperative mandate.

At the core of this organisation, the institutions designed to distribute help among the poor members of the Garde played a very important role. The Conseil de Famille which distributed help to the *necessiteux* could thus break the captain who refused to recognise its authority.[141] The *gardes* could also address the municipality and claim their own political legitimacy and reassert their specific republican jurisdiction by threatening to use their weapons. Within besieged Paris citizens in arms carried more weight than unarmed ones, and in practice rations were not 'the expression of equality'.[142]

Those who still had employment during the siege could find themselves in a more difficult situation even than if they had to rely on the army or the municipality for their survival. Few employers could afford to imitate the Rothschild bank in creating a private ambulance[143] and increasing salaries by 50 per cent for the

---

137 VdP, VD6/1333/1, Rapports journaliers au maire de Paris, Vème, 1/10/1870; L. Veuillot, *Paris pendant les deux sièges* (2 vols, Victor Palmé, 1871), vol. 1, pp. 267–73.
138 Lucile Newman makes the point that hunger may be caused by the failure of food-entitlement even in periods of relative wealth. L. Newman (ed.), *Hunger in History: Food Shortage, Poverty and Deprivation* (Oxford, Blackwell, 1990), pp. 5–7.
139 Morillon, *L'Approvisionnement de Paris*, p. 126.
140 VdP, VD6/1796/1, Service de boucherie du Xe arrondissement, containing complaints about the abuse of Garde Nationale rights.
141 VdP, VD6 1711 and Vbis 1 H3 7, procès verbal du conseil des familles.
142 VdP, VD6 730. 5. The argument goes both ways: the rich did not suffer the same physical privations; M. P. Johnson, *The Paradise of Association: Political Culture and Popular Organisation in the Paris Commune of 1871* (Ann Arbor, University of Michigan Press, 1996).
143 A. Job, *Malades et blessés de l'hôpital Rothschild pendant le siège de Paris, 1870–1871* (A. Delahaye, 1871).

duration of the siege.¹⁴⁴ The petite bourgeoisie was often identified as the class that suffered the most from the siege. While their fate was in no way worse than that of their working-class neighbours, contemporaries identified a cultural inadequacy to cope with this type of crisis. While the income of many *rentiers* virtually collapsed as a consequence of the war, they could not take advantage of the charitable safety net without debasing themselves. They usually remained better dressed and housed than most, however, and if they suffered from hunger, few died of starvation.

The lodging crisis which afflicted Haussmannian Paris only increased during the siege and became one of the key political priorities of the government. Most factories had closed down, demand and supply had dried up in most trades and work was so slack that very little income was now disposable to spend on rent. The government avoided a general crisis of trust and commerce by imposing a moratorium on business debts and rent from 1 October, renewable after three months until March 1871.¹⁴⁵ The landlords lost their income for the period of the siege, or rather they owned bad debts that had little value in the case of the poorer section of the population.¹⁴⁶ This measure was undoubtedly necessary in the context. In real terms it also presented a political liability by deferring the resolution of the problem to a later date. This financial freeze on the economic crisis was bound to lead to a financial *débâcle* when the moratorium would be lifted and when six months worth of rents, debts and charges would be due. This situation did indeed arise brutally when the armistice government insensitively attempted to revert to its normal *laissez-faire* doctrine. This measure was necessarily unpopular and came far too quickly after what was perceived as a shameful surrender. It also affected a much wider section of the population than the government had anticipated and greatly contributed to the social unrest that sustained the Commune.

During the siege, however, the housing crisis contrasted with the misuse of many empty apartments. Various motions were put forward to make better use of the homes of the rich who had fled in the early days of September. These flats were opened for investigations and municipalities like the V *arrondissement* took measures to use them as refugee shelters in spite of the government's reluctance.¹⁴⁷ Churches and empty buildings, cellars and the Pantheon were used as bomb shelters, but the humid and dark accommodation they provided could not

---

144 Marthold, *Mémorandum*, p. 150.
145 *Recueil officiel des actes du Gouvernement*, p. 423; M. du Camp, *Les Convulsions de Paris* (4 vols, Hachette, 1878–80), vol. 1, p. 40.
146 C. Ballot, *Des effets de la guerre à Paris et en France sur le louage, la propriété et les divers contrats* (Maresq, 1871)
147 VdP, VD6/1542/1, Réquisitions de logements du Ve, 7/10/1870, and 18/01/1871. Municipalities had a difficult choice to make. Either they made a requisition of private houses and furnished accommodation (*hôtel meublé*), or they had to repress a large vagrant population and become unpopular.

lead to any unwelcome appropriation. The constant shelling of the left bank of Paris killed few Parisians but it did damage a number of buildings, usually uninsured, and the Parisians once again turned to their government. Refugees who could present a number of compensation claims, those wounded and permanently crippled were assimilated to soldiers wounded on the battlefield.[148]

These measures added to the sum of financial liabilities that made the naturally cautious accountants of the government shiver. The knowledge of forthcoming war indemnities of up to 6,000 million francs, announced in September 1870 during the early Franco-German negotiations, conspired with the prevalent ideology to keep the government's proactive intervention to the minimum. Devolving to the municipalities most of the practical powers and the freedom for new initiatives was only a devolution of credits accounted for separately from the national expenditure and repayable by the city and not the state.[149] This led to a greater level of public debts in Paris than in the provinces. This caution explains why the Parisian central municipality waited until 25 October to spend the 3 million francs lent by the government to the communes of the Seine department (including Paris) since 12 September to finance bread distribution among the poor.[150] While the centre preferred to balance the books, the *arrondissements* could indulge in more direct welfare spending. Paris was directly accountable for its debts but not, it seems, each *arrondissement*.

This freedom and the separate if not conflicting political agenda of the municipalities made for inter-*arrondissement* competition rather than co-operation. This 'Napoleon of Notting Hill' situation led to a number of artificial crises, when one *arrondissement* suffered from the lack of food, or blamed another for its lax policies. It also led to contrasting conservatism and vociferous radicalism. On the other hand, the interventionist policies implemented for the first time by various municipalities left their seeds in the French municipal practice.[151] The elections of mayors during the Commune and later, with the Conseil Municipal during the Third Republic, meant that it was in the administrators' best interest to create a directly identifiable type of management which might not reflect and channel governmental priorities. Allan Michell has shown how the municipalities could

---

148 Inhabitants of Strasburg or Metz did not receive the same benefits.
149 G. Massa-Gille, *Histoire des emprunts de la ville de Paris* (Ville de Paris, 1973), pp. 308–23.
150 AAP, 542 Foss 95.
151 Most of the research on welfare and poverty provisions deals with the Third Republic and national legislation, see R. G. Fuchs, 'Morality and poverty: public welfare for mothers in Paris, 1870–1900', *French History*, 2:3 (1988) 288–95; S. Elwitt, *The Third Republic Defended: Bourgeois Reform in France, 1880–1914* (Baton Rouge, Louisiana State Univerity Press, 1986); J. H. Weiss, 'Origins of the French welfare state: poor relief in the Third Republic, 1871–1914', *French Historical Studies*, 13:1 (1983) 47–78; also H. Hatzfeld, *Du Paupérisme à la sécurité sociale, 1850–1940* (Armand Colin, 1971).

foster a policy like systematic anticlericalism into the mid-Third Republic until it became national debate.[152]

While the most cumbersome siege welfare policies were not maintained, it certainly came to the notice of municipal councils that their fund-raising efforts had been successful and often brought in unexpected profits on welfare expenditure. The municipal ambulances and soup kitchens which served a clear political purpose also buttressed the *arrondissements'* coffers. In the III *arrondissement,* for instance, the fund-raising activities raised 25,257 francs, 11,699 of which were given to municipal ambulances, 8,125.10 were spent on various necessary provisions and 5,432 francs were discreetly absorbed by the *arrondissement* municipality. Other accounts show that the municipality kept nearly a third of its charitable income.[153] While the responsibility for the war, the defeat, the rationing even fell on the government, the real proactive rationing powers, charity visits and policing practices were initiated by the self-serving municipalities. They allied charity and self-government democracy into the small-scale replication of the state of emergency; they shaped the experience of the siege of Paris but never shouldered any of the blame for it. These politics of care remained the source of political legitimacy and popularity in Paris.[154] Central welfare authorities in Paris like the Assistance Publique slowly slipped under the control of the Conseil Municipal. The Conseil Municipal then acted as a powerful counterpower to the state in the early years of the Third Republic.[155] Moreover, the interventionist and environmentalist policies developed by the civic administration provided an experimental ground for economic and social reforms that only became law in France ten or twenty years later.

While economic historians have pointed out the interventionist traditions born out of the Jacobin war policy tradition revived by the 4 September regime,[156] they have on the whole failed to notice that it was perhaps on the micro-scale that the rhetoric of interventionism and the politics of care carried the more weight and shaped a political culture which held the centre responsible while acting independently from it: a centralisation of thoughts rather than practice.

152 A. Mitchell, 'Crucible of French anti-clericalism: the conseil municipal of Paris, 1871–1885', *Francia,* 8 (1980) 395–405.
153 Ferré, A*mbulances municipales du troisième arrondissement,* pp. 5–6, 33.
154 A. De Bonnard, *Organisation de la vraie république* (Berthélémy, 1870).
155 M. Le Mansois Duprey, *L'Oeuvre sociale de la municipalité Parisienne 1871–1891* (Imprimerie municipale, 1892), pp. x–70.
156 P. Levillain and R. Riemenschneider (eds), *La Guerre de 1870–1871 et ses conséquences* (Bonn, Bouvier Verlag, 1990).

6 Revolutionary society and medicine

The role of 'medicine' in France often surprises the student of French history who has constantly been told that France was *the* centralised country stifled by state interventionism. *La médecine* itself is often presented unproblematically as a reified social and intellectual component of French society under the all-encompassing shadow of the state. This unidimensional presentation of 'bodies' like *le corps médical* hides more than it reveals. Readers may share in Robert Gilpin's despair: 'the complexity of French Society in general, which is accompanied by insufficient knowledge of how it really functions, is discouraging'.[1] To add to this pessimistic vision, Suleiman rightly reminded us, the French system of government was and still is infinitely more complex than a strictly statist model would suggest.[2] Some vital areas of government in the legal domain (for instance, the notaries, the *avoués*, the *huissiers*) remained controlled by venal offices well into the twentieth century. The abolition of the few surviving 'private civil servants' of the French state is not on the political agenda even now. In Suleiman's words, it is useful to think of French centralisation as the concentration of jurisdiction rather than the concentration of 'effective power'.[3] The state was therefore central in the organisation of French medicine because it was at the heart of all jurisdictions and because a centralised state could be most easily taken over by professional interests. This last point does not indicate undue cynicism, but illustrates a reciprocal relationship between state and professional status.

As Stuart Jones has noted, the cult of the state and its pivotal role in the political discourse, perhaps more than the reality of state administration, was what made nineteenth-century France so distinct from Britain.[4] The awe in which originally autonomous areas of French life held the state explains why various agencies structuring daily life were so anxious to be recognised and assimilated to the state. To become part of the state jurisdictional portfolio was the guarantee of a protected and monopolistic status which could be reinforced over time. Medicine was thus largely self-regulated through a strict hierarchy inspired by and mimicking the authoritarian forms of government France knew in the nineteenth century.

---

1 R. Gilpin, *France in the Age of the Scientific State* (Princeton University Press, 1968), p. 78.
2 E. N. Suleiman, *Private Power and Centralization in France: The Notaires and the State* (Princeton University Press, 1989), pp. 16–30.
3 Suleiman, *Private Power and Centralization in France*, p. 17.
4 H. S. Jones, *The French State in Question: Public Law and Political Argument in the Third Republic* (Cambridge University Press, 1993), pp. 6–54.

The 'institutions' of medicine, the Academy of Medicine and the faculty, had their share of jurisdiction over what increasingly became a professional 'body' in the nineteenth century. Moreover, since the emergence of legal medicine, medical experts could act, within narrow parameters, in legal cases or be invited to judge on health-related cases on behalf of the French government.[5] In other words, the state relinquished part of its jurisdiction to a private group which, by then, had almost merged with the state as a pool of experts.

This apparent contradiction between an essentially centralising state and a multiplicity of autonomous groups working beside the state may only be deemed a contradiction in a rigidly statist view of centralisation. This chapter will show that autonomous and semi-autonomous groups working with and towards the state were, in France at least, powerful agents of the state and tied to the most legitimate government through a complicated set of reciprocal arrangements. In 1871, when the Commune of Paris and the elected Versailles government competed for public recognition, medical choice would overwhelmingly demonstrate the strength of this bond.

The government of France was, by philosophy, non-interventionist in matters of health and sanitation, not only because *laissez-faire* was the best way of managing a low-tax budget, but also because to intervene would alienate powerful and faithful servants of the state. Current debates (of the 1990s) on the *sécurité sociale* prove that when the state attempts to reform a mostly private medical system it can be slowed down and eventually challenged by doctors posing as defenders of the common good. On the other hand, the current medical staff's political attitude is not simply a pose but really expresses their unwritten position in the French state. For historians, the many attractions of a society abiding by a set of written codes make them forget how much France also works with an unspoken common law beyond legal *jurisprudence* or case books.

This chapter will explore the ties between the state and medicine, between centralising but autonomous institutions and an ostensibly decentralising but interventionist revolutionary regime. While the Commune of Paris was always essentially chaotic and unstable, fractionate and often ineffective, it still stated a great number of key objectives regarding health and social provision.[6] For Commune leaders, welfare issues were intrinsically attached to religious and educational reforms which constituted the most consensual aspects of its policies. The first section of this chapter thus deals simultaneously with the secularisation of the 'giant hospital' described in Chapter 4 and the reforms attempted by the

5 F. E. Foderé, *Traité de médecine légale et d'hygiène publique* (De l'imprimerie de Mame, 2nd edn, 1813), pp. xi–xv; M. Foucault (ed.), *Moi Pierre Rivière ayant égorgé ma mère, ma soeur et mon frère* (Julliard, 1973), pp. 205–7.
6 C. Rihs, *La Commune de Paris, sa structure et ses doctrines, 1871* (Geneva, Librairie Droz, 1955; Seuil, reprint, 1973).

Communard administration. The second part shows how medical practitioners and 'mandarins' failed to subscribe to this political and social project and instead chose to serve the government *outside* Paris. The penultimate section is devoted to the agony of the Commune and the massacres that took place in the last week of May 1871. The conclusion will seek to define the inheritance of the Commune for medical reforms in Third Republic Paris.

Towards secular medicine

The Commune obviously owed a tremendous amount to the politics of care outlined in the previous chapter. Communards, for instance, felt the need to reinstate the regulation of the sale of meat in spite of an ineffective blockade. From 11 May 1871, the Commune decided to regulate butchers directly[7] in order to stop adulteration and to fix the prices.[8] There was no tangible need for this type of measure after the end of the siege. However, as a symbolic social measure tampering with free trade and the monopoly of large butchers and maintaining the rights of the state to intervene in such matters, the Commune legislation renewed the social compact between local administration[9] and people which had been at the basis of the war effort.[10] Other important reforms of the Commune, and more representative of its social ideals, were the combined reforms of the pension rights of the guards and their families, a continuation of 4 September measures and reminiscent of the *ateliers nationaux* of 1848. These rights had such an important application that they virtually provided a form of unemployment benefit for those who volunteered in the citizens' army.[11]

The amendment of bankruptcy legislation and the moratorium on debts and rents went in the same direction. Figure 8 published after the war by Cham (Amédée de Noé), the author of the *Folies de la Commune*, contrasts ironically the state of devastated Paris with the policies initially developed in the Communard political discourse.[12] Rent reform was also combined with a moratorium on the Mont-de-Piété or municipal pawn shops which had long provided that buffer of

---

7 Municipal regulations ceased around 28/02/1871. VD6/1796/1, Service de boucherie du Xe arrondissement. Monopolies of distribution and retail were abolished in an effort to protect the small dealers. VD6/1506/3.
8 *JORC*, 11/05/1871.
9 Rihs, *La Commune de Paris,* pp. 26–34.
10 VdP, VD6/1506/3, VIIe arrondissement, Report on the lower quality of beef since the institution of large retailing practices in 1848.
11 A. Morillon, *L'Approvisionnement de Paris en temps de guerre, souvenirs et prévisions* (Perrin, 1888), pp. 117–18. Morillon made the comparison between the 2 francs and 25 centimes of the married *gardes nationaux* and the 2 francs paid to the workers of the Ateliers Nationaux of 1848 as the cause of the Commune and June days respectively.
12 G. J. Sanchez, 'The challenge of right-wing caricature journals: from the Commune amnesty campaign to the end of censorship, 1878–1881', *French History*, 10:4 (1996) 451–89; R. J. Goldstein, 'Censorship of caricature in France, 1815–1914', *French History*, 3:1(1989), 71–107.

Figure 8 *Don't blame the Commune, it was about to solve the housing and rent problem!* 1871

credit which enabled employers to shed and hire staff on low wages.[13] During the siege of Paris the government had taken a number of measures which forbade the selling of goods held for mobilised soldiers, and enabled people to recover essential and cheap belongings (worth less than 20 francs), pawned since the beginning of the war.[14] This decision taken on 1 October 1870 was detailed ten days later and specifically related to shirts and bedding.

The Commune claimed these measures and also attempted to go much further in abolishing the Mont-de-Piété altogether.[15] The general purpose of the reforms was to raise the wages and social conditions of the workers while leaving the general employment laws untouched in the name of the sacrosanct budgetary orthodoxy. The Commune always stated that it intended to abolish pauperism through work.[16]

This was the paradox of the Commune that it remained tangled in a confusion of revolutionary aspirations and attempts at finding a legitimacy in the management

13 The Mont-de-Piété administration attached to the Assistance Publique provided loans at 9 per cent on the artefacts deposited. A. Fleury, 'De l'Assistance Publique à Paris' (Thèse de doctorat, Faculté de droit, Rousseau, 1901), p. 43; M. Le Mansois Duprey, *L'Oeuvre sociale de la municipalité parisienne 1891–1871*, p. 125; E. Deschodt, *Histoire du Mont-de-Piété* (Le Cherche-Midi, 1993).
14 *Recueil officiel des actes du Gouvernement* (Librairie Administrative de Paul Dupont, 1871), pp. 326, 457, 535.
15 *Les 31 séances officielles de la Commune de Paris* (Joseph Floch, 1970), 25/04/1870, pp. 86–97.
16 *JORC*, 12/04/1871.

of the available legal and economic tools. Born from a conflict with the state, the Commune respected its forms and attempted to appropriate its administration.[17] In spite of this cautiousness, the situation left very little scope for such hesitation and the daring innovations and revolutionary actions could not be balanced by the Commune's political moderation. The high mortality rates of January continued unabated and the spring, always a season of high-priced cereals, was marked by constantly high morbidity. While matters of health and social welfare were only rarely debated in the official sessions of the Commune, the practice of the Commune illustrates a number of priority reforms. The first was to take control of the Assistance Publique, putting Treillard, an aged and affable man, in control. Treillard was a life-long opponent of the regime of Napoleon III and he had led a battalion of veteran volunteers during the siege.[18] Beyond his republican credentials, he did not have the administrative *gravitas* necessary to rule such a complex machinery of ambulances, hospitals and voluntary hospitals and services. To domesticate such a complex and largely hostile administration, Treillard followed the Communard practice of sending clear symbolic revolutionary messages.

His first priority was thus to secularise the hospitals of Paris. This reform followed the general policy of the Commune and reflected the lively anticlericalism of the ultra-republicans, some of whom had ruled *arrondissements* during the siege. The XI and the north-eastern *arrondissements* had already been engaged in a secularist crusade for several months before Treillard's reform.[19] As one of the Commune's nine ruling committees explored the secularisation of education,[20] hospitals could not possibly be left out of the reform.[21] Above Treillard, Adolphe Clémence so-called Roussel, elected member of the Commune for the IV *arrondissement*, was at the cutting edge of the symbolic *de-Christianisation* of religious ambulances and hospitals.[22] To launch the campaign in style he destroyed all the crucifixes of the Red Cross ambulance at the Palais de l'Industrie. This violent measure was immediately effective and most ambulances then chose to remove all religious symbols from their wards rather than attract the Commune's attention.[23]

---

17 R. V. Gould, *Insurgent Identities: Class, Community and Protest in Paris from 1848 to the Commune* (Chicago University Press, 1996), pp. 135, 153.
18 VdP, VD6/1333/1, Rapports journaliers au maire de Paris, mairie du Ve, lettre du citoyen Treillard, chef du bataillon des vétérans du quartier du jardin des plantes et du quartier St Victor, 19/11/1870.
19 ASSAT, box 63/3, Ambulance municipale du XVIIe, letter 4/12/1870 to Larrey. *Ambulances municipales du XVIIe arrondissement,* report to Baron Larrey by Dr Angelot.
20 O. Marion and L. Perrin, 'La Commune et l'Église' (Mémoire de Maîtrise, Université Paris X–XII, 1981), p. 53.
21 *JORC*, 30/03/1871.
22 *Rapport du Comte de Beaufort* (Paul Dupont, 1871), p. 6.
23 J. d'Arsac, *Les Frères des écoles chrétiennes pendant la guerre de 1870–1871* (F. Curot, 1872), p. 262; H. R. Blandeau, *Patriotisme du clergé catholique et des ordres religieux pendant la guerre de 1870–1* (Lecoffre, 1873).

Throughout the Commune era the secularisation process was heavy-handed, unevenly applied and took on some *carnivalesque* features.[24] At Saint-Laurent the dusty skeletons found in the crypt were exhibited as 'victims of clericalism', 'tortured' with evil-looking ancient prosthetic instruments.[25] Rigault's zealous policemen also invaded the Picpus convent, found three insane nuns locked in safety cells, and a medical thesis on midwifery which suggested that the convent nuns might be more worldly than usually assumed.[26] The gutter press rapidly made the link between vice, madness, medicine and clericalism. The visiting consultant of this aged congregation of Picpus ran away while the nuns were locked up with the prostitutes of Saint-Lazare. This practical joke was a crude piece of propaganda inspired by trash literary tropes but it served a wider purpose.[27] The Communard Prefect of Police, Raoul Rigault, played on the well-established association of medicine and clergy in people's minds.[28] The secret languages of medicine[29] and religion had conspired together to lock women in the convents and lunatic asylums which Rigault denounced as the new Bastilles serving bourgeois families.[30]

Communard iconoclasm and radical politics were threatening to all forms of establishment. In fact the anticlerical line of the Commune went as far as choosing hostages principally among the religious personnel of the archbishopric of Paris, starting with Archbishop Darboy[31] whom Raoult Rigault hoped to exchange for the leader of his faction, Blanqui.[32]

This hostage-taking policy resulted in the blood-bath of the end of May, when as the Versailles armies advanced these men were executed summarily.[33] Even in its early stages, this secularisation was resented as an aggression and followed a militant atheist agenda. Within established hospitals this reform went

24 F. Bournand, *Le Clergé pendant la Commune, 1871* (Tolra, 1892).
25 M. du Camp, *Les Convulsions de Paris* (4 vols, Hachette, 1878–80), vol. 1, p. 196.
26 Marion and Perrin, 'La Commune et l'Église', pp. 92–3.
27 G. Da Costa, *La Commune vécue* (2 vols, Quantin, 1903–5), vol. 2, pp. 247–8.
28 L. Wilette, *Raoul Rigault : 25 ans, Communard, chef de la Police* (Syros, 1984), p. 135.
29 *Le Soir* in October 1870 launched a fierce assault on psychiatric medicine. *GMP*, 25 (1870) 537. The 1838 law had given more prominence to one of the few specialisms of French medicine. J. Goldstein, *Console and Classify: The French Psychiatric Profession in the Nineteenth Century* (Cambridge University Press, 1987), pp. 276–321.
30 See J. Donzelot, *La Police des familles* (Éditions de Minuit, 1977).
31 The Gallican Darboy had been republican until 1857 and only supported the Empire by opportunism. This profile made him least likely to find much conservative backing in Versailles. J.-O. Boudon, 'Une Promotion épiscopale sous le Second Empire', l'abbé Darboy à l'assault de Paris', *Revue d'histoire moderne et contemporaine*, 39:3 (1992) 476–81.
32 C. Prolès, *Les Hommes de la révolution de 1871* (Chamuel, 1898), pp. 46–59.
33 See AEP, Fre I, *Copie de dépositions reçues en 1871 par M. Le Vicomte Laverdo, Juge d'instruction à Paris*. Testimonies from surviving ecclesiastics imprisoned with Darboy were at the origin of Darboy's cult as a martyr of the Catholic Church.

beyond removing the crucifixes from the wards and abolishing morning prayers; it endangered basic medical provision. Until the 1880s, France did not have a professional nursing group comparable to that created in Britain by St John's House and, after the Crimean war, by the followers of Florence Nightingale.[34] Most nurses belonged to religious orders of a kind that had long been associated with hospitals. During the siege, voluntary ambulances and emergency hospitals had, if anything, reinforced this clerical involvement. Churchmen, Petits-Frères des Pauvres, Frères des Écoles Chrétiennes had all been involved in voluntary ambulances. The latter had been particularly prominent during the siege of Paris.[35] While their enthusiasm and self-sacrificing practices led them to accept little or even nothing by way of remuneration, they prevented the creation of secular professional nursing careers. Even though some hospitals already used non-religious medical staff, the nursing ideals followed religious discourses of self-sacrifice.[36]

Religious orders were not uniformly admired, however, even by doctors. Their open proselytising intentions made them suspicious to deeply anticlerical socialists and radicals. As Jacques Léonard pointed out, nuns in the provinces were often competing fiercely with the local physician and constituted the most organised form of 'quackery'.[37] Even moderates or ex-Bonapartists like the Protestant Tardieu were critical of the religious orders' intentions and suspected a hegemonic agenda on health care.[38] In line with these anxieties and following secularist policies, Treillard sacked all hospital nuns with the immediate result that hospitals lost a great proportion of their medically trained staff. Three days after the 'nationalisation' of Red Cross ambulances on 15 April, members of religious orders were asked to stop their work.[39] The replacement staff provided by the Commune was distinguished more by its republican enthusiasm than by its ability to dress wounds.[40] Ultra-republican women and socialist women of the Union des Femmes pour la Défense de Paris et les Soins aux Blessés, led by, among others, Elizabeth Dmitrieff or Louise Michel, had already identified health care as an area women

---

34 S. Borsa and C. R. Michel, *La Vie quotidienne des hôpitaux en France au dix-neuvième siècle* (Hachette, 1985), p. 183.

35 Comte Gazon de la Peyrière, *L'Église de France devant l'invasion prussienne* (Régis Ruffet, 1872), p. 33.

36 Abbé E. Domenech, *Histoire de la campagne de 1870–1871* (Lyons, Salut Public, 1871), p. 72.

37 J. Léonard, 'Religieuses et médecins au XIXème siècle', *Annales ESC*, 29 (1977) 887–907; also E. B. Ackerman, *Health Care in the Parisian Countryside, 1800–1914* (New Brunswick, N.J., Rutgers University Press, 1990), pp. 41–3.

38 A. Tardieu, *Huitième ambulance de la Société de Secours aux blessés, campagne de Sedan et de Paris* (Delahaye, 1872), pp. 18, 21–2, 33.

39 d'Arsac, *Les Frères des écoles chrétiennes*, pp. 260–1.

40 *Rapport du comte de Beaufort*, p. 10. Beaufort stressed that the nurses were recommended rather than imposed on the society.

could invest and use for political purposes.[41] These radical movements only perpetuated the action of the Association des soeurs de France, a secular nursing movement, reserved to women over the age of twenty-five, meant to staff siege ambulances.[42] During the Commune secular nurses and assistants became as many political agents in the hospital, looking for malingerers and spying on conservative medical staff,[43] who sometimes rejected them successfully.[44]

Wounded soldiers and even some members of the Commune petitioned against any hasty decision in vain. Nuns and monks, brothers and priests eventually had to dress up as 'civilians' in order to resume their ministry[45] and eventually escape in April.[46] More importantly the Commune attacked the fundamental tenets of hospital provision in Paris. Historians of French medicine are often keen on stressing the secularist or even anticlerical tendencies of French science and medicine in the nineteenth century. What materialistic physicians may have thought remained locked in the secret of their hearts and most made passing references to God, even if only to the 'great architect'.[47] For the administration of the Assistance Publique, religion was at the origin of its mission and most hospitals had had a prior religious purpose. The various orders and deaconess orders had specific health care or social missions: the deaconess order of widows, Dames du Calvaire, cared for cancer patients,[48] the brothers of Saint-Jean-de-Dieu catered for the insane, Abbé Roussel and his followers educated poor orphans (even, after the war, Communard ones), the Saint Paul order dealt with the Blind, the Petites-Soeurs des Pauvres catered for senile paupers, and so forth. The exhaustive list of religious orders dealing with specific aspects of welfare would be much longer. This sample illustrates the intricate bond between public and private, secular and religious charity in Paris in 1870.[49] The administration under the Second Empire had undoubtedly been

---

41 P. Durand, *Louise Michel : la passion* (Messidor, 1987), p. 16; J. Rougerie, *Procès des Communards* (Archive Juillard, 1976), p. 112. This type of mobilisation worked alongside more directly military organisations such as the Légion des fédérées; M. P. Johnson, 'Citizenship and gender: the Légion des fédérés in the Paris Commune of 1871', *French History*, 8:3 (1994) 276–95; E. Schulkind, 'Socialist women in the 1871 Paris Commune', *Past and Present*, 106 (1985), 124–63; L. Michel, *La Commune histoire et souvenirs* (2 vols, Maspéro, 1970), vol. 2, pp. 7–15; G. Gullickson, *Unruly Women of Paris: Images of the Commune* (Ithaca, Cornell University Press, 1996); C. G. Moses, *French Feminism in the Nineteenth Century* (Albany, State University of New York, 1984), pp. 190–4.
42 F. Sarcey, *Le Siège de Paris, impressions et souvenirs* (Lachaud, 1871), p. 284.
43 AAP, 542 Foss 80, Rapport de l'ambulance des Magasins-Réunis, 21/07/1871, p. 5. This hospital occupying the empty department store of the Magasins-Réunis was centrally located and under the close control of Cluseret's Comité Central.
44 A. Motet, *L'Ambulance militaire de Reuilly* (Delahaye, 1872), p. 24.
45 *Bulletin de la Société française de secours*, 10 (1871) 433.
46 *L'Union médicale* (8/06/1871) 349.
47 P. Guillaume, *Médecins, église et foi depuis deux siècles* (Aubier, 1989), pp. 49–52.
48 P. Pinell, *Naissance d'un fléau* (Métaillé, 1992), pp. 37–42. The Calvaire was not really a religious order but was an association of Catholic widows.
49 du Camp, *La Charité privée à Paris*, pp. 24–41, 81, 156, 164, 213, 251.

religious and the ultramontane Empress Eugénie had been the active patron of many new institutions which confused religious and secular activities.

The second most urgent reform initiated by Treillard and his friends of the army, Rastoul and then Courtillier, was to enrol all medical men in the Garde Nationale to staff war ambulances and battalions.[50] From 17 April, a list of 'volunteers' appeared in the *Journal officiel* enlisting doctors and students as medical officers and surgeons. Some 130 doctors were thus appointed as *chirurgiens majors*, with 168 citizens, medical students for the most part, as *aides-majors*. In order to find the number of recruits needed, considering the large number of defections, the Commune eventually authorised on 27 April any student with five registrations and successful examinations to practice with the full title of doctor and be regularised later.[51] *Officiers de santé*, second-rate medical practitioners, were also authorised to join in. The lists published by the Commune included a very high percentage of students, foreign and French, and rather fewer established medical men. In effect they had very little influence over the later development of the Communard medical services.

Many medical officers appointed to such and such a service never enrolled, or the battalion they were supposed to join only existed on paper or in the minds of the mostly powerless Communard military leaders Cluseret,[52] Rossel[53] or Delescluze.[54] Many established doctors were either reluctantly dragged into the Commune or resigned at the earliest opportunity, thinking that 'if there is a stupid way to risk one's life, it is to risk it for such people'.[55] Students with eight registrations also became *chirurgiens majors* as a matter of course in the first weeks of May;[56] some joined in and formed the basis of the skeletal Communard sanitary services.

The faculty of medicine had refused to renew the teaching, and the students' meetings organised by Paul Reclus (the brother of Élie and Élysée Reclus) on

---

50 On the largely ineffective reorganisation of the army medical services under the Commune see SHAT, Ly 123, 11/04/1871, batallion ambulances; 14 and 17/04/1871, creation of an autonomous medical service (compagnie d'ambulance); 19/04/1871 reform of the latter; 30/04/1871 another reform.
51 *Les 31 séances officielles de la Commune de Paris*, 27/04/1871, pp. 98–100.
52 Gustave Paul Cluseret (1823–1900) was an adventurer who served in the French, US and Garibaldian armies before becoming briefly the Commune *délégué à la guerre* (3–30 April 1871). See *Mémoires du Général Cluseret* (3 vols, Jules Lévy, 1888), vol. 3.
53 Louis Nathaniel Rossel (1844–71), was perhaps one of the few real military talents of the Commune. The Communard rejection of military authoritarianism and militarist discipline made traditional military organisation virtually impossible. See *Mémoires et correspondance de Louis Rossel* (P. V. Stock, 1908); É. Thomas, *Rossel 1844–1871* (Gallimard, 1967); *Louis Nathaniel Rossel, papiers postumes recueillis et annotés par Jules Amigues* (Lachaud, 1871).
54 Charles Delescluze (1809–71), Jacobin republican and the most respected member of the Commune, served as the *délégué à la guerre* for the last eighteen days of the Commune and died on the barricades. M. Dessol, *Un Révolutionnaire jacobin : Charles Delescluze (1809–1871)* (Marcel Rivière et Cie, 1952).
55 D. J. Joulin, *Les Caravanes d'un chirurgien d'ambulances* (E. Dentu, 1871), p. 86.
56 *JORC*, 9 and 17/05/1871.

17 April 1871[57] proved to be lukewarm to Communard ideals.[58] A student meeting which invited Paul Broca to discuss medical reforms with the Commune followed the academician's leadership and abstained from any further involvement.[59]

Because of a lack of enthusiastic or even credible partners, the reform of the faculty and Academy was buried. Furthermore the Commune leadership felt the need to thank the handful of academicians who did not desert the flagship institution of the French mandarinal structure: 'whatever their political opinions, they show their patriotism in continuing their work'.[60] At a lower level the Commune was not in a position to rationalise the ambulance network which had already been systematically reshuffled after the end of the Franco-Prussian war, as seen in Chapter 4. The official reorganisation of 13 April 1871, which on paper created ambulance squads (*compagnie d'ambulance*) composed of 20 doctors, 60 students, 10 carts and 120 stretcherbearers, did not materialise on the ground.[61] Private ambulances remained. Only a handful of symbolic Communard ambulances were created. Some of the most symbolic demonstrations of the Commune like the Tuilerie concerts where the celebrated singer La Bordas sang 'la Canaille ... et bien! j'en suis' [the scum ... I am one of them]', were given ostensibly for the benefit of ambulances.[62]

Throughout the second siege of Paris, the Commune had to rely on the same politics of care outlined in the preceding chapter to maintain some of its support. Treillard took over the reform of Bureaux de Bienfaisance, noting that they provide 'no satisfaction to our feelings of civic solidarity. They were in the past, yesterday even, the instrument of a struggle against social ideas under clerical influence.'[63] His reform followed the debates on state intervention and his proposal would have resulted in a tighter and denser network of Committees of Public Assistance based on notions of citizenship rather than charity.

Another unfulfilled project of 1 May reformed the Assistance Publique along the great lines of Jules Ferry's democratic plans.[64] The premature fall of the Commune meant that these reforms never matured or became effective. In other

---

57 The Commune had previously made a solemn call to *internat* students. *JORC*, 16/04/1871.
58 L. Fiaux, *Histoire de la guerre civile de 1871* (Charpentier, 1879), p. 290. On the intellectual environment of the Reclus family see J. Harvey, 'Medicine and politics: Dr Mary Putman Jacobi and the Paris Commune', *Dialectical Anthropology*, 15 (1990) 107–17. I am indebted to Mark Jenner for this reference.
59 *Le Courier médical* (26/05/1871); Martin Johnson in *The Paradise of Association: Political Culture and Popular Organisation in the Paris Commune of 1871* (Ann Arbor, University of Michigan Press, 1996), pp. 145–8, confused the grand plans and the discourse of a minute group with what they achieved.
60 *JORC*, 2/05/1871.
61 *JORC*, 13/04/1871. AAP 542, Foss 119, 6/05/1871. Rossel's organisation did not work either.
62 L. Baron, *Sous le drapeau rouge* (Nouvelle Librairie Parisienne Albert Savine, 1889), pp. 118–19.
63 AAP, 542 Foss 7, *Rapport du Citoyen Treillard ... à la commission des finances et à la Commune de Paris*.
64 AAP, 542 Foss 8, *Proposition de Loi (01 mai 1871), sur l'organisation des commissions administratives des hospices et hôpitaux civils*.

respects the Commune was a weak master. The medical staff were given if anything more freedom in the management of their institutions, and beyond the duty of accepting Communard soldiers, they did not change much. The paradox of the Commune was that it never went as far as really contesting the power given by high levels of expertise. The ideals of the French Revolution which stressed merit as the source of a fair social hierarchy meant that it was difficult for Commune leaders, often themselves self-educated or under-educated, to contest the Parisian medical establishment or its prestige.

Far from acting on the commendations of pre-war reformers, the Commune attempted to reopen the medical schools and teaching hospitals, leaving the political structure untouched and under the vague threat of a medical reorganisation report.[65] Communards did not emulate the great upheaval of revolutionary medicine in the 1790s which validated all medical practice and any form of medical training. The major reforms ventured by the Commune's education committee, led by the likes of Jules Vallès, a handful of primary school teachers and two doctors (Goupil and Robinet), dealt mostly with technical education, secular primary schooling and free education.[66]

Before 1870 the education market was marked by the fierce competition between secular and clerical schools.[67] Jules Andrieu who sat on that committee later explained that he attributed the initial military defeat against German states to French deficiencies in terms of education.[68] Communard policy-making reflected their analysis of the causes of the defeat and a life-long involvement in fighting dictatorship and followed some of the policies of the radical *arrondissement* mayors of the siege of Paris.[69] Secular educational policies had been in place in the XI *arrondissement* of Paris since 3 October 1870 (even though this measure probably led to the replacement of the mayor Mottu ten days later and to his re-election on 6 November).[70] After 1880, one finds many of these interpretations and even some of the policies on the agenda of the moderate left governments.

The sum of these tentative reforms made for a patchy and provocative package which combined the mobilisation of medical services and the integration of ambulances to the army in contravention of the Red Cross voluntarist ideals. Secularist reforms and intrusive interventionism also contrasted with the deferential *laissez-faire* of earlier regimes in medical matters. Considering how

65 *JORC*, 18/04/1871.
66 M. Dommanget, *L'Instruction publique sous la Commune* (EITE, 1929).
67 J. Gaillard, *Paris la ville, 1852–1870* (Lille, H. Champion, 1976), p. 281; Y. Déloye, *École et citoyenneté* (Presses de la Fondation Nationale des Sciences Politiques, 1994), pp. 18–20; R. D. Anderson, *Education in France, 1848–1870* (Oxford, Clarendon Press, 1975).
68 J. Andrieu, *Notes pouvant servir à l'histoire de la Commune* (Payot, 1971), p. 31.
69 On the political role of the mayors of Paris see D. E. Griffin, 'Adolphe Thiers, the mayors and the coming of the Paris Commune of 1871' (unpublished thesis, Santa Barbara University, 1971).
70 J. de Marthold, *Mémorandum du siège de Paris 1870–1871* (Charoray Frères, 1884), p. 89.

unattractive the Commune reforms were to most doctors, it is not too surprising that many either passively resisted or openly defied the Commune.

Doctors against the Commune

Major opposition to the Commune took the form of evasion of duty as advised by Versailles. The notes transmitted at the end of March explicitly stated to 'stay at one's post as long as it was possible to make it function without the agents of the Commune. To leave it immediately if they were to intervene in any way.'[71] Wurtz, the dean of the faculty, left his position on 1 April, obeying the Versailles orders and showing the example to follow.[72] A great number of practitioners abandoned their patients and their hospital services in the wake of the insurrection. The Commune had to take remedial action and announced triumphantly: 'the Versailles Government has disorganised all the administrative services. It did not anticipate our will to mend and save everything.'[73]

Assuming an insurrectional legitimacy as the true expression of the Republic, the Commune took on the burden and duties of previous administrations with a vengeance. It claimed that '1,500 active republicans do the work of 10,000 people, a real crowd of parasites'.[74] Treillard attempted to re-establish Assistance Publique hierarchy and to match, as far as possible, like with like.[75] On 11 May a number of conservative medical men like Verneuil, Broca or Worms made a solemn appeal to their colleagues, mailing each and every one:

> My dear colleague,
> the hospital situation and medical staffing crisis worsens every day because so many practitioners are missing (around ⅓). Those of us whose duty it is to stay in Paris are doing everything in our power to face this situation and avoid some regrettable interference. In spite of their good will, in spite of their willingness to replace missing colleagues, they cannot fulfil their duties completely. A decree of 10 May creates a commission of three doctors, alien to our medical services, who have all powers to change and replace staff.[76] We are convinced that we, doctors, can by being here, by our regular work, the evidence of our beneficial work prevent most effectively dangerous innovations. We, the commission, representing our colleagues in Paris, pray you to return in the shortest possible time to renew your service and take your share to our common duties.
> Signed C. Laillier, Hospital of Saint Louis, signed by Broca, Guerin, Verneuil, Gosselin, Duply, Maissenet, Trélat, Jules Worms, Bernutz, Leven, Briquet ...[77]

71 AAP, 542 Foss 68.
72 *Le Courier médical*, (15/04/1871).
73 *JORC*, 3/04/1871.
74 *JORC*, 3/04/1871.
75 AAP, 542 Foss 64, letter to Clérin and Desgrands, 25/04/1871.
76 Treillard's commission was composed of Drs Régnard, Gallaud and Levraud. Régnard had been an intern. *JORC*, 10/05/1871.
77 Fiaux, *Histoire de la guerre civile*, p. 579.

This call for a medical united front against any Communard interference was remarkably disingenuous about its clear objectives. The mandarins intended to offer the appearance of efficiency to prevent any reform from without. As far as Parisian mandarins were concerned, the Commune replaced previous regimes in their most negative aspects by attempting to intervene directly. The greatest threat came from the successively ineffective 'medical services' on which Pyat, Vermorel or Tridon were supposed to sit.[78] Like many other high-handed reforming bodies, these failed to inspire any practical change or to obtain any support. Part of this failure comes from the fact that, in spite of its ostentation, the Commune could and would not provide the status, honours or pensions which used to oil the fragile mechanisms of the Assistance Publique. Because it did not find a radical alternative establishment or alternative pools of expertise, the Commune backed down when the medical establishment threatened to resign *en masse*.[79]

Calls to doctors to be humane and forget their political opposition to the regime to help the wounded were renewed so often that they proved *a contrario* that they were in vain.[80] The resistance to the Commune went beyond corporatism when the cash funds at the disposal of the Assistance Publique were smuggled at night or when malingerers were hidden from Communard conscription. These two instances illustrate active forms of resistance to the Commune.

The major problem of the Commune was to group a sufficient number of trained soldiers for the defence of Paris. Malingering seems to have been encouraged by doctors and hospital managers on a large scale.[81] The *Journal officiel de la république* (edition of the Commune) repeatedly denounced this treacherous behaviour in vain.[82] When Communard soldiers walked into ambulances they were shouted out by the medical experts, who exhibited an unsurpassed zeal for their patients. In fact, many patients occupied beds unduly and were not returned to their now revolutionary fighting units. Some 120 malingerers were thus hidden in the Magasins-Réunis, under the nose of a Communard garrison, while in the Necker hospital the administrative staff did its best to isolate the wounded soldiers from revolutionary ideas and censored all Communard newspapers.[83] When the Commune was to reclaim the unused weapons kept in hospitals, doctors and administrators sabotaged or dispersed the weapons. A medium-size ambulance like the Assistance Publique Magasins-Réunis held over 100 chassepots and 600

78 *JORC*, 19/04/1871.
79 *L'Abeille médicale* (8/05/1871).
80 *JORC*, 29/04/1871.
81 *L'Union médicale* (8/06/1871).
82 *JORC*, 9/04/1871.
83 AAP, 542 Foss 80, Rapport de l'Hôpital provisoire des Magasins-Réunis, 21/07/1871, p. 19; Rapport de l'hôpital Necker, 14/07/1871, p. 15.

rounds of ammunition. The medical staff destroyed the ammunition and tried to hide the weapons.[84] On 4 and 5 April, as well many other times during the second siege, the Commune attempted in vain to obtain accurate records of the number of soldiers occupying hospital beds.[85] This type of constant dissimulation and systematic concealment illustrates best how medical practitioners felt tied to the 'legitimate' government and acted as a secret army within the Commune.

In some sense this medical behaviour was not new and hospitals had been used to hide the troops in times of insurrection as in 1848. In his 1880 parliamentary speech, Hippolyte Larrey recalled an incident when the medical staff had used their scientific status to protect a squad of regular soldiers against the insurrection.[86]

The administration of the Assistance Publique, following government orders and medical leadership, also demonstrated vigorously its loyalty to the Versailles government. Broca, who had fostered the French school of physical anthropology and craniology, organised the most active resistance to the Commune.[87] Four days after the insurrection, Broca decided to hide the bulk of the Assistance Publique's cash reserves. A functionary then went to Versailles to obtain the authorisation to take the money there. While Rigault's men became suspicious of their action, they still managed to hire a cart and load it with bread and food for the Hospice des Ménages. When the cart arrived at the gates, the functionaries played on the good feelings of the guards ('this food is for the poor invalids') and, taking advantage of the relative calm between the two governments, went through and escaped to Versailles.[88] As a belated measure of retaliation the Hospice des Ménages was turned into a Communard fortress.[89]

In other cases the petty officials took a less clear line, stole the money and ran away with the remaining cash.[90] Directors who chose to remain were sworn-in by Treillard while being threatened and spied on from Versailles. Many chose to

---

84 AAP, 542 Foss, 80, Hôpital provisoire des Magasins-Réunis, 21/07/1871, p. 1.
85 AAP, 542 Foss 112, Letters from Dr Herzfeld and Bancette.
86 Baron H. Larrey, *Discours prononcé par Monsieur le baron Larrey le 14 juin 1880 au sujet du projet de loi sur l'administration de l'armée* (Librairie des Publications Législatives, 1880), pp. 62–3.
87 One cannot attribute a theory to a set of circumstances, but Paul Broca's stance on the Commune was unusually muscular and signalled a departure from his optimistic views on degenerescence of 1867. 'Sur la prétendue dégénérescence de la population française', *Revue des cours scientifiques de la France et à l'étranger*, 4 (1867) 305–9; Y. Conry, *L'Introduction du darwinisme en France au XIXième siècle* (J. Vrin, 1974), pp. 326–34; W. H. Schneider, *Quality and Quantity: The Quest for Biological Regeneration in Twentieth-Century France* (Cambridge University Press, 1989), pp. 15–17; F. Schiller, *Paul Broca explorateur du cerveau* (Berkeley, University of California Press, 1979), pp. 186–216, 315–17. This intellectual biography is remarkably poor on Broca's life in 1870–71.
88 AAP, 542 Foss 34, Report on the transfer of Assistance Publique funds to Versailles 30/03/1871. Written by Guillon who, with Vertujol, took most of the risks, 29/06/1871.
89 AAP, 5425 Foss 80, 4/05/1871.
90 AAP, 542 Foss 80, Affaire Leduc, 2/06/1871.

escape before an imminent arrest at the end of April 1871, only to find that their ambiguous behaviour had already been denounced in Versailles by the doctors working in their hospitals.[91]

Cases of whole-hearted co-operation were rare and mostly refer to the natural tendency of lower-ranking administrators to obey the power in place. Some noted that the edicts emanating from Treillard 'seemed to be from the traditional authorities, it is the powerful embrace of administration. . . . The machine continues to work by itself.'[92] Hospital staff who had not left managed large institutional structures, often crowded by the return of patients from the provinces since the end of the war. Treillard was not heavy-handed beyond replacing a number of hospital administrators on political grounds. His edict of 14 April 1871 showed a certain realism as to the extent of the co-operation he anticipated from the hospital staff: 'the political spirit must be banished from the hospital to leave more room for devotion and solidarity. I mean by this that any employee who will voice views within a hospital against the current political order triumphant in Paris, will be immediately replaced.'[93]

He then tried to manage the hospital service with an integrity unusual for the period. Along with Jourde, the too respectful negotiator of loans with the Banque de France,[94] Treillard was often mentioned in Communard history texts as a model of probity. Invested with the administrative spirit and sense of duty which emanated from the Assistance Publique, Treillard repeatedly attempted to stop food requisitions effected at the expense of the administration by Communard *arrondissement* municipalities.[95] Among the few remaining archives of the Commune, his books of accounts were scrupulously kept, and each entry was justified until 23 May 1871.[96] When the army arrested him on 25 May and executed him in the Polytechnique school, rue de la Montagne Sainte-Geneviève, his widow returned the funds, a very substantial 53,012 francs and 86 centimes, and the books in her possession to the colonel in charge of the local municipality.[97] No other instance of incongruous and heroic probity could perhaps sum up best the limitations of the Commune revolution than the idea of a widow bringing back the account books and spare cash to the man who murdered her husband, and the

---

91 AAP, 542 Foss 80, Report of 2/05/1871, by Dr Dubisay on the Maison municipale de Santé.
92 L. Gallet, *Guerre et Commune 1870–1871, impressions d'un hospitalier* (Calmann Lévy, 1898), p. 187.
93 AAP, 542 Foss 80, Rapport sur l'hôpital de la Charité, July? 1871, also including a letter from Treillard, 12/04/1871.
94 F. Jourde, *Souvenirs d'un membre de la Commune* (Brussels, H. Kistemaeckers, 1877).
95 AAP, 542 Foss 85. The Commune actually respected the financial integrity of the Assistance Publique far more than the previous government.
96 AAP, 542 Foss 23, Register of Commune incomes.
97 Fiaux, *Histoire de la guerre civile de 1871*, p. 548. The Treillard incident is actually often quoted in accounts of the Commune to prove its integrity.

murderer thanking her and respecting her gesture more than the man he had killed. The bourgeois sanctity of the state and public funds was never challenged by the Commune.

When they realised that the administration would not embrace their political ideals, Communards had to choose between practical considerations and dogmatic positions. The two polarities were similarly attractive and explain the tension between *laissez-faire* and direct management which largely contributed to more proactive forms of resistance. Military hospital staff were also torn between what they considered to be their duty towards their patients and the contradictory orders from the Commune and the army.[98] The Red Cross organisation was in the same dilemma and could only extricate itself by eventually taking sides with Versailles. The initiative came from the Commune, which rightly identified the Red Cross organisations, working in close contact with the army since 31 December 1870, as potential traitors. On 15 April 1871 Cluseret accused the Red Cross of collusion with the enemy and seized its material. The Count de Flavigny, both an aristocrat and a known Bonapartist, was then put in a difficult situation and only escaped through the intervention of Delescluze.[99] Count de Beaufort, Chenu, Demarquay and many other Assistance Publique and volunteers leaders remained in Paris to protect the patients and the belongings of the society.[100] Chenu himself was briefly imprisoned in early April[101] and many were put in a difficult position when the French Red Cross voted a specific budget to help the Versailles army's medical services.[102] In spite of Paul Rastoul's efforts as the director of ambulances,[103] their autonomy was maintained throughout the conflict but eventually ended up being more contested by advancing Versailles troops than by Communards.[104] The Freemason ambulance of Rue Cadet of the Grand Orient obedience was thus taken between the crossfire of the army and the Commune.[105] Freemasons had generally supported the Commune and had even demonstrated in its favour and conversely many leaders of the Commune were Masons. To follow Tombs's arguments on 'prudent revolutionaries', it is striking that even the most politically and philosophically close medical practitioners, like the Freemasons, chose to sit on the fence and declined to embrace openly Communard policies or

---

98 ASSAT, box 63/2, Note au médecin en chef du Val-de-Grâce, 26/04/1871.
99 E. Delessert, *Épisodes pendant la Commune* (Charles Noblat, private circulation,1872), p. 60.
100 *Compte rendu... du conseil d'administration siégeant à Versailles*, p. 4.
101 *Bulletin de la Société française de secours*, 10 (1871) 431.
102 Delessert, *Épisodes pendant la Commune*, p. 64.
103 On Rastoul's work and that of his replacement Courtillier see SHAT, Ly 123.
104 Paul Rastoul (1835–75), was a *montagnard* extreme republican and had managed simultaneously his political and ambulance activities in the X *arrondissement*. He became director of the inspectorate on 24 April 1871 and immediately attempted to discipline ambulances in vain. *JORC*, 24/04/1871; B. Noël, *Dictionnaire de la Commune* (Fernand Hozon, 1971), vol. 2, p. 198.
105 *Bulletin du Grand Orient de France*, 26 (07–08/1870) 380, 392.

reforms. The Mason ambulance had remained independent and secularist (if still theist) in its own rights.[106] When the Versailles troops arrived, Louis Ormières, a young Mason under the patronage of Dr de Saint-Jean, protected his patients by calling on the mayor and Masonic sympathies.[107] For most doctors the narrative of the war against the Commune became a liberation narrative and the fall of the Commune was witnessed with barely concealed relief.[108]

The agony of the Commune

Not all independent ambulances could rely on Masonic links. To the great surprise of their medical staff, voluntary ambulances were treated with some suspicion by the advancing armies.[109] The term *'internationale'*, which was an integral part of the Société de Secours' (Red Cross) name, now lent itself to dangerous confusions with the socialist *internationale* generally held responsible for the insurrection.[110] In some instances a massacre was only narrowly avoided. The same logic which had justified the desertion of hospitals and ambulances at the beginning of the Commune now turned against those who had made more ethically grounded choices or who had served Versailles from within the Commune. Government troops expected complete solidarity from the doctors they met but they initially treated all Parisians with great suspicion.

The killing of a military surgeon, Dr Pasquier, in the early days of the war against the Commune had been used to maximum propaganda effect by Versailles and some of the early massacres were in direct reprisal. Among Communards' prisoners, doctors were apparently more highly prized and Robert Tombs reports of an order from MacMahon specifically excluding army medical officers from the sweeping summary executions of May.[111]

Whatever MacMahon had ordered, in one case at least Versailles troops talked of killing doctors 'like your people who have murdered our emissary Dr Pasquier at Courbevoie'.[112] During the assault a Communard nurse of the Vanves fort was executed on 18 May.[113] During the Bloody Week one prominent Communard and doctor, Dr Tony Moilin, ex-member of the Ambulance

---

106 A. Combes, 'Les Elus francs-maçons de la Commune de Paris', *Chronique d'histoire Maçonnique*, 27–28 (1981) 25–33.
107 F. Court, *Louis Ormières (1851–1914), et l'ambulance du Grand Orient de France en 1870–1871* (Imprimerie Nouvelle, 1914), pp. 5–9.
108 *Compte rendu ... du conseil d'administration siégeant à Versailles; Bulletin de la SSBATM*, 10 (1871) 435.
109 AAP, 542 Foss 80, Rapport de l'hôpital provisoire des Magasins-Réunis, 21/07/1871, p. 19.
110 J. Furley, *Épreuves et luttes d'un volontaire neutre* (Jean Dumaine, 1874), p. 2.
111 R. Tombs, *The War Against Paris, 1871* (Cambridge University Press, 1981), pp. 184–5.
112 Delessert, *Épisodes pendant la Commune*, p. 7.
113 *JORC*, 19/05/1871.

Commission of the Central Committee of the VI *arrondissement*, was arrested on 29 May while he attempted to make his way home. Moilin was put against a wall and shot in the great execution centre of the Luxembourg gardens.[114] The pro-Commune literature is particularly insistent on ambulance massacres, which put the Versailles army's action on the same level as the Prussians' in terms of 'atrocities'. There is a lot of evidence to corroborate these stories. While there was undoubtedly a general cover up after the events, the massacre of Communards in their sick-beds seems to have taken place in some institutions, probably with the consent or the passive acceptance of the medical staff. Pierre Dominique, an early Marxist historian of the Commune, quotes a series of incidents in the last week of the insurrection. The people, staff and patients in the ambulance of rue d'Allemagne, the Seminary of Saint Sulpice, were all executed, between sixty and eighty people in all.[115]

Pierre Dominique believed in high casualty figures of around 40,000 dead, which, in the curious debates always found in cases of civil war, would make the Versailles regime more guilty than if they had simply executed a quarter of that number![116] As Robert Tombs pointed out, it is now virtually impossible to count retrospectively the victims of May 1871.[117] Estimates for the population of Paris during the siege varied between 1,600,000 and 2,200,000. The variations between a low estimate of 10,000 and a high one of 30,000 or even 40,000 killed is impossible and perhaps insignificant to verify in detail; historians will never agree on what Lissagary called 'the balance-sheet of bourgeois vengeance'.[118]

While the exact number of victims in the Saint Sulpice massacre remains difficult to ascertain, Dr Faneau, who was not a Communard or socialist, did get executed. In the courtyard of the hospital Saint-Antoine, Communards were taken from their beds and shot.[119] Dr Dolbeau, accused by Lissagaray of giving away the Communards of his wards to the firing squads at the hospital Beaujon, became the focus of student demonstrations in 1872.[120] The director of the Ménages hospice was also almost shot for being still at a managerial post under the Commune.[121] More isolated murders are more difficult to identify. We are left with many war memoirs in which medical men witnessed that only their energetic reaction had

---

114 Fiaux, *Histoire de la guerre civile de 1871*, p. 561.
115 *Le Soir* (12/06/1871). This massacre was justified on the ground that a shot was fired from the ambulance.
116 P. Dominique, *La Commune* (Grasset, 1930), pp. 280–94.
117 Tombs, *The War Against Paris*, pp. 190–1. This debate is perhaps one of the least interesting relating to the Commune: 38,000 prisoners were taken, 11,000 tried, 5,000 deported to New Caledonia.
118 P. O. Lissagaray, *The Paris Commune* (New Park Publications, 1976), p. 352.
119 R. Durand-Fardel, *L'Internat en médecine et en chirurgie des hôpitaux et hospices civils de Paris* (Steinheil, 1904), p. 130.
120 P. Darmon, *La Vie quotidienne du médecin parisien en 1900* (Hachette, 1988), p. 49.
121 Gallet, *Guerre et Commune*, p. 245.

saved their patients from the bayonet of governmental troops which prove, *a contrario*, that the practice may have been more generalised than can be ascertained. Doctors often report their powerlessness as the army made arrests randomly in the streets and then systematically with the Parisian police's help and detailed knowledge of neighbourhoods and individuals.[122] Other instances of direct violence on helpless patients, sabotaging their wound dressing or even unnecessarily wounding the patient to exercise a form of punishment on them, are reported in Communards' accounts: 'At the ambulance of Vincennes the surgeon stabbed me in the wound with his lancet'.[123] Anecdotes such as this one may well be a simple transfer of their sufferings as the expression of the surgeon's vindictiveness. The penultimate issue of the *Journal officiel*, on 23 May, poignantly contained one such story of moral torture: 'a wounded woman asked Dr Maisonneuve: 'Will I have much more time? – No, but our gallant soldiers will still have enough to exterminate your husband's battalion before you go.''[124]

On the other hand, the chaos of the Bloody Week of May allowed a number of prominent Communards to escape dressed up as ambulance staff. Medical complicity at Saint-Antoine, where some atrocities took place still, enabled Jules Vallès to escape death.[125] While several unfortunate bearded gentlemen were shot because they looked like him, Vallès, freshly shaven, combed and wearing blue-tinted glasses, went into hiding.[126] Civilian administrators of the Assistance Publique like Möring attempted to stop the massacres by trying to impose a general policy allowing investigations and even the guarding of prisoners in hospitals, but forbidding medical men or administrators to surrender patients to the firing squads.[127] In the last days of the Commune, the mythology of a medical resistance to the communists grew on an unprecedented scale. One of the most notable and symbolic anecdotes, narrated at length in the press, was the story of *internes* from the nearby Hôtel-Dieu saving Notre-Dame Cathedral from the incendiaries.[128] The story claimed that a handful of *internes* stopped the iconoclastic whims of an officer, 'the blond type and German looking', who attempted to start a fire from the floor of the Cathedral.[129] The portrayal of the Communard officer as a proto-Prussian fitted with the assimilation of the Commune with the

---

122 A. Flamarion, *Le Livret du docteur, souvenirs de campagne contre l'Allemagne et contre la Commune de Paris* (Le Chevalier, 1872), p. 160.
123 This is the testimony of the rather unreliable Maxime Lisbonne (1839–1905), quoted in E. Monteil, *Souvenirs de la Commune, 1871* (Charavay Frères, 1883), p. 188.
124 *JORC*, 23/05/1871.
125 Durand-Fardel, *L'Internat en médecine*, p. 131; J. Vallès, *L'Insurgé* (Messidor, reprinted 1990), pp. 332–7.
126 Fiaux, *Histoire de la guerre civile de 1871*, p. 573.
127 Gallet, *Guerre et Commune*, p. 257.
128 *L'Abeille médicale* (29/05/1871).
129 *L'Union médicale* (1/06/1871) 344–5.

Prussian invaders. The story was good to a point but there were many problems in the details. The bonfire of a few seats and pieces of cloth built by the altar would have had some difficulty in reaching the ceiling and the roof. The evidence available soon reduced the incident to the more modest status of a mere innocuous desecrative bonfire or barbecue. It nevertheless survived in the medical history of the glorious episodes of the 'liberation of Paris' and together with two administrators killed by stray Communard bullets, a few cases of wrongful arrests, and a wounded nun, it represented the high point of the Assistance Publique's physical resistance to the Commune.[130] Foreign observers like John Furley of the British Red Cross described the Notre-Dame fire as a simple encampment where the altar served as a kitchen table.[131]

In another revealing incident Dr Mohé was later credited with saving the Admiralty's centre by evacuating his patients very slowly and stopping the incendiaries' presumed activities.[132] An ambulance was also credited with saving the Luxembourg Palace.[133] Dr Joulin also used the Red Cross flag to protect private property from incendiaries.[134]

Commentators all spoke approvingly of this political use of hospitalised patients. More importantly, the medical press and principally the editors of the conservative press scrutinised long lists of the medical men whose names had been published in the Commune's official lists from 17 April until 19 May, much to the embarrassment of those who had been named officers of such and such a battalion. Some, like Dr Souchard, a major of the Commune, inserted a message in *L'Union médicale* to certify that they had resigned from the Communard functions as soon as appointed 'and wished to make it known'.[135] The medical press soon obliterated the memory of any such collaboration and denounced the few doctors who had been involved in political structures of the Commune as 'a few instances of failings and aberrations among our ranks, luckily a very small number indeed and for the most part debased people [*déclassé*]. Their expiation has been cruel enough. Let us throw a veil on what is already the past.'[136] Amédée Latour, the conservative editor *L'Union médicale*, added: 'one cannot find these names in the directories of the profession ... it was not the best part of our profession. ... Too many doctors without patients become, alas, necessarily the auxiliaries of riots and insurrections.'[137]

130 AAP, 542 Foss 9, June 1871. L. Nass, *Le Siège et la Commune, essais de pathologie historique* (Plon, 1914), pp. 316–21.
131 Furley, *Épreuves et luttes*, p. 495.
132 Fiaux, *Histoire de la guerre civile*, p. 512.
133 *Le Soir* (12/06/1871).
134 Joulin, *Les Caravanes d'un chirurgien*, p. 94.
135 *L'Union médicale* (12/06/1871) 360.
136 *La Lancette française* (4/06/1871).
137 *L'Union médicale* (27/06/1871) 424.

The restored order felt sufficiently self-confident to avoid vindictive purges after the May massacres. Only a handful of hospital administrators were sacked for their alleged sympathy with the revolutionaries.[138] The less prominent figures took a low profile and saw with apprehension the Assistance Publique come back from Versailles:

> An agent of the Assistance Publique came from Versailles. As a refugee there since the month of April he does not seem to be fully aware of what happened and of our state of mind. He does not blame us for having stayed at our office over these two months, but he is not far from it. . . . we are suspect [*nous sentons le roussi*] and we are somewhat linked to the Commune.[139]

French medicine belonged socially and ideologically with Versailles. Even though some of the Communard initiatives seemed to follow radical aspirations, they stopped short of a real upheaval and lacked the legitimacy and durability which could have gathered some support among doctors. The private civil servants of the state had behaved impeccably against the revolutionaries. This did not mean that the Commune reforms had died with the Communards. Free 'safety-net' medical care, secularised hospitals and state interventionism were to return ten to twelve years later during the republicanisation of the Third Republic, and be promoted in Paris by the republican government 'in waiting' of the Conseil Municipal of Paris.[140]

Conclusion

The Commune's shyness to address directly the more mundane issues of welfare, health and employment was largely the result of the war. Over the seventy-six days of the Parisian revolution it hardly had enough time to implement durable reforms, and Chapter 9 will show how some of the most direct measures were self-contradictory. Beyond the difficult circumstances, the Communards' constant wrapping in historical precedent and their blurred reading of 1793 did not allow them to address the most vital questions. The co-operative and mutuality aspirations of the Commune could not in themselves replace the paternalistic politics of care developed during the first siege.[141] The socialist aspirations often summed up as *la sociale* were not really about social or socialist reforms but increasingly about modes of government and modes of political representation.[142] The Commune itself lacked the electoral legitimacy of the Versailles government; it

---

138 AAP, 542 Foss 68. The Assistance Publique was fairly lenient.
139 Gallet, *Guerre et Commune*, p. 212.
140 Le Mansois Duprey, *L'Oeuvre sociale de la municipalité*, pp. 103–9; A. Mitchell, *The Divided Path: The German Influence on Social Reform in France after 1870* (Chapel Hill, University of North Carolina Press, 1991), p. 130; L. Andrieux, *A travers la République* (Payot, 1926) p. 169.
141 Johnson, *Paradise of Association*, pp. 140–3; J. Rougerie, *Paris Libre, 1871* (le Seuil, 1971), pp. 183–4.
142 A. Rifkin and R. Thomas (eds), *Voices of the People* (Routledge and Kegan Paul, 1988).

lacked the background of expertise the French had come to expect from their rulers. Only two members of the Commune were doctors, for instance; many more had been obscure political militants before the events. Within the time given and considering the resources it gave itself, the Commune failed to deliver more than symbolic measures about pawning goods, providing health care or reforming and secularising education. The fact that the whole state apparatus betrayed them, and that even non-governmental institutions chose to take sides against the Commune, was largely a result of this original inadequacy.

The *corps médical*, the informal 'brotherhood' of medical men, was deeply divided along professional, religious and political lines, but the Commune failed to attract the sizeable portion of the profession which might have benefited from educational and statutory reforms. The mixture of direct interventionism and decentralisation was unappealing to men whose training and ethos emphasised, in spite of nepotistic and corporatist practices, individualism, independence and a meritocratic hierarchy. Nevertheless all the points touched on by the Commune were to prove to be thorns in the side of the medical world of the early Third Republic. As Jack Ellis and Jacques Léonard have shown, medical expertise became increasingly represented in post-war French parliamentary politics.[143] The idea of secularising hospitals was completed first in Paris but only after a long up-hill struggle.[144] From Laennec hospital, made secular in 1878,[145] to the Charité in 1888,[146] the municipal authorities revived the secularist project of the Commune and increasingly claimed its revolutionary legacy.[147] Another key revolutionary project of the Commune was to create a professional nursing career path for republican nuns.[148] This particular enterprise was fostered by Charcot and his anticlerical disciple Bourneville.[149] The famous and formidable

---

143 J. Léonard, *La Médecine entre les savoirs et les pouvoirs* (Aubier Montaigne, 1981), pp. 280–3; J. D. Ellis, *The Physician-Legislators of France: Medicine and Politics in the Early Third Republic, 1870–1914* (Cambridge University Press, 1990); Léonard, 'La Médicalisation de l'État : l'exemple des premières décennies de la IIIe république', *Annales de Bretagne*, 86:2 (1978) 313–20.

144 Léonard, *La Médecine*, p. 288.

145 P. Feuillet, *De l'Assistance Publique à Paris* (Berger Levrault, 1888), pp. 38–9.

146 Le Mansois-Duprey, *L'Oeuvre sociale de la municipalité*, p. 105; E. M. Acomb, *The French Laic Laws 1879–1889* (New York, Columbia University Press, 1941); A. Mitchell, 'Crucible of French anti-clericalism: the Conseil Municipal of Paris, 1871–1885' *Francia*, 8(1980), 395–405.

147 A. des Cilleuls, *Historie de l'administration parisienne sous la Troisième République* (Picard Fils et Cie, 1910), p. 178. AN, F/ICI/170, The Conseil Municipal on building a monument to honour executed Communards, 23/12/1883 – 14/08/1895; Johnson, *Paradise of Association*, pp. 212–13.

148 Le Mansois Duprey, *L'Oeuvre sociale de la municipalité*, p. 106. Three nursing schools were created in Paris, at the Salpêtrière 1878, Bicêtre 1878 and Pitié 1881.

149 V. Leroux-Hugon, *Des saintes laïques, les infirmières à l'aube de la Troisième République* (Sciences en Situation, 1992); J. Goldstein, 'The hysteria diagnosis and the politics of anti-clericalism in late nineteenth-century France', *Journal of Modern History*, 54:2 (1982) 209–39; K. Schultheiss, 'Gender and the limits of anticlericalism: the secularisation of hospital nursing in France, 1880–1914', *French History*, 12:3 (1998) 229–45.

matron Marguerite Bottard, serving for forty-eight years, allegedly without a day's break, became, perhaps against her will, an icon of republican virtues to oppose nun-nurses.[150] This opposition illustrates the way in which anticlerical institutions mimicked religious ones and aimed at beating religion on its own moral and social ground.[151]

Similarly many of the educational ideas developed during the Commune were taken on board by the Ferry administration.[152] The crisis of French education became a recurrent problem for all governments from 1871.[153] The reform of medicine following Pasteur's pamphlet and many reports on German medicine proved to be a protracted and difficult issue. The relationship between the state and the *corps médical* (medical establishment, the medical press) evolved from a relationship of trust and dependency fostered by *laissez-faire* policies, and grew more strained. Increasingly more interventionist policies curbed and undermined the rights and ideological status of medical men in French society to make them ever less faithful servants of the state. After a short-lived honeymoon with the early Third Republic in the 1880s and early 1890s, which saw the reinforcement of the medical monopoly on matters of health and the end of the *officiat de santé*, state patronage turned into a set of directives.[154] This call to medical expertise at low cost caused the bond that tied the *corps médical* to the body politics eventually to break down into a deeply entrenched and corporatist conflict of vested interests.

The law on free municipal medical assistance which came late in 1898 provoked a furious uproar from medical practitioners. They criticised the low profile and low cost approach of the state which intended to pass on to medical practitioners the burden of minimal health standards without giving them a proportional role in the state through a special ministerial office. Had the latter been established it would also have been perceived as state-mingling. They also reacted to the loss of their independent status and to the privileged position that their charitable work, increasingly a compulsory part of their profession, used to

---

150 Darmon, *La Vie quotidienne du médecin parisien*, p. 94; Y. Knibielher *et al.*, *Cornettes et blouses blanches* (Hachette, 1984), pp. 47–60; J. Guillermand, *Histoire des infirmières* (France Sélection, 1988).

151 This made the co-operation between Catholic charity and the state difficult at least until 1914. N. Rovitch, *The Catholic Church and the French Nation, 1589–1989* (Routledge, 1990); H. Rollet, *L'Action sociale des catholiques en France 1871–1914* (Desclée de Brouwer, 1958); T. B. Smith, 'Republicans, Catholics and social reform: Lyon, 1870–1920', *French History*, 12:3 (1998) 246–75.

152 K. Auspitz, *The Radical Bourgeoisie: The 'Ligue de l'Enseignement' and the origins of the Third Republic, 1866–1885* (Cambridge University Press, 1982).

153 The German model of higher education was scrutinised with a lot of attention as the French first figured their crisis to be predominently a crisis of elites; E. P. Dreyfus-Brisac, *L'Université de Bonn et l'enseignement en Allemagne* (Hachette, 1879); L. Fiaux, *L'Enseignement de la médecine en Allemagne* (Baillière, 1877).

154 Léonard, 'La Médicalisation de l'état', pp. 313–20.

provide them with: 'we want to be the masters of our own charitable work and we want to receive in exchange the consideration to which we are entitled'.[155]

The restoration of moral order which followed the crushing of the Paris Commune was never as thorough as religious leaders hoped for and believed in.[156] Calls to miracles baffling medical science and grand civic and religious gestures of redemption like the building of the Sacré Coeur of Montmartre only expressed the aspirations of an artificially prominent religious portion of the population.[157] The elections of the 1870s slowly eroded the monarchist majority in Parliament, which was unable to find a suitable monarch. In medical circles, the old elite of the Empire retained its grasp on the Academy and the medical nepotistic system unabated. Only slowly, and perhaps more because of a natural generation process, did the new 'princes of science' replace the old guard of the art. The 'moral order' restoration had very little to restore in medicine that would not re-establish itself from within, as if their institutional weight was in itself enough to prevent factors of change.

An ironic conclusion for this chapter could be in one of the minor immediate effects of the war, rich, however, in symbolic value, like the bombing of the Salpêtrière hospital. After the relentless bombing of January 1870, female hysterics had to be moved out of the derelict ward they shared with epileptics to find suitable accommodation in the services of Dr Charcot.[158] Charcot then successfully resisted attempts to return them to the psychiatric wards and, over fifteen years, developed his theories from his abundant practice.[159] Coincidentally Charcot led the struggle for the secularisation of hospitals, and became a symbol of a truly 'national' and republican medicine. His work on madness included such militant gems as a reading of mystical occurrences as unrecognised hysterical

---

155 L. Salomon, *Le Pauvre et son médecin devant la loi sur l'assistance médicale gratuite* (Chamuel, 1898), pp. 35, 40, 108; M. L. Hildreth, *Doctors, Bureaucrats and Public Health in France 1888–1902* (New York, Garland, 1987), pp. 36–106
156 *Le Mouvement médical*, 9 (13/08/1870).
157 J. Gadille, *La Pensée et l'action politiques des évêques français au début de la Troisième République* (2 vols, Hachette, 1967), vol. 1, pp. 228–36.
158 *Les Médecins des aliénés de Bicêtre et de la Salpêtrière à Monsieur le Préfet de la Seine* (Martinet, 1875), p. 7. The alienists wanted to see hysterics reintegrated to the epileptic ward and the rebuilding of the buildings lost in 1870. This petition was entirely aimed at Charcot's appropriation of an entire nosological category of insanity. Also see M. S. Micale, 'Hysteria male/hysteria female: reflections on comparative gender construction in nineteenth-century France and Britain', in M. Benjamin (ed.), *Science and Sensibility: Gender and Scientific Enquiry, 1780–1945* (Oxford, Basil Blackwell, 1991).
159 M. S. Micale 'The Salpêtrière in the age of Charcot', *Journal of Contemporary History*, 20 (1985) 703–31; G. Didi-Huberman, *Invention de l'hystérie* (Macula, 1982), p. 20. Charcot's career depended closely on Gambetta's and he owed his chair in 'clinic of nervous diseases' to Gambetta's patronage. G. Guillain, *J.M. Charcot, sa vie, son oeuvre* (Masson et Cie, 1955), pp. 17–18; M. Bonduelle, T. Gelfand and C. G. Goetz, *Charcot: Constructing Neurology* (New York, Oxford University Press, 1995), pp. 98–9.

fits.¹⁶⁰ While the French flocked to Lourdes and saw in prayers the redemption of defeat, Charcot exhibited the photographs of his pet hysterical patient, Rosalie Leroux, in Bernadette Soubirou-like poses, mocking thus the mystic visions of Lourdes.¹⁶¹ The symbolic revenge of the Commune could seem almost complete had it not been that 'mass hysteria' itself became a highly fashionable analytical tool to describe revolutionary events and particularly the great fires of May 1871. While it cannot be said that the secularisation of French medicine would not eventually have taken place without the war and Commune, it seems almost certain that the civil war sharpened ideological divisions and brought to the fore the religious question over many more vital issues.¹⁶² The religious question maintained the illusion of movement over the permanence of institutional structures.¹⁶³

160 C. G. Goetz, 'Visual art in the neurological career of Jean Martin Charcot', *Archives of Neurology*, 48 (1991) 421–5; J. Lalouette, 'Charcot au coeur des problèmes religieux de son temps. A propos de *la foi qui guérit*', *Revue Neurologique*, 150 (1994) 511–16.
161 Bonduelle, Gelfand and Goetz, *Charcot*, pp. 171–7.
162 P. A. Bertocci, *Jules Simon: Republican Anticlericalism and Cultural Politics in France, 1848–1886* (Columbia, University of Missouri Press, 1978), pp. 175–80; J. M. G. Roberts, *The Paris Commune from the Right* (Longman, 1973), pp. 9–11.
163 On the reinforcing role this antinomic pairing state/church had for the republican state see Jones, *The French State in Question*, p. 10; R. Rémond, *L'Anticléricalisme en France* (Brussels, Complexe, 1985); M. Ozouf, *L'École, l'église et la République* (Cana/Jean Offredo, 1982).

7 The dynamics of humanitarianism and the making of the Red Cross

The 1995 British Red Cross anniversary emphasised the respectability acquired with age rather than its origins and the war of 1870.[1] One of the reasons for this silence may be the uneven and controversial results of the involvement of the then new humanitarian movement in the Franco-Prussian war. The literature devoted to the history of humanitarianism is usually more sceptical on early achievements than the hagiographic literary production originating from Geneva. Even in the hagiographic literature, 1870 generally comes across as a difficult time, the teething problems of Dunant's noble invention.[2] A recent critic, John Hutchinson, makes the same point, partly because his revisionist account of the Red Cross movement encompasses the same progress narrative and chronology, and also because he relies so heavily on the work of Léon LeFort who fell out with the French Red Cross early in 1870.[3]

The 1870 war saw the first application of a Utopian project for which national organisations worked within established 'trans-national solidarity' which endured even after the crisis ended.[4] Taking over the older forms of relief which were expended occasionally after a flood or some other major natural disaster, the new agencies structured a common ideology reminiscent of ancient Christendom. This relief work built on nearly two hundred years of religious work like that carried out by religious groups such as the Quakers in Ireland.[5] To consider war on a par with natural disasters was not a universally acceptable idea. Quaker humanitarian agencies thus did not join in the Red Cross enterprise and instead developed a specific pacifist opposition to the movement[6] and attempted to build a peaceful post-war French society. While this is in itself a fascinating story, it has already been told and it never

---

1 See 1995 Red Cross campaign. Dr Cabanès, *Chirurgiens et blessés à travers l'histoire* (Albin Michel, n.d., 1925?); V. Swain, 'Franco-Prussian war 1870–1871', *British Medical Journal*, 3 (1970) 511–14.
2 P. Boissier, *Histoire du comité international de la Croix Rouge, de Solférino à Tsoushima* (Geneva, Institut Henry Dunant, 1978), pp. 351–65; V. Segesvary, *La Guerre Franco-Allemande de 1870–1871* (Geneva, L'Age de l'Homme, 1971).
3 J. F. Hutchinson, *Champions of Charity: War and the Rise of the Red Cross* (Oxford, Westview Press, 1996), pp. 105–49.
4 M. Huger and J. Picket, *Le Comité international de la Croix Rouge* (Geneva, A. Paten, 1985), pp. 9–14.
5 H. E. Hatton, *The Largest Amount of Good: Quaker Relief in Ireland, 1654–1921* (Kingston and Montreal, McGill-Queen's University Press, 1993), pp. 3–44.
6 H.A.U., *On the New Laws of War and the Succour to the Wounded* (n.p., 1865).

constituted more than a drop in the ocean of the war effort.[7] Though the 1870 war was only a step in the centuries-old Quaker action, it had far more importance in the subsequent developments of the Red Cross and led to a long-term militarisation of civilian relief agencies analysed by John Hutchinson, and arguably to the complex war machine described in Daniel Pick's work.[8] It certainly shaped many recognisable features in the contemporary Red Cross movement in France and abroad.

Some of these features have been the targets of constant criticism since the 1960s and the Red Cross has not been through the past 129 years unscathed. The founders of new forms of medical interventionism like the post-1968 'French doctors' of Médecins sans Frontières and Médecins du Monde have been unkind to the Red Cross ideal. They denounced its failures in the 1980s disasters and condemned the methods as a 'humanitarian trap', the organisations and practices as 'strategies of complacency' and its transnational co-operation as an 'impossible ideal'.[9]

The most important criticism of the Red Cross in the twentieth century concerns its lack of independence towards nation-states, their military and bureaucracy. The second generally dwells on the Red Cross's social structure and bureaucracy modelled on established class systems. The third tackles its alleged coyness about pacifism and questions its slack definitions of humanitarianism.[10] Keeping these three polemical points in mind, the first part of this chapter will narrate the genesis of contemporary humanitarianism; the second part will expose the history of various forms of established Red Cross organisations in France and the social tensions dividing them; the third part will be more widely concerned with the extent and national dimension of the Red Cross civilian medical war effort; and the concluding section will then tackle the major conflicts between the army and medical services, and look at the ideological cement of the voluntary movement in wartime and post-war France. Through humanitarian mobilisation, the boundary between the military and the civilian sphere – in effect, between the social orders of war and of peace – became more blurred and porous than ever before; at the same time it also became more central to thinking about the nature of civilisation.

---

7 W. K. Sessions, *They Chose the Star: An Account of the Work in France of the Society of Friends War Victims Relief Fund from 1870 to 1875* (York, Ebor Press, 1991), pp. 1–75. The London Committee also distributed food to the municipal administration of Paris. AdVP: VD6/1591/2. Relief work included sending a steam plough to Nancy, seeds and cattle. Sewing classes and various other duties continued the Quaker work until 1875 when it stopped after an expenditure of around £100,000 or 4 million francs. X. Long, *Rapport au sujet de la répartition des secours faite par la Société anglaise des Amis (Quakers)* (n.p., 1872). In comparison the German Red Cross alone gathered over 70 million francs. French accounts are more difficult to assess considering the diversity of organisations. G. Moynier, *La Croix Rouge, son passé, son avenir* (Sandoz et Thuillier, 1882), p. 107.

8 D. Pick, *War Machine: The Rationalisation of Slaughter in the Modern Age* (New Haven, Yale University Press, 1993), pp. 88–109.

9 A. Destexhe, *L'Humanitaire impossible ou deux siècles d'ambiguïté* (Armand Colin, 1993); J-C. Rufin, *Le Piège* (Pluriel, Lattès, 1986), pp. 33–5.

10 I. Vichniac, *Croix Rouge : Les stratèges de la bonne conscience* (Alain Moreau, 1988).

Humanitarianism

The *Oxford English Dictionary* indicates that in the nineteenth century the word humanitarianism had mostly a negative connotation akin to 'bleeding-heart liberal'. One finds this usage of the term in the most violent critics of the French Red Cross.[11] To avoid confusion I intend to use 'humanitarianism' in its modern meaning of 'humanitarian help', as the expression of a modernist sensibility bringing the respect for basic 'rights' in warfare, as discussed in the work of Geoffrey Best or Tom Laqueur.[12]

The Red Cross reformulated these enlightenment views and became the embodiment of 'humanitarianism' and medical ethics at war. It also followed closely the Geneva Convention which guaranteed the 'neutrality' of medical staff on the concerned.[13] The concept of neutrality in war was not really new in 1870.[14] Yet, even though there were significant historical precedents, neutrality as a contractual obligation between two enemies was first extended to civilians during the Franco-Prussian war. This simple axiom of the new laws of war still led to real and disingenuous confusion. Early in the war the Prussian government stated that the war was a war on the French imperial government and not on the French people.[15] This statement ignored French political realities and specifically French revolutionary traditions revived after 4 September 1870 like the *levée en masse* and war *à outrance*. The status of the wounded and sick of a given army – neutral but not yet civilian – was another confused notion.[16] The whole concept of neutrality originated from a strict understanding of the unwritten right of the people

---

11 '3: One who advocates or practises humanity or humane action, one who devotes himself to the welfare of mankind at large, a philanthropist. Nearly always *contemptuous*, connoting one who goes to excess in his humane principles', *Oxford English Dictionary*.

12 T. Laqueur, 'Bodies, details, and the humanitarian narrative', in L. Hunt (ed.), *The New Cultural History* (Berkeley, University of California Press, 1989), pp. 176–204; G. Best, *Humanity in Warfare: The Modern History of the International Law of Armed Conflict* (Methuen, 1983), pp. 31–74.

13 W. MacCormac, *Souvenirs d'un chirurgien d'ambulance* (J. B. Baillière et Fils, 1872); *Notes and Recollections of an Ambulance Surgeon* (J. A. Churchill, 1871), p. 89; Anon., *Un Mois dans les lignes prussiennes du 15 août au 19 septembre* (E. Dentu, 1871).

14 A. Forbes, *My Experiences of the War between France and Germany* (2 vols, Hurst and Blackett, 1871). Naval warfare had been regulated very since the declaration of Paris in 1856. F. Piggott, *The Declaration of Paris* (University of London Press, 1919).

15 *Circulaire du délégué du ministre des affaires étrangères aux agents diplomatiques de France*, 29/11/1870, in *Recueil officiel des actes du Gouvernement* (Librairie Administrative de Paul Dupont, 1871), pp. 575–8.

16 Soldiers were 'neutral', could be kept in ambulances and cared for, but remained prisoners. The Geneva Convention had not clarified this point. During the Italian wars of the 1850s the French had exchanged wounded prisoners with the Austrians and the 1870 practice seemed a regression in this respect. L. LeFort, *Oeuvres*, ed. Félix Lejars (2 vols, Félix Alcan, 1895–96), vol. 2, p. 20; L. C. A. de Beaufort, *Étude sur la Société française de secours aux blessés des armées de terre et de mer et sur la convention de Genève* (Imprimerie Administrative de Paul Dupont, 1870), pp 37–48.

(*droit des gens*), including the right to property and life for the non-combatant civilians.[17]

Any rigid division of society in two separate spheres civilian/military was impossible to sustain over a long period. Civilian society meshed in with the military. Uniforms superficially covered a civilian identity; conversely armed civilians seemed out of place. Women, for instance, like the professional nurses of the English model or French nuns, *bourgeoises* or actresses, enjoyed simultaneously a renewed emphasis on the sanctity of women and mothers, and an important role in military ambulances.[18] The military tradition of the Second Empire itself was also based on nation-making wars, particularly in Italy.[19] The concept of neutrality was therefore at odds with political and military traditions, yet it reflected a traditional manner of considering war as an extension of diplomacy combined with the new humanitarianism.[20] Although Prussian high-commanding officers had territorial aims in mind from the beginning of the war, the way war was meant to be led excluded civilians. The French government's call for every male French citizen to arm demonstrated that the French did not fully comprehend the global implications of Genevan neutrality.[21]

Prussian and other German troops always refused military status to guerrillas and armed civilians.[22] Occupying armies considered them as the equals of spies, and executed hostages and partisans' families.[23] When Prussian, Bavarian

17 For an early example see C. de Martens, *Causes célèbres du droit des gens* (2 vols, Leipzig, F. A. Brockhaus, and Paris, Ponthieu and Cie, 1827). I am indebted to Andrew Jones for this reference. Individual rights were not discussed in an international convention until the Hague congresses of 1899 and 1907. D. A. Wells, *War Crimes and Laws of War* (University Press of America, 1984), pp. 44–5; and J. B. Scott, *The Hague Conventions and Declarations of 1899 and 1907* (Oxford University Press, 1915); C. Richet, *Les Guerres et la paix, étude sur l'arbitrage international* (Schleicher, 1899). For a clear definition of the *droit des gens* see François Guizot, *L'Église et la société chrétiennes en 1861* (Michel Lévy Frères, 1861), pp. 109–12, which clearly states that: '*Hors du droit des gens, il n'y a que l'état révolutionnaire qui est la barbarie jetée au travers de la civilisation*', p. 112.
18 A. Summers, *Angels and Citizens: British Women as Military Nurses* (Routledge and Kegan Paul, 1988), pp. 125–33.
19 J. Jaurès, *La Guerre franco-allemande de 1870–1871* (Flammarion, [1908] 1971), especially Chapter 2.
20 R. Cooter has noted the linguistic militarisation of medicine since 1870, and it could be noted that the reverse is also true. See R. Cooter, 'War and modern medicine', in W. F. Bynum and R. Porter, *Companion Encyclopedia of the History of Medicine* (2 vols, Routledge, 1994), vol. 2, pp. 1536–73, p. 1563.
21 German occupants constantly denied a military statute to *francs-tireurs* even when they had been authorised by the French state. AdVP, VD6/1529 and in AN F9/1348. I. P. Troinin, 'Questions of guerrilla warfare in the law of war', *American Journal of International Law*, 11 (1946) 534–62.
22 G. Best 'Restraints on war by land before 1945', in M. Howard (ed.), *Restraints on War: Studies in the Limitation of Armed Conflict* (Oxford University Press, 1979), pp. 17–39, p. 33.
23 M. Howard, *The Franco-Prussian War: The German Invasion of France, 1870–1871* (New York, Dorset Press, 1990), pp. 251–2.

or Saxon troops (whom the French only gradually considered as one German collective entity) shot down villagers after short-lived resistance, on the sole grounds of them having broken the rules (or so-called laws) of war, they were applying a strictly defined understanding of legitimate enemies. This view contrasted modern warfare to the Prussian *Nationalverein*, when German volunteers resisted French occupation in 1813. During this episode the French occupants had been pitiless and had hanged a number of them. Forgetful of this, French historians of the generations following 1870 echoed the French press of 1870, and argued that such violence after the Geneva Convention demonstrated the hypocrisy of the Prussian government.[24]

The Geneva Convention encoded the neutrality of ambulance staff on the battlefield, but they could not be more protected by its provisions than civilians were by unwritten ones. Many of the early incidents of the war were due to the French using buildings near the front-line as ambulances, in which their medical staff ignored the Genevan rules and did not wear suitably stamped Red Cross armbands.[25] When the front-line receded, the ambulance became a stronghold that an advancing enemy needed to destroy.[26] This pattern occurred several times during the war and the whole staff of the ambulance either died in the action or was executed soon afterwards.[27]

These executions were the logical consequence of the Geneva Convention: by letting soldiers use their ambulance as a stronghold they had breached the terms of the convention. The press mediated and created this indignation and readers only grasped war aims through an identification with the horrors of war. In a way, the horrors of war, unilaterally attributed to the opposite side, justified retrospectively the war itself.[28] The breaking of the rules induced indignant reports of massacres. 'The other' was the barbarian, the rule breaker. The concept, expressed

24 *The Times*, 15/09/1870, reported the first massacre of civilian population by the Bavarians. E. A. Gavoy, *Études de faits de guerre : Le service de santé militaire en 1870, hier, aujourd'hui, demain* (Paris and Limoges, Henri Charles Lavauzelle, 1894), p. 21. Simultaneously the Germans published reports of the attack on a German ambulance in Bazeilles. Dr Weill, manuscript report, ASSAT, box 64/30, 'à Stuttgart', p. 9. A meeting in Brussels in 1874 attempted to solve the vexed question of the status of irregular warfare. P. Karsten, *Law, Soldiers and Combat* (Westport, Greenwood Press, 1978), pp. 22–3.
25 Dr Weill, 'Rapport', ASSAT, box 64/30.
26 A. Flamarion, *Le Livret du docteur, souvenirs de campagne contre l'Allemagne et contre la Commune de Paris* (Le Chevalier, 1872), p. 25; F. Bron, *Histoire d'une ambulance sur le champ de bataille* (Lyons, Vingtrinier, 1872), pp. 10–11.
27 F. Christot, *Le Massacre de l'ambulance de Saône-et-Loire, 21 Janvier 1871* (Lyons, Vingtrinier, 1871); for the German side, C. Lüder, *La Convention de Genève au point de vue historique, critique et dogmatique* (Erlangen, E. Besold, 1876), pp. 231–3.
28 S. Audoin-Rouzeau, 'Guerre et brutalité, 1870–1918, le cas français', *European Review of History*, 0 (1993) 95–108. On this mirroring of national identities see M. Jeismann, *Das Vaterland der Feinde, Studiem zum Nationalem Feindbagriff und Selbstrerständnis in Deutschland und Frankreich, 1792–1918* (Stuttgart, Klett-Cotta, 1992), pp. 161–298.

in French by *neutralité*, has a broader meaning than the English 'neutrality'. While killing was legitimate during a war, only some targets were fair game.

The Genevan Red Cross later conducted investigations into these executions.[29] Pictorial representations of such massacres were particularly damaging for the German image abroad. The images used to illustrate a Catholic history of the war are representative of the French production of 'German atrocities' propaganda.[30] It is because they are clichés that they are interesting. Figure 9 is a reworking of Goya's *The Third of May 1808: Execution on Principe Pio Hill* (1814), akin to Manet's *The Execution of the Emperor Maximilian* painted in 1868.[31] The executed stand in the light, the firing squad is in the dark corner of the picture. Light falls on the victims; the criminals stand in darkness. Scenes of looting in the background confirm a return to barbaric behaviour. Behind one of the victims, a gun sticks out, explaining clearly the excuse for this execution.

Figure 10 is more complex and fractured; the meaningful elements present themselves in a dislocated order, related to each other but yet not necessarily correlated. The picture is on its own a summary of several scenes of atrocities which took place in Wissembourg. The Red Cross flag on a broken pole is at the centre of the picture, on the right a woman protects a wounded soldier with her body. This is a typical neo-classical pose taken from an image of the imploring mother in King Herodius's 'massacre of the innocents'. This woman is also protecting a *Turco* (a north African native soldier) and could also stand as a metaphor for France. On the floor the imploring wounded seem already more dead than alive. The Bavarians appear barbaric, one staggering with a bottle of wine in the one hand and a sword in the other. The whole picture revolves around the Red Cross flag and is loaded with an emotional appeal that a normal battle scene would not have. The term 'atrocities' attached to the killings struck an emotional chord. Defeated but victimised, the losers pulled over their wounds the humanitarian blanket marked with the Red Cross.

There is some truth in these accounts. Red Cross flags near the troops provided useful aims to gunners, for instance, and the siege situation created another impossible dissociation between legitimate targets and civilian ones.[32] In

---

29 German governments reacted violently through Bismarck's telegram (9 January 1871), and later in an extended denunciation of the numerous French breaches of the Convention. *Les Violations de la Convention de Genève*. The need for an appropriate jurisdiction, acting at government level, was felt and exposed as early as 1872; see G. Moynier, *Notes sur la création d'une institution judiciaire internationale* (Geneva, Comité International, 1872).
30 A. Wachter, *La Guerre de 1870–1871, histoire politique et militaire* (E. Lachaud, 1873).
31 The work of Goya was often mentioned in accounts of the war. H. E. Beaunis, *Impression de campagne, 1870–1871 siège de Strasbourg, campagne de la Loire, campagne de l'Est* (Félix Alcan and Berger Lerrault et Cie, 1887), p. 4.
32 M.-R. Brice and Capitaine Bottet, *Le Corps de santé militaire en France, son évolution, ses campagnes, 1708–1882* (Paris and Limoges, Berger Lerrault, 1907), p. 375.

Figure 9 A. Darjou, *The Looting and Massacre of Bazeilles by the Bavarians*, 1873

Figure 10 A. Darjou, *Wissembourg – Massacre of the Wounded in Farms Converted in Ambulances*, 1873

Strasburg, in Metz and later in Paris, Krupp shells could not distinguish between children and soldiers. Even if the French had started the war by shelling Saarbrücken, the Prussians refined the night-time shelling of besieged cities to an art which had great psychological impact.[33]

The Prussian Crown Prince himself feared that the January shelling of Paris would undermine the German cause and would provoke a negative reaction in Europe.[34] His fears were political and humanitarian. He well perceived the emotional impact of shelling civilians, but his attitude denoted a form of civilian sensitiveness which was echoed and amplified through the media of Europe. Shelling civilians did not kill in large numbers, especially compared with the slaughter of the open battlefield, yet it killed the archetypal innocents, women and children.[35] Children and women were the victims needed to construct the image of the enemy as melodramatic villain.[36] Gunners embodied a force of evil victimising, from a distance, innocent beings. This genre provided the French with a suitable sort of clear-cut opposition between forces of evil and of good.[37] The French then consistently used this schematic layout to reverse their historical position from aggressor to victim.

The shelling of major Paris buildings included the south bank hospitals, most of which were within range like the Salpêtrière or the Val-de-Grâce. The Salpêtrière practitioners sent a useless petition to the German headquarters protesting against the barbarity of attacking hospitals. Meanwhile Larrey used German prisoners as human shields.[38] Brutality was answered with cynicism. Premeditated and unpremeditated physical violence was not the only bone of contention between the French and the Prussians after the war. Both sides accused the other of using forbidden weapons. Both countries had signed the 1868 St Petersburg Convention prohibiting explosive bullets.[39] This convention paradoxically ignored much more

---

33 The Prussian press had first used the shelling of Saarbrücken to stir public indignation against the invading French army. The arguments were simply reversed when, in turn, the Germans invaded France. See Wachter, *La Guerre de 1870–1871*, p. 160; Brice and Bottet, *Le Corps de santé militaire en France*, p. 404.
34 A. R. Allinson (ed.), *The War Diary of the Emperor Frederick III, 1870–1871* (Westport, Greenwood Press, 1971), pp. 244–58. 'I thought of the innocent people who have to suffer for this curse of war; but above all I cannot get over the thought of the children who may possibly be hit.'
35 Assimilation of civilian victims to soldiers, decree of 11/01/871, *Recueil officiel des actes du Gouvernement*, pp. 12–13.
36 J. L. Smith, *Melodrama* (Methuen, 1973); J. Przybos, *L'Entreprise mélodramatique* (J. Corti, 1987).
37 E. Carlton, *Massacres: An Historical Perspective* (Scolar Press, 1994), pp. 4–10.
38 C. Laurent, 'Histoire de deux prisonniers allemands à Paris', *Annales politiques et littéraires* (1911) 304–6, 338–9, 358–9, 378, 404–6.
39 G. Moynier, *Le Droit des gens, études sur la Convention de Genève pour l'amélioration du sort des blessés dans les armées en campagne* (Cherbuliez, 1870).

destructive modern weaponry used during the war: the Krupp gun enabled the Prussians to fire more shells than had been thought possible in the past; the French mitrailleuse sent out dozens of murderous 50 g conical lead bullets; the bullets of French rifles, with an effective range of over a mile, often caused incredible wounds, sometimes the exit wound exceeding 'the size of a saucer'.[40] This modern weaponry was deemed regular but the not yet developed exploding bullets presented an alternate source of horror.[41] Several army and Red Cross commissions launched enquiries into their supposed use,[42] but none found any evidence to support the allegations or prove the existence of the fanciful 'poisonous bullets'.[43] The most devastating wounds were more probably due to projectiles at the end of their 'useful' firing range 'bouncing' on bones within the body and tearing the flesh open.

The Germans also accused the French of using a new sort of weapon which increased the barbarisation of warfare: native colonial troops. The German press treated the French 'Turcos', or later 'Negroes', as the incarnation of barbarity at war. The barbarisation of warfare was presented on both sides as a unilateral crime. Each side presented the conflict as the struggle of civilisation against the barbarians.

French commentators focused more than the Germans on cruelty in war and unnecessary violence.[44] Through the description of war incidents based on the violations of the diversely understood rules of war, there was a genuine process of popular appropriation of the motives of the war.[45] Commentators presented the war as a conflict of civilisation, of ideas, of humanist values, and in its unravelling found its legitimacy: 'France will regain the certitude of representing what is Right in a struggle from which the winner, whatever it does, will appear only as the incarnation of strength'.[46] The complex apportioning of

---

40 MacCormac, *Souvenirs d'un chirurgien d'ambulance*, p. 112.
41 ASSAT, box 62/4, Baron Larrey's letter on explosive bullets to the French foreign office.
42 SHAT, Lu 1, *Rapport sur le fonctionnement du Service de santé militaire*, October? 1870, p. 13, which states that unexploded projectiles were extracted from wounds at the battle of St Privat.
43 The official inquiries led after the war were negative and pointed out that no material evidence was brought forward. J. E. Rochard, *Histoire de la chirurgie française au dix-neuvième siècle* (J. B. Baillière et Fils, 1875), p. 860; E. Saint-Edme, *La Science pendant le siège de Paris* (E. Dentu, 1871), p. 34.
44 Criminals, thieves, murderers or rapists were severely punished by armies in a stable position but on the move discipline went after the morale of the troops and crimes could remain unnoticed or unpunished.
45 A similar process emphasizing German atrocities took place in 1914–15. J. Horne and A. Kramer, 'German "Atrocities" and Franco-German opinion, 1914: the evidence of German soldiers' diaries', *Journal of Modern History*, 6611 (1994) 1–33; R. Harris, '"The Child of the barbarian": rape, race and nationalism in France during the First World War', *Past and Present*, 141 (1993) 170–206.
46 Wachter, *La Guerre de 1870–1871*, p. 4.

responsibility boiled down to a banal story of good and evil. Indignation at violations of impossible rules shielded the horrors of war with isolated anecdotes.[47] The general character of the nations in the conflict was evoked, never individual responsibilities. German cruelty was condemned, but no German officer was singled out as a criminal.[48] This finer apportionment of blame did not happen in spite of at least one famous American precedent. Captain Henry Wintz, commandant of Andersonville confederate prisoner camp, had been prosecuted and sentenced to death under article 59 of General Order 100 after the American Civil War.[49] Six years later, neither the French nor the Germans actually thought of qualifying brutal war action as the criminal behaviour of a few. On the other hand, paradoxically, the mass slaughter on the battlefield was neglected in favour of *faits divers*, of little scenes of anonymous human cruelty which readers and spectators could comprehend. The war had not become any more brutal yet brutality had become a focus of representations as the counterpoint of humanitarianism. Humanitarianism structured a new legal vocabulary required to write about war. The Red Cross organisations had played an important role in this new approach to a modern warfare which reached out and had deep implications at all levels of society.

Official movements

The history of the Red Cross is familiar and Henry Dunant's *Souvenir de Solferino* remains a cornerstone of the history of humanitarianism.[50] Nineteenth-century French historians of humanitarianism found eighteenth-century instances of neutrality at war and inscribed the Geneva Convention in the long sequence of

---

47 H. de Condé, *La Prusse au pilori de la Civilisation* (Brussels, Devillé, 1871); Anon., *Comment les Français font la guerre* (Berlin, C. Duncker, 1871); C. A. Daubant, *La Guerre comme la font les Prussiens* (Plon, 1871); A. Marteau, *Le Droit prime la force* (Librairie Internationale, 1876); *Recueil de documents sur les exactions, vols. et cruautés des armées prussiennes en France* (Bordeaux, Férot et Fils, 1871); A. Vavasseur, *La Paix honteuse ou le droit des gens selon les prussiens* (Lacroix, Verboeckhoven et Cie, 1871); Némésis, *Crimes, forfaits, atrocités et viols commis par les prussiens sur le sol de la France* (André Sagnier, 1871); A. de la Guéronnière, *La Prusse devant l'Europe* (Brussels, Office de Publicité, 1870). A popular history of the war written by A. Michiels, *Histoire de la guerre franco-prussienne et de ses origines* (Alphonse Picard, 1871) contained only two illustrations demonstrating the violation of *droit des gens*: the robbery of Alsatian farmers by German peasants and the shooting of a French surgeon bandaging a wounded soldier, pp. 1 and 69.

48 T. Meron, *Human Rights and Humanitarian Norms on Customary Law* (Oxford, Clarendon Press, 1989); Howard (ed.), *Restraints on War*; P. Bohannan, *Law and Warfare: Studies in the Anthropology of Conflict* (Austin, University of Texas Press, 2nd edn, 1980); Wells, *War Crimes and Laws of War*, p. 65.

49 H. J. Schroeder (ed.), *Disciplinary Decrees of the General Councils* (Herder, 1937).

50 H. Dunant, *Convention de Genève : un souvenir de Solférino* (Hachette, 6th edn, 1873).

enlightened progress.[51] Perhaps because of a misreading of the American experience,[52] the American Civil War was often presented as the first instance of a successful 'liberal', free-enterprising administration of help to wounded soldiers. Thomas Evans, Napoleon III's American dentist, exposed the American model to the French public as early as 1865. Evans's book ran to five editions between 1865 and 1867 and contributed to the promotion of medical neutrality at war.[53] He later imported personally some American material for the Exhibition of 1867. He eventually contributed to the creation of an American ambulance in Paris in October 1870.

The Geneva Convention dated from 1864 and had been first applied during the Duchies war against Denmark in 1864 and on a larger scale during the Austro-Prussian war of 1866.[54] These short wars were merely semi-experiments for only the Prussians had signed the Convention and abided by its rules. The Franco-Prussian war thus came as the first full-scale application of the convention. Symbolically linked with the text of the convention, but not strictly part of the convention, was the Société de secours aux blessés des armées de terre et de mer.[55] In 1870, a few months before the war, the Société de secours remained inoperative for the foreseeable future. It was a rather informal club of medical men who had personally experienced war like Chenu,[56] and benevolent aristocrats like

---

51 Early conventions were aristocratic gestures by noblemen in the eighteenth century and had little relevance to modern war. Yet the constant recall of these precedents had a purpose in the post-war conflict against the Red Cross. George Sand claimed Henry Arrault's work published in 1861, *Notice sur le Perfectionnement de matériel des ambulances volantes*, was at the origin of the humanitarian movement. Lüder, *La Convention de Genève*, p. 37; Moynier, *Le Droit des gens*, pp. 38–9; Best, *Humanity in Warfare*, pp. 32–120.

52 E. Leboulaye, 'De la médecine militaire en France et aux États-Unis', *Revue des Deux-Mondes* (15/12/1869).

53 T. W. Evans, *La Commission sanitaire des États Unis* (E. Dentu, [1865] 5th edn 1867); *Essais d'hygiène et de thérapeutique militaire* (E. Dentu, 1867); *History of the American Ambulances in Paris during the Siege of 1870–1871* (Baillière, 1873); M. Charenton, 'Le Dr Thomas W. Evans, dentiste de Napoléon III et les dentistes de son époque' (Thèse de doctorat, dentaire, Université de Paris, 1936).

54 The Austro-Prussian war of 1866 was the first experiment of its kind and gave the opportunity for a first hagiographic campaign directly linked to Florence Nightingale's legend. Mme W. Monod, *La Mission des femmes en temps de Guerre* (Bellaire, 1870); *Les Héroines de la charité, Soeur Marthe de Besançon et Miss Florence Nightingale* (Bellaire, 1873). The same book was published twice under two different titles but the German equivalent of Florence Nightingale was eluded to for the 1873 edition.

55 The Red Cross was not mentioned in the Convention. Although clearly associated, it needed flags and signs stamped by military authorities to be able to gain access to the battlefield. Only a revision of the Convention in 1878 gave an almost complete monopoly to the Red Cross while it became subordinate to the military authority in Prussia. Moynier, *La Croix Rouge*, pp. 46–7.

56 J. C. Chenu had experienced the Crimean war as an army surgeon and was the main statistician of French warfare and casualties: *Aperçu historique, statistique et clinique* (2 vols, Hachette, Dumaine, Masson, 1874).

Viscount de Melun. Under the imperial patronage it had become a tax exempt *association d'utilité publique* on 23 June 1866. Napoleon III insisted on a stand at the Universal Exhibition of 1867 and on an international congress. In the midst of this display of wealth, the congress delegates had theoretical views on the eventuality of war. The early French Société de secours lived without means. It did not have a clear purpose in the absence of national war[57] under the patronage of the dictator who claimed his Empire meant peace. The 1870 war ended this uncertainty.

In July 1870 the Société de secours started canvassing for money with little results in the first month.[58] The public did not appear to understand the need to complement army services with civilian ambulances. It is quite significant that fund-raising only took off after the defeats early in August 1870. It is also significant that in one year foreign gifts amounted to virtually half the total income at the disposal of the French Société. The French Société de secours became an international investment fund in humanitarian causes and a form of surrogate diplomacy for neutral powers. The Red Cross blossomed throughout Europe and could serve a variety of less philanthropic purposes including gathering medical intelligence.[59] The British, Dutch, Irish,[60] Italian, Austrian and Belgian committees sent various ambulances to France to help the wounded and observe the effects of modern warfare. Many of the staff of the British ambulances, for example, were on leave from the British army.[61] Other nations were represented by handfuls of students taking it on themselves to represent their nation on the battlefield.[62] The war thus became a stage for national representation even when, as was the case for

57 The 1870 war became a major challenge across Europe. On the measures taken in Belgium and on training schools established after the war see Z. Z. Merchie, *Guerre de 1870–1871* (Brussels, Manceaux, Muquardt, Delahaye, 1876), pp. iii, 145.
58 N. Elias, *Über den Prozess der Zivilisation, Soziogenetische und psychogenetische Untersuchungen* (2 vols, Basel, Haus zum Falken, 1939); E. de Billy, *Rapport à la commission des finances à l'assemblée générale des fondateurs de la SSBATM* (Imprimerie Nationale, 1873), p. 7.
59 Merchie, *Guerre de 1870–1871*, Chapter 3.
60 The Irish ambulance served complex nationalistic purposes and had a chaotic existence. Many of its orderlies joined the French army and the remaining ambulance was viewed with suspicion by the Germans and taken prisoner. *Report of the Irish Ambulance Committee of Dublin, Irish Ambulance Corps for the Service of the French Wounded* (Dublin, Browne and Nobu, 1871), pp. 5–27. The Irish ambulance is unique in choosing to support only one side in the conflict. J. Fleetwood, 'An Irish field-ambulance in the Franco-Prussian war', *Irish Sword*, 18 (1964) 137–48; M. A. Leeson, *Reminiscences of the Franco-Irish Ambulance* (Dublin, M'Gleshan and Gill, 1873).
61 For instance, Gordon, Captain Douglas Galton, General Vincent Eyre, Major Jones, Captain Brackenbury, Captain Newill, Major Wyatt etc. See: 'Opérations de la Société nationale anglaise pendant la guerre franco-allemande 1870–1871,' in *Rapport des sociétés étrangères sur leurs activités durant la guerre de 1870–1871* (SSBATM, 1873), pp. 56–78; C. A. Gordon, *The Siege of Paris: A Medical and Chirurgical Study* (Baillière, Tindall and Cox, 1872).
62 J. W. S Johnson, 'Relations médicales entre la France et le Danemark', *Bulletin de la Société française d'histoire médicale*, 10 (1911) 434–6; J. Grange, *Mort et obsèque de Monsieur le Docteur Arendrup : médecin danois, mort au service de la France* (*Union médicale*, 1871).

the Irish or the Romanians, these nations had no real autonomous existence yet.[63] Foreign observers subsequently published important analyses and medical observations of the effects of war. The Russians paid special attention to high velocity bullets, the Italians cared about train-hospitals, etc.[64]

From the wider public's point of view, this financial and sentimental investment expressed the capitalist construction of a civilising process in Norbert Elias's meaning of the word. There was a clear shift from an individual aristocratic gesture to an anonymous philanthropic fund. It also reflected the parallel growth of international media and finance. From the start the Red Cross involved highly complex financial tools transferring large funds across Europe and the world into the heart of the conflict.[65]

At a national level, French conservative newspapers like *Le Gaulois* undertook to raise money for similar purposes. The public subscription started at the beginning of the war soon gathered a lot of momentum: 352,141 francs by 21 July, 669,293 by 3 August, 1,000,637 by 21 August after the first heavy defeats and the battle of Gravelotte. Newspapers published patriotic lists of subscribers, street collections became a familiar sight and Parisian shops' coin boxes gathered large public donations.[66] With the proceeds, they created another structure called the Comité de la presse.[67] Although originally meant to be only a fund-raising group, it grew to become a rival organisation to the Société de Secours.[68] The editorial of *Le Gaulois* on 23 August signalled the break between the two organisations:

> Today we address to the Count of Flavigny, president of the international society ... a letter asking to return to us the ambulance funded at our expenses for this above mentioned society. In this letter we thank warmly the Count of Flavigny and we regret to withdraw from his custody an equipment that now needs to be used...[69]

The internal politics of the Société de Secours were the cause of this split. The administration, originally put under the responsibility of Nélaton, a high-class

---

63 A. D. Petrescu, 'La Participation des médecins et pharmaciens roumains à la guerre de 1870 et à la Commune', *Revue médicale et pharmaceutique*, 20 (1970) 229–31.
64 O. Geifelieder, *Voienno Khirourgitscheskiïa Nablïoudeniïa vo Vremia niemiezko-franzousskoi voiny 1870–1871* (St Petersburg, 1873). E. B., *I treno-ospedali della Germania nella guerra di 1870–1871* (Florence, 1872); J. H. Plumridge, *Hospital Ships and Ambulance Trains* (Seeley, Service and Co., 1975), p. 86. Twenty-one trains moved 90,000 casualties in France and Germany in 1870–71.
65 Billy, *Rapport de la commission des finances*, pp. 11–2. Thirty sovereign nations including Japan and Mexico contributed to the Red Cross funds.
66 *Le Gaulois* (24/07/1870 to 21/08/1870). Various newspapers associated themselves with the conservative and populist *Gaulois*.
67 *Le Gaulois* (17/07/1870).
68 *GMP*, 25 (1870) 487.
69 *Le Gaulois* (23/08/1870).

surgeon with a prominent university chair,[70] was placed under aristocratic management backed by Chenu. Major benefactors clearly meant to associate their names to the action undertaken with their money and their connections.[71] This significant seizure of power worked in two directions. Firstly, non-medical men entered the Société de Secours as administrators or delegates,[72] spoiling medical hopes of complete independence in the management of 'their' ambulances. Secondly, funds were more liberally and indiscriminately distributed than originally planned.[73] The removal of Nélaton as head of the Red Cross was the real cause of the conflict, but the Comité de la presse committee accused the Red Cross of being unable to use their money, while a month later the same committee would accuse the same Red Cross of wasting their funds. The most vociferous critic of the Red Cross was Léon LeFort, who, according to Chenu, resented losing the salary and status he had bullied out of the Red Cross in its early days. In his own words, he had lost any faith in an amateurish aristocratic tea party and became its fiercest critic.[74]

Money and 'value for money' took on a vital importance in the debate between the two organisations, structuring the Red Cross as a consumer-based charity.[75] A way of justifying the expenditure was to create a large number of ambulances to cope with the sorry state of the army. This was a conscious move to adapt the Société de secours to the *levée en masse* of universal conscription. The Société de secours tried to match modern armies, creating more ambulances and field hospitals favouring quantity rather than quality. To follow the new war effort and multiply ambulances implied ever-increasing funds drawn from untapped civilian reserves. It also widened the range of experts admitted to join this self-selected elite group. 'Unknown' members of the medical establishment became the head of provincial field-hospitals.

This neglect of scientific and bourgeois hierarchy encouraged medical men of high prestige to join the Presse organisation rather than the Société de

---

70 Auguste Nélaton (1807–73), had operated on Garibaldi in the past but was in 1870 mostly famous as one of Napoléon III's private surgeons.

71 The coup overthrew Nélaton and replaced him with a committee of founding members of the Red Cross composed of Comte de Flavigny and Viscomte de Melun for the aristocratic side and Dr Chenu for the medical side. See A. Tardieu, *Huitième ambulance de la Société de Secours aux blessés, campagne de Sedan et de Paris* (Delahaye, 1872), p. 8; G. Wyrouboff, 'Les Ambulances de la Société Française de Secours aux blessés pendant la guerre de 1870–1871', *Philosophie positive*, 6 (1875) 379–403, p. 386.

72 Tardieu, *Huitième ambulance*, p. 91.

73 E. Domenech, *Histoire de la campagne de 1870–1871* (Lyons, Imprimerie du Salut Public, 1871), p. 58.

74 Chenu, *Aperçu historique, statistique et clinique*, vol. 2, pp. x–xii.

75 Some titles reflect this attitude using the phrase 'balance humanitaire'. J.-B. V. Autier, *Notre balance humanitaire, ou compte rendu de l'emploi de notre temps* (Montdidier, A. Radenez, 1872).

Secours.[76] The Presse provided some high-profile newspaper coverage, some adventure and the public recognition of well-established status.[77] From the first month the issues of social status played a prominent part in internal politics and in shaping a prestigious public image fitting with war-wounded heroes. In reality, the two organisations became unwittingly complementary: one worked on the home front with household names like Ricord, while the official Société de secours could call for foreign moneys through the well-established networks of upper-class sociability.[78] Although coherent, this complementariness was implicit and there was a deep dissension between the two associations.

This original social split at the top of the humanitarian organisations was not the only one. A deeper and more bitter division separated 'first and second class' medical men. There were obvious rivalries about whom might get accepted in the Société de secours ambulances.[79] This rivalry became more obvious when the main ambulances of Paris published a list of 'authorised' surgeons of talent. This exclusive list rejected most medical[80] volunteers from the lower parts of the medical world.[81] This revived furious arguments dating from the Second Empire: 'We are the medical democracy, we want a medical republic and we will not stand that the revolution was won to favour privilege.... No more oligarchy, no more princes of science, no more unfair and humiliating distinctions, let us leave to the clerics the privilege of their divided clergy.'[82]

At a time of high political instability the Société de secours and its twin proved to be socially and politically useful for established medical men who owed

---

76 The staff of the Presse was upper-class and familiar with the *salons*. The main organiser of the committee was Philippe Ricord (1800–89), surgeon of Napoléon III. M. Guignard, 'Philippe Ricord, sa vie son oeuvre 1800–1889' (Thèse en médecine, Paris VII-Lariboisière, 1978); P. Ricord, *Les Ambulances de la presse, annexes du ministère de la guerre pendant le siège et sous la Commune, 1870–1871* (J. B. Baillière, 1873).

77 Dr G. Bitterlin, *La Croix rouge aux avant-postes de la Marne, 1870–1871* (St Maur, Vigot Frères, 1912), pp. 17–18.

78 Foreign appeals were under the high patronage of kings and queens in Italy, Belgium and the Netherlands. In Britain, the main foreign contributor, the Lord Mayor of London, led the subscription to help the Paris people, while Queen Victoria offered her patronage and financial contribution and the Prince of Wales presided over the society. *Rapports des sociétés allemandes et britanniques* (SSBAMT, 1873), pp. 56–8; Merchie, *Guerre de 1870–1871*, p. 140.

79 The call to medical men took place in July to complement army ambulances paid for by the army itself. The Red Cross constituted its own ambulances later in July and in August, creating sedentary ambulances during the siege of Paris as late as January 1871. M. Lévy, *Notes sur les hôpitaux baraques du Luxembourg et du Jardin des Plantes* (J. B. Ballière, 1871), pp. 5–6.

80 *Gardes nationaux* elected their medical officers. Most medical officers elected were general practitioners with a limited number of second-class medical men called *officiers de santé*. G. Carrot, 'La Garde Nationale 1789–1871, une institution de la Nation' (Thèse de doctorat de 3ième cycle, Université de Nice, 1979), pp. 222–4.

81 The Commission d'Hygiène et de Salubrité published a list of sixty-six authorised surgeons on 10 October 1870.

82 *GMP*, 25 (1870) 541–2.

their position to the rampant nepotism of the previous government. Closing their ranks to the lower-ranking, and often more politically radical medical men, they whitewashed their institutional prominence with war heroism. The Société de Secours and the Presse provided a rare opportunity to obtain honours like the Légion d'honneur from whatever government might exist after the war.[83] 'This bright ribbon that looks so good over a black coat has become a means of corruption, tempting vain and vulgar ambitions; it has become the price of the most shameful begging and the most revolting servitude, the mark of a lack of honour',[84] wrote a medical journalist who did not obtain one. Some of the numerous war accounts used in this study prove, on closer examination, to be nothing but a portfolio justifying an award.[85] When the desirable ribbon proved to be scarce, the Société de secours commemorative medals became second best. Being red and white, their ribbon could be woven with more red than white and be confused with the red Légion d'honneur. At best the Société de secours and the Presse served as a social ladder, at the very least they turned into a social scaffolding which certainly prevented leading men from falling with the Second Empire.[86]

The societies also filled in a political gap. Voluntary organisations could flourish and develop their own public image and 1870 became the golden age of voluntary movements acting almost totally independently from a weak state and army.

Voluntary movements

To try to understand the complex relation between organised voluntary movements, the army and the administration, one needs to stress the state of chaos in which both the French state and army were. In the first section of this chapter I have mentioned the institutional forms of mobilised civilian medical effort, but those represented but a fraction of the civilian medical war effort and their call to unity went against many vested interests. In the political vacuum of 1870, voluntary associations offered a unique opportunity for free enterprising humanitarianism. The Société de secours and the Comité de la presse had directly financed 217 ambulances in August 1870, including three gathered in Brussels, thirty-one regional ambulances and about eleven 'flying ambulances' and eight hospitals, in total 4,210 beds.[87] This compares rather poorly with the 1,291 other ambulances created in

---

83 The government's decision of 28/10/1870 to limit the Légion d'honneur to military services provoked an uproar in the medical press. See *Recueil officiel des actes du Gouvernement*, p. 472; *Union médicale* (29/10/1870). Immediately after the armistice Baron Larrey wrote 272 letters supporting medical applications.
84 *L'Abeille médicale* (26/12/1870), leader.
85 E. Delessert, *Épisodes pendant la Commune* (Charles Noblet, private circulation, 1872), pp. 71–4.
86 Pasteur himself came under severe criticism for his stance at the end of the war: *GMP*, 26 (1871) 76.
87 A. Cochin, *Le Service de santé des armées avant et pendant le siège de Paris* (A. Sauton, 1871), p. 41.

Paris alone.[88] The flag bearing a red cross validated the independent existence of hundreds of ambulances supported by religious orders, municipal authorities, companies,[89] rich philanthropists like Wallace[90] or Rothschild,[91] Jewish, Protestant (748 beds),[92] and Freemasons' organisations,[93] or even individuals. These Parisian ambulances represented 25,182 beds, an average of 19.5 beds per ambulance.[94]

This proliferation of flags bearing a red cross,[95] of ambulances devoted to wounded soldiers rather than sick ones, to officers rather than mobilised peasants, remained largely uncontrolled.[96] The rationale seems also to have been more than a purely voluntary impulse.[97] The Geneva Convention explicitly protected ambulances and personnel from requisitions and invading armies. While the French army was totally unaware of the benefits of the convention until late into the war,[98] civilians appropriated the most immediately applicable 'war insurance' measures it contained.[99] This 'war insurance' also fitted with customary *droit des gens* protecting private and neutral property at war. In a play published in Melun and obviously targeting local notables, the anti-hero states:

> *Fortoison*
> In the foreseeing of a disaster, I have had a stroke of genius and I have written to the high authorities to offer my house as an ambulance.
> *Madam*
> An ambulance here?
> *Fortoison*

---

88 Chenu, *Aperçu historique, statistique et clinique*, vol. 1, pp. 101–267.
89 ASSAT, box 63/3, 'Rapport sur le service des ambulances pendant le Siège de Paris dans la 5ème section', par M. Barberet, Médecin Général, p. 12 (unnumbered).
90 His ambulance was called 'Lord Hertford' in memory of Richard Wallace's father. T. Auger, *Le Siège de Paris, rapport les services rendu par l'ambulance de feu le Marquis de Hertford* (Parent, 1871).
91 A. Job, *Malades et blessés de l'hôpital Rothschild* (A. Delahaye, 1871), p. 8.
92 H. Monod, *Rapport du comité évangélique auxiliaire de secours pour les soldat blessés ou malades, 1870–1871* (Sandoz and Fischbacher, 1875), p. 7.
93 F. Court *Louis Ormières, 1851–1914, et l'ambulance du Grand Orient de France en 1870–1871* (Imprimerie Nouvelle, 1914); *Bulletin du Grand Orient de France*, 26 (1870) 380, 392.
94 ASSAT, box 63/1, Répartition des hôpitaux et ambulances de la ville de Paris.
95 Foreign observers were quite sarcastic about this enthusiasm: G. H. Boyland, *Six Months under the Red Cross with the French Army* (Cincinnati, Robert Clarke and Co., 1873), p. 232; Chenu, *Aperçu historique, statistique et clinique*, vol. 1, p. xxxii; Flamarion, *Le Livret du docteur*, p. 113; G. Peltier, *L'Ambulance N°5* (Delahaye, 1871), p. 28.
96 Tardieu, *Huitième ambulance*, p. 18.
97 The voluntary impulse seems to have been strong, however, and even cynical observers did not dismiss off-hand the kindness of strangers. J. Bonnefont, *Ambulances internationales et privées* (Bureau de l'Union Médicale, 1871), p. 2.
98 SHAT, Lu 1, Memorandum from the Ministry of Foreign Office to the Ministry of War following a reminder from the Swiss Federal council on the terms of the convention (20/07/1870), 25/08/1870.
99 J. Furley, *Épreuves et luttes d'un volontaire neutre* (Jean Dumaine, 1874), p. 59.

> Certainly, and this very morning I have received the authorisation and the insignia which will make the head of such an institution both respected and recognised....
> That way they will never dare to enter anywhere.[100]

Even official Red Cross literature had to clear its name from these practices:

> These people do not calculate what a gaping wound or a broken limb may represent in terms of heroism or suffering, but what they [the wounds] may contain in terms of protection against the advancing enemy and their requisitions. We will never be, at any cost, the society for the exploitation of the sick and wounded.[101]

In some instances, like the particularly harsh occupation of Le Mans, this systematic conversion of the town into a hospital did not protect house-owners from the invading army or their brutal exactions.[102] This cynical approach to humanitarian work was not the only impulse behind the creation of ambulances. The proliferation of ambulances also implied a polyphony of specific humanitarian discourses working on different paradigms. Charitable agencies and religious ones used the Red Cross flag in their proselytising.[103] A Protestant preacher thus stated that 'beyond our care we had to remember the religious work we sought to carry on' using daily scripture readings.[104] Henri Monod candidly admitted that 'this spontaneous move [towards an ambulance] has been most helpful for the cause of Protestantism, because it powerfully undermined the prejudice, ignorance and ill-will against our faith'.[105] The ambulances also fitted in a wish to become part of the republican war effort, in Nord's terms, to be active in the 'republican moment'.[106]

During the difficult battles, local priests, relatively unsolicited by their often hostile flock (when they were not Muslim *Turcos*), found in ambulance work a rewarding work which enabled them to satisfy their Saint-Sulpician sentimental taste for sufferings and martyrdom while gently bending the ears of the patients:

100 C. Monteuil, *Helfen den Verwundeten, épisode de l'invasion de Melun* (Melun, Herisé, 1873), pp. 8, 12.
101 SHAT, Lu 1, *Circulaire au comité de la délégation de Tours*, 4/02/1871, p. 514.
102 SHAT, Lu 1, *Rapport de monsieur le conseiller de préfecture Boulanger à monsieur le comte de Flavigny, l'oeuvre du comité du Mans*, 20/07/1871, pp. 18–19; 1992. L. Boulanger, *Compte rendu des travaux du comité de secours de la Sarthe* (Le Mans, Imprimerie E. Monnoyer, 1871); A. E. Mordret, *Rapport sur le service militaire de santé, guerre de 1870–1871 dans la ville du Mans* (Le Mans, E. Monnoyer, 1872).
103 On this issue see N. Isser, 'Protestant and proselytisation during the Second French Empire', *Journal of Church and State*, 30 (1988) 51–70.
104 A. S. de Doncourt (Comtesse Drohojovska), *Souvenirs des ambulances* (Lille, Lefort, 1872), p. 25; Monod, *Rapport du comité évangélique*, pp. 8, 65.
105 Monod, *Rapport du comité évangélique*, p. 17.
106 P. G. Nord, *The Republican Moment: Struggles for Democracy in Nineteenth-Century France* (Cambridge, Mass., Harvard University Press, 1995), pp. 78–87, 106–7; speech of the secretary of the Jewish *consistoire* (18/12/1870), *Le Journal du Siège de Paris* (*Le Gaulois*, March 1871), p. 332.

'Only yesterday did I understand my true place in the ambulance . . . I provide the patient with consolations and encouragement while their wounds are dressed. I elevate his soul to God, and then I lower it gently towards the consoling duties of a Christian.'[107] Freemasons acquired social visibility and integrated humanitarianism in their secularist philosophy. Notables gained social inviolability in the civil war climate and practised charity in a new guise. Individuals avoided the military service and requisition orders while showing patriotism. Junior medical practitioners in the overcrowded urban medical market secured well-deserved custom out of their war effort.[108] Municipalities used ambulances to re-establish their political authority after years of repression. They also made occasional profits from donations.[109]

The government only attempted to create order out of this chaos at the very end of December 1870, a month or so before the armistice. The model that eventually emerged at the end of the war maintained the Société de Secours' nominal independence from the army and gave it a total monopoly over humanitarian issues, sanitarian inspections (first attempted on 20 October) and fund-raising.[110] Voluntary ambulances were simply registered by the Société, which was then accountable to the army. In some other instances the Red Cross replaced helpless authorities. The Girondin ambulance, for instance, filled the vacuum left by the state and, ignoring its original military focus, actively worked to relieve poverty, hunger and diseases. 'We do not believe that we are exceeding our mission by treating the civilian population too.'[111]

More interestingly, the events linked to the Paris Commune in 1871 ended this independence on both sides. The Commune nationalised the Société and incorporated it to the revolutionary army, while the government exerted far more control over the voluntary effort.[112] These unexpected forms of institutionalised and militaristic humanitarianism were the result of the 1870 war experience. Most European countries eventually followed suit, and like the Prussian government in

---

[107] AEP, 5b2 10, weekly letter from Abbot Rincazaux to the Archbishop of Paris from the fort of Saint Denis, 2/10/1870. AEP 4 B244, André Belin, 'Les Aumôniers de 1870: essai de reconstitution de l'ordre de bataille des aumôniers de l'armée et de la marine française pendant la guerre de 1870–1871', typescript, 1972.

[108] This became the major criticism of humanitarian action during after the war. C. de Montesson, *Souvenirs d'ambulance, 1870–1871* (Le Mans, Monnoyer, 1885), pp. 80–2; Chenu, *Aperçu historique, statistique et clinique*, vol. 1, p. xxxii.

[109] T. Ferré, *Rapport sur les services des ambulances municipales du troisième arrondissement pendant le siège de Paris, 1870–1871* (Rigal, 1872), p. 33.

[110] *Recueil des décrets, statuts, règlements et instructions concernant la société de secours aux blessés militaires* (Siège de la Croix Rouge, 1936), decree of 31/12/1870, p. 36.

[111] F. de Luze and A. Labodie, *Rapport au comité départemental pour la Gironde* (Bordeaux, n.p., 1871), p. 13.

[112] *Opérations du conseil d'administration siégeant à Versailles* (Société de Secours, 1872), p. 4. This nationalisation provoked an international outcry and the French Red Cross thus doubled its income.

1878, subordinated the Red Cross to military command.[113] This was an explicit condemnation of free enterprise in the age of universal conscription and warfare.[114] In the early 1880s army administrators could thus proclaim confidently that 'the Red Cross has no longer any purpose'.[115] The conscription of medical practitioners through the reform of the military service in the 1880s seemed to justify this claim. The Red Cross survived nevertheless, getting ever closer to the military, because it could serve the national war effort in other and primarily ideological ways.[116]

Ideology

The Société de Secours' ideological ground became increasingly unstable during the war. The soft Christian internationalism of Geneva gave way to more effective forms of 'mobilising' discourse centred on national priorities.[117] In a perverse manner, moreover, the Société owed its wealth and influence to the continuation of the war. The voluntary effort was part and parcel of the republican revival of the 1792 people's war and call to public opinion to support the continuation of war. This revolutionary appeal was initiated, as in 1792, by an ideological statement about the national integrity of France and a call for the defence of liberty across Europe. The revolutionary government continued the imperial war but gave it new meanings and called in universal principles of right: a feature with which we are familiar in the twentieth century but which in 1870 was reminiscent of the great revolutionary wars. Ambulance work became an integral part of national cum republican revival. Medical authors clamoured: 'Salute gladly the return of Liberty and applaud this pacific revolution that will become with our heroic national war the greatest glory of our generation.'[118] Indeed it could be argued that the display of generosity and the extravagant expenses incurred to establish ambulances were as many morale-boosting measures. In besieged Paris, starved of any real news, ambulance activities provided a focus for an exuberant press. Journalists could gloss over the heroic wounded heroes, the saintly nurses, since the closure of theatres actresses like Sarah Bernhardt or semi-professional nurses belonging to religious orders or secularist movements.[119] At a more fundamental

---

113 Moynier, *La Croix Rouge*, p. 46.
114 *Le Mouvement médical* (15/10/1870), 543.
115 E. Delorme, *Traité de chirurgie de guerre* (2 vols, Félix Alcan, 1888–93), pp. 342, 360.
116 A. Buchet de Chauvigné and M. Collet, *Rapport sur le service de l'évacuation des militaires blessés et malades presenté à Mr l'Intendant de Première Classe Guérin* (Lefebvre, 1875), p. 14.
117 S. Pietrowski, *La Guerre et la Société de secours aux blessés militaires des armées de terre et de mer* (E. Dentu, 1870), p. 43: 'today national hatred disappears to be replaced by the curative dogma of humanitarianism ...'.
118 *GMP*, 25 (1870) 483.

level, the issue of humanitarianism, the too often violated rules of war,[120] conspired to the creation of a conflict of *ideology*, a conflict between *realpolitik*[121] and civilising ideals.[122] The interpretative frame of humanitarianism was in contradiction with the practices of warfare. Using the language of humanitarianism one could only conclude by emphasising the growing barbarisation of warfare. It built a self-perpetuating analysis. Humanitarianism needed war to be expressed, yet war was the negation of humanitarian feelings.

This appropriation of humanitarian principles worked on a purely national basis (i.e. the French vs. Barbarians) and went against transnational principles. The acrimonious debates in post-1870 Europe seemed to condemn the Red Cross movement. It has nevertheless survived another 129 years. To explain this survival, most hagiographers of the Red Cross seem to argue that the humanitarian principles eventually won. Hutchinson's view rejoins my own analysis and points out that the humanitarian discourse became autonomous in Geneva from the national experience.[123] The Société played a crucial role in post-war France through its action during the 1871 Commune civil war. During that crisis it defined future humanitarian action in similar circumstances and it contributed to post-civil war mending of the social fabric. The Red Cross movement, in its diverse forms, took sides during the civil war against Paris and joined forces with the government, 'to whom our sponsors and donators called us to take our resources'. Red Cross ambulances kept valid soldiers and priests hidden.[124] The nation implied in the nationalistic ideology of the Red Cross movement was not a socialist nation. The Commune had tried in vain to obtain neutral status for their military medical services and to sign the Geneva Convention.[125] It failed to obtain the nominal legitimacy needed to do so. The emblem of the red cross itself became common to both sides and thus facilitated communication between sides. To solve

---

119 H. A. Wauthoz, *Les Ambulances et les ambulanciers à travers les siècles* (Brussels, Lebègue, 1872?), p. ix; I. de Crombrugghe, *Journal d'une infirmière pendant la guerre 1870–1871* (H. Plon, 1872), p. 10; J. Jurgensen, *Le Soir du combat, récit d'une infirmière, poème* (Geneva, Durafort, 1871); P. and H. de Trailles, *Les Femmes en France pendant la guerre et les deux sièges de Paris* (F. Polo Libraire, 1872).

120 Lüder, *La Convention de Genève*, pp. 227–63.

121 Jeismann, *Das Vaterland der Feinde*, pp. 161–295.

122 Lüder, *La Convention de Genève*, p. 18, on the hatred and fundamental opposition which rose during the second period of the war on both sides. Also see Elias, *Uber des Prozess der Zivilisation*, especially vol. 1, chs. I and II on the differences between German *Kultur* and Anglo-French *Civilisation*. On Elias see R. Robertson, 'Civilisation and the civilizing process: Elias, globalisation and analytic synthesis', *Theory, Culture and Society*, 9:1 (1992) 211–27.

123 Boissier, *Histoire du comité internationale de la Croix Rouge*, pp. 353–83.

124 *Opérations du conseil d'administration siégeant à Versailles*, pp. 5–6; Gallet, *Guerre et Commune*, p. 257.

125 *JORC* (19/05/1871). In fact the Commune joined on 13 May; A. Vidieu, *Histoire de la Commune* (Dentu, 1876), p. 336. *Rapport du comte de Beaufort*, pp. 27–8.

this problem, the Société abandoned without hesitation the symbol on its identity cards.[126] The civil war imperatives took precedence over humanitarian ones. This first instance of civil war set the trend for all forthcoming internal conflicts in which the Red Cross movement later became involved.[127]

The ultimate form of national identification took place after the war when the Red Cross used some of its war dowry to establish itself as a 'patriotic and humanitarian institution' (in that order of priority) commemorating the fallen soldiers and indicating the path for national reconstruction.[128] On 16 January 1872 the French Red Cross, as it became then known instead of the socialist-sounding Société Internationale, organised a solemn ceremony in the Cathedral of Notre-Dame in Paris. On the outside of the Cathedral, two large shields bore the 'fatal dates' 1870–71 over a large black draping. The organisers had covered the inside walls in black. The Cathedral was entirely in mourning. The crowd gathered inside wore mourning outfits. Members of Parliament, generals (Marshal MacMahon), members of the government (General de Cissey, Jules Simon), Parisian personalities (the mayors of Paris *arrondissements*, Madame Thiers) and bourgeois. This was a mass for the dead, a requiem. In the heart of the transept, an empty coffin covered in black was resting. Count Serurier, Mr Huber-Saladin (from Switzerland),[129] Viscomte de Melun, Count de Beaufort, Dr Chenu and Dr Ricord (the heads of the competing branches of the French Red Cross) were the pallbearers. On both sides the Comte de Flavigny, Baron Mundy (from Austria), founding members of the Red Cross, a few representatives from the civilian medical men, army medical men, nurses and invalid soldiers stood silently. In the nave, just above the pillars of the church, large white shields painted with red crosses and Red Cross flags contrasted with the black hangings. There were no national flags to be seen, only the ominous Red Cross.

The coffin was empty and had a metaphorical purpose.[130] It stood as a symbol of 'the officers, non-commissioned officers, soldiers, *gardes mobiles* and *gardes nationales* who died during the Franco-Prussian war'. Among the guests were the princes and princesses of the Orléans branch of the royal family that had lost the throne in 1848. The Archbishop presided and a famous preacher gave all the meaning to the three-hour ceremony:

---

126 *Opérations du conseil d'administration siégeant à Versailles*, p. 7.
127 Moynier, *La Croix Rouge*, pp. 172–3.
128 *Opérations du conseil d'administration siégeant à Versailles*, p. 2, 'Oeuvre de Patriotisme et d'Humanité'.
129 Huber-Saladin had represented Switzerland at the Paris Congress to revise the Geneva Convention in 1867. Boissier, *Histoire du comité internationale de la Croix Rouge*, p. 331.
130 On the purpose of images to mediate knowledge see R. Chartier, 'Le Monde comme représentation', *Annales*, 44:6 (1989) 1505–18, p. 1514.

Socialist utopians wanted to negate suffering: but one can find suffering even among our voluptuousness, above our wounded pride, below our unsatisfied greed, everywhere people are suffering even in pleasure... After each disaster France redresses herself through the [sacrifice] of martyrs' blood.... France will not die, She will be again the soldier of God and Civilisation.[131]

In occupied Lorraine a similar form of ritual was to be enacted by the ladies of Metz under the patronage of Mgr Dupont des Loges on 8 September each year. The rites of commemoration and *revanche* deeply rooted themselves in the traditional support for the Red Cross and humanitarian work. [132] Many post-Commune sources show this desire to forget which was at the heart of Renan's discourse and which is at the heart of Benedict Anderson's analysis of national identity. Books like Jules de Marthold's chronological account of the war suddenly bridged the gap of the Commune by stopping their chronology at the armistice and starting it again at the religious ceremony of Notre-Dame in January 1872. The statue of Strasburg at the Place de la Concorde remained shrouded in black: 'Facing the Strasburg statue veiled in mourning, a wounded but not dead people, thinking of what its past requires of present times, burning with hope, with all its undiminishing faith, honourable, their flag in mourning, can contemplate the future.'[133]

Conclusion

The Red Cross, the altar and the army formed an unholy trinity in the confusion of post-war France, and this social and ideological alliance prefigured the reorganisation of the civilian voluntary effort as a natural complement to new forms of conscription. The Red Cross, recognised and honoured at the end of the war, reflected faithfully the reactionary hierarchy which controlled France after the Commune. It differed, however, from Mr Thiers's government in that it devoted itself to the preparation of the next European war.[134] The prospect of forthcoming wars transcended gender limits but not class boundaries: a ladies' and a women's organisation targeted the relevant sections of society. The Union des dames françaises (1879) and the Union des femmes de France (1881) were united in the

---

131 J. Grange, *Compte rendu du service funèbre célébré à Notre-Dame de Paris* (Chaix, 1872), pp. 3–10. *Le Gaulois* (16/01/and 18/01/1871); J. de Marthold, *Mémorandum du siège de Paris 1870–1871* (Charovay Frères, 1884), p. 305.
132 F. Roth, *La Lorraine annexée (1870–1918)* (Nancy, Presses Universitaires de Nancy, 1976), pp. 99–100.
133 Marthold, *Mémorandum*, pp. 305–8: 'Devant la statue de Strasbourg voilée de deuil, un peuple meurtri mais non point mort, songeant à ce que son avenir exige de son passé, de toute l'ardeur de son espoir, de toute la constance de sa foi, honneur sauf, crêpe au drapeau, peut regarder demain.'
134 C. Bonnard, *1870–18??, Vichy ambulance ; son rôle pendant la prochaine guerre* (Vichy, C. Bougarel, [1872], 1890, 1891).

Comité Central de la Croix Rouge only in 1892.[135] In answer to my own original problematic I would like to propose the following points in conclusion.

The Red Cross restructured social hierarchies within a pyramidal institution after the war. In the process of the war and of the Commune revolution, the Société de Secours' independence and the substance of its internationalist ideology perished. In Comte de Beaufort's words: 'if the cause to which these societies contribute is international, their character is national'.[136] Even as it allied itself to the pursuit of nationalist projects, however, the Red Cross was able to ensure its survival by exploiting its international connections and developing its role as a channel for transnational corporate charity and surrogate diplomacy. It found new missions which relieved the state from unpleasant duties such as the repatriation of prisoners and refugees.[137] During the conflict the Red Cross had used its international connections to publish, from October 1870, a regular list of wounded prisoners kept by the Germans.[138] The international agency in Basel especially played a major part in the sending of parcels and mail to prisoners, and eventually their repatriation from Germany[139] and from the remains of the Bourbaki army left in Switzerland.[140] The Société also moved wounded Parisians to the provinces of France, negotiating independently with the German authorities. In the words of the *intendant général*:

> evacuations to the provinces have been authorised after some negotiations between the International Society and Prusse, therefore it is this society which organises the convoys and designates the doctors who will accompany the wounded. I cannot therefore oblige Mr the Dr in Chief and favour the doctors he commended for this mission.[141]

One could attribute this successful survival to the important part the associations took in sustaining the war effort financially and ideologically.

> It [the Red Cross] will be an active charity serving misery [*sic*]. Those who cannot serve the country taking arms should serve it with their generosity, so that becoming

---

135 Y. Knibiehler *et al.*, *Cornettes et blouses blanches, les infirmières et la société française* (Hachette, 1984), pp. 51–5.
136 Beaufort, *Étude sur la société française*, p. 7.
137 A mission prevalent in the following conflicts: G. H. Davis, 'National Red Cross societies and prisoners of war in Russia 1914–1918', *Journal of Contemporary History*, 28:1 (1993) 31–53.
138 SHAT, LT 28, *Liste des blessés français recueillis par les troupes allemandes* (Geneva, Georg, 1st list, 30/10/1870). This list completed the full list of wounded soldiers published by the national Red Cross committees since mid-August.
139 S. Pietrowski, *Rapport général, campagne de 1870-1, armée de Sedan – armée de la Loire* (Imprimerie Centrale des Chemins de Fer, A. Chaix, 1871), p. 31; A. Quesnay de Beaurepaire, *De Wissembourg à Ingoldstat* (Firmin Didot, 1891).
140 SHAT, Lu 1, Rapport du Pasteur Sohler à son excellence le ministre de la guerre sur l'ambulance du collège of Montbeliard.
141 ASSAT, box 62/6, Les Convalescents, congés et dépots, various letters.

active or honorary members of this society through a yearly subscription, they will still be soldiers to the nation.[142]

Serving *malheur*, in unison the poor and the unhappy, misery and unhappiness became a para-military slogan for the Red Cross officials. Henry Dunant's Utopia had become the platform for the gradual integration of non-combatant civilians in the age of mass war. The 1870 chaos definitively enslaved the humanitarian agenda to national and military ones. The Red Cross then served to blur the boundaries between war and peace – a function it would further fulfil by mobilising, not just for war, but also for natural disasters like the Toulouse floods in the 1870s. By blurring these boundaries, the Red Cross became an integral part of the management of manpower in the age of the new mass armies. It thereby demonstrated the existence of a civilian push towards 'total war' before a military 'pull' could be organised.

After the war the Red Cross chose to develop two symbolic new activities: it created a permanent structure meant to train civilians to the requirements of a forthcoming war, and it set up a Red Cross museum in Les Invalides in Paris, in the same building as Napoleon I's tomb.[143] This was a suitable location for more than one reason. Les Invalides encapsulated the benefaction of the French monarchy to the wounded, the glory of the Empire and the centrality of war in the making of the French nation.[144] Overall, at the heart of the military establishment and so close to many layers of symbolic *lieux de mémoire,* the museum reminded all that 'the Red Cross during a war can only be the servant and never the master'.[145]

142 Grange, *Compte rendu du service funèbre,* p. 10.
143 Boissier, *Histoire du comité international,* p. 287. The idea of a museum and of a permanent training ambulance had been discussed since 1867, only three years after the foundation of the movement. Grange, *Rapport sur l'ambulance de Bougival, projet d'ambulance permanente de perfectionnement*; Billy, *Rapport à la commission des finances* pp. 62, 97.
144 P. Triare, *Dominique Larrey et les campagnes de la Révolution et de l'Empire, 1766–1842* (Tours, Alfred Mame et Fils, 1902), pp. 717–23; G. L. Niox, *The Hôtel des Invalides* (Delagrave, 1924).
145 Lüder, *La Convention de Genève,* p. x.

8 Defeat embodied: the severed limbs of the nation

This chapter deals with issues of representations and discourse around the 1870 war. It dwells on the embodiment of defeat and focuses on victims and war casualties who, in the hands of their surgeons, became living symbols of defeat, and, to a certain extent, living representations of the nation. It is the contention of this book that the defeat of the flesh became the central metaphor of French representations of the war after 1870. By considering metaphors in medical and social practice, this chapter intends to show how porous cultural boundaries were between the literary and the scientific and how metaphors mattered in post-war reconstruction. It is therefore also about what happened to these people after the war, when their maimed bodies became grotesque reminders of the defeat. By looking at the embodiment of war, many recent historians have undertaken a history of the self at war, and have attempted to locate the war experience in the continuum of individual lives. When wars end, those whose flesh is scarred, torn or mutilated carry with them and on them the expression of war violence. As Jay Winter and Joanna Bourke have shown for the First World War, thin layers of identities can peel off from individuals, masculinity and a productive 'labourer' identity can be similarly scarred and damaged.[1] In an attempt to decode the significance of war wounds in society after war ends, this chapter will consider two different but related issues that arose during and after the war.

The first one is the vital debate on conservative surgery, which, set in the political and symbolic context of 1870, acquired a great deal of importance. In this section I would argue that French anthropomorphic representations of the nation and/or the Republic,[2] so well described for Marianne by Maurice Agulhon, applied in this medical discussion.[3] The loss of Alsace-Lorraine, this 'amputation of the national territory', echoed painfully the sufferings of mutilated soldiers. The political contest between a party of peace and a party of war also mirrored the medical debates around conservative surgery.

---

1 J. Winter, *The Great War and the British People* (Macmillan, 1986); J. Bourke, *Dismembering the Male: Men's Bodies, Britain and the Great War* (Reaktion, 1996), pp. 33–75.
2 T. J. Clark, *The Absolute Bourgeois: Artists and Politics in France, 1848–1851* (Thames and Hudson, 1973), p. 64. The ambivalence and the constant confusion of France and Marianne, the symbol of the Republic, singularly reinforced the political legitimacy of the latter.
3 M. Agulhon, *Marianne au combat, l'imagerie et la symbolique républicaines de 1789 à 1880* (Flammarion, 1979) and 'Esquisse pour une archéologie de la république : l'allégorie civique feminine', *Annales*, 28 (1973), 5–34.

The second theme of this chapter is its logical and literal continuation and deals with the fate of soldiers and civilians who, against all odds, survived their wounds, their surgeons and the threat of gangrene. The establishment of charitable funds immediately after the war and the dispensation of none-too-generous pensions cannot hide the fact that French society wished to forget those people, to ignore their plight and shame their unproductive bodies. This section will mostly look at the fifteen years after the war when the desire to forget was strongest. The *revanche* spirit which grew from the murky political field of the late 1880s and 1890s only used these veterans and their wounds on occasions. In spite of their claims to commemorative medals, they were hardly recognised as being relevant to the new political and social order. They remained the expression of defeat and hopeless cases at that.[4] Healthy Alsatian children and women in full traditional costume[5] evoked stronger images of a united regenerated France to come than ageing men on crutches.

Bodyloss

In this first part I wish to tackle a set of representations from my original approach beset with medical and surgical issues. From the surgical, the analysis will move on to the application of the surgical discourse to politics, and, though metaphorically, to its impact on representations of the French nation during and after the 1870 war.[6] French nation-images and even the concept of nation itself changed as an outcome of the act of remembering the war.[7] The reification of the struggle between 'France' and 'Germany' was rapidly narrowed down to the struggle between a Prussian soldier and a French one. After the summer of 1870 this French soldier, France, was wounded and the struggle that carried on took heroic and desperate dimensions. When impromptu ambulances opened their bedrooms to the soldiers they usually favoured wounded bodies rather than sick ones. Some

---

4 After the First World War, on the other hand, such ritualistic use of war veterans even suffering bad facial wounds became more common and part of the explicit cost of the victory. S. Delaporte, *Les Gueules cassées, les blessés de la face de la grande guerre* (Noêsis, 1996), p. 41; J. Dollimore, 'Death and the self', in R. Porter (ed.), *Rewriting the Self: Histories from the Renaissance to the Present* (Routledge, 1997), pp. 249–61.

5 The cult of things Alsatian grew considerably after the war and was further disseminated by a flood of migrants who chose to remain French. E. Beaujort, *L'Héroïne d'Alsace, récit en vers* (Lachaud, 1871); É. Bergerat, *Le Petit Alsacien, poème* (A. Lemerre, 1871); *Les Cuirassiers de Reischoffen* (A. Lemerre, 1870); *Strasbourg, ode* (A. Lemerre, 1871); *Poèmes de la guerre* (A. Lemerre, 1871); E. Magnan, *Angéla ou l'Alsace enchaînée* (Ghio, 1884); L. Baron, *Le Petit Alsacien, poème patriotique* (E. Dentu, 1885)

6 C. Digeon, *La Crise allemande de la pensée française* (Presses Universitaires de France, 1959); A. Mitchell, *The Divided Path: The German Influence on Social Reform in France after 1871* (Chapel Hill, University of North Carolina Press, 1991).

7 B. Anderson, *Imagined Communities* (Verso, 2nd edn, 1991), pp. 197–203.

of this choice might have been based on a rational assessment of the dangers presented by a 'foreign body' in the confined atmosphere of the home. Alternatively it seems that the sick room, so pervasive in nineteenth-century culture, could not share in the national military legend as well as a war wound. Unlike war scars, the horrifying skin of smallpox victims could not be read like a map of military achievements. Thus, originally the concern with the wounded soldier was a fad.[8] 'Soldiers wounded on the battlefield have a sort of poetic aura.'[9] From a fad, the treatment of the soldier's wound became, perhaps indirectly, the embodiment of fundamental national choices.

The medical debate that triggered my enquiry is older than the war but is still very typical of the debates of the 1870s. Should one cut swiftly through the flesh and amputate a damaged limb before any infection sets in, or should one practice conservative surgery? The first option, also named primary amputation, was reminiscent of the days of heroic surgery, the 'great surgery' or 'war surgery'.[10] When the patients seemed to have recovered from the initial shock of the wound, their leg or arm fell within seconds, forever detached from their body. Such an operation took place in the vicinity of the battle: 'While excited by the combat and yet within sound of the cannon, the soldier or sailor willingly parts with a limb which a few hours of reflection would make him desire to run the risk of preserving, and upon which he fixes all his attention.'[11] This sudden and crude intervention, with or without anaesthetic,[12] left the patient in a state of shock but, supposedly, relieved.[13] When the effects of chloroform or morphine faded the victims woke up to live the rest of their lives in a different body.[14]

The second method, conservative surgery, was reminiscent of the 'modernist' urban hospital practice of the time. The patient was kept under scrutiny and avoided an operation unless it became clear to the surgeon that the

---

8   A. Tardieu, *Huitième ambulance de la Société de secours aux blessés, campagne de Sedan et de Paris* (Delahaye, 1872), p. 94. M.-R. Brice and Capitaine Bottet, *Le Corps de santé militaire en France, son évolution, ses campagnes 1708–1882* (Paris and Limoges, Berger Levrault, 1907), p. 399.
9   H. Monod, *Rapport du comité évangélique auxiliaire de secours pour les soldats blessés ou malades, 1870–1871* (Sandoz and Fischbacher, 1875), p. 28.
10 L. J.-B. Béranger-Féraud, *Le Baron Hippolyte Larrey, 1808–1895* (Fayard Frères, 1899), p. 24.
11 G. H. B. Macleod, *Notes on the Surgery in War in the Crimea* (John Churchill, 1858), p. 362.
12 *Report of the Operations of the British National Society...* (Hanson & Sons, 1871), p. 12. Dr Poncet in Strasburg also used anaesthetics, but few others seemed to dare to weaken temporarily their patients. J. E. Rochard, *Histoire de la chirurgie française au dix-neuvième siècle* (J. B. Baillière et Fils, 1875), pp. 489–90.
13 A. Juguriano, 'Des avantages de l'amputation à la suite des blessures de guerre' (Thèse de doctorat, Faculté de médecine de Montpellier, 1872).
14 E. Bancel, *Relation médico-chirurgicale du siège de Toul* (Nancy, Berger Levrault, 1873), p. 60. Some surgeons used morphine injections and hypodermic needles. *Report of the Operations of the British National Society*, p. 12.

limb was lost to gangrene, pyaemia or 'hospital rot'.[15] Only in those drastic circumstances did an amputation take place, a 'secondary amputation' which cut off what was no longer a limb but a mass of purulence and infection. There were intermediate options available to conservative surgeons, a resection (the ablation of the joints) or an excision (the ablation of a section of the bone).[16] The surgeon then placed the damaged limb into an apparatus created with the purpose of reconstituting its original shape.[17] This reinforced plaster apparatus became the site of a merciless 'combat' between the surgeon and evil,[18] the multitude of possible infections and contamination lurking in the 'hospital air'.[19] The pus leaking from small drain pipes connected to the wound would then act as a barometer of the state of the wound. Doctors would then argue on the colour, fluidity and smell of these liquids.

Both sets of practices were common during the 1870 war. However, the latter set of practices was later associated with Listerian antiseptic practice,[20] while historians of medicine and medical authors alike glossed over the former collection of embarrassing butchers.[21] To them, the 1870 war became the earliest incarnation of 'modern' war medicine looking forward to the 'Pasteurian revolution' rather than backwards to Gallen and Ambroise Paré.

The methodological choice between conservative and heroic surgery was almost exclusive. While it did happen that conservative surgeons had to cut off an irredeemably destroyed limb with a primary amputation, the opposite was rarer and heroic surgeons hesitated to 'risk' conservative surgery. This conflict of practice may still appear as the conflict between the 'modern', concerned about the patients in uniform, and the 'ancient' who could not care less. The dividing line is more blurred than it looks. Looking more closely at the supporters of both methods, one

15 The origin of 'hospital rot', gangrene etc. was still hotly debated. A. Trémeau de Rochebrune, *Essai de statistique médicale* (Savy, 1871), p. 36.
16 A. A. Chipault, *Fractures par armes à feu, expectation, résection sous-périostée, évidemment, amputation* (G. Baillière, 1872).
17 There are at least sixty-three doctoral theses on related topics from the faculties of Montpellier and Paris in the years immediately following the war: A Malinas, 'Conservation dans les fractures des membres' (Thèse de doctorat, Faculté de médecine de Paris, 1872); M. Chaules, 'Résections dans la continuité des os longs des membres à la suite des coups de feu' (Thèse de doctorat, Faculté de médecine de Paris, 1872); M. Gircourt, 'Plaies et Résections de l'épaule' (Thèse de doctorat, Faculté de médecine de Paris, 1872), etc.
18 J. C. Chenu, *Aperçu historique, statistique et clinique* (2 vols, Hachette, Dumaine, Masson, 1874), vol. 1, p. 491.
19 *Report of the Operations of the British National Society*, p. 102; C. A. Gordon, *Lessons on Hygiene and Surgery, from the Franco-Prussian War* (Baillière, Tindall and Cox, 1873), pp. 47–57, 123; M. Berkeley-Hill, *Treatment of the Sick and Wounded: Illustrated by Observations Made at the Seat of War* (James Walton, 1870), pp. 9–16; Tardieu, *Huitième ambulance*, pp. 72–3.
20 E. Lantier, *L'École antiseptique conservatrice* (Moulins, E. Auclaire, 1889), p. 9, and *Conservation des membres blessés par armes à feu perfectionnées* (Asselin, 1872).
21 J. de Blonay, *1870 : une révolution chirurgicale* (Geneva, Delta, 1975).

finds that their choice did not reflect their clinical training or lack thereof. For instance, the application of recent Listerian methods or Pasteurian theories of germs was very uncommon on either side,[22] and there is no evidence that either conservative surgeons or radical ones had a grasp of their principles and uses.[23] The antiseptic issue was a side issue of this debate, and in spite of what the later historiography made of it, its use remained limited.[24] A radical surgeon, MacCormac,[25] and a conservative surgeon, Demarquay, both tried to use Listerian methods.[26] Many more on either side did not. This conflict was not the superseding of one practice by another more effective one. The real issue was elsewhere. Proponents of primary amputations had a simple and powerful argument: if you postpone amputation, the limb will become infected and you may lose your patient. A limb was not worth the risk. They also stressed the contrast between 'the usually healthy look of these men [lower limb primary amputees] with the miserable appearance of those on whom conservative surgery had been practised'.[27]

Proponents of conservative surgery had a slightly weaker argument: that to save the limb was to save the man within the body. A cripple was no use to society. Apart from those fundamental issues of medical ethics (in the absence of the patients' informed choice), the real issue was that of the allocation of resources involved in one or the other method. Conservative surgery was time-consuming, expensive, and arguably unsuited to the military tactical choices. The view that conservative surgery was a risk, a gamble, an experiment and, perhaps, a fad, justified many rebuttals of the conservative theory and practice. This notion of risk has to be questioned here. It seems strange that in the war context, entirely composed of calculated and fortuitous risks, medical people saw it as their duty to limit the risk to their patient. They presented the continuation of the struggle on the damaged limb as a risk avoided by amputation. An amputation would get rid of the useless limb and the meaningless conflict with one blow. The logic may seem twisted but it was not uncommon: 'in some instances the results obtained from its adoption [conservative surgery] have been scarcely *less* deplorable than those of

---

22 Careful readers of the medical press were surprisingly aware of the theories but often found the procedures too complicated or unapplicable. L. Vaslin, *Étude sur les pansements des plaies et l'hygiène des blessés* (Anger, Germain & Grassié, 1878).
23 Berkeley-Hill did not see one instance of the use of Listerian methods during the early months of the conflict. Berkeley-Hill, *Treatment of the Sick and Wounded*, p. 31. Some experimented at the outbreak of the war, but the haste of those experiments illustrates how unfamiliar French medical practitioners were with the practice. *GMP*, 25 (1870) 455; T. Bonjean, *L'Emploi de l'ergotine sur les malades et les blessés de l' Armée du Rhin* (Germer Baillière, 1870), pp. 34–6.
24 C. Ryan, *With an Ambulance during the Franco-German War* (John Murray, 1896), p. 96.
25 William MacCormac's authoritative work was translated into French, Italian and German within twelve months of the original publication in English. *Souvenirs d'un chirurgien d'ambulance* (J. B. Ballière et Fils, 2nd edn, 1872).
26 *Report of the Operations of the British National Society*, p. 107.
27 'The Surgery of the War', *The Lancet*, 2 (20/10/1870) 619.

capital operations'.[28] Charles Gordon, a British observer, who principally tried to synthesise contradictory accounts of the war and war surgery, attempted to accommodate both views. If secondary amputations gave decent results, Gordon, quoting Pirogoff, approved of conservative surgery where practicable; otherwise he would defend the logic of neutralisation, the amputation which cut the limb, and hence retrieved the soldier from war.[29] Amputation may not have given brilliant results but it always gave swift and definitive answers.

Dr Chenu, leader of the French Société de Secours, among others, argued that the life of soldiers and their potential recycling, after being wounded, mattered to the army. The survival of the soldier could mean the continuation of war. Chenu characteristically refused to separate war medicine from war. His was less a concern with petty tactical issues of present resources than with serving the wider strategic problems of the continuation of war and preserving the human material.[30] Chenu also favoured a generous deployment of the superavailability of medical staff and resources brought by the Red Cross to enable conservative surgery.[31]

This disproportionate funding enabled civilian and military medical men to experiment with conservative surgery, particularly in places where beds were superabundant.[32] Yet not everybody experimented, and those who did were severely criticised for doing so. Proponents of radical surgery argued that too much effort and too many resources were spent on futile exercises. 'The logic and the necessities of war demand that all should be done for valid men, i.e. the destruction of the enemy and therefore Victory, before anything can be done for the wounded. It is barbaric but true.'[33] Also against any linear and positivistic reading of this debate, the statistical evidence collected by Chenu himself showed disastrous rates of survival after either sort of surgery.[34]

This global overview and simplification may have given the mistaken impression that conservative surgery was the stuff of civilian medicine, strongly rejected by army surgeons. It is true that the formidable means of civilian medicine

28 Gordon, *Lessons on Hygiene*, p. 190.
29 Gordon, *Lessons on Hygiene*, pp. 132, 191.
30 J. C. Chenu, *De la mortalité dans l'armée et des moyens d'économiser la vie humaine* (Hachette, 1890), p. 50.
31 E. Decaisne, 'Le Siège de Paris au point de vue de l'hygiène et de la chirurgie', *Revue Scientifique*, 20 (11/11/1871) 468–71.
32 Mundy, for example, used two beds per patient, dressing the wound with carbolic acid, and it was noted 'not only in wards but as applications in cases of wounds and operations'. Gordon, *Lessons on Hygiene*, p. 45; A. Maffitt, *A Manual of Instruction for Attendants on Sick and Wounded in War* (National Society for Aid to the Sick and Wounded, 1870), pp. 42–69.
33 L. Chapplain, *De l'Intendance du corps médical militairè et de la mortalité dans l'armée* (Librairie Jean Dumaine, 1872), p. iii.
34 Earlier statistical work on the subject include E. Spillmann's *Études statistiques sur les résultats de la chirugie conservatrice* (P. Asselin, 1868).

mobilised in the war effort made conservative surgery possible. It is not so that surgical opinions diverged solely according to the professional background of the practitioners. Chenu quoted experienced surgeons who blamed an inexperience of war or even the juvenile audacity of heroic surgeons:[35] 'Were they not scared by these wounds they had never seen before, and, for some of them, more audacious than experts, did they not use their knives on limbs that could have been saved?' 'The older I become, the less I amputate', said the academician Velpeau.[36] Baron Larrey, a fervent Bonapartist, head of the army services, commended surgeons more happily to the Légion d'honneur if they had defended conservative surgery during the conflict.[37] In his later parliamentarian speeches he made a political and emotional point of defending conservative surgery during and after the war.

On the other side of the political spectrum, one finds a coalition of diverse interests: enemies of the Red Cross, established civilian medical practitioners, strong militarists attached to the autonomy of the army, and fanatical proponents of virile attitudes towards suffering. All defended the view that a short cut is better than a protracted bedridden agony, that a limited loss is better than death itself. Politically most belonged to an aggregate of factions ranging from the Orleanists to opportunistic republicans. This political mapping becomes possible through the analysis of individual convictions, particularly on the issue of the continuation of the conflict, which had become the main element in the crystallisation of French politics.

The French Red Cross found its origin and justification in the war. The enthusiasm of most of its activists had natural affinities with a form of revived 1792 patriotism reacting against the invasion.[38] Transcending their original political background, most of its members associated themselves with the conflict. The Bonapartists, also bred on a diet of identification between people and nation, nation and territory, like the left-wing republicans were not ready to give away 'one inch of our territory, nor one stone of our fortresses'.[39] It was principally those who worked either in the army or in the Red Cross who took daring initiatives like conservative surgery. In this paradoxical debate in which both sides accused the other of recklessness and haste, they made the political point of

35 M. Sarazin, *Récits sur la dernière guerre franco-allemande* (Berger Levrault & Cie, 1887); Brice and Bottet, *Le Corps de santé militaire*, p. 397.
36 Chenu, *Aperçu historique, statistique et clinique*, vol. 1, p. 490.
37 J. C. Chenu, *Rapport au conseil de la Société française de secours aux blessés des armées de Terre et de Mer* (Le siège, 1876), p. xxxvii; ASSAT, box 62/17.
38 For instance *La Guerre illustrée* published calls to the Armée du Nord dating from 1792 and stressed the relevance of revolutionary patriotism, 20 (1/10/1870). See B. Taithe 'Reliving the Revolution: war and political identity during the Franco-Prussian war', in B. Taithe and T. Thornton (eds), *War: Identities in Conflict* (Stroud, Sutton, 1998), pp. 141–56.
39 Jules Favre's famous address to the French diplomatic services of 6 September 1870: 'Our soldiers swear to be worthy of their heroic brothers of Alsace and to die like they did', *Recueil officiel des actes du Gouvernement* (Librairie Administrative de Paul Dupont, 1871), p. 370.

presenting conservative surgery as made of caution: 'while *éliminatrice* surgery seems outstanding in the way it cuts through limbs and problems, conservative surgery calculates and does not decide anything *a priori*. While the former is based on a rapid decision, I was about to say a *brutal* decision, the latter is based on circumspection, not on shyness but on prudence.'[40]

Conservative surgery encouraged 'Nature's healing efforts'.[41] Conservative surgery could, in the perspective of a long war of attrition, provide a fair return on casualties who would have been irretrievably lost if subjected to primary amputations. Their opponents opposed what they saw as a vain struggle against reality and as the denial of the total defeat of September 1870. Radical surgery accepted the unavoidable, saved more lives and seemed cheaper and decisive. Surrender on German terms would also meet the same conditions in spite of the fact that the German terms after September 1870 meant the loss of a safety zone made of Alsace and northern Lorraine.

I do not intend to argue that the two analyses, the medical and the political, were in any way consequential from one another or even consciously correlated. They were two tropes of national discourse, two metaphors linked semantically and ideologically into the meta-narrative of war. This fundamental political choice recurred in the professional and private life of many individuals. The choice of continuing the struggle against unfavourable odds overlapped in two distinct professional and political fields. This conflict of views could also be found in later historiographical accounts of the war. One side counted the lost opportunities of the conflict and blamed them for the humiliating defeat, while the other would describe in fatalist terms the inexorable move towards the defeat from either 1789, 1852, or 1866 onwards.[42] The narrative of crisis faced that of *fatum*, of national decline. As a royalist delegate of the Red Cross confided in his diary: 'All great amputations, after a period of good hope end with gangrene or haemorrhage. It is alas a sad consequence of the physical and moral depression of our soldiers since the beginning of this war.'[43] Could it be true that French flesh did not resist surgical interventions any more?[44]

The link between the two fields of surgical theory and national ideology was semantic and particularly to be found among the gems of metaphors: if for a medical chronicler war was 'nothing but a giant vivisection',[45] the defeat was alike

---

40 Chenu, *Aperçu historique, statistique et clinique*, vol. 1, p. 491.
41 E. Grellois, *Histoire médicale du blocus de Metz* (J. B. Baillière, 1872), p. 65.
42 C.-O. Carbonell, 'Les Historiens français chroniqueurs de la guerre franco-allemande et de la Commune, naissance du nationalisme historiographique, 1871–1875', *Bulletin de la société d'histoire moderne*, 13 (1974) 37–56.
43 A. Mony, *Notes d'ambulance, août 1870 – février 1871* (Plon, Nourrit et Cie, 1909), p. 324.
44 L. LeFort, *Oeuvres* ed. Félix Lejars (2 vols, Félix Alcan, 1895–96), p. 117.
45 H. E. Beaunis, *Impressions de campagne, 1870–1871, siège de Strabourg, campagne de la Loire, campagne de l'Est* (Félix Alcan and Berger Levrault et Cie, 1887), p. 2.

the 'throes of death', the loss of Alsace-Lorraine an amputation. These metaphors did not simply illustrate the author's view. As Christiane Sinding and Roger Cooter have pointed out, the medical language structured an epistemological status for medical knowledge which applied throughout society.[46] The rules of the 'linguistic turn' taken by the historiography since the 1980s apply here. These metaphors may only have been metaphors but because of their nature they were transposable and particularly suited to create coherent representations of the post-war situation. The prominence of sentimentalism in most of the literature dealing with the war was a way of coming to terms with a collective shock.[47] It was a manner of understanding and appropriating the national issues as personal grief. Quicherat writing to Jules Michelet found medical metaphors best expressed his feelings: 'One cannot believe it sometimes; then when one must face reality, one falls prostrated; it is the consequence of painful operations on weak organisms.'[48]

James Nisbet's Catholic tale of the conflict embodied the French drama: the soldier is first wounded: 'after taking the dismembered limb in his left hand and kissing it, he said, "with these hands I have kept my poor and aged mother", and not till then, the tears coursed down'. Later he dies: 'and Peace was made at once – the terms, complete surrender; in return, the fullness of the immortal God was now his portion; rest, liberty, and love his lot forever!'.[49] The recurrence of such body metaphors was made possible by the strong anthropomorphism of French republican body politics and national identity. I would also argue that the medicalisation of French political representations extended to the historiography and representations of the Commune and of the nation at large. The image of Marianne, incarnating the French Republic, dominated anthropomorphical French body politics very early on. This anthropomorphism grew into an artistic convention during and after the conflict in the works of Falguière, Meissonier, Puvis de Chavanne.[50] At another level, the close identification made during the French Revolution of territory with the nation, territory with the Republic, and of Marianne with France within its 'natural' borders, was common among republicans and Bonapartists in 1871. This series of reifications and identifications structured the French national imagery. Arguably, this identification rooted their nationalism around a common ideal of national integrity as defined in all French constitutions. After the 4 September revolution, enthusiastic republicans around Gambetta attempted to

46 C. Sinding, *Le Clinicien et le chercheur* (Presses Universitaires de France, 1991), pp. 149–50, 237; R. Cooter, *Surgery and Society in Peace and War* (Macmillan, 1993).
47 For instance, the sickly sweet novellas of Alphonse Daudet, *Les Contes du Lundi* (Maxi Poche Classiques Français, [1873] 1995).
48 J. Quicherat to J. Michelet, 7/07/1871, quoted in Digeon, *La Crise allemande*, p. 48.
49 J. Nisbet, *Wounded in War: A Tale of August 1871* (n.p., 1871), p. 12.
50 P. Sesnot, *1870–1871, l'année terrible* (Musée d'Orsay, 1994), pp. 5–12. France, Marianne, the spirit of the siege are all represented in the painting of Puvis de Chavanne or the sculpture of Falguière.

revitalise French enthusiasm with revolutionary speeches, imagery, and representations dating from 1792–93.[51] After the surrender of January 1871, only the extreme left and the Commune used this form of suddenly dated revolutionary language.

In this context the loss of a province, like Alsace-Lorraine,[52] especially Alsace-Lorraine, could only be represented as a loss of *national* territory, a geographic fragment of national identity and as an amputation. Alsace-Lorraine, although linguistically mostly Germanic, had long been a hotbed of French nationalism, a strong Bonapartist area and with an abundant supply of volunteers and soldiers.[53] *The Marseillaise*, recently reintroduced as a national anthem during the war, had been written in Strasburg for the armies of the Rhine.

The left and Bonapartists, in an unlikely alliance, were in a majority in favouring a war of attrition, *la guerre à outrance*, until the Germans' defeat or until they renounced any territorial gains.[54] While Gambetta managed to create army after army from very little, the moderate Thiers represented the peace party at the Franco-German negotiating table.[55] The 4 September government knew the cost of defeat from late September 1870 and chose to postpone the surrender until late January. It took six months to defeat the partisans of war. Those days lived in the expectation of a miracle were the days of conservative surgery. Eventually Adolphe Thiers and his supporters won and the French lost most of the territories claimed by the German high command. When Thiers read the act of armistice at the Bordeaux assembly, Zola reported: 'It seemed to me that I saw in Mr. Thiers' hand the tool of the surgeon whom, amidst tears, severs a limb and dresses a wound with all his energy'.[56]

This metaphor of Thiers 'the surgeon' practising heroic surgery with dexterity and calm, chopping off Alsace-Lorraine and then the Commune from the French body politics, can be found in a diversity of texts favourable to Thiers, ranging from Zola in 1871 to Bernard von Bülow, later Chancellor of Wilhelm II.[57] The urgency of this surrender was justified by the unwillingness of the provinces to risk a worse defeat than the one already perceived. A direct political

---

51 J. P. T. Bury, *Gambetta and the National Defence: A Republican Dictatorship in France* (Longmans, 1936), p. 179.

52 D. Fustel de Coulanges, *L'Alsace est-elle allemande ou française?* (E. Dentu, 1871).

53 F. Roth, *La Lorraine dans la guerre de 1870* (Nancy, Presses Universitaires de Nancy, 1984), on the revanche in Lorraine, pp. 99–100.

54 L. Dupont, *Tours et Bordeaux, souvenirs de la république à outrance* (E. Dentu, 1877), pp. 307, 414. 'They [the representatives from Alsace-Lorraine] wished that the interest of France be sacrificed to that of their province.'

55 'Circulaire du délégué du ministre des affaires étrangères aux agents diplomatiques de France', 29/11/1870, *Recueil officiel des actes du Gouvernement*, pp. 575–8.

56 E. Zola's article in *La Cloche* (5/03/1871) and J. Kayser (ed.), *La République en marche* (Fasquelle, 1956), p. 66.

57 B. von Bülow, *Memoirs, 1849–1897* (London and New York, Putnam, 1932), p. 473.

consequence of this surrender was the revolution in Paris, while most of France elected moderates and royalists to Parliament in Bordeaux. The Chambre des Députés met in the municipal theatre which Zola compared to an operating theatre: 'Let us leave as soon as possible this red theatre lit in broad daylight like a vault, this ward where France had a limb amputated!'[58]

Adolphe Thiers himself felt the need to use medical metaphors the day he became the leader of the provisional government to explain the constitutional vagueness of his temporary republican regime: 'when we have taken from the field this wounded hero we call France; when we have dressed his wounds, given him his strength back to him, we will leave him to himself; and, recovering then, sane again [liberté de ses esprits], he will tell how he wishes to live'.[59] Thiers, unlike Zola, chose to express his political anthropomorphism in male terms. France was not the republican Marianne but that wounded soldier who, near the battlefield, does not enjoy his full sanity, and upon whom primary amputation should take place. The diminished responsibility and the constitutional weakness of the nation justified a decisive act. This metaphor was immediately taken on by the authorities of the French Red Cross who carried on using it even after the Commune and the civil war. Comte E. de Flavigny started his report investigating the future of the Red Cross in those terms: 'Our ambulances are now disorganised and our hospitals vacated [by the soldiers], but we must still care for "this wounded hero we call France" and all our united efforts will not go amiss to help a convalescence.'[60]

Almost simultaneously, another set of medical metaphors appeared to deal with the new national crisis created after the beginnings of the Commune in March 1871: that of the obsidional fever (fever created by a long siege) and that of collective madness.[61] The latent temporary insanity implied in Thiers's analysis became a universal causality in Maxime du Camp's analysis of the Commune.[62] Similarly the conflict between Versailles and Paris oscillated on both sides between negotiated settlement and open conflict, between mending the body politic or severing the opposition from it.[63] Zola again summarised in La Débâcle the meaning of the agony of a Communard:

58   Zola, in Kayser (ed.), La République en marche, p. 69.
59   'Discours du Chef du pouvoir exécutif de la République Française', 22/02/1871, in Recueil officiel des actes du Gouvernement, pp. 83–6.
60   E. de Flavigny, Bulletin de la société française, délégation du conseil central de la société à Tours (13/06/1871).
61   Dr Legrand du Saulle, 'L'État mental des parisiens pendant le siège de Paris', Chronique Médicale (1896) 77–80, 119–21, 147–51; P. Lidsky, Les Écrivains contre la Commune (François Maspéro, 2nd edn, 1982), p. 54.
62   M. du Camp, Les Convulsions de Paris (4 vols, Hachette, 1878–80) and Les Ancêtres de la Commune (Charpentier, 1877).
63   P. G. Nord, 'The party of conciliation and the Paris Commune', French Historical Studies, 15:1 (1987), 1–35.

Remember what you told me, the day after Sedan, when you said it wasn't bad to be slapped from time to time.... And you added that when one had some rot somewhere, a rotten limb, it was better to leave it on the floor, felled by an axe, rather than die of it as of cholera.... I often thought about that conversation since I found myself by myself, locked in this demented and miserable Paris.... Well, I am the rotten limb you cut off. ....[64]

After the early days of May, the initiative was in the hands of Versailles. Adolphe Thiers had long believed French political turmoil originated in some identifiable and 'surgically' removable sections of Paris.[65] Politicians of the majority, around Adolphe Thiers, blamed the Communards for much of the defeat of France in 1870, as the symbols of alcoholism, syphilis, degeneracy and as the legitimate target for the violent purge from French body politics of May 1871.[66]

Medically speaking, the victory of conservative surgery was principally retroactive and historiographical in the 1880s and 1890s.[67] Politically speaking, the defeat was complete in the short term. By 1873, the Bonapartists had lost hope in a restoration, the republicans saw the adulteration of their hopes into a republic dominated by monarchists, meanwhile those who had survived the Commune suffered in the harshness of prison life in New Caledonia.

With hindsight, nevertheless, the French historiography was kinder to the losers than to the moderates. The latter had sacrificed two provinces and the symbols of national unity to the altar of social stability in the hope of a religious and moral regeneration of France. The radicals had wanted to find in the war itself the modalities of a social and political regeneration. The medical debate happened to have a similar dynamic and an overlapping metaphorical lexicon. This overlapping had at least another consequence in the increase of the numbers of MPs practising medicine. As Jacques Léonard and later Jack Ellis have noted, the French Parliament saw the rise in a whole generation of GPs, physicians and surgeons.[68] Yet this rapid rise from 5 per cent to 12 per cent of the lower house did not reflect, for at least the first twenty years of the Third Republic, a similar increase in parliamentary awareness of sanitarian or health-related issues.[69] The usual notability status attached to provincial medical luminaries had not been such a powerful

---

64 E. Zola, *La Débâcle* (La Pleïade, reprint, 1990), p. 907.
65 A. Thiers, *Notes et souvenirs de Monsieur Thiers, révolution du 24 février* (n.p., 1902), p. 48.
66 D.-J. Joulin, *Les Caravanes d'un chirurgien d'ambulances pendant le siège de Paris et sous la Commune* (E. Dentu, 1871), p. 86.
67 E. Delorme, *Traité de chirurgie de guerre* (2 vols, Félix Alcan, 1888–93), vol. 2, p. 356. 'The experience of the 1870 war consecrated anew the practice of conservative surgery.' Or the self-proclaimed pioneer Lantier, *L'École antiseptique conservatrice*.
68 J. Léonard, *La Médecine entre les savoirs et les pouvoirs* (Aubier Montaigne, 1981), pp. 280–8; J. D. Ellis, *The Physician-Legislators of France: Medicine and Politics in the Early Third Republic, 1870–1914* (Cambridge University Press, 1990).
69 Mitchell, *The Divided Path*, pp. 88–93.

electoral argument before the war either. I would suggest that the relevance of medical men for the electorate increased with the accentuation of the forms of national anthropomorphism mentioned earlier. Apart from the scientific alternative to the Catholic Church that many medical candidates, often *libre penseurs* or militant anticlericalists, offered to the electors, they also presented a curing alternative to prayer for the nation at large.[70]

After the conflict, the Catholic Church, in a redemptive mood reminiscent of the 1815 restoration,[71] launched a massive movement of public subscriptions to erect expiatory buildings across France.[72] High above the urban landscape and political turmoil the Sacré Coeur de Montmartre in Paris, Notre-Dame de Fourvière in Lyons and Notre-Dame de la Garde in Marseilles dominated the three cities where Communard politics had once ruled.[73] The need to expiate came from an analysis of the atheistic horrors of the Commune and also from the prophetic message represented by the defeat itself.[74]

This conflict of ideologies confronted the two major allegories of the French nation: Marianne and the Virgin Mary.[75] St Napoleon's day under the First and Second Empires, for example, had been fixed on 15 August, the day of the Annunciation, the traditional day of the Virgin Mary.[76] Medical men offered in their own personae the secularist recourse to national reconstruction. Georges Clemenceau, in his Parisian free practice at 20 rue des Trois Frères, opened in July 1871, posed as a secularist saint.[77] Similarly, Émile Combes won over his electorate in the Charente department, a Bonapartist stronghold, by his charitable practice.[78] Jean Moreau, the 'doctor of the poor', also made it in Creuse through

70 *GMP*, 25 (1870) 483: 'the studies he has been through bent him towards Liberal ideas ... He is therefore called to contribute to the general movement happening now. ....'.
71 A. Chalanet, *Les Bienfaits de la guerre et les leçons de la défaite* (Lyons, Mérat, 1871), p. 11.
72 A. Mitchell, *Victors and Vanquished: The German Influence on the Army and Church in France after 1870* (Chapel Hill, University of North Carolina Press, 1984), pp. 121–8, 159–69.
73 D. Harvey, *Consciousness and the Urban Experience* (2 vols, Oxford: Basil Blackwell, 1992), vol. 1, pp. 221–50; R. A. Jones, 'Monuments as ex-voto, monuments as historiography: the basilica of Sacré Coeur', *French Historical Studies*, 18:2 (1993) 482–502.
74 *Apparitions prophétiques d'une âme du purgatoire à une religieuse d'un monastère en Belgique en 1870, par l'auteur des 'voix prophétiques'* (Bruxelles, 1871); prophetic statements abounded such as the Blois prophecy, the prophecy of Avignon and other apparitions of the Virgin Mary. *Le Salut public* (Lyons) (1/11/1870); *Le Réveil de la province, journal Limousin* (Tulle) (19/11/1870); J. Gadille, *La Pensée et l'action politiques des évêques français au début de la Troisième République* (2 vols, Hachette, 1967), vol. 1, pp. 229–37.
75 This conflict can often be found on *monuments aux morts:* D. G. Troyansky, 'Monumental politics: national history and local memory in French *monuments aux morts* in the Department of Aisne since 1870', *French Historical Studies*, 15:1 (1987) 121–41.
76 Agulhon, *Marianne au combat*, pp. 74, 157–208.
77 J. D. Ellis, *The Early Life of Georges Clemenceau, 1841–1893* (Lawrence, Regent Press of Kansas, 1980), p. 60.
78 J.-M. Mayeur, *Les Débuts de la IIIième République 1871–1898* (Nouvelle Histoire de France, Le Seuil, 1973), p. 91.

his disinterested practice of medicine.[79] The relevance of their 'science' or 'art' was less important than the charitable values and the hope of cure they incarnated. While Thiers and his allies offered a period of *recueillement*, a period of moral meditation or even a time of prayer and atonement for a God-given scourge,[80] nationalists of the left and right would offer a period of *redressement*, a period of convalescence to cure war wounds.[81]

Outliving war

At the more prosaic level of lived experience, war victims met a diversity of fates. The ones who died on the open fields found a resting place in cemeteries located near the battlefield and their resting place marked the topography with locations of remembrance which could later be exploited. Originally dumped in common mass-graves, army officers made sure that their respective troops remained separate in the afterlife and later had them segregated even in the most difficult circumstances such as the siege of Metz.[82] The army had toyed with the idea of cremating corpses but had bowed to religious pressure. In a short note, Larrey compared in two columns the advantages and disadvantages of cremating bodies:

Advantages:	Disadvantages:
replaces burials: prophylactic against typhus and epidemics, suppresses the risk of deleterious miasma from the buried corpses, preserves from bad burial practices and grave robbing, preserves remains for the families.	religious and social opposition, against our customs and family mourning; medical objections: difficult to manage, lack of means, dangers of fires, nature and quantity of gases released, dangers of suffocation.[83]

Considering these objections the army did not dare to cremate bodies until the massacres of the Commune and had to cope with modified civilian and customary practices.[84] In Paris soldiers who died in hospital, in the hands of conservative or radical surgeons, were buried at the Assistance Publique's expenses or privately in

---

79 Ellis, *The Early Life of Georges Clemenceau*, p. 64.
80 *Lettre de Mgr l'évêque de Nîmes au clergé de son diocèse sur les enseignements et les consolations attachés par la Providence à nos derniers désastres* (Nîmes, Soustelle, 1871).
81 This emphasis on redressement led to the development of sports in France: P. Arnaud (ed.), *Les Athlètes de la République* (Toulouse, Privat, 1987) and *Le Militaire, l'écolier, le gymnaste* (Lyons, Presses Universitaires de Lyon, 1991).
82 Grellois, *Histoire médicale du blocus de Metz*, p. 88.
83 ASSAT, box 62/8, Handwritten note.
84 T. A. Kselman, *Death and the Afterlife in Modern France* (Princeton University Press, 1993), pp. 65–124; M. Wheeler, *Heaven, Hell and the Victorians* (Cambridge University Press, 1994), pp. 50–68; D. Ligou, 'L'Évolution des cimetières', *Archives de sciences sociales des religions*, 39 (1975) 61–77.

local cemeteries.[85] A special commission convened from 19 September attempted to identify and send to the families the various corpses, but this action was limited by the constraints of siege warfare and the total isolation of provincial soldiers in Paris, many of whom did not speak French and could not be easily identified.[86] To solve the problem, photographic records were systematically taken. A few generous ambulance-keepers afforded the expenses and later informed the families of their own accord.[87] Prisoners in Germany found their final resting place there as well and were later re-buried thanks to a subscription of the Oeuvre des tombes jointly paid by public subscription and by Red Cross funds.[88] The society eventually initiated memorial inscriptions in the churches of their towns and villages and added to privately funded memorial publications.[89] Even discharged soldiers who died in hospitals mostly escaped the investigative scalpel of medical students because the faculty was closed,[90] the morgue full, and post-mortem dissections meaningless.[91] The scope for medical observation at the expense of soldiers proved rather disappointing for medical experts and in contradiction to international hopes in the 'goodness of war'.

This superabundance of corpses and the lack of an effective burial organisation turned this debate on its head. The shallow graves of the Franco-Prussian war literally emerged as an important health issue in 1871. The conclusions of the Comité consultatif d'hygiène aux ministres de l'agriculture et du commerce linked directly the bad burial practices due to the urgency of battlefield burials and the sick curiosity of Parisian bystanders:

---

85 AAP, 542 Foss 4, 29/12/1870, Report on the burial of soldiers whose bodies are not claimed back. The Assistance Publique later claimed back the expenses from the army.
86 AAP, 542 Foss 120, Commission pour l'enlèvement des morts.
87 J. P. Bonnefont, *Ambulances internationales et privées* (Bureau de l'Union Médicale, 1871), p. 2.
88 F. L. C. A. de Beaufort, *Questions philanthropiques – transport des blessés – hôpitaux– appareils. Assistance aux mutilés pauvres, etc* (Imprimerie Nationale, 1875), pp. 137–8. Vovelle sees the 1870 war as an intermediary stage in the celebration of war casualties; while buildings were relatively unevenly distributed, the funds were national. M. Vovelle, *La Mort et l'Occident de 1300 à nos jours* (NRF, Gallimard, 1983), p. 649.
89 P. d'Albigny, *Le Livre d'or du département de l'Ardèche, contenant la liste des enfants de ce département morts en 1870–1871* (Privat, Roure, 1879); C. de Lacroix, *Les Morts pour la patrie, tombes militaires et monuments élevés à la mémoire des soldats tués pendant la guerre* (l'auteur, 1891), for later developments see J. M. Winter, *Sites of Memory, Sites of Mourning: The Great War in European Cultural History* (Cambridge University Press, 1995).
90 Civilian corpses were stored at the great *morgue* of Clamart from which hospital teachers routinely dissected unclaimed corpses. The availability of fresh corpses for anatomical purposes since the French Revolution had long been a great attraction of studying in Paris. R. Durand-Fardel, *L'Internat en médecine et en chirurgie des hôpitause et hospices civils de Paris* (Steinheil, 1904), pp. 107.
91 The officers regularly sent corpses to Clamart well into the civil war. AAP, 542 Foss 121, 26/04/1871.

> There are in suburban communes some graves where the corpses are literally breaking the surface of the ground and whose extremities rise above the ground, others whose putrefied and blown up abdomens emerge and display the dreadful spectacle of fly larvae eating a human being. A crowd looking for strong emotions is going, especially on Sundays, to these burial fields, and one of us [member of the committee] saw the bystanders search with their walking sticks, or even their hands, the few inches of ground above the corpses, uncovering body parts without any apparent disgust and releasing the most atrocious stench.
>
> For the sake of morality and decency as well as for sanitation, we must stop as soon as possible this dreadful spectacle.[92]

The conclusions of this report came two days after the Commune insurrection and projected in this disgust a number of fears which were not simply linked to hygienic principles. These searching fingers might have been looking for a friend, a son, a brother buried in haste, for their features lost forever. They may conceivably have been digging for curiosity's sake. The fact that only the latter possibility was contemplated by the committee showed that the real, metaphorical corruption was with the Parisians themselves, who seemed so unaffected by the stench of rotting flesh. The Communard crowds digging the corpses of a lost war make for a powerful political image to which more corpses were to be added.

The Communards, far from being carrion crawlers, had a specific cult of death too,[93] and, emulating in this the revolution of 1848, paraded funeral processions throughout the town, showing the deepest respect for their war victims.[94] During the Commune the Assistance Publique's amphitheatres routinely resumed their dissection work discreetly and behind closed doors. The administrators feared a violent mob reaction to the dissection of soldiers.[95] The outrage at the display of bones and mummified corpses from various churches and nunneries further illustrates this point. Documents fail to discuss the manner in which Communards buried their enemies. As their war was essentially made of retreats and little ground was gained after the first few weeks of the insurrection, the issue may not have arisen often. On the other hand, the repression of the Commune proved violent beyond death. The corpse of Raoul Rigault, unceremoniously shot at the entrance to his hotel, was exposed to the public, spat at, robbed and battered until a stranger covered his face with his coat. Other key Communards' corpses

---

92 'Rapport du Comité consultatif d'hygiène aux ministres de l'agriculture et du commerce' quoted in its entirety in O. du Mesnil, 'L'Hygiène pendant le siège de Paris', *Annales d'Hygiène*, 2nd series, 35 (1871) 413–28, pp. 421–4.
93 Vovelle, *La Mort et l'Occident*, pp. 625–50.
94 D. Marion and L. Perrin, 'La Commune et l'Église' (Mémoire de Maîtrise, Université de Paris X–XII, 1981), pp. 80–1, 90–1; P. O. Lissagaray, *History of the Paris Commune of 1871* (New Park Publications, 1976), p. 273; G. Jeamenet, *Paris pendant la Commune* (Neuchâtel, Le Guillaume, [1871] 1968), p. 57.
95 AAP, 542 Foss 121, 26/04/1871.

were only grudgingly surrendered to their families on their undertaking to keep the place of the burial discreet if not secret. Corpses were distributed throughout the various cemeteries, and while some expenses figures remain, the exact location of many of these mass graves was kept secret. Louise Michel describes the scene thus: 'All those buried in haste were swollen beneath the earth, like the germinating harvest, they were rising, breaking the surface.'[96] The Versailles government, like following republican governments, knew that graves had too much political meaning, especially when they gave opportunities for subscriptions to build monuments, statues and celebrations of anniversaries. The Second Empire had had its share of political trouble around tombstones from Baudin to Victor Noir.[97] It is highly symbolic that the *mur des fédérés*, a site of executions in the Père Lachaise, remained in the historiography as the symbol of the last days of the Commune, in spite of the fact that it was not the last stronghold of the Commune. Figure 11 shows how important matters of burials had become when corpses, still wearing their red scarves, escape from the mass grave. In the same spirit the French republican governments would resist the erection of monuments to the Commune voted by the Conseil Municipal of Paris until the late 1890s.[98]

War survivors, crippled and wounded, could not be disposed of so easily. Their broken bodies, which had been so fashionable during the war and especially during the siege of Paris, lost their attractiveness in the aftermath of the peace treaty and the end of the insurrection. Many remained in hospitals and ambulances well into 1872, then, gradually, they were moved out of Paris to provincial convalescence hospitals and then they were discharged into the care of their families or whoever wanted them.

From the outset of the war funds had been voted to help the victims of the conflict. Fifty million francs were set aside for that purpose and attributed to a Commission pour la distribution des secours merging with another imperial institution, the strangely named Caisse des offrandes nationales (fund for national donations), which had provided very small pensions since 1860 from 50 francs for a crippled private to 500 francs for a disabled general.[99] From the 50 million francs from the state one had to add 12 million in donations. Of this, only 27 million was

---

96 L. Michel, *La Commune, histoire et souvenirs* (2 vols, Maspéro, 1970), vol. 2, p. 66; also see Jeamenet, *Paris*, p. 193.
97 A. Ben Amos, 'Molding the national memory: the state funeral of the Third Republic' (Ph.D. thesis, University of California, Berkeley, 1988), pp. 83–5; also see on Mgr Darboy's funeral, p. 150.
98 AN, F/ICI/170, 'Délibération du conseil municipal pour l'érection d'un monument aux fédérés fusillés en 1871'.
99 A.-H. O. de Riencourt, *Les Militaires blessés et invalides* (2 vols, Jean Dumaine, 1875), vol. 2, p. 85; idem, *Insuffisance des pensions accordées aux militaires blessés* (Lachaud, 1872); idem, *Instructions pour le service de l'oeuvre des pensions militaires* (Abbeville, Paillart, 1883); idem, *Manuel des blessés et malades de guerre* (Dumaine, 1876); ASSAT, box 65/2–3; E. Dupuy, *De la situation des invalides en Allemagne et en Autriche Hongrie* (Librairie Jean Dumaine, 1874).

Figure 11 *Le Mur des Fédérés: You need regiments to guard corpses like these!* 1873

spent, most of it through the *garde nationale's secours* or unemployment benefits during the war.[100] To these barely touched funds one had to add the Légion d'honneur, which, beyond the honour it bestowed on the recipient, also entitled them to a very modest pension. Wounded soldiers received remarkably little from funds often raised in their names and using images of their plight. While generally acknowledged, this situation was not dealt with by the state but through specific charities in the first instance. Adolphe Thiers's wife led a parliamentary and aristocratic association to help the crippled: the Oeuvre des amputés de la guerre.[101] This organisation, based on *dames patronesses,* members of the charitable middle class,

[100] Riencourt, *Les Militaires blessés et invalides*, vol. 1, p. 31.
[101] ASSAT, box 65/1, *Circulaire de l'oeuvre des amputés de guerre.*

used familiar charitable networks and Catholic connections to raise 168,287 francs, which were almost entirely employed to equip some 1,651 crippled soldiers with artificial limbs and help another 2,781.[102] Comte de Beaufort had also created a small society in 1868 for the poor cripples in order to equip them with limbs of his own design.[103] After the war, Baron Larrey became its president and gave new impetus to this small fund. One of the great advantages of a fund for the cripples was that 'charity cannot be misguided, a mutilation cannot be simulated'.[104]

Foreign organisations and Red Cross committees[105] also directed their remaining funds towards the making of several, often competing designs of artificial limbs.[106] Since November 1870 the French Red Cross had made the provision of artificial limbs one its policies alongside a funeral service and a floral wreath.[107] These measures prepared simultaneously three forms of war commemoration: the dead would be honoured, the grave marked and the crippled mended. The Red Cross also distributed the official honours bestowed to the dying before creating its own Red Cross medals for the humanitarian volunteers. Beyond the symbolic measures, most of the practical help towards rehabilitating the maimed bodies of 1870 veterans came from charitable funds and not from the state.

There were many types of artificial limbs and prostheses.[108] Costly facial disfigurements, artificial jaws, palates and noses were designed by dentistry firms to solve the most hideous cases of disfigurement which provoked mixed reactions of horror and pity.[109] The unfortunate Étienne Rouland, aged twenty-five, who lost his chin and lower jaw 'from the second molar to the left to the third on the right side of his jaw', spent seven months dribbling, his tongue hanging loose, until a military dentist obtained his custody to experiment on him with a complex prosthesis. His prosthesis, composed of a palate, false teeth held together with gold attachments, and a silver chin holding to the neck through a leather and latex

---

102 Riencourt, *Les Militaires blessés et invalides*, vol. 2, pp. 100–1.
103 *L'Assistance aux mutilés pauvres*, bulletin trimestriel, 1883–88.
104 Beaufort, *Questions philanthropiques*, p. 118.
105 L. de Cazenove, *Compte rendu des travaux du comité sectionnaire lyonnais de la Société française de secours aux blessés et malades des armées de terre et de mer* (Lyons, Imprimerie de Bellan, 1872), p. 16.
106 Boulogne English Committee SASW, *Red-Cross Operations in the North of France, 1870-2* (Spottiswoode and Co., 1872), p. 31; G. Moynier, *La Croix Rouge, son passé, son avenir* (Sandoz et Thuillier, 1882), pp. 129–30.
107 *Bulletin de la Société française de secours aux blessés militaires des armées de terre et de mer*, rapport de M. le Docteur Chenu, 10 (1871) 425.
108 E. Spillmann and G. Gaujot, *L'Arsenal de la chirurgie contemporaine* (2 vols, J. B. Baillière et Fils, 1867–72); G. Fajal, 'L'Histoire des prothèses et des orthèses' (2 vols, Thèse de doctorat de médecine, Université de Nancy (1), 1972), vol. 2, pp. 9–160; Fajal rightly remarks that there is a different type of prosthesis per patient.
109 Appareil Delacroix for instance. Facial disfigurement through diseases and accidents had long been treated this way.

harness, was both costly and extremely strange.[110] Behind the latex lips, under the fake beard, silver tubes enabled the saliva to be sucked back into the throat.[111] Each case of facial disfigurement or even amputation required the same enthusiastic ingenuity and philanthropic expenses.[112] Dr Delalain concluded his report on Private Rouland by stating: 'I have done everything in my power for this boy to be satisfied. I am happy if I have contributed to prove once again the benevolent solicitude of most doctors in the military service de santé for their patients.'[113] Delalain stressed the difficulties he had overcome to be allowed to treat Rouland. Such an expenditure of time and resources was allowed by the army eventually, but did not become army policy. By stressing the gratuitous nature of this type of effort, the army medical services reinforced the philanthropic status of military medicine while avoiding the establishment of a costly precedent. During the First World War, on the other hand, the number of facial wounds and disfigurements led to a very different approach to the question of facial prostheses.[114]

For the limbs prices ranged from the crudest wooden stumps at 20 francs, to more complex articulated wood, metal and leather implements like Comte de Beaufort's design at 30 francs,[115] or those of the orthopaedic firm Werber which replaced forearms for 15 francs and whole arms for 30.[116] These inventions claimed to re-establish some of the functions of the lost limbs. Beaufort used complex systems and mechanical traction to enable these limbs to function

---

110 S. Maillet, 'Des origines de la prothèse jusqu'à la prothèse adjointe totale' (Thèse de doctorat d'état en médecine, Université de Paris (6), Broussais Hôtel-Dieu, 1986), pp. 66–100, 110–15. Some earlier experiments by Gunning during the American Civil War had mostly dealt with artificial noses. In France the slow developments of dentistry made this sort of treatment a rare occurrence until the end of the nineteenth century. See F. Busquet, 'La Prothèse nasale dans l'oeuvre de Claude Martin' (Thèse de médecine, Université de Lyon, 1974), pp. 3–18; P. Haik, 'L'Histoire de la prothèse en rapport avec l'évolution des techniques et des matériaux' (Thèse de doctorat de chirurgie dentaire, Université de Paris (7), 1991); T. Delaume, 'Contribution à l'étude de la prothèse totale: son évolution du XVI au XIXe siècle' (Thèse de chirurgie dentaire, Université de Strasbourg (1), 1988).

111 See the 'Album de prothèses maxillo-faciale' written by Charles Delalain, displayed in the Bibliothèque Centrale du Service de Santé.

112 Facial plastic surgery is a later development of specialisation in France pioneered by Hippolyte Morestin (1869–1919), in the decade immediately before the First World War. B. Boutroux, 'Hippolyte Morestin, 1869–1919' (Thèse de doctorat d'état, Université de Nancy I, 1978); N. Nessakh, 'Histoire de la chirurgie plastique, reconstructive et esthétique' (Thèse de doctorat, Université de Besançon, 1995).

113 ASSAT, box 62/14, 'Note remise à Monsieur le Baron Larrey by Ch. Delalain', 55 bataillion of Mobiles, June? 1871.

114 J. Martinier and L. Lessurle, *Prothèses restauratrices bucco-faciale et traitement des fractures des maxilliaires* (J. B. Baillière et Fils, 1915).

115 Comte de Beaufort had been perfecting a number of designs since the the late 1840s, and was almost alone in this field. See *Recherches sur la prothèse des membres* (P. Asselin, 1867), p. 3.

116 Riencourt, *Les Militaires blessés et invalides*, vol. 1, pp. 314–38; Beaufort, *Questions philanthropiques*, pp. 113–14. Over the period 1871–73 Werber delivered 564 artificial limbs; other French makers produced the same models on a smaller scale. Other limbs came from abroad.

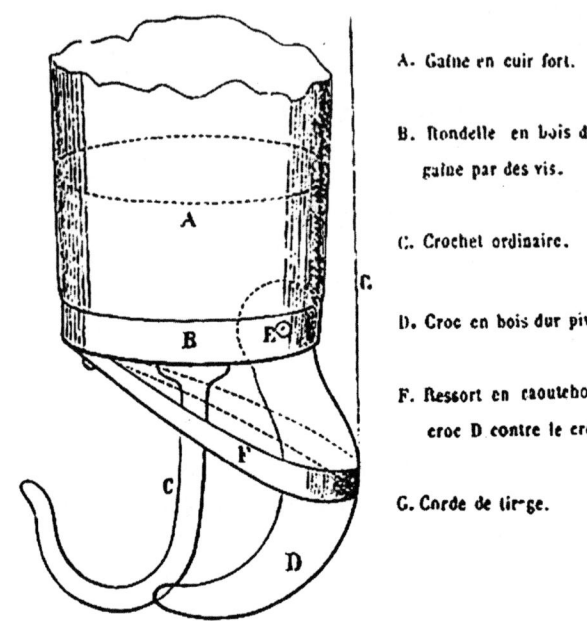

Figure 12 The hand as tool: 'Crochet-pince' – the de Beaufort working-class prothesis

correctly. The hand especially was controlled by minute ropes linked to the stump. In spite of the artist's impressions, these implements looked and functioned crudely like tools attached to the body. Beaufort's machines had fixed fingers and a thumb which turned the 'hands' into a clamp (see Figure 12).[117] The assumption was that the wounded needed to convert their bodies into productive units, into mobile tools which would allow them to resume their mostly physical occupations. Jean-François Montes has noted that the concept of a specific professional re-education tailored for the needs of the war-wounded or for those suffering from accidents did not really exist in France before 1870.[118] Beaufort's research into low-cost technology made the crucial difference between prostheses and 'professional prostheses' by developing a worker's clamp which had no pretensions to imitate a hand: 'the worker can, at the end of the day, leave the ungracious implement in his workshop or factory'.[119]

The evidence suggests that people were not provided with a set of interchangeable body parts fitting to a specific employment or various social

117 Beaufort, *Recherches sur la prothèse*, pp. 66–78.
118 J. F. Montes, 'La Réhabilitation professionnelle et l'emploi des mutilés du travail et des mutilés de guerre en France de 1898 à 1957', in F. O. Touati (ed.) *Maladies, Médecines et Sociétés* (2 vols, Recherches, L'Harmattan, 1993), vol. 2, pp. 253–67.
119 Beaufort, *Recherches sur la prothèse*, p. 90.

circumstances until the First World War.[120] Workers received the sturdy body-tool apparatus which compensated for the loss of industrious body-parts; officers received the less useful but aesthetically more pleasing fake arms with which writing and normal social interaction were possible (see Figures 13, 14 and 15).[121] The army administration adopted Beaufort's complicated models for their staff from 1864. Only officers would be retained in service after an amputation at that stage, while the Assistance Publique adopted both the 'arm with a useful hand' and the articulated clamp-hook costing a fraction of the more realistic prosthesis.[122] Crudely summed up, there was an assumption that the body could be itemised and replaced mechanically and financially.

Beyond replacing flesh with wood and leather there was no attempt to understand that an unfamiliar body, an unknown body, could be alienating and destructive for the tooled individuals. The medical literature noted this issue in terms of tolerance and patience. Some of the technical choices at the time of the operation itself mattered. The German circular method using 'flaps' of flesh was described as an improvement on the Lisfranc–Dupuytrens methods which produced stumps ending with painful raw muscle scars. J. H. Porter, who won the Queen of Prussia's essay for the most useful guide on 'the practical treatment of the wounded at war', commended Teale's operation which 'aimed at a better stump' cushioning the muscle tissues with fat and skin.[123] Even when treated with the greatest care, the body itself rebelled against the new attachments and tools. Irritations, callosity, tumours even, could grow in any space between the flesh and the leather and could make the prosthesis unbearable to wear. By this constant interaction between the flesh and the prosthesis, the '*invalide*', the crippled, often remained perpetually ill.

Even in the more successful cases of conservative surgery, inoperative arms were only 'capable of very little use and a source of constant anxiety, lest it receive injury'.[124] Their illnesses not only came from the scars but also from the missing limb itself which still existed in their minds and made them suffer from ghost rheumatism or gout.[125] In practical terms it also meant that the care specific to

---

120 P. Rozan, *Blessés de guerre, prothèse et orthèse professionnelles* (Berger Levrault, 1919); Bourke, *Dismembering the Male*, p. 47. Bourke points out that British cripples were not provided with artificial limbs at state expense until the welfare state.
121 Beaufort, *Questions philanthropiques*, pp. 102–3. Beaufort always made a point of printing the manuscript letters he received from the recipients of his charity using one of his artificial arms.
122 Beaufort, *Recherches sur la prothèse*, p. 95.
123 J. H. Porter, *The Surgeon's Pocket Book* (Harrison and Sons, 4th edn, 1875), pp. v, 158, 166, 189.
124 Berkeley-Hill, *Treatment of the Sick and Wounded*, p. 29.
125 The 'phantom limb' phenomenon was often observed almost as a psychological curiosity. More detailed studies of the real sufferings coming from phantom limbs were published during and immediately after the Second World War. B. Cronhalen, 'Phantom limbs in amputies', in *Acta Psychiatrica et Neurologica Scandinavia* (Copenhagen, 1951), supplement 72; J.-M. Octave de Lassard, 'Les Membres fantômes des amputés' (Thèse de la faculté de médecine de Paris, 1944).

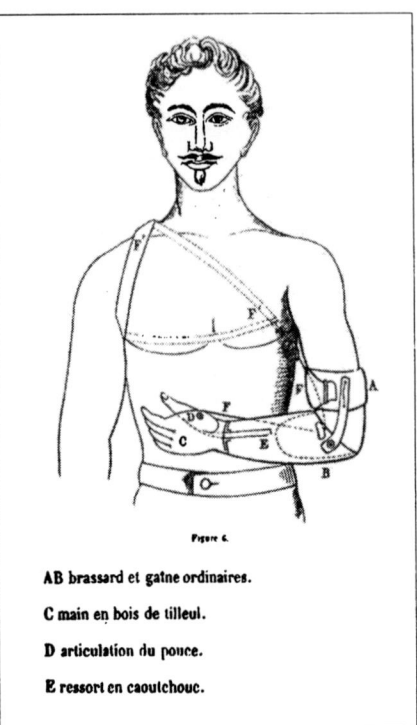

Figure 13 The wooden limb as ornament – the de Beaufort middle-class prothesis

AB brassard et gaîne ordinaires.

C main en bois de tilleul.

D articulation du pouce.

E ressort en caoutchouc.

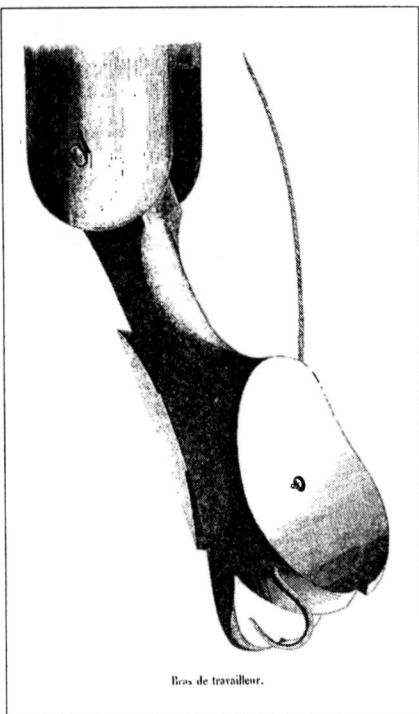

Bras de travailleur.

Bras de travailleur. — Côté gauche.

Figures 14 and 15 Labourers' arms – note that workers' bodies and faces do not appear and that illustrations of protheses at work usually refer to agricultural labour

Table 15 **Pension rights awarded after the war**

Category	Pension rights (francs)
1st and 2nd class: constant care	780 (blindness or two limbs)
3rd and 4th class	600 (one limb lost or two damaged)
5th and 6th class	500 (use of one limb or smaller injuries)
Orphans, ascendants	0
Unregistered in time	discretionary 180

Source: Anne-Honoré Olivier, Comte de Riencourt, *Instructions pour le service de l'oeuvre des pensions militaires, rédigées en 1879 et revues en 1883* (Abbeville, Paillart, 1883), p. 7. For blindness see H. -J. Nimier, *Les Blessures de l'oeil pendant la guerre de 1870–1871* (Archives de Médecine et de Pharmacie Militaire, 1889).

those who had lost a limb could be much more costly and longer than was first thought. The Swiss charities in Basel that added to their repatriation mission the distribution of prostheses, recognised that two identical artificial limbs were often necessary per amputee.[126] Beyond this initial expenditure maintenance work or replacement expenditures would continue for the patient's lifetime. Regardless of the long-term implications, Madame Thiers's foundation ran out of goodwill and funds in 1874, three years after the end of the war. The state administrations themselves intended to settle the issue and their budget once and for all as soon as possible after the conflict.

Debts of honour were much more costly for the state and pension rights had to be paid to the wounded of both the war and the civil war. Unlike the veterans of 1830 whose poverty had been so forcefully depicted by Daumier, 1870 veterans were entitled to a meagre pension pro-rata to their losses.

Here again the figures given in Table 15 illustrate the itemisation of the body and a very narrow understanding of their usage in society. The basic assumption before a case could be processed was that the individual could be defined as a 'cripple' (*infirme*), i.e. someone without the ability to earn a living. This definition only applied to privates and non-commanding officers. Officers would enter a different category, either by being employed in spite of their handicap, or by being entitled to a retirement pension. These figures were purely related to production and loss of income, rather than to suffering and inconvenience. Pension rights had also been attributed to the Parisians who had suffered from the siege and the bombing. Strasburg or Metz civilian victims were not treated so generously and did not obtain pension rights. Claiming this money was difficult and slow. After the defeat most regimental archives were either lost or destroyed. Many units only lasted a few weeks; *francs-tireurs* units were even more difficult to track down. So much so that many soldiers returned home empty-handed and without the means

[126] Cazenove, *Compte rendu des travaux du comité sectionnaire lyonnais*, p. 47.

of claiming back their pension rights or even unaware that military pensions existed. Indeed from the few accounts left to us by the patients themselves, some were more likely to receive the unpaid bills relating to their treatment than a medal or a pension. Charles de Montesson, for instance, was wounded at the battle of Coulmiers on 9 November 1870. Being an officer and a gentleman he was taken in by a small private ambulance for the nine months his broken leg took to heal. On his departure the grateful civilian he had become left 250 francs to pay some of the medical expenses, only to receive a further bill for 600 francs when he returned home.[127]

The *sociétés de secours mutuels* (friendly societies) which had maintained their services in spite of the loss of income during the war were unable to pay compensation on war wounds.[128] More generally, after the immediate aftermath of the conflict, enthusiasm, support and funds dried up.

In 1875 a number of aristocratic figures like Comte de Beaufort and Comte de Riencourt, who had already been involved in the Red Cross, started to campaign for the public recognition of unknown war heroes. Their campaign for better prostheses and pensions was based on traditional aristocratic values dating from the foundation of Les Invalides by Louis XIV. These two openly royalist figures obviously thought it their social responsibility to champion the cause of good Frenchmen and they redefined their social position in humanitarian terms.[129] Their birth rights acquired meritocratic value through the practice of thinly veiled old-style charity using the new language of humanitarian work and sickly sentimentalism. In a speech to the twin association *L'Oeuvre* for the poor cripple, Beaufort finished his speech thus: 'This is how, ladies and gentlemen, you make smiles of happiness replace tears. To the thanks of the poor cripple will be added ours, as, through your precious donations, we have the privilege of being the humble brokers [*mandataires*] of charity.'[130]

The first campaign was against the petty administrative deadlines which stated that wounds unregistered by 1875 were not to be recognised by the state. Riencourt, Beaufort and their friends sent a *Manuel des blessés et malades de guerre* to all the 35,000 mayors of France. In 1876 this set of guidelines was followed by a letter to all Protestant and Catholic clergy and obtained another deadline in 1877 for state registrations. By January 1877 they had dispatched another 80,000 copies of their circular and had contributed to the opening of 1,500 cases previously unrecorded. Riencourt estimated the unrecorded war victims at

127 C. de Montesson, *Souvenirs d'ambulance, 1870–1871* (Le Mans, Monnoyer, 1885), p. 86.
128 J. Bernet, *La Mutualité et la guerre* (Etampes, Société Régionale d'Imprimerie et de Publicité, 1962), p. 4.
129 Beaufort, *Questions philanthropiques*, p. ii. The book was dedicated to his Royal Highness the Duke of Nemours.
130 *L'Assistance aux mutilés pauvres* (01/1888) 292.

another 6,500 in 1882. From 1878 onwards the Oeuvre des pensions militaires became the voluntary organisation in charge of the propagation of information and the defender of pension rights against the administration.[131] One of their principal targets were the local Commissions de réforme which 'united with the Commissariat' in its crusade against malingerers. Army-appointed doctors were treated with the same contempt as the pen-pushers in central administrations.[132] These campaigns had some success in winning over a few more pension rights and in keeping the issue alive. The newly established Republic was not allowed to forget that it had originated in a defeat.

The political aims and the motivations of this campaign are quite difficult to decipher. There is clearly an anti-administrative slant to these writings, and there is also the expression of disgust at the manner in which the war soon lost its centrality in public debates. The none-too-comfortable moral order of the early days of the Third Republic left little time to think sympathetically of the defeats of the Empire *and* the Republic. Pension rights were an expense careful administrators were keen to reduce. Systematic destruction of regimental records every seven or eight years eventually simplified the task by making regular archives almost as poor as the republican army ones had been in 1870. The administrative hurdles in the way of any applicant appeared like a disgrace to these aristocrats and retired officers who cultivated a very romantic and personal vision of the nation. Heroism and duties were analysed as reciprocal obligations between the state and the individuals. The petty-mindedness of officials and the dust-gathering routines of the administration served a dishonourable purpose for these aristocrats. Service and masculinity were deeply imbricated in their vision of citizenship and were at the heart of a vision of veteranship.[133] Because these notions remained embedded in charitable practices and hierarchical structures, they never achieved a subversive status resembling the veterans' organisations which blossomed in continental Europe after the First World War.[134]

Nineteenth-century war veterans had always played a minor part in the twilight of a bygone age. The soldiers from Napoleon I's army who came to weep by the fallen Vendôme column when the Commune pulled it down were perceived as remnants and ruins of a distant past. Their political significance after the fall of the Second Empire was minor. War-wounded veterans of the 1870 war could potentially have a much greater role after the loss of Alsace-Lorraine. The writings of

---

131 Riencourt, *Les Blessés oubliés*, pp. iii–viii.
132 Riencourt, *Les Blessés oubliés*, p. 24.
133 I. Woloch, *The French Veteran from the Revolution to the Restoration* (Chapel Hill, University of North Carolina Press, 1979), p. 195. The notion of *armée morte* used for revolutionary veterans did not recur in 1870. Veterans acquired a more silent identity voiced by self-appointed spokespersons like Beaufort.
134 N. Barr, 'The British Legion after the Great War: veterans or civilians', in Taithe and Thornton (eds), *War*, pp. 213–33.

Paul Déroulède, Alphonse Daudet, Maurice Barrès, or even Émile Zola emphasised the physical dimension and consequences of the war on the survivors. *Souvenirs* societies in Alsace-Lorraine, local museums, monuments and the excruciating Sedan day on the other side of the border all contributed to the making of a *revanche* spirit glorifying another war. In this imagery, veterans tend not to be the mutilated ones. Unlike the *gueules cassées* of the twentieth century inter-wars, 1870 cripples slowly disappeared from sight and lost some of their war specificity.[135] In practice their war experience lost its importance.

The loss of Alsace-Lorraine had far more meaning than their individual suffering.[136] National memory could on the one hand be constantly stimulated collectively by referring to common anthropomorphic imagery, and on the other be dull, indifferent and ignorant of human costs. Arguably exalted memories of war cannot comfortably cope with crude images of warfare and suffering.

Conclusion

The superimposition of national and social priorities onto individual ones in time of war made for coherent choices often transcending the limits of a professional or political field. There was a consistency between ideology and praxis. This set of representations also turned into a hall of mirrors reflecting actions and ideologies so that it becomes futile to argue that one preceded the other. The crisis was that of a loss, of the war, of a province, losing touch, losing the national and individual integrity, the physical and moral integrity. The heroic act of the surgeon cutting away dead flesh turned into that of the butcher chopping off what cannot be used. If it is true that all nations are narration, a last literary example might suitably conclude and summarise this argument.[137] In Zola's *La Débâcle*, the best novel on the war, there is a scene of striking emotional strength during which the surgeon of Sedan cut through flesh for hours.

> The fear of haemorrhages made Bouroque amputate immediately... at the feet of the corpses, severed limbs lay pell-mell, legs and arms formed a heap, everything that was cut off and trimmed out, everything felled on the operating tables, the butcher's broom swept up, pushing into a corner the rubbish, flesh and bones.[138]

While the sufferings often do not stop after the loss of a limb, the conspicuous silence that surrounded the issue of Alsace-Lorraine in post-1870 France was

135 S. Delaporte, *Les Gueules cassées, les blessés de la face de la grande guerre* (Noêsis, 1996). For a Second World War equivalent see D. Gerber, 'Anger and affability: the rise and representation of a repertory of self-representation skills in a WWII disabled veteran', *Journal of Social History*, 27:1 (1993) 5–28.
136 Fajal, 'L'Histoire des prothèses et des orthèses', vol. 1, p. 128.
137 E. Said, *Imperialism and Culture* (Chatto and Windus, 1993), pp. xii–xxx.
138 Zola, *La Débâcle*, p. 673.

made of unspoken resentment. Resentment of the enemy, resentment of a series of violent losses, resentment of oneself. Remembering to forget, French politics revolved around this lost territorial and *therefore* national integrity, remembering the land,[139] forgetting the men.

139 Poetic rhetoric structured this imagery of borders see: H. Baye, *La Frontière, essais de poésie* (A. Lacroix, Verboeckhoven & Cie, 1871); Bergerat, *Strasbourg*.

9 Seeds of defeat: alcohol and syphilis

The enemy within is always blamed for the collective defeat as the rotten apple corrupts the barrel, and doubts weaken the heart and the arm. Not everybody believed in the revolutionary songs of September 1870, or those of March 1871. Indeed some provincial French people reluctantly carried on the war and many harshly judged Gambetta's frantic actions to create army after army, regiment after regiment. At a medical level, the preceding chapters have shown that French flesh under the knife did not heal well, went septic and was prone to sudden attacks of hospital rot and septicaemia. The superiority of German soldiers was emphasised by British observers and Frenchmen alike. The invaders paraded their 'broad chest', their sturdy bodies and strong features. They had coarse manners and a unique ability to drink large amounts of alcohol without showing the signs of a debilitating drunkenness.[1] The French soldiers, on the other hand, let themselves down by drinking their way to a hospital bed. The merchants of gloom constantly compared the victors with the vanquished, the soldiers standing for the nations.

Most texts written immediately after the wars focus their concerns on three scourges with which historians of the *fin de siècle* are very familiar: syphilis, tuberculosis and alcohol. As Robert Nye has shown about France, these diagnostics of contamination and addiction structured to a large extent the French *fin de siècle*. The academic debate mentioned in the conclusion of Chapter 4 represented the most scientific and rational aspect of these fears. More popularly the siege was perceived as the source of a specific form of madness fostered by abuses of alcohol, political speeches, unemployment and licentiousness. Maxime du Camp among many others, but more emphatically than most, denounced the Commune as the grotesque child of this insanity. Others saw the Commune as an aberration and as the product of the collective madness that seized over-excited brains after a long confinement and the abuse of alcohol. Paul Lidsky has depicted this literary down-pouring of abuse and excuses which revealed less than it hid, which was far less about understanding and far more about condemning and erasing.[2] Alcohol could also be held directly responsible for the physical degradation of individuals. Alcohol-induced septicaemia and delirium combined to kill the wounded drunkard.[3] The secondary

---

1 *The Lancet*, 2 (3/09/1871) 349, 579; A. Flamarion, *Le Livret du docteur, souvenirs de campagne coutre l'Allemagne et contre la Commune de Paris* (Le Chevalier, 1872), p. 30.
2 P. Lidsky, *Les Écrivains contre la Commune* (François Maspéro, 2nd edn, 1982), pp. 24–76.
3 A. Poncet, *Le Siège de Strasbourg (1870) hôpital militaire, service de la première division des blessés* (Montpellier, Boehm et Fils, 1873), p. 77.

literature has, on the whole, tended to take these pessimistic diagnostics at face value and retrospectively attribute to them the momentum of the war. Ground-breaking studies of the French temperance movement like Patricia Prestwich's book followed this tradition and start in 1870 when they really focus on the more animated turn-of-the-century debates.[4] The literature on syphilis and prostitution has, on the whole, been more interested in representation than practice, and dwells often heavily on the strident scaremongering of the late nineteenth century.[5] The literature on tuberculosis deals mostly with the later period and the golden age of the sanatorium.[6]

The importance of the war in this medical historiography is contradictory and often paradoxical. While the defeat seemed to provoke the most pessimistic forecast and juiciest soundbites, it did not have the same clear-cut impact on practices. While 1870 often seems a good turning point, the impact of the war is frequently diffusely avoided. In the post-Foucauldian historiographical trends, shifts take place, epistemological breaks happen, they do not deserve to be explored historically. In Quêtel's history of syphilis, knowledge seems self-propelled, discovery and paradigmatic changes stand proud of any social causalities or parallel political developments.[7] While the war in itself did not cause anything, new social and political priorities of the war meant that medical and political agencies re-distributed responsibilities and zones of control between themselves. The military perception of society, with its insistence on discipline and battle fitness, certainly shaped the historical meanings of the defeat and pointed at ready-made explanations and pre-existing but often marginal medico-social fears.[8]

Of the three emblematic scourges syphilis, alcohol and tuberculosis, only the former two were clearly identifiable to explain military inferiority among volunteers and were undeniably consequences of carelessness and excess.[9] Tuberculosis on the other hand, like rickets, was seen as an opportunistic disease

---

4 P. E. Prestwich, *Drink and the Politics of Social Reform: Antialcoholism in France since 1870* (Palo Atto, Cal., Society for the Promotion of Science and Scholarship, 1988).

5 D. S. Barnes, *The Making of a Social Disease: Tuberculosis in Nineteenth-Century France* (Berkeley, University of California Press, 1995), pp. 74–111.

6 P. Guillaume, *Du désespoir au salut : les tuberculeux au XIXe et XXe siècles* (Aubier, 1986).

7 The history of sexuality cannot be written in one country and some of the importance changes that took place in post-1870 regulation France need a broader perspective. See B. Taithe, 'Consuming desires: female prostitutes and "customers" at the margins of crime and perversion in France and Britain c. 1836–1885', in M. Arnot and C. Usborne (eds), *Gender and Crime in Modern Europe* (University College London Press, 1999).

8 Ruth Harris rightly points out that the *fin de siècle* did not see the invention of fears of heredity, madness and crime but a renewed emphasis on these issues. *Murders and Madness: Medicine, Law and Society in the Fin-de-Siècle* (Oxford, Clarendon Press, 1989), p. 51.

9 The three were often represented together see *Art and Information to Prevent Disease: France in the Early Twentieth Century: Tuberculosis, Venereal Disease and Alcoholism* (Atlanta, Department of Health and Human Services, 1993).

of both alcoholism and syphilis,[10] and remained chronic and difficult to track down and prevent while paradoxically receiving later more attention than either syphilis or alcoholism.[11] This chapter will thus look first at the social construction of drunkenness and alcoholism and then analyse the measures taken to contain the spread of syphilis.

In the first instance the fears and the legislation targeted not alcoholism in the modern sense but drunkenness and drunken antisocial behaviour. In the second instance the practice of the regulation of prostitution in Paris went through a tumultuous year and was significantly altered by the war experience and military priorities. On the whole these seeds of defeat pinpointed easy scapegoats and the same dangerous classes which had haunted bourgeois views of society since the 1830s.[12] Yet this prognosis of French decline allowed for hope in the future. Both alcohol and venereal disease could be medically transposed, studied, and, supposedly, socially contained. This chapter argues that, in spite of atavistic fears found in French literature from Gobineau to Zola, such a clear diagnosis left much scope for remedial action and expert professional advice. In other words, the crisis had a dynamic side-effect and reinforced claims to expertise and the rise of a French 'technocracy'. When Jules Andrieu found in the defeat and the Commune a proof of his views on the terminal decline of 'Latin races', he added the caveat 'unless France, regenerated by education, became the last and invincible lead'.[13]

From the cabaret to the grave

Many historians have questioned the consumption figures which made France the leader of per capita alcohol consumption in the world, while social historians have paid much attention to the different social practices attached to alcohol.[14] Regional variations in patterns of alcohol consumption are quite astonishing, while the various types of alcohol consumed reflected the absence of a national market.[15] Wine, the hygienic drink recommended by Dr Onimus of the hygiene commission, was produced very extensively across France before the philoxera

---

10 D. Nourisson, *Le Buveur du XIXe siècle* (Albin Michel, 1990), pp. 184–5.
11 Guillaume, *Du désespoir au salut*, pp. 112–15; M. E. Teller, *The Tuberculosis Movement: A Public Health Campaign in the Progressive Era* (New York, Greenwood Press, 1988), pp. 10–12.
12 L. Chevalier, *Classes laborieuses et classes dangereuses* (Plon, 1958); B. M. Ratcliffe, '*Classes laborieuses et classes dangereuses à Paris pendant la première moitié du dix-neuvième siècle*? The Chevalier thesis reexamined', *French Historical Study*, 17:2 (1991) 542–74.
13 J. Andrieu, *Notes pouvant servir à l'histoire de la Commune de Paris en 1871* (Payot, 1971), p. 31; A. de Quatrefages, *La Race prussienne* (Hachette, 1871)
14 Popular history is particularly attentive to alcohol: P. Fouquet and M. de Borde, *Le Roman de l'alcool* (Seghers, 1985), pp. 159–60; *Histoire de l'alcool* (Presses Universitaires de France, 1990); *L'Alcool, boire et déboire* (Hachette, 1991).
15 D. Nourisson, *Le Buveur du XIXe siècle* (Albin Michel, 1990), pp. 1–45.

disaster of the end of the century. Cider and cider-based spirits were predominant in the north-western provinces, beer in the north and the east, and a multitude of spirits were produced by privileged *bouilleurs de crus* who distilled themselves their own fruits and by the great alcohol industry converting sugarbeet into various synthetic drinks.

Both small-scale or industrial production found various outlets, from the dance halls of the suburban areas of Paris to the cafés and bistros of the smallest Commune. The recent literature has, on the whole, been quite descriptive and poured scorn on bourgeois fears while emphasising the centrality of the café and bistro experience for the French working class.[16] Warm and friendly bars make for nostalgic accounts of tightly knit communities and brotherly working-class sociability. The flip side of that coin is the recent literature on crime and domestic violence which often replicates late-nineteenth-century observations by pointing at the bistro as the cause of violent behaviour.[17] From another, more detached perspective, increased alcohol consumption figures could also be analysed as the index of rising living standards. The 1902 parliamentary enquiry made that assumption and, under intense lobbying from the wine-producing areas of France, took the reassuring view that wine drinking was a necessary part of French diet.[18] This attitude cannot be said to be threatened, and in spite of Prestwich's great amazement the general perception of an alcohol problem in France in the later years of the nineteenth century did not lead to harsh legislative measures or stringent alcohol retailing control. The story of French temperance movements, like that of French Protestant churches with which they often were associated, remains a minority interest in the current historiography.

In this context the rhetoric of 1870–71 could ring particularly hollow were it not for the fundamental difference one has to draw between the concepts of alcoholism and drunkenness. As Sournia and Prestwich pointed out, the term alcoholism entered Dechambre's French medical dictionary in 1865, thirteen years after its translation from the Swedish work of Magnus Huss which itself dated from 1849.[19] In other words, the medical nosology followed recent developments and created a category of substance abuse specific to alcohol very late in the history of alcohol consumption in Europe. Alcohol excess by 1870 had been well identified and discussed for a very long time. Experiments conducted in the 1860s showed

---

16 M. C. Delahaye, *L'Absinthe, histoire de la fée verte* (Nancy, Berger Levrault, 1983); H. M. de Langle, *Le Petit monde des cafés et débits parisiens au XIXe siècle* (PUF, 1990); A. Corbin, *Time, Desire and Horror: Towards a History of the Senses* (Cambridge, Polity Press, 1997).
17 D. Nourisson, 'La France alcoolique des années 1870' (*Rapports d'activité*, centre de recherches d'histoire quantitative, 1984), pp. 264–72.
18 Prestwich, *Drink and the Politics of Social Reform*, p. 23.
19 J.-C. Sournia, *A History of Alcoholism* (Oxford, Basil Blackwell, 1990), p. 69; Prestwich, *Drink and the Politics of Social Reform*, p. 38.

that animals injected with large doses of alcohol died painfully. On the human scale of things, a major difference was made between industrial alcohol such as absinthe or *gnole*, spirits, and food-alcohol such as wine. Wine was considered a nutrient of great importance and rich of vital elements. The medical advice on alcohol distributed by the Commission d'hygiène in October 1871 was thus somehow contradictory as sobriety figured prominently in the introductory notes while in the following pages wine was deemed to be only second best to a nourishing soup. A few pages later, alcohol was supposed to favour the loss of body heat. Like most medical texts on nutrition in 1870, this pamphlet made a clear and commonly held distinction between alcohol food and alcohol recreation.[20] Absinthe or spirits were the almost exclusive stuff of bar drinking patterns while wine could be drunk at home, in the workplace or in a more congenial setting.[21] Some of this ingrained attitude would later undermine the Association française contre l'abus des boissons alcooliques founded in 1872.

The role played by alcohol during the siege of Paris and the Commune is difficult to assess critically as most of the available evidence is not strictly contemporary to the events and is informed by the counter-revolutionary medical discourse on alcoholism and atavism.[22] From the bulk of the primary material it appears that the armies that went to war rarely went thirsty and received much encouragement and libations on their way to Sedan. The spectacle of drunken squadrons and regiments was deplored on the one hand but also signalled a lively national support for the war. Wine was an important part of the soldiers' rations and remained so during the war. In volume, however, the half-litre of wine compared poorly with a qualified worker's daily consumption of 2 to 6 litres.[23] When the bread became poorer in texture the municipal authorities of the VIII arrondissement distributed free wine to compensate for the loss of quality and nutritive value.[24]

There is also no evidence that soldiers consumed more alcohol than previous armies had in the past, and there is no evidence that many suffered from alcohol intoxication. There is, on the other hand, evidence that alcohol distribution contributed to and reflected the organisational nightmare of the mobilisation of

20 Prestwich, *Drink and the Politics of Social Reform*, p. 37.
21 'Health Condition of Paris', *The Lancet*, 2 (2/09/1871) 342.
22 F. Dumoulin, 'Le Débat sur l'alcoolisme après la Commune (1871–1887)' (Mémoire de Maitrise, Paris X, Nanterre, 1979); S. Barrows 'After the Commune: alcoholism, temperance and literature in the early Third Republic', in J. M. Merriman (ed.), *Consciousness and Class Experience in Nineteenth-Century Europe* (New York, Holmes and Meier, 1979), pp. 205–18; M. R. Marrus, 'Social drinking in the belle époque', *Journal of Social History*, 2 (1974) 115–41; Nourisson, *Le Buveur du XIXe*, pp. 208–9.
23 Nourisson, *Le Buveur du XIXe*, p. 35.
24 VdP, VD6/1586/3, *Histoire des services ordinaires et extraordinaires du huitième arrondissement durant le siège*, 1874, p. 75.

July 1870. As seen in Chapter 2, this failure to organise successfully was much deeper and more structural than a few impromptu street-parties. The war accounts which almost always stress the embarrassment of too much heavy drinking paradoxically emphasise the Germanic heavy drinking habits. Alcohol fell short of being a viable explanation for the French defeat when the coarser and stronger teutonic warriors could eat poor food and drink 'enormous quantities of alcoholic liquors ... without intoxication' while still belonging to a disciplined and efficient war machine.[25]

Alcohol did acquire an important rhetorical purpose in explaining the siege fever (*fièvre obsidionale*), the madness of besieged crowds. Here again there is nothing really surprising emerging from contemporary accounts. Wine was stocked in large quantities near Jussieu, and Paris also had breweries and distillers to produce more alcohol. The government, however, did not assess alcohol reserves as being much in excess of normal consumption for three months. On 31 December 1870 rumours abounded that wine was going to be requisitioned by the government and only be available on ration cards.[26] Wine was rationed to soldiers. Observers stress the fact that soldiers crowded the cafés and that enterprising alcohol dealers had opened their stalls and bars (*estaminets*) near the walls in order to provide for the army to such an extent that the military high command had to close them down.[27] There is no doubt that even watered down and adulterated alcohol could have strong effects on a weakened and starved frame. Adulterated drinks provoked cases of:

> furious drunkenness. . . . After ingesting a certain quantity of spirit, not a large quantity according to witnesses, this drunkenness was followed by a violent delirium which made the treatment of these men very difficult; after their evacuation to the Beaujon Hospital, the man named Fergner died there two days later after showing unusual signs of cerebral excitation.[28]

Surgeons bathing in blood and repeatedly failing their operations did not hesitate to blame the bad patients.[29] Bad patients could 'neither stand their disease nor the prescribed treatment'.[30] This image could then easily be applied to the political

25 *The Lancet*, 2 (3/12/1870) 791; 1 (28/01/1871) 133.
26 P. Ch. Joubert and A. de Vresse, *De la défense de Paris pendant le siège au point de vue de l'alimentation* (Arnault de Vresse, 1871), p. 22.
27 ASSAT, box, 62/17, General order to canteens, 6/10/1870.
28 ASSAT, box, 63/4, Letter from Médecin en Chef du 5e secteur to the admiral Du Quilio, 6/11/1870.
29 O. Faure, *Genèse de l'hôpital moderne, les hospices civils de Lyon, 1802–1845* (Lyons, Presses Universitaires de Lyon, 1982), p. 191. To blame the patient for the high hospital mortality was not uncommon even in peace time. What is different here is the direct link between a mental state and a substance abuse.
30 L. Fiaux, *L'Hygiène militaire, esquisses historiques et médicales à propos d'un bataillon de la garde mobile de l'armée de Paris* (Victor Rozier, 1871), pp. 49–50.

turmoil in Paris. By December academicians started to make direct comparisons and implicit descriptions. Overexcited speech and revolutionary behaviour betrayed the influence of drink: 'the rapid speech, the jerky delivery, betrays the cerebral over-excitement which only a doctor can recognise ... having firmly diagnosed alcoholism, I gave a fatal prognosis.'[31]

However, army discipline did not collapse because of alcohol consumption but rather because it was never forcefully enacted in the first place. Citizen-soldiers who drank as civilians drank in uniform. The idleness of military life and chronic unemployment combined with the cold made the bars all the more attractive. There is little doubt that desultory drinking took place among soldiers; some even brawled and fought under the influence of alcohol during their rest time. It is difficult to judge how many participated in these displays of public drunkenness. Relatively few were prosecuted but this might reflect more on the weakness of the police and army discipline. The only real figures available show that liver failure and other directly alcohol-related diseases decreased considerably over previous years and remained relatively rare.[32]

With the closure of theatres, ballrooms and operas, cafés and *estaminets* remained alone to provide Parisians with drink and rumour, wine and politics. The role of alcohol in the physiology of revolutionary enthusiasm had been well documented in past revolutions. The historiography following Michelet had clearly associated the September prison massacres of 1792 with drink.[33] In 1870, like in 1792, revolutionary meetings often took place in common rooms available to the working class and turned the café into a hot bed of alcohol consumption and radical agitation. French radicals knew this and, like Gambetta, later defended the bistro as the symbol of working-class democracy.[34] The 4 September government's ambivalent position towards radical clubs and cafés reflected a certain empathy with the more libertarian aspects of revolutionary democracy and a knowledge that drink and politics were vital revolutionary rights for their popular support. This conjunction of alcohol and politics was not heavily stigmatised during the siege. Similarly the unfitness of the French army could only be partially attributed to the *dive bouteille*. The locus of concern during the siege was drunkenness and not alcoholism. One is tempted to paraphrase Mary Douglas and argue that drunkenness could be defined as heavy drinking out of place. Many of the charges of drunkenness could simply be attributed to the illusions of universal conscription and mobilisation. The ultimate danger was mentioned in places:

31 *BAIM*, 35 (1870) 974.
32 ASSAT, box 63/2, Register of death taking place in December 1870 Hôpital du Gros Caillou, 6/01/1871. Only 0.9 per cent of the deaths were related to alcoholism.
33 J. Michelet, *Histoire de la Révolution Française* (2 vols, Robert Laffont, [1847; 1868] 1979), vol. 1, pp. 847–8.
34 Prestwich, *Drink and the Politics of Social Reform*, p. 18.

soldiers might forget their role under the influence of drink and fraternise during a battle, or after a surrender.[35] The problem of drink and discipline became the universal excuse for the failures of the citizens' army. Paris was a city infinitely more complex than the largest military camp and the various types of soldiers – *gardes mobiles*, regular soldiers and *gardes nationaux sédentaires* and *de marche* – did not share a common identity or respect of military hierarchies.

On the other hand, popular perceptions of middle- and upper-class excesses were also deeply exaggerated. The alcohol lamps which burnt by the windows of the Grand-Hôtel ambulance to heat dressings and herbal teas were widely perceived as being the blue flames of punch bowls. The Préfecture de Police was seized under the political pressure of club denunciations and Chenu had to demonstrate that orgies did not take place at the Grand-Hôtel.[36] This debate about alcohol consumption reveals the chasm that opened between classes during the siege and the deep doubts about each other's morality and sanity.

Maxime du Camp and a generation of naturalist writers from Daudet to Zola are largely responsible for historical views of the siege and the Commune as the combined climax of working-class excess and imperial corruption. They were supported in their analysis by a whole literature of medical history and collective psychology which took over the naive physiology of revolutionary enthusiasm, going as far as calling it the '*morbus democraticus* or democratic madness'.[37] To explain better the political turmoil of 1870–71, conservative medical writers invested it with teleological meanings and medical jargon.[38] They often presented the Commune as an orgy or the overflowing of a moral sewer. The police and armies of the Commune were more specifically targeted by this bilious literature. Raoul Rigault, aged twenty-five, Chief of Police and one of the key leaders of the Blanquist wing of the Commune, became the most criticised individual of the insurrection.

Rigault belonged to the bohemian society of the Latin Quarter and while being the son of a high-ranking official had spent his student days studying the police.[39] After the 4 September revolution he managed to become part of the police administration of de Kératry. Following Blanqui he then took part in the 31 October insurrection and was sacked. After 18 March, Rigault and his friends took over the Préfecture de Police and re-established its functions as a political and crime-prevention instrument. Here again, there is not much evidence left of Rigault's

---

35 H. E. Beaunis, *Impression de campagne, 1870–1871, siège de Strasbourg, campagne de la Loire, campagne de l'Est* (Félix Alcan and Berger-Levrault et Cie, 1887), p. 63.
36 *Bulletin de la Société française de secours aux blessés militaires des armées de terre et de mer, Rapport de M le Docteur Chenu*, 10 (1871) 409.
37 A. Brierre de Boismont, *L'Union médicale* (24/06/1871); idem, 'A lunatic asylum during the siege of Paris', *The Lancet*, 1 (4/03/1871) 301–2.
38 J. B. V. Laborde, *Les Hommes et les actes de l'insurrection de Paris devant la psychologie morbide* (G. Baillière, 1872).
39 C. Prolès, *Les Hommes de la révolution de 1871* (Chamnel,1898), pp. 12–33.

police action and most of his archives were destroyed in the fire of May 1871. His friends and subordinates belatedly supported his action while the socialist radicals like Lissagaray and the Marxist historiography in general condemned him for being a dissipated amateur.[40] One of the more striking aspects of his administration was his reluctance to change his lifestyle and end the student feast of his youth. Rigault seen drunk in the company of his mistress presented ample evidence of the Commune's folly. His men and the guards themselves sometimes used their power to arrest at random a variety of people and drink at the public's expense. To some the Commune turned into a perpetual feast of freedom and transgression; for most, however, alcohol filled the hours of unemployment and boredom.[41]

Here again the nature of the evidence is so sketchy that the picture remains impressionistic. Communards may have drunk more than customary or they may not. Or perhaps they drunk more openly, more improperly than their Versailles counterparts. Their drunkenness, using our earlier definition, was more real in those terms. To a certain extent these issues are irrelevant. Alcohol became a fundamental analytical tool, beside multifarious and enigmatic international socialist plots, to explain the Commune and the final *auto-da-fé* of May 1871. Drunkenness had run the city like a carnival of violence; the more innocuous forms of sociability had turned into brawling and crime. Café politics had been allowed to run the city into self-destruction.

The shift of analysis from drunkenness to alcoholism, and from misplaced behaviour to atavistic and hereditary behaviour, took place after the war and was heavily medicalised from the onset. The Academy of Medicine's debates on alcohol concluded immediately after the end of the civil war and issued a stern warning as to the physical and social consequences of prolonged alcohol abuse.[42] The prize for the best medical essay in 1872 was awarded to best study of the very political topic of alcoholic deliria and their treatments.[43] Later an important congress in 1878 was devoted to the issue of alcoholism.[44] It seems unnecessary to add much to the already large literature devoted to the concept of degeneracy and hereditary diseases.[45] The 1870 war could certainly be analysed as the acid test of racial theories from Gobineau to Bénédicte Morel.[46] The fact that alcohol became

---

40 P. O. Lissagaray, *History of the Paris Commune of 1871* (New Park Publications, 1976), pp. 180–1.
41 L. Baron, *Sous le drapeau rouge* (Nouvelle Librairie Albert Savine, 1889), p. 74.
42 T. Gallard, *Leçons de clinique médicale* (J. B. Baillière et Fils, 1872), pp. 7–9.
43 V. Magnan, *De l'alcoolisme, des diverses formes de délire alcoolique et de leur traitement* (Delahaye, 1874).
44 A. Rabuteau, *Des alcools et de l'alcoolisme : extraits des comptes rendus du congrès international de 1878 pour l'étude des questions relatives à l'alcoolisme* (E. Donnaud, 1878).
45 J. Borel, *Du concept de dégénérescence à la notion d'alcoolisme dans la médecine contemporaine* (Montpellier, n.p., 1968).
46 B. Morel, *Traité des dégénérescences* (J. B. Baillière, 1857); Nourisson, *Le Buveur du XIXe siècle*, p. 215–26.

clearly identified as a source of insanity that could be passed on to following generations is in itself interesting.

More interesting, however, is the fact that so little was done about it in France. The fundamental piece of legislation concerning alcohol was passed in 1873 and aimed principally at the social manifestations of heavy drinking: public disorder and drunkenness. Six months earlier the army had made public drunkenness a punishable offence only for privates.[47] The real political danger was in the lower classes' drunkenness not in alcoholism. Medicalised fears focused on atavism and alcoholism had more literary outcomes in Zola's *L'assommoir* in 1877 and in a multitude of medical doctoral theses.[48] The temperance movement in France never found the religious and social backing it enjoyed in America or Britain. Strong economic pressure also prevented the passing of further legislation. *Fin de siècle* anxieties which have so often been emphasised in the recent development of the historiography may well have been inflated beyond measure.

Early Third Republic France survived the war; the feeling of inferiority and the fear of decline one finds in literary sources were not often translated into practical action or radical reforms. The debate on alcoholism in the 1880s and 1890s carried less weight than that on drunkenness and moral danger of the 1870s. Maxime du Camp's work reflected much more clearly a political anxiety building on forty years of social fears, while Émile Zola's extrapolated on controversial contemporary medical evidence. As Robert Tombs recently argued, the social anxieties crystallised in 1871 focused reform discourses from before the war and gave a lot of impetus to the modernisation of France around its educational and Parisian elite.[49] The discourse on alcoholic heredity and national decline was sterile and could only serve when republicans were in opposition. With the republicanisation of the Third Republic it acquired an aesthetic and literary value but only a minor political role. The other seed of defeat which this chapter discusses is in itself very different. The regulation of prostitution changed in practice during the war and ideologically after the war.

Syphilis

When Émile Zola portrayed *Nana*'s death at the onset of the 1870 war, her dead body displayed the most exaggerated medical and metaphorical symptoms of the

---

47 Nourrisson, *Le Buveur du XIXe siècle*, p. 260.
48 E. Lancereaux, 'De l'alcoolisme et ses conséquences au point de vue de l'état physique, intellectuel et moral des populations' (Thèse de doctorat, Faculté de Paris, 1878); E. Monin, *L'Alcoolisme: étude médicalo-sociale* (Octave Doin, 1889).
49 R. Tombs, *France 1814–1914* (Longman, 1996), pp. 72–5.

historically correct smallpox, yet his description borrowed heavily from the register of syphilis-pox:[50]

> Venus was rotting. It seemed as though the poison she had assimilated in the gutters, and on the carrion tolerated by the roadside, the leaven with which she had poisoned a whole people, had but now remounted to her face and turned it into corruption. The room was empty. A great despairing breath came up from the Boulevard, and swelled up the curtains.
> A Berlin, à Berlin, à Berlin![51]

This anxious ending to the imperial feast figured in the writings of intellectuals, historians, journalists and diarists.[52] The links between contagion and defeat underpinned all forms of narrative and assumed a protean identity.[53] Always different, yet always the same, the sense of defeat informed a multitude of stories. In Émile Zola's biological narrative of defeat, the curse of heredity involved the substance of individuals and their flesh.[54] By studying syphilis during the war one can reflect on a story which turned an individual disease into a symptom *and* an analytical category of French decadence and *fin de siècle*.[55] The process leading to this identification developed in two simultaneous phases. The first was the decline of syphilis as a social and class issue in civilian society. The second was its rise as a national problem in besieged Paris.

A disease is only identified when its nature, vectors, symptoms and dangers are ascertained. Syphilis was deeply associated with one group of people presenting the optimum risk of contagion: prostitutes. The link between the two was especially strong in France and the danger of prostitution had become almost synonymous with the danger of syphilis. As François Buret stated in the late 1880s: 'it can be safely asserted that these diseases are as old as prostitution itself and a necessary privilege of that pursuit'.[56]

In 1870 France had a sophisticated system of municipal police regulation of prostitution. The disease justified the controlling of semi-criminal elements of the population. A political economy of vice had evolved in which prostitutes were the hostages of the police and had to act as informers. They represented a social

---

50 P. Wald-Lasowski, *Syphilis, essai sur la littérature française au dix-neuvième siècle* (Gallimard, 1982).
51 E. Zola, *Nana* (Living Library, 1946), pp. 467–8.
52 C. Digeon, *La Crise allemande de la pensée française* (Presses Universitaires de France, 1959), pp. 113–318. For instance the royalist L. de Montesquiou, *1870, les causes politiques du désastre* (Librairie Française, 2nd edn, 1979).
53 On Renan's reconstruction see B. Anderson, *Imagined Communities* (Verso, 2nd edn, 1991), pp. 187–206.
54 D. Pick, *Faces of Degeneration: A European Disorder* (Cambridge University Press, 1989), pp. 74–96.
55 P. Citti, *Contre la décadence* (Presses Universiatires de France, 1987).
56 F. Buret, *Syphilis Today and Among the Ancients* (3 vols, Philadephia and London, Baillière, 1889–92), vol. 1, p. xi.

danger and the statistical basis of a minimalist sanitarian approach. From the time of the Consulate (1802) onwards, Paris had a specific and highly sophisticated police system to check prostitutes, whether in brothels or on the street. As Erica Marie Benabou has shown, the system of the *police des moeurs* before 1789 was originally political.[57] The Napoleonic Préfecture de Police in Paris, including the *police des moeurs,* controlled many functions normally attributed to the municipalities. It was divided in two divisions with several *bureaux,* each tackling different issues. The first division had five *bureaux,* the first being the criminal police and the *Sûreté* (the political police), the second being the *police des moeurs* controlling prostitution.[58] The third, fourth and fifth dealt with foreigners and management of prisons, lunatic asylums and children's homes respectively. The second division of the police was dealing with statistics, buildings, vehicles, markets, and anything related to public hygiene.

Prostitutes belonged to the first division. They lived on the margin of society among the criminals, among the students, among opponents to the successive authoritarian regimes of the French nineteenth century. Police administrators used prostitutes as informers in their chess game against political and criminal organisations. The hygienic rationale was backed by fortnightly visits to the Dispensaire de Santé of the Préfecture or at 'home' in brothels. The hygienist rationale had never been prevalent in the practice of regulation but it increasingly became a useful shield to deflect critics and closer examination. The work of Parent-Duchâtelet justified the *police des moeurs* with hindsight as a sanitarian measure and integrated it within the positivist arsenal of the public health movement.[59] This logic was so powerful that the issues were never dealt with from another point of view. The necessity of police regulation was always the premise of any examination of the social effects of syphilis and prostitution. Alain Corbin named this framework of regulationism in Paris 'a constraining pattern of analysis of prostitution and syphilis'.[60]

The *police des moeurs* collected names and summoned all the 'working girls' of Paris to register and be examined once a fortnight (1802). Only later did it define the aim to contain prostitution in police-controlled brothels (1804), 'seminal sewers', where men could safely and quickly relieve themselves of their lust.

---

57 E.-M. Benabou, *La Prostitution et la police des moeurs au XVIIIe siècle* (Perrin, 1987); A. Parent-Duchâtelet, *De la prostitution dans la ville de Paris* (J. B. Baillière, 1836); C. J. Lecour, *La Prostitution à Paris et à Londres* (P. Asselin & Cie, 2nd edn, 1872).

58 B. F. Martin, *Crime and Criminal Justice Under the Third Republic: The Shame of Marianne* (Baton Rouge, Louisiana State University Press, 1990), pp. 39–124.

59 A. F. La Berge, *Mission and Method: The Early-Nineteenth-Century French Public Health Movement* (Cambridge University Press, 1992), pp. 188–240.

60 A. Corbin, *Les Filles de noce, prostitution (XIXe siècle)* (Aubier, 1978). See also the more detailed study J. Termeau, *Maisons closes de province, l'amour vénal au temps du règlementarisme à partir d'une étude du Maine-Anjou* (Le Mans, Cénomane 1986).

This first policy on brothel containment failed and an increasing number of prostitutes resorted to living on their own. The balance between freelance prostitutes, *en carte*, and women in brothels was about even by 1870. Beyond the registered prostitutes an unknown quantity of women and men (who were never registered) practised prostitution illegally.[61] The scandal of prostitution paraded openly in the streets and the police increasingly had to justify their action in terms of hygiene.

If a police doctor found an 'unhealthy' woman at the Dispensaire de Santé, he sent her to spend six weeks at Saint-Lazare. Saint-Lazare was a prison for women and a lock hospital. Statistical evidence on syphilis came mostly from such penal institutions and from the army. The powerful central administration of charities and public hospitals of Paris, the Assistance Publique, had also established two specialised hospitals since 1836, that of the Midi for the men and Lourcine for the women.[62] Both hospitals practised 'lock-ins', but not on a compulsory basis. People with money could either resort to private practice or attend as day patients.

Soldiers (mostly professional before 1870) resorted to specialised brothels and had access to the Midi. They made up the only other possible source of statistics on syphilis apart from prostitutes.[63] They were a 'high-risk group' contained in a disciplinary environment. Every syphilitic soldier was punishable and liable to give the name and address of the presumed source of infection.[64] The prostitute-customer couple, the recurrent 'site' for syphilis infection, was saturated with defiance and betrayals.

Reports on the workings of regulation never dealt with the dark side of regulation (although some radicals denounced it). They were unanimously positive on the principles, if not on the material power given to the police. The containment of prostitution/syphilis was altogether spatial, temporal and social: prostitutes lived in brothels or small streets, they came out at certain hours, and the police made sure prostitutes would not climb the social ladder. Class boundaries were secured in police records. Medical and police reports exaggerated the perfect co-operation of the police with medical men. Police regulation worked on a shoe-string, did not properly pay the medical staff they had to use and often questioned their integrity.[65] However unstable or inefficient regulation was on the

---

61 APdP, Db 590, 591, 636 Police des moeurs; Da 223 *filles publiques insoumises,* Da 230 on homosexuals.

62 A. E. Pignot, *L'Hôpital du Midi et ses origines, recherches sur l'histoire médicale et sociale de la syphilis à Paris* (n.p., 1885).

63 J. Garin, *De la police sanitaire et de l'assistance publique dans leurs rapports avec l'extinction des maladies vénériennes* (Rapport à la Société Impériale de Médecine de Lyon, Masson, 1866), p. 16.

64 APdP, Da 225, Lettre au colonel commandent les encampements de Sèvres et Saint Cloud, 29/08/1871.

65 See APdP, series Da 223–232, W. Acton, *Prostitution Considered in its Moral, Social and Sanitary Aspects in London and other Large Cities* (John Churchill, 1857).

Table 16 Breakdown of the people evicted from Paris in August 1870

	French people in *meublés*	Foreigners in *meublés*
July	160,126	35,650
2 September	135,857	29,102
1 October	93,996	8,365
Difference	66,130	27,285

Source: C. J. Lecour, *La Prostitution à Paris et à Londres* (P. Asselin et Cie, 2nd edn, 1872), pp. 296–300.

streets, the principles were part of the imperial order. In that civil order, syphilis was a curable and perhaps even morally useful lesser evil.[66]

Regulationism was a syllogism which implied that the police socially contained a disease.[67] This containment seemed as secure and intangible as the police itself and one had to wait for an upheaval to see it crumble. The 4 September revolution, the *mobilisation générale* and the *levée en masse* meant that every fit man turned into a soldier. Politically marginal, the republican government, legitimated by the mob, was overtaken on its left by socialist, Blanquist and Proudhonist clubs.[68] These Parisian pressure groups were particularly active among volunteers of the Garde Nationale and the Garde Mobile.[69] The soldiers were the people. The people were in arms. This enormously enlarged the representativeness of medical statistics and the size of the 'high-risk' group.

In August 1870, as the prospects of a siege increased, the administration started to prepare Paris discreetly. One of the first aims was to clear Paris of 'useless mouths.' The military governor of Paris decided to send away to the provinces all people renting furnished accommodation (*meublés*, a sign of economic precariousness) on 24 August 1870. Lecour calculated the number of people sent away and his figures are presented in Table 16.

Lecour estimated that out of this large population around 1,000 were known prostitutes. The administration also deported over 3,000 criminals out of Paris, 250 of whom were registered prostitutes afflicted with venereal disease (VD). In

---

[66] Philippe Ricord claimed to be able to cure syphilis with the help of his mercury pills. M. Guignard, 'Philippe Ricord, sa vie, son oeuvre, 1800–1889' (Thèse de doctorat, IHU Lariboisière, 1978). Some attacked his complacent views: P. Yvaren, *Des métamorphoses de la syphilis* (J. B. Baillière, 1854).

[67] J. Harsin, *Policing Prostitution in Nineteenth-Century Paris* (Princeton University Press, 1985), pp. 241–79.

[68] P. H. Hutton, *The Cult of the Revolutionary Tradition: The Blanquists in French Politics, 1864–1893* (Berkeley, University of California Press, 1981), pp. 64–99.

[69] J. Casevitz, *Une Loi manquée: la loi Niel 1866–1868, l'armée française à la veille de la guerre de 1870* (Presses Universitaires de France, 1959); T. J. Adriance, *The Last Gaiter Button: A Study of the Mobilisation and Concentration of the French Army in the War of 1870* (Westport, Greenwood Press, 1987); G. Carrot, 'La Garde Nationale 1789–1871, une institution de la nation' (Thèse de doctorat de 3i ème cycle, Université de Nice, 1979).

the trains, among the deported paupers were the lunatics of Bicêtre and the prostitutes of Paris. A few hundred syphilitic prostitutes ended up in provincial prisons and about a thousand 'healthy' ones were deported to the provinces. While the army tried to empty Paris, suburban populations including paupers and prostitutes took refuge within the walls. Meanwhile, the army grew enormously. To nearly 100,000 *mobiles* were added up to 400,000 improvised *gardes nationaux* and around 70,000 remnants of the defeated imperial army: 570,000 soldiers out of a total population of around 2,200,000.[70] Some men, either too old or too young, gathered in guerrilla units on the outskirts of the city.

The army administration saw this situation as rotten at the core. Officers could not control their troops, their discipline or their health. The male–female and the military–civilian ratios changed dramatically. Fresh soldiers had no experience of discipline and felt overwhelmed by their political power. They invaded the brothels at their disposal. Some were vandalised. Some were burnt.[71] Chaos rose up from the seminal sewer. There was a shift in representation of the customers, from potential victims of the prostitute's syphilis to vandals. This shift took place over the whole period of the war and the Commune. The war exaggerated collective behaviour: it made prostitutes less visible and busier. When all economic activity was on hold, prostitution and alcohol consumption increased among the troops.[72] Or rather those who were in uniform exhibited exaggerated behaviour by normal army standards. The concept of soldier and mobster became confused.

Shifting regulation

The decline of civilian forms of regulation dates from August 1870. At that stage, most of the police enrolled in the Garde Nationale and surrendered their police tasks for the defence of the city. The republican government was defiant of the police.[73] All the bribes and financial rewards policemen used to receive in the exercise of regulation created a situation of promiscuousness from which neither prostitutes nor policemen benefited, the former being associated with informers

---

70 These numbers were debated and estimates ranged from 308,000 (L. Berthier, *Histoire de la guerre*, p. 340 to Gal. Vinoy's 570,189, quoted in A. Wachter, *La Guerre de 1870–1871, histoire politique et militaire* (E. Lachaud, 1873), p. 593.

71 *Gardes nationaux* often tried to break in at illegal hours. This was due to the fact that brothels often had a bar. Brothel-keepers (always women) often protested through the police to the military authority. APdP, Da 225, 'Lettre aux autorités militaires'.

72 Corbin, *Les Filles de noce*, pp. 206–30.

73 Édouard de Kératry, who directed the service of the Préfecture de Police on 19 September 1871, wanted the abolition of the Préfecture and of the metropolitan force in favour of purely municipal police forces. *Le 4 septembre et le gouvernement de la Défense Nationale* (Librairie Internationale A. Lacroix, Verboeckhoven et Cie, 1872).

(which they often were) and the latter with pimps (which they sometimes were).[74] The government sought to abolish the Préfecture de Police, but eventually simply curbed its powers.[75] In the new context, many registered women thought that regulation had ended with the Second Empire. They subsequently petitioned to disregard regulation as a thing of the imperial regime:

> *Monsieur le Préfet,*
> An inspector of your administration came to us, in our homes, this morning to constrain us to go to the sanitarian visits accustomed to the women of Paris (special class). We answer to you, Mr le Préfet, that we will object to going there any more because we have properties and live a settled life [*en nos meubles* made the difference between people lodging in furnished hotels and estate owners], in our homes, because we contribute and we even lodge some *mobiles* and because we do not want to depend, as we used to, on the above administration because it behaved absurdly towards us and threw dishonour at the whole of our family. It is high time to end all these things [*autres temps, autres moeurs*] and we hope that the *Republic* will overturn all these absurdities.[76]

This letter was signed by nearly a dozen brothel-keepers and is an interesting sociological document. The odd style, impossible to translate in places, points out a research and a choice of powerful words expressing indignation, calling on family values (when the word family could also cover a trade) and even making a pun on the Latin phrase *O Tempora, o Mores* with the word *moeurs* taking the meaning of usage and morals, as in *police des moeurs*. Through their war effort brothel-keepers expected to reintegrate society. Their exclusion was therefore self-represented as relative to their social usefulness. In entering the war effort, or as seen elsewhere in donating generously to charities, prostitutes and brothel-keepers expected to become respectable. With respectability would have come different relations with the police. Police protection could be sought against the mob of soldiers, who in turn had become the vectors of infection and the source of social unrest.

As the police gradually collapsed, the hospital committee of Paris emptied its wards to welcome the troops and the paupers. Lourcine and the Midi were both turned into war hospitals. When casualties rose dramatically in December and January, locked-in syphilitic patients became out-patients. Since the police were unable and unwilling to enforce any real repression,[77] the rationale of locking up disappeared. There was a short-lived attempt at restoring police control after the

---

74 The police archives contain many denunciations of infected prostitutes by other prostitutes; there is also a large number of denunciations of corrupt doctors and policemen. APdP Da 530, denunciations.
75 E. Cresson, *Cent jours à la Préfecture de Police, 2 novembre 1870 – 11 février 1871* (H. Plon, Nourrit et Cie, 1901), pp. 28–30, 71.
76 Lecour, *La Prostitution*, p. 310.
77 Cresson, *Cent jours à la Préfecture*, p. 116.

riot of 30 October, but the newly appointed Prefect realised that the hospitals were saturated, the police powerless and regulation unpopular. Moreover it had been made clear to him by the new government that the administration of the imperial police should disappear.[78] Within the civilian administration of Paris the fear of contagion did not prevail. The disease was associated with the containment of prostitution within socially acceptable boundaries. Syphilis appeared relatively innocuous in the short term compared with the impending famine. The social risk of prostitution also shrunk in proportion to the social unrest caused by the war.

Meanwhile, the army found itself having to manage the existence of a very wide cross-section of society. This management induced the consideration of diseases including syphilis. The coexistence of two worlds, the civilian and the military, was never more apparent than in the response of each to the prevalent venereal diseases. From the month of October onwards the army administration became concerned about the spread of syphilis among their scattered troops. An order dating from 9 December instructed the commanders of the nine sectors to contain the circulation of criminals and prostitutes from sector to sector.[79] It closed the brothels near the walls and created its own military lock hospital at the Ivry hospice for the terminally ill.[80] It was not the only military hospital outside the city walls, but it was one of the two, with the smallpox hospital of Bicêtre, to be within the Prussian cannon range. Indeed, in January, it was to be the only military hospital under enemy fire *not* to be evacuated.[81]

In this military reconstruction of regulation, the nearly always full lock hospital was a place of infamy. Venereal disease was not only a professional disease of soldiers (even in this case when they were not really professional soldiers), it was also a solid case for punishment. Some 1,000 beds were reserved for people suffering from venereal infections. This is by all accounts an enormous number when you consider the large turnover due to short treatments and the fact that it was virtually full from the first day of its operation to the last.

Figures available represent a sample based on the few remaining data found at the ASSAT (the sheets were used as filing wrappers). They illustrate two important points. First, the daily movement (admissions and discharges) was considerable: 112 people left the hospital after VD treatment in a single week in January while 101 entered the hospital; 202 convalescents left while 216 entered. These statistics are too incomplete to draw any conclusions about the average length of time spent at Ivry, but if they were in any way representative the turnover must

---

78 Cresson, *Cent jours à la Préfecture*, pp. 28–30, 71.
79 SHAT, Li 3, Papiers du Gouverneur Militaire de Paris, *Memorandum to the 9 secteurs*.
80 There is no written trace of who decided to create the lock hospital but it was roughly when Larrey came back to Paris in September. The terminally ill had been transferred to several hospitals like the Salpêtrière and the Hôtel-Dieu. See ASSAT, box 63–65; AAP, 542 Foss 108, Foss 109 and Foss 78.
81 This is particularly striking when other hospitals were evacuated as soon as the first shells fell on them. See AAP, 542 Foss 2, Minutes of the Conseil Général des Hospices.

have been quite fast. Over the period of the siege around 2,000 men would have been treated at Ivry, and up to 3,200 convalescents. Second, officers and non-commissioned officers chose not to stay in the hospital to recover if they could avoid it. This would create a 10 per cent difference between the people treated and the people considered as convalescents, which could be explained by a number of military patients with VD treated for something else in a civilian hospital and sent there to recover. The number of in-patients, being on average 876 under treatment for a total of 1,000 beds, represents a high level of occupancy. A similar number of convalescents camped around the hospice. This is only a sample but reports seem to show that there is no reason why there should have been more or less cases of VD in January than in any other months.[82]

In non-specialised services the number of patients was small: thirty-one cases of syphilis were recorded for the fourth sector, for instance, out of a total of 1,628 patients described in the statistics produced in March 1871. Such low rates show that either syphilitic patients went undetected or they were directed towards this specialised institution.[83] Other statistical accounts of venereal diseases in the army outside Paris put at around 4 per cent the number of soldiers infected reporting to their doctor. With this caveat in mind the rate could either be judged as encouraging or as threatening.[84]

In Paris, on the other hand, Louis Fiaux claimed that venereal diseases represented between $\frac{1}{6}$ to $\frac{1}{5}$ of the sick cases in some Garde Mobile battalions.[85] He thus only became a lifelong opponent of regulationism precisely because of his fear that the system might actually contribute to the spreading of syphilis by giving the impression that regulated prostitutes were healthy. Louis Fiaux, who later became a member of the Conseil Municipal de Paris, contributed greatly to renewed fears of syphilis in the 1880s and 1890s.[86] The impact of this war experience was probably greater on the army itself. The Ivry hospice was of considerable importance among the military hospitals since the Service de Santé directed by Baron Larrey created only two types of specialised hospitals: the venereal hospital and the smallpox hospitals of Gros Cailloux, in the city, and Bicêtre and Vincennes outside Paris but protected by fortresses. The exclusion of VD from the city is all the more striking when assimilated to highly contagious smallpox. Syphilis was not the type of disease which spreads in the wind but, like smallpox, it was seen as worth isolating from Paris, even more strictly than typhus for instance. We therefore have this antithetical evolution of civilian medicine rating VD low on the scale of emergencies

82 ASSAT, box 63–64–65, the information is scarce and left unclassified.
83 ASSAT, box 63/4, 'Recapitulative descriptions of the wounds justifying admittance to the ambulances of the 4th Sector'.
84 A. Doyon, *Notes et souvenirs d'un chirurgien d'ambulance, deuxième ambulance lyonnaise* (Lyons, Imprimerie A. Vingtrinier, 1872), p. 44.
85 Fiaux, *L'Hygiène militaire*, pp. 73–5.
86 L. Fiaux, *Les Maisons de tolérance : leur fermeture* (Georges Carré, 1892), pp. 152–5.

while military medicine considered it a priority. The main difference was the extent to which the army scale was permeated with disciplinary measures aimed at the prostitutes' customers, the wider social group.

As war contributed to re-centre all the priorities of society towards the war effort, a certain number of aspects of everyday life changed their meanings to be clearly assumed as part and parcel of the military administration. The treatment and prophylactic of VD became a specifically military concern. Syphilis touched at the core of masculinity.[87] It affected male vitality and potency.[88] This weakening involved not only a given soldier at a given moment but also the weakening of the whole army. Considered superficially, a soldier with gonorrhoea or even syphilis in its primary stage was perfectly able-bodied, and if it were not for the fear of contagion (the vectors of which remained undefined) he could stay at his post. When syphilis was viewed through the magnifying glass of decay, defeat and loss of vitality, it appeared as the ultimate military danger: the loss of the fighting spirit, the expression of decadence. The image of Hannibal's army becoming weak and effeminate in the arms of Capuan prostitutes recurred from a common stock of classical education and readings of Titus Livius. The hereditary dangers of syphilis were also present in the advice given to the soldiers:

> Beware of the women lurking near the camps; they are *almost always ill*. Many soldiers of the mobile are married; most sedentary guards are, they must KNOW that one instant of forgetfulness and weakness may bring in their families *a rightly dreaded disease*; for which *a cure is never certain* and *which will strike its victims even among their children*.[89]

In spite of these stern warnings the *gardes* often colluded with prostitutes. A notorious instance of this collusion took place in the 'no-man's land'. The Parisian 'no-man's land' was mostly composed of allotments and gardens, fields and farmland just outside Paris, which meant that as the famine progressed it became the only possible source of fresh vegetables. This was particularly important at a time when scurvy developed as a relatively important epidemic.[90] Hospital staff tried to gain access to these fields to collect the precious vegetables at their own risk.[91]

---

87 R. A. Nye, 'Honor, impotence and male sexuality in nineteenth-century French medicine', *French Historical Studies*, 16:1 (1989) 48–71; *Maculinity and Male Codes of Honour*.

88 Flaubert argued 'that pox should not be contracted too young' as the character was not fully developed. This was also a view expressed in old textbooks like that by Fernet d'Amiens. This concern rejoins that over masturbation expressed in the eighteenth century by Tissot, *L'Onanisme, dissertation sur les maladies produites par la masturbation* (Geneva A. Chapuis, 1760); J.-P. Aron and R. Kempf, *La Bourgeoisie, le sexe et l'honneur* (Brussels, Complexe, 1984).

89 *L'Union médicale* (12/11/1870) 587.

90 E. Decaisne, 'Le Siège de Paris au point du vie de l'hygiène et de la chirurgie', *Revue Scientifique*, 20 (1/11/1871) 468–71, p. 469; C. A. Gordon, *Le Siège de Paris au point de vue de l'hygiène et de la chirurgie* (J. B. Baillière, 1871), p. 8.

91 H. Gallet, *Guerre et Commune 1870–1871, impressions d'un hospitalier* (Calmann-Lévy, 1898), pp. 289–90.

There, they found the guerrilla troops would not readily let them through. The privilege of the access to open fields was disputed between the hospital staff and the starved prostitutes of Paris, who, in exchange for their services, risked their lives to harvest potatoes, carrots and cabbage.

This anecdote has symbolic value. Scurvy was a disease, like syphilis, symbolising decay and physical corruption. In Paris the appearance of scurvy was yet another sign of the fall. The cure and prevention of scurvy was only possible through a radical improvement of the diet, hence the importance of no-man's land vegetables. To have to contest these precious aliments with the living symbols of decay and disease was perceived as another illustration of declining standards of morality. The blame was put on the volunteers. Their corruption explained the impossibility of executing General Trochu's hypothetical military plan. Their shortcomings were used to justify the apathy of the huge and amorphous Paris army. The country had sunk so low that its only defence was the mob dressed up as 1792 volunteers.

Symbolic regulation and prohibition

Communard policies best incarnated these historical confusions. In Rigault's ex-Préfecture were the *police des moeurs* and civilian regulation. The Commune's position relative to vice and prostitution in particular was highly ambiguous and contradictory. The Proudhonist mayors of the XI and XIV *arrondissements* condemned prostitution unequivocally as a remainder of the imperial corruption and sex exploitation of the poor by the rich.[92] This prohibitionist position had been held before the Commune by Louise Michel's XVIII *arrondissement* women's committee created on 20 November. Michel's views on the abolition of regulation were aimed at brothel houses and were representative of the socialist minority of the Commune.[93] Strict prohibition was in no way an invention of the Commune but was developed earlier in Proudhon's and Fourier's analysis of sexual exploitation. Because of the Commune's diversity, these measures were only applied in parts of the city.[94] These socialist ideas were enacted in a repressive manner as any prostitute could be arrested for public immorality by any of the *gardes nationaux*, i.e. by her neighbour, her lover or any man of Paris since most of them were in the army.

The practice of the Blanquist leaders in charge of the police was different. The Commune police administration only gradually came into existence and was soon involved in spy hunting and political arrests. From the ex-Préfecture de Police's point of view, the regulationist system still existed and was working more or less with the same structural problems encountered during the first siege, i.e.

92 *JORC*, 4–15/04/1871.
93 M. Borel d'Hauterive, *Les Sièges de Paris* (Dentu, 1871), p. 328.
94 This gave rise to many ironic comments on how prostitutes could walk the streets in one *arrondissement* and sleep in another.

the lack of staff and hospital room at Saint-Lazare. Some 279 prostitutes soliciting without legal registration (medical examinations were not carried out) were locked in.[95] The *gardes nationaux* settled a post at Saint-Lazare and the nuns who worked there were either dismissed or ran away. There was no discipline and the medical staff left at the earliest opportunity, according to the procedures established by Versailles. Versailles sabotaged regulation under the Commune in making certain that the necessary elements would go missing. Yet, in spite of all these difficulties Rigault had recreated a form of regulation system.

Prostitutes were brought to the examination centre where they were recorded but not examined. This confusion between administrative regulation and medical examination has been encountered earlier; it was reinforced within the Commune's practice. Rigault understood regulation purely as a political tool and as a way of enacting police control over a semi-criminal fauna, wishing to maintain this symbol of law and order.[96] His use of regulation was purely to restore law and order. He eventually had to 'recall the previous inspectors of the vice squad to resume the surveillance of prostitutes that had been in practice under previous administrations'.[97]

Paradoxically for a terrorist organisation, the ex-Préfecture de Police gave a strong sense of parody to regulation. The examination centre became the focus of large crowds[98] who entered these places from which they had been kept away for so long and had been drilled to fear.[99] There was a very important cathartic element in the Commune's celebration of liberty. The invasion of working administrations was inspired by curiosity and by the unique feeling of being the masters of it all. In the case of regulation, the machine was well-known but not understood. Entering it, they just acted as students in the medical amphitheatre: they wanted to witness the great show of power.

Raoul Rigault and his friends, who had most of the 'real' power during the Commune, did not abolish the *police des moeurs* but they reduced it to what they thought it was: a record office. In doing so they showed little interest in VD itself but very much more in law-and-order enactment. As in a carnival, the Commune authorised the revealing of the nature of things through derision. Policemen, after the Commune, reported the fraternising of prostitutes and so-called policemen in the accomplishment of that parody of regulation and they explained it as lust

---

95 L. Faze, *Histoire de la guerre civile de 1871* (Charpentier, 1879), p. 301.
96 G. Da Costa makes a point in saying how well law and order were maintained during the Commune. Da Costa, *La Commune vécue* (3 vols, Quantin, 1903–5), vol. ii, pp. 295–310.
97 P. Cattelain, *Souvenirs inédits du chef de la sûreté sous la Commune* (Juven, 1900), p. 69.
98 Large crowds of *gardes nationaux* had guarded the centre during the siege, commenting loudly on the women coming in, cheering or insulting them. The crowds' feelings towards the prostitutes were always mixed with scorn, or even frank hatred. See Police Archives, Da 225–230; Lecour, *La Prostitution*, p. 310.
99 Cattelain, *Souvenirs inédits du chef de la sûreté*, p. 113.

unrestrained.[100] It was not. On the contrary, when the Commune had any will to legislate on sexual matters it proved authoritarian and prudish. What happened to the regulation services was part of the parody of a world turned upside down. The attitudes presented one major difference. When prostitutes were chased from their neighbourhoods, when they were registered, it was never for sanitarian reasons. Syphilis was not part of the problem and the fate of the Ivry hospice illustrates this point.

The great hospital of Ivry was suddenly dismantled. The manager of the hospital had long run away, and the *gardes nationaux* moved in and guarded the administration and the patients of the hospital. The lock hospital was doublelocked: the control of VD was complemented by a political control of the soldiers locked in, with the eventual forced enrolling of any cured patient. Under threat, the financial director thought he was going to be executed, and he took the decision to move the hospital by night to Vincennes in the east of Paris.[101] Ivry was set in the limits of the Commune's zone of influence, while Vincennes was shared between the Prussians and the Commune. Under duress the pox and smallpox hospitals merged, uniting all the agents of decay in one institution. The major part of the army regulationist administration chose to escape the Commune and there is no sign that the Commune tried to reconstitute any military regulation.[102]

Conclusion

Before 1870, regulation in Paris functioned in pre-Darwinian[103] times in a world where syphilis could be contained.[104] Regulation according to Duchâtelet and

---

100 Lecour, *La Prostitution*, pp. 327–30. He accused the Communards of having had orgies at St Lazare. It seems very odd that sane men should choose infected women to have intercourse with and Lecour's accusation belongs to the same Versaillais discourse on unrestrained vice as Maxime du Camp's *Les Convulsions de Paris* (4 vols, Hachette, 1878–80).
101 ASSAT, box 65/6. The financial director seems to have panicked after sending scared letters on 16 and 18/04/1871. On 6 May he ran away from Vincennes with the payroll of the hospital.
102 The new army formed from Versailles created its own field lock hospital and after the invasion of Paris settled it into a barrack hospital at Courcelles which was found to be difficult to control. Later the venereal patients were moved right out to Compiègne. The structure of army regulation did not change and these various institutional moves did not seem worth any more elaborate description. Ivry was converted into a penal institution receiving all the wounded and sick Communards found in the Paris ambulances and hospitals in May 1871. ASSAT, box 65bis/13.
103 Darwinism or Lamarckian evolutionary theories allied with Darwinism usually supported a right-wing political discourse which some, like Dramard, tried to undermine by allying evolutionary theory and socialism. L. Dramard, *Transformisme et socialisme* (Bureaux du Prolétaire, 1882); P. J. Bowler, *Charles Darwin: The Man and His Influence* (Cambridge University Press, 1990), pp. 167–76.
104 Even alternative theoreticians of syphilis like Alexandre Auzias-Turenne (1812–70), who warned whoever cared to listen against the prevalence of syphilis, had a ready-made answer to the disease. Auzias-Turenne, *La Syphilisation* (Germer Baillière, 1878). D. Beyer Perett, 'Ethics and error: the dispute between Ricord and Auzias-Turenne over syphilisation, 1845–1870' (unpublished thesis, University of Stanford, 1977); Also See B. Taithe, 'The rise and fall of European syphilisation: the debates on human experimentations and vaccination of syphilis, c. 1845–1870', in F. Eder, L. Hall, G. Hekma *et al.* (eds), *Sexual Cultures in Europe* (Manchester University Press, 1999).

Ricord was not enjoying the hegemonic domination described by Quêtel or Corbin in 1870 and there were more signs of a polyphonic discourse on the nature of the venereal dangers.[105] The old certitude on contagion, cure or containment were severely undermined by new, military-based and racially concerned perspectives. The events of 1870 occurred between two congresses devoted to the dangers of venereal diseases. The 1867 Parisian congress was still dominated by the Ricord–Auzias debates on the nature of syphilis,[106] but the 1873 congress in Vienna witnessed more debates on regulationism and the long-term dangers of syphilis.[107] The moderate optimism of Philippe Ricord gave way to Fournier's syphilophobia of the 1880s and Zola's catastrophist heredity.[108] The experience of the defeat sunk in and gradually permeated all sorts of political and medical analyses, just as the war itself acquired a real historical importance and shaped French identity.

The *outrance* of the 1870–71 war and Commune[109] was to play a determinant role in the pessimism developed in Zola's naturalistic novels.[110] Even though Zola never mentioned the disease by its name in the Rougon–Macquart series, his friends were more adventurous.[111] Guy de Maupassant in *Le Lit 29* even portrayed a women dying of her own *guerre à outrance*: having been raped and contaminated by the Prussians, she patriotically decides to spread the disease among their officers.[112]

In the context of *guerre à outrance* in Paris, two interpretative models faced each other: the police and the traditional model of regulation and the more catastrophist and scaremongering model of military regulation. The army management was not merely concerned with social problems and unrest but with the fight for survival. The improvised army did not correspond to normal army standards. The circumstances shaped anew medical issues into social and collective crises. This construction of a new scourge happened with tuberculosis or cancer after 1914 and happened on a smaller scale with syphilis after 1870.[113] In the period preceding the

105 J. A. H. Depaul, *De la syphilis vaccinale* (J. B. Baillière, 1865).
106 APdP, Da 230, the policeman in charge of producing a report on over ten hours of debates concluded 'there will be nothing left from this debate except the fact that venereal disease is spreading alarmingly'.
107 H. Mireur, *La Syphilis et la prostitution dans leurs rapports avec l'hygiène, la morale et la Loi* (Masson, 2nd edn, 1888), pp. 2, 8, 200–1.
108 A. Fournier, *L'Hérédité syphilitique* (Masson, 1891); B. Nevins, *On Hereditary Syphilis* (Liverpool, *The Medical Enquirer*, 1878).
109 Lidsky, *Les Écrivains contre la Commune*.
110 Wald-Lasowski, *Syphilis*; C. Quêtel, *History of Syphilis* (Cambridge, Polity Press, 1990).
111 J. Pierret, *L'Imaginaire décadent (1880–1900)* (Presses Universitaires de France, 1977), pp. 12–19.
112 P. Garcia, 'Les Idées médicales à travers l'oeuvre de Guy de Maupassant' (Thèse de doctorat en médecine, Université de Lyon (1), 1987), pp. 168–70.
113 P. Pinell, *Naissance d'un fléau, histoire de la lutte contre le cancer en France 1890–1940* (Métaillé, 1992), pp. 115–30.

emergence of eugenics as a coherent discourse,[114] the regulationists articulated a discourse and a practice of exclusion and social containment rooted in the analysis of dangerous classes from the 1830s.[115] While police regulation acted as a form of social control of lust, army regulation created universal rules applying to all active males. The danger crossed class boundaries and overwhelmed primitive forms of social policing. There was an important shift in the meaning of regulation.

Medical regulation took on dramatic forms. The integration of hereditary concerns into the treatment of syphilis deepened with new approaches to brain diseases. From a closely specified disease located around the genitals and the mouth, syphilis turned into a causal disease ramifying its symptoms and consequences to the whole of the body. The seminal sewer was not the only one put at risk, the nervous system and brain were too, especially since the 'discovery' of syphilitic paralysis or cardiovascular syphilis.[116] Syphilitic insanity, which came to be diagnosed among many eminent artists in post-1871 France, extended, through them perhaps, the dangers of syphilis to the whole of society.[117] This was the metaphorical extension of the ontological growth of the disease: syphilis became more dangerous, less visible (tertiary symptoms are not visible), and more contagious after Fournier described tertiary syphilis as contagious.[118] The accidental transmission of syphilis between glass-makers illustrated the new dangers of this shameful yet discreet plague.[119] The group at high risk had also widened from the small number of professional soldiers to the universal crowd of mobilised citizens.

Many other diseases enjoyed metaphorical status, but only this new syphilis implied such drastic evolutionary and historical consequences.[120] When the revolutionary rhetoric backfired and 1870 Frenchmen compared poorly with their

---

114 French eugenics have always been an oddity in French thinking. The French obsession with quantity dwarfed but did not exclude concerns on the quality of the new born. See A. Béjein, 'Néomalthusianisme, populationisme et eugénisme en France de 1870 à 1914', in J. Dupâquier (ed.), *Histoire de la population française* (Presses Universitaires de France, 1988), pp. 481–8; A. Carol, *Histoire de l'eugénisme en France, les médecins et la procréation, XIXe–XXe siècle* (Seuil, 1995); K. Offen, 'Depopulation, nationalism and feminism in fin-de-siècle France', *American Historical Review*, 89:3 (1984) 648–78.
115 H. A. Frégier, *Des Classes dangereuses de la population dans les grandes villes* (J. B. Baillière, 1840); Lidsky, *Les Écrivains francais contre la Commune*, p. 24.
116 This link between syphilis, sexuality and madness was in fact recurrent throughout the history of the disease. Yvaren, *Des métamorphoses de la syphilis*, pp. 33–71.
117 Guy de Maupassant, Paul Verlaine and Flaubert among many others suffered from syphilis, and in Maupassant's case it was reputedly a case of hereditary syphilis. They were also abusing a number of substances: alcohol, opium, ether, etc. C. Quêtel, *Le Mal de Naples* (Seghers, 1986), p. 207; Garcia, 'Les Idées médicales', pp. 3–41.
118 A. Fournier, *De la contagion syphilitique* (Delahaye, 1860).
119 J. W. Scott, *The Glassworkers of Carmaux* (Cambridge, Mass., Harvard University Press, 1974), pp. 42–3.
120 See M. B. Adams (ed.), *The WELLBORN Science: Eugenics in Germany, France, Brazil and Russia* (Oxford University Press, 1989).

romantic 1792 ancestors, their collective failure was the sum of their individual deficiencies.[121] The defeat was in their flesh.[122] Their decadence was sexual, reproductive and hereditary. The 'Commune orgies' added to this rich mythology.[123] Some texts went as far as describing the whole political movement as an instance of prostitution, describing the agents of the Commune as *souteneurs* or pimps.[124]

In spite of this scaremongering which contributed to the individual and collective crisis called the French *fin de siècle*,[125] the test of practice shows that regulationism could enjoy a second lease of life with a different rationale, a stronger medical and military backing but with the same resources, staff and routines as before the war. Similarly the fear of alcoholism had to be weighed against the sum of vested interest in the politics of the bistro and the economics of wine- and spirit-making. In both cases the regeneration of France could be initiated with low-scale reforms and minor investments. To compare analytical categories with the tools of policy-making is certainly unfair on the former. Readers will be aware that an ecological awareness does not make for immediate reforms of the car industry, and that an AIDS scare can be both very real and very underfunded. What mattered more perhaps than the actual practice in the immediate aftermath of the war, was a radical and deep-seated change of attitudes. The numerous debates against regulationism and alcohol consumption did not make the French a people of teetotal prudes, but French policies towards the imaginary or real causes of the defeat were no longer characterised by a wish to contain and maintain a *status quo*, but instead by a desire to reform which remained, for the most part, discursive.

121 J. D. Ellis, *The Early Life of Georges Clemenceau 1841–1893* (Lawrence, Regent Press of Kansas, 1980), p. 8.
122 L. Le Fort, *Oeuvres*, ed. Félix Lajars (2 vols, Félix Alcan, 1895–96), vol. 2, p. 117.
123 Popular historians of the period 1871–80 often analysed the Commune solely as a symptom of syphilitic madness and accused every Commune leader of being contaminated with syphilis. C. A. Dauban, *Le Fond de la société sous la Commune* (Plon, 1873); du Camp, *Les Convulsions de Paris*, vol. 1, pp. 73–84; P. de Saint-Victor, *Barbares et bandits* (Michel Lévy Frères, 1872).
124 Anon., *Les Souteneurs de la Commune – Prussiens et Bonaparte* (Librairie Générale, 1871).
125 E. Showalter, *Sexual Anarchy: Gender and Culture at the Fin-de-Siècle* (New York, Viking, 1990), pp. 1–18; E. Weber, *France, Fin-de-Siècle* (Cambridge, Mass., Harvard University Press, 1986).

10 Conclusion: war stories

Many of the readers of this book will only have a mediated and intellectual understanding of war and even of the military with its cult of discipline and sacrifice as moral values. My parents, to whom this book is dedicated, will never read it; my father died as I completed the manuscript, and hence this conclusion took on a more personal dimension. My father fought many wars: colonial wars, the war against Nazism, and half-hidden wars that were almost civil wars or brotherly wars. In some respect one's childhood is always bathed in the stories of the older generation, always growing, fed on the previous generation's historical imagination or lack thereof.[1] My own childhood was spent partly listening to the same stories, partly attempting to extract new stories, many of which stemmed from the eighteen years of war my father fought. Most stories were not simply war stories and did not relate to warring incidents. In most instances, there was no gore but an exhilarating sense of adventure and the exotic. There were also stories that did not come out, that remained unspoken, and which, now, will never be told. A French child thirty years ago, even growing up in the heart of the military establishment, rarely heard tales of Algeria.

I grew up playing Second World War games on military training fields, throwing dummy grenades among the broken tanks, yet I was ignorant of the deepest scars in my father's life. Even now I am not sure when and where my uncle died in Algeria. Benedict Anderson's second edition of *Imagined Communities* states that remembering and forgetting have a symbiotic and dynamic dialectic which is at the heart of national identity. William Keylor, like Carbonell before him, has reflected on the political role played by French historians in shaping the regeneration of images of France.[2] The wars my father remembered and the ones he forgot could have been very close to the ones he heard of as a child, the wars my grandparents and great-grandparents remembered, and the ones they forgot. The 1870–71 wars are among those which, even now, leave few people indifferent if they know anything about them at all. That a recent Parisian colloquium on the Franco-Prussian war has found a quiet, neutral, acceptable and almost indifferent tone to discuss a national war 127 years ago should not have surprised the British reviewer.[3] It would be surprising,

---

[1] E. Deschaumes, *Souvenirs d'un lycéen de 14 ans pendant le siège de Paris, 1870–1871* (Firmin Didot, 1890).
[2] W. R. Keylor, *Academy and Community* (Cambridge, Mass., Harvard University Press, 1975), pp. 36–41; C.-O. Carbonell, 'Les Historiens français chroniqueurs de la guerre franco-allemande et de la Commune', *Bulletin de la société d'histoire moderne*, 13 (1974) 37–56.
[3] R. Tombs, 'L'année terrible 1870–1871', *Historical Journal*, 35:3 (1992) 713–24.

however, if a similar French conference on the Commune achieved this equipoise. For thirty years, when the Third Republic shifted from being the 'regime that divided least the French' to being the regime that could unite them best, the Conseil Municipal de Paris structured a cult of municipal independence which stretched back to the fifteenth-century prevost Étienne Marcel who betrayed his king for his city and was commemorated in the Commune as the revolutionary spirit of Paris. In Jacques Rougerie's beautiful phrase, the 'Parisian people in 1870 seemed more prisoner of its memory than aware of its future'.[4]

This line applied to the Commune, but also, and perhaps even more so, to the previous episode of the war. Since then the Commune has taken on an ambiguous role in the hagiographic pilgrim's progress of the French left. The cries of their revolt, and the agony of the martyrs of an indiscriminate repression, echoed painfully in 1971 for a centenary bathing in post-1968 moral order, but this historiographical revival was short-lived and the memory of the Commune lingers on in socialist politics. A Marxist interpretation has been its undoing, and now that Karl Marx's work is more often found in large piles of remaindered Russian editions, the Commune has taken on an ideologically dated iconic gloss.[5]

In this emotionally loaded atmosphere it is certainly not surprising that the French historiography has neglected so much of the Anglo-American input. The fundamental political narratives of 1870–71 have an internalist logic and lead to a divisive but basically French-centred introspection. As the French approach their second *fin-de-siècle* malaise and still refuse to remember and understand the Algerian war,[6] perhaps could they attempt to solve some the deepest political scars of their past, most of which date from 1870?

In this book I have argued that starting from the stifling abundance of semi-recollections and partial histories which aimed at hiding and disguising, a certain type of history could be attempted using the medical standpoint and through the lenses of the social history of medicine and the history of the body. This wide angle on the politics of social practices, militarisation, care, food, centralisation, humanitarianism and body representations did not exhaust the full potential of the meanings of war. I am well aware of this, but it opens the full range of issues for further research. The final section on body representation sought to convey the forms taken by the sense of defeat. A sense of defeat embodied was not simply illustrative of ideological dogma but was also formative of and structuring intellectual constructs such as decadence, *fin de siècle* and renewed racialist theories.

---

4   J. Rougerie, *Procès des Communards*, (Archives Julliard, 1976) p. 240.
5   K. Marx, *La Commune de Paris* (Savelli, [1871] 1976).
6   J.-P. Rioux and J.-F. Sirinelli, *La Guerre d'Algérie et les intellectuels français* (Brussels, Complexe, 1991); H. Lebovics, *True France: The Wars over Cultural Identity, 1900–1945* (Ithaca, Cornell University Press, 1992), pp. 5–8; B. Stora, *La Gangrène et l'oubli, la mémoire de la guerre d'Algérie* (La Découverte, 1992), pp. 187–276.

The full intensity of the wars of 1870–71 must be re-discovered and re-cast at the centre of the making of French 'modernity'. The subtle processes of militarisation described in practical terms about the welfare provisions, the Red Cross or even intellectual constructs led to the greater penetration of images of defeat in the fabric of French culture.

All of those who have lived through an armed conflict, or even lived close enough to touch the survivors of such a human tragedy, know that a war never works entirely *for* you but does much *to* you. The high politics of July 1870 or the summer of 1914 float later like a surreal mind game. Those who lived the war realised that there was no such thing as a 'self' to come back to at the end of the conflict. There was no such thing as a stable self and only the nostalgia of the pre-war days anchors this illusion of a civilian identity in wartime. Medicine, care, health acquired an agonising centrality in focusing ideas of the self, concepts of identity on the locus of the body. However, as Chapter 8 has shown, even bodies can have a transient form. They are not an empty canvas on which peaceful images can be projected. War becomes them and the military language summons the vision of collective bodies, *corps d'armées* etc., marching to a planned sacrifice. The *imagined communities* of warfare acquire an individual and collective physical expression, a real-flesh embodiment which dies with the last survivor and which cannot be translated painlessly in words.

The endless tide of war writings published in the life-time of survivors of the war attempted to preserve for all what all had shared in. The calendars established of the war events and the diversity of anniversaries offered hundreds of possible commemorations and celebrations and a diversity of *lieux de mémoire*.[7] Yet this multiplication of attempts illustrates *a contrario* how powerless words were to communicate a corporeal memory. What had been heard, felt, touched, smelled, or even tasted of war inhabited these texts, and in a desperate race against time their authors tried to project this collective fragment of their lives into a glorified and refined form of history. Few challenged the concept of war itself and fewer even dared contest the importance of this war. Unlike 1914, 1870 happened and was only debated within an analysis of defeat.[8] To write a story that could mirror some of their concerns while questioning the narrative structure of their lives was in a sense easy and difficult at the same time: it is easy to be incisive and cut through the Gordian knots of their existence; it is difficult to allow empathy to dictate the work, and difficult to ignore the callousness inside us which can make history such a shallow and smug affair. I have attempted to navigate treacherous waters and it is not in my power to decide whether my story has failed to do justice to this silent crowd of witnesses.

7 H. Gallet, *Les Anniversaires de la guerre de 1870–1871* (Garnier Frères, 1895).
8 S. Hynes, *A War Imagined* (New York, Atheneum, 1991), pp. 353–82.

The superstructure of this story, the self-imposed boundaries of this book, were those of the sieges of Paris. To cut this picture into two parts – the war and the civil war – did not seem fully justifiable. It is the fundamental result of war that civilian society dissolves itself into the military and assumes the simplified choices and uncompromising values imposed by the brutal struggle. Because the fight is altogether simpler, more basic, brutal and meaningless than any other form of social organisation, social, religious and civilian values regress and hide despondently on one side of the Manichean organisation of the collective psyche. All civilian values, values of civilisations, take sides and justify the struggle. From July 1870 the war appeared different. It was not only the first conflict in fifty-five years between two of the greatest continental powers,[9] it also became a 'modern' war, a war of alleged 'modernity'. Its 'modernity' lay in the real causes of the conflict: the principle of national unity in Germany versus old French politics of intervention in the German sphere. Its modernity also resided in the technology: the Krupp guns, the mitrailleuse, the chassepot rifle, (the French were perhaps the more innovative during the war), hot air balloons, electric projectors lighting up enemy troops, armoured trains, ersatz milk and meat. Most of all, the notion of human 'progress' was expressed in 'feelings': to the horrors of war answered the sentimental Red Cross, the impossible rules of war.

The rise of humanitarianism as an aid to war, as a form of mobilisation and nationalism even, functioned along those lines. The violations of the rules of war, however illogically, ended up justifying war. Within French society the war also called for the state to assume a patriarchal and protective role that it had neither the ambitions nor the ability to fulfil. The politics of care, the duty to care, came to the fore when the state proved unable to deliver the victory that justified the war effort, the self-censorship and the collective emotional and physical investment in war. *La sociale* and the Commune grew from the war and from the siege because so much of government and legitimacy became attached both to a hypothetical victory and to the duty of caring for the city at war. The failure to deliver the war, the unwillingness to deliver *la sociale,* this new social compact between citizen-soldier and state guarantor of social and political rights, prompted the 18 March insurrection.

When the Commune started around the guns of Montmartre, the latter stood less as weapons than as symbols of sacrifice, as the Parisians' side of the sham deal they had with *their* government. The emergence of the Commune, altogether the expression of community ideals, Utopian socialism and municipal forms of government, reflected a greater trust in the smaller and caring forms of government. The defeat of the Commune owed as much to its own inability to recreate a military discipline opposed to all its principles, as to its inability to command

9 F. R. Bridge and R. Bullen, *The Great Powers and the European States System 1815–1914* (London and New York, Fontana, 1980).

respect and obedience from all the necessary but often independent servants of the state. The medical world largely refused to follow the Commune and even conspired in its downfall. This was partly due to social class solidarity, but it was also the result of a successful assimilation of the medical establishment and hierarchical ways into the structure of the state.

What the war revealed about the national integration, the understanding of government and the assimilation of social values in politics and medicine was only part of this story. What the war became in the collective and political imagination described in Chapter 1 was largely the result of how it was described, how it was organised and discussed during the conflict. The languages of defeat were not autonomous from the acts. The evidence, perhaps even the necessity of an incoming defeat, was integrated to the way the war was conducted from early August onwards. A similar study of the way the army was mismanaged and under-used by pessimistic, mediocre, routine-prone officers is certainly both possible and much needed. In this book, the medical debates on amputation, alcohol and venereal diseases served the same purpose. In any discussion of amputation the nature of the patient came to be discussed: his lack of resilience and all the hereditary burden of a tired nation would favour gangrene in his wounds, septicaemia in his blood. Gobineau's work and the whole corpus of degeneracy studies weighed on the mind of surgeons. Those who argued that not to intervene was the most heroic and wise decision, those who wanted clear cuts, felled limbs and peace and rest, could have been members of the Bordeaux assembly discussing the terms of the peace and the loss of Alsace and part of Lorraine. The doubts they voiced about the decline of the French race echoed until the next war, only to bounce back at us in current political discussions.

The radicalisation of all debates of the importance of venereal diseases and substance abuse in French society also reflected, on the one hand, the imposition of military discipline over a large cross-section of French society, and on the other, fears about the enemy within, the search for that elusive agent of defeat, that traitor and scapegoat. While it might be tentative, to say the least, to attribute the whole of the rise of anti-Semitism and even the Dreyfus affair to this quest for the enemy within, there are a number of hidden connections between them. The Third Republic found its ideological boundaries in its founding moment. The failure of the politics of care, the violence exerted against one's own (after all Communards were primarily and intensely republicans), and the inability to recognise the legitimacy of opposing political cultures all contributed to poison the atmosphere of this most syncretic of regimes.[10] Historians have largely tended to consider the

---

10 J.-P. Machelon, *La République contre les libertés* (Fondation Nationale des Sciences Politiques, 1976); B. F. Martin, *Crime and Criminal Justice Under the Third Republic: The Shame of Marianne* (Baton Rouge, Louisiana State University Press, 1990)

Second Empire as a deep freezer of French political culture, a tendency recent work by Hazareesingh and others has considerably undermined, but there is another danger in seeing the Third Republic as the only possible continuation of a regime of slow democratisation.[11] In 1870 the full range of possibilities was open and it is the middle ground of politics, the National Defence government's political field, which suffered most.[12] The sense of defeat that later condemned the Bonapartist to a minor role also undermined all forms of conciliatory politics and peace with oneself.[13] The history of high politics failures has been written over and over again. The slow victory of republicanism over reactionary Bonapartism, hesitating and feeble legitimism, has long been described.[14] Less obvious are the mechanics of French internecine struggles. This book might provide some of the threads and add to a richer tapestry including the full range of gendered, age-related and embodied experiences.[15] The penultimate chapter headed in this direction and asked to recast fairly familiar stories of French *fin-de-siècle* anxieties in the light of the trauma of 1870.

Syphilis came out of the war a more frightening disease, and alcohol a new social and medical scourge responsible for the defeat, the Commune and much more besides. They became tropes of the metaphorical language of defeat and self-explanatory elements making sense of the war narratives. When they appear in any description of the siege (syphilis is often veiled and associated with debauchery, or insanity), they come tautologically before the conclusion in the redeeming fires and sacrifices of May 1871. The defeat of the flesh was largely a metaphorical construct directly linked to the material experience of the wars. As such it remained a metaphor and an analytical tool, supported by and supporting much medical evidence and grand narratives.

From a detached historical viewpoint, I would argue that little comfort came from medicine, that humanitarianism and the politics of care were only ways in which these wars penetrated more deeply into French culture, and shaped

---

11 S. Hazareesingh, *From Subject to Citizen: The Second Empire and the Emergence of Modern French Democracy*, (Princeton University Press, 1998) pp. 313–21; L. Hamon (ed.), *Les Opportunistes : les débuts de la République aux républicains* (Maison des Sciences de l'Homme, 1991).

12 This is particularly obvious in the writing of the conciliation party: J. Adam, *Nos Angoisses et nos luttes, 1871–1873* (Alphonse Lemerre, 1907), p. 83; P. G. Nord, 'The party of conciliation and the Paris Commune', *French Historical Studies*, 15:1 (1987) 1–35.

13 P. A. Bertocci, *Jules Simon* (Columbia, University of Missouri Press, 1978); J. Rothney, *Bonapartism after Sedan* (Ithaca, Cornell University Press, 1969).

14 J. Gouault, *Comment la France est devenue républicaine* (Armand Colin, 1954); R. R. Locke, *French Legitimists and the Politics of Moral Order in the Early Third Republic* (Princeton University Press, 1974).

15 R. Harris, *Murders and Madness: Medicine, Law and Society in the Fin-de-Siècle* (Oxford, Clarendon Press, 1989); R. Nye, *Crime, Madness and Politics in Modern France: The Medical Concept of National Decline* (Princeton University Press, 1984); A. L. Shapiro, *Breaking the Codes: Female Criminality in Fin-de-siècle Paris* (Stanford, Stanford University Press, 1996).

CONCLUSION: WAR STORIES

Figure 16 The fortieth anniversary of the first fight of 1870: the German Colonel von Villiez honours the grave of French NCO Pagnier

lop-sidedly French collective memory. I do not believe this war to be unique in any respect. In every war there is always at least one of the two sides which resents its own defeat. Perhaps it is the narrative nature of defeat to be a tale of resentment, grievance turned inwards and against one's own people which does not enable those war stories to become therapeutic. Returning to Figure 3 in my opening chapter (p. 18), it is by 1910, when the veterans on both sides started to look decidedly tired, that a senile form of memory developed into the *revanche* ideology, which, to a certain extant, led to the First World War. Among pages of endless *grandes manoeuvres* and imminent war reports, veterans on both sides became a more prevalent feature. In Figure 16 the soldiers of both armies went to honour the first victim of the war on either sides. The flowers and the speeches they delivered had a special meaning for them all. The war had harvested their youth as it had killed these two soldiers. Youth and war became entangled in rosy nostalgia: 'The older we grow, the pleasanter do the memory of early dates become and there are none to which I turn with greater happiness than those of 1870–71.'[16] The morbid tourism which basked in the war atmosphere of 1870 turned into literature.[17] The relics, the museums and the monuments remained central to this senile form of memory, while the graphic literature of war had taken all the subtlety and violent colours of contemporary illustrated tabloids. The 1870 war had sunk to the level of a dark fantasy calling for an expiatory battle and the lust for victory.[18] Colonial images had only been derivative and a blue African map never compensated for the mourning purple or black of the lost departments on maps of France.[19] Only a new continental epic narrative could supersede the defeat stories of 1870–71 and put them to rest.[20]

Reviving these stories and writing this book has been an often harrowing experience because fear is contagious, because between the lines of the wildly optimistic newspapers and journals of the siege, one can read the doubts, the hatred, the darker emotions brewing in the confinement of a winter siege. Within the wall-like boundaries of war stories, the words gradually betrayed the knowledge that defeat had to be accepted, that food would run short, that the cold would freeze the hearts and the hands, that *any* hope would dwindle and die.

16 H. Rundle, *With the Red Cross in the Franco-German War, 1870–1871* (Werner Laurie, 1911), p. ix.
17 War tourism and voyeurism fed the red cross with a large number of volunteers. H. Templer, *A Labour of Love under the Red Cross during the Late War* (Guernsey, LeLièvre and London, Simkin, Marshall and Co., 1892), p. 30.
18 W. Broyles Jr., 'Why men love war', in Francesca M. Cancian and J. W. Gibson (eds), *Making War, Making Peace* (Belmont, Cal., Wadsworth Publisher, 1990), pp. 29–37.
19 R. Aldrich, *Greater France: A History of French Overseas Expansion* (Macmillan, 1996), pp. 102–14; D. P. Silverman, *Reluctant Union* (Harrisburg, Pennsylvania University Press, 1972), p. 69; E. About, *Alsace, 1871–1872* (Librairie Hachette, 1906), p. 241.
20 W. R. Fryer, 'The war of 1870 and the pattern of Franco-German relations', *Renaissance and Modern Studies*, 18 (1974) 77–125.

Bibliography

Archival, newspapers and manuscript sources

I have used many Parisian archives to write this book, and newspapers and journals have added to the wealth of material. Many newspapers have also a file in the police archive which throws some light on the level of political surveillance to which they were subjected. *Paris journal*, Archives de la Police, Db139; *L'Avenir national*, Db147; *L'Abeille médicale, journal de médecine humaine, vétérinaire et revue des sciences*; *Le Courrier Médical et la réforme médicale*; *La France médicale et le Paris médical*; *La Gazette hebdomadaire*; *La Gazette médicale de Paris (3rd series, 25 & 26)*; *La Gazette des hôpitaux civils et militaires ou la lancette française*; *Le Journal de médecine mentale*; *Le Journal de la société de statistique de Paris*, 1872–73; *Le Mouvement médical, annales de l'hydrothérapie scientifique*, 1870–1871; *L'Opinion médicale*, 1869–1871; *La Presse médicale*, 1870–1871; *La Tribune médicale*, 1870–1871; *L'Union médicale*, 3rd series, 1870–1871; *La France*, Db140–1; *La Guerre illustrée, La Nation souveraine*, Db 153; *La Patrie*, Db144; *La Presse*, Db143; *Le Français*, Db 145; *Le Gaulois*; *Le Journal de débats*, Db149; *Le Journal de Paris*, Db150; *Le Journal officiel de la République*, édition de la Commune, 19 March–23 May 1871; *Le Pays*, Db151; *Le Rappel*, Db142; *Le Siècle*, Db152–3; *Le Soir*, Db146; *Le Temps*, Db1548; *Gazette des ambulances de l'armée du Rhin*, 16 August–8 September; *Gazette de l'armée, La Décentralisation (Lyons)*.

The major archival deposits of Paris have been used and in particular the following *cotes*. Archives Nationales: Dossiers des Commissaires de Police, les émigrés Polonais et l'Internationale, AN F7 12708; Ministère de l'Intérieur Janvier–Juin 1871, AN FIC1 131; Communards Amnistiés et Libérés, AN F7 12713 bis. Archives de l'Assistance Publique: all the archives relating to the war and the Commune have been classified in 1991 under the register 542 Foss which goes from 542 Foss 1 to 125. Archives du Service de Santé des Armées de Terre et de Mer: here again all the archives have been collated in a series of 'boxes' 62, 63, 64, 65, 65 bis, 66. The archives at the Vincennes Service Historique des Armées de Terre are also well organised and mostly under the label La 1–78, Lb 1–78, Lc 1–5, Ld 1–34, Le 1–59, Lf 1–14, Lg 1–7, Lh 1–13, Li 1–129, Lj 1–8, Lk 1–3, Ll 1–4, Lm1–48, Ln 1–17, Lo 1–79, Lhs 1–28, Lq 1–17, Lr 1–11, Lt 1–29, Lu 1–151, Lv 1–28, Lw 1–35, Lx 1–103. Another more detailed inventory exists for the

Commune, previously Ly 1–26. The Archives de la Préfecture de Police de Paris have suffered from the fires of May 1871 but still contain important quantities of material mostly listed in the series Ba, Db and Da. The archives of Paris also suffered greatly from the fires but enormous files are still accessible at the Archives de la Ville de Paris in the series of material deposited by *arrondissement* town-halls ranging from VD6 715 to VD6 2696, deposits from 1860 onwards. The Archives Episcopales of the archbishopric of Paris are not so well organised but contain the files of Mgr Darboy and the elements relating to his death; other interesting files are the reports to the bishop from many army chaplains. The Archives of the Grand Orient de France are now mostly available at the Bibliothèque Nationale: an inventory exists. I have also used some regional archives, notably the Archives Départementales du Rhone (Lyons), de la Creuse (Guéret), de la Haute Vienne (Limoges), de la Corrèze (Tulle), de l'Hérault (Montpellier). In all these regional archives the files studied belonged mainly to the M and R series. I also used the Archives Municipales de Montpellier.

Books, articles, pamphlets and official documents published before 1914

All French and English titles are published in Paris and London respectively unless otherwise specified. Obviously redundant publication details such as Oxford, Oxford University Press have been simplified to Oxford University Press.

Abbaie, Dr, *Les Prussiens à l'Isle–Adam et à Parmain du 16 au 30 septembre 1870*, Masquier et Cie, 1871.
About, Edmond, *Alsace, 1871–1872*, Librairie Hachette, 11th edn, 1906.
Académie de Médecine, *Mémoires sur la transmission de la syphilis par la vaccination et la vaccination animale*, J. B. Baillière, 1865.
Académie de Médecine, *Bulletin de l'Académie de Médecine*, 35(1870) and 36 (1871).
Acton, William, *Prostitution Considered in its Moral, Social and Sanitary Aspects in London and other Large Cities*, John Churchill, 1857.
Adam, Juliette, *Nos Angoisses et nos luttes, 1871–1873*, Alphonse Lemerre, 1907.
Aguilé, Jules, *Lettres d'un conscrit pendant la guerre, poésies*, Sillé le Guillaume, Besnardeau, 1875.
Aiguy, M. d', *Quel Gouvernement la France se donnera-t-elle?*, Lyons and Paris, Félix Girard, 1871.
Albigny, Paul d', *Le Livre d'or du département de l'Ardèche, contenant la liste des enfants de ce département morts en 1870–1871*, Privat, Roure, 1879.
Albiousse, Lt-Colonel d', *Le Drapeau du Sacré-Coeur, campagne de France, zouaves pontificaux*, Rennes, Hauvespre, 1871.
Allard, Abbé Julien S., *Les Zouaves pontificaux, ou journal de Mgr Daniel, aumônier des zouaves*, Hugny, 1880.
Alpy, Henri Marie, *Le Coût de la laïcisation des hôpitaux de Paris*, Le Sage, 1892.

Amanieu, Clémer, *Récits anecdotiques, campagne de 1870–1871, sept cent lieues en sept mois à travers la France, la Belgique et la Suisse*, Sauvaître, 1888.
Ambert, Général Joachim, *Le Baron Larrey*, Casse & Dumaine, 1863.
Ambert, Général Joachim, *Gaulois et Germains, récits militaires. I l'invasion; II après Sedan; III la Loire et l'Est; IV le siège de Paris*, 4 vols, Bloud et Barral, 1883–85.
Amigues, Jules, *La France à refaire : la Commune*, Lachaud, 1871.
Amigues, Jules, *Louis Nathaniel Rossel, papiers postumes recueillis et annotés par Jules Amigues*, Lachaud, 6th edn, 1871.
Amigues, Jules, *Les Aveux d'un conspirateur bonapartiste. Histoires pour servir à l'histoire de demain*, Lachaud et Burdin, 1874.
Andréoli, Émile, *Le Gouvernement du 4 septembre et la Commune*, A. Bocquet, 1871.
Andrieu, Jules, *Notes pouvant servir à l'histoire de la Commune de Paris en 1871*, Payot, 1971.
Anon., *Apparitions prophétiques d'une âme du purgatoire à une religieuse d'un monastère en Belgique en 1870, par l'auteur des 'voix prophétiques'*, Brussels, n.p., 1871.
Anon., *Comment les Français font la guerre. Recueil de faits pour servir à l'histoire des moeurs et de la civilisation au XIXe siècle*, Berlin, C. Duncker, 1871.
Anon., *Les souteneurs de la Commune – Prussiens et Bonaparte*, Librairie Générale, 1871.
Anon., *Les Violations de la Convention de Genève par les Français en 1870–1871*, Berlin, C. Duncker, 1871.
Anon., *Recueil de documents sur les exactions, vols et cruautés des armées prussiennes en France*, Bordeaux, Férot et Fils, 1871.
Anon., *Un Mois dans les lignes prussiennes du 15 août au 19 septembre par un chirurgien aide major de la Société internationale de secours aux blessés*, E. Dentu, 1871.
Anon., *Extrait des causes célèbres de tous les peuples, le maréchal Bazaine, relation complète*, Lebrun, 1874.
Anon., *Grands cadres, petits tableaux, 1870–1871. Gravelotte, Sedan, campagne de la Loire, par un chirurgien*, Coulommiers, Brodard, 1877.
Appia, Louis, *Un chirurgien à l'ambulance*, Geneva, Cherbuliez, 1859.
Appia, Louis and Gustave Moynier, *La Guerre et la charité, traité théorique et pratique de philantropie appliquée aux armées en campagne*, Geneva, Cherbuliez, 1867.
Arago, Étienne, *L'Hôtel de Ville au 4 Septembre et pendant le siège*, J. Hetzel, 1871,
Armagnac, L., *15 Jours de campagne, août–septembre 1870, étapes d'un franc-tireur parisien de Paris à Sedan*, Hachette, 1889.
Arnold, Julius, *Anatomische Beiträge zu der Lehre von den Schuss-Wunder gesammelt während der Kriegsjahre 1870–1871, in den Reservelazarethen zu Heidelberg*, Heidelberg, F. Bassermann, 1871.
Arsac, Henri, *Les Mercenaires ou les zouaves pontificaux en France*, Reims, Imprimerie Coopérative, 1872.
Arsac, Joanni d', *Les Frères des écoles chrétiennes pendant la guerre de 1870–1871*, F. Curot, 1872.
Artilleur de la batterie du Pas-de-Calais, *Histoire d'une batterie de volontaires du Pas-de-Calais, armée du Nord*, Lille, A. Noël, 1921.
Assolant, Alfred, *Le Docteur Judassohn*, E. Dentu, 1873.
Astrie, Théophile, *Le Siège de Paris en 1870 et 1871*, Le Bailly, 1871.
Atkinson, F. M. (ed.), *Memoirs of M. Thiers, 1870–1873*, George Allen, 2nd edn, 1915.

Auger, Théodore, *Le Siège de Paris, rapport sur les services rendus par l'ambulance de feu le Marquis de Hertford*, Parent, 1871.

Autier, Jean-Baptiste Victor, *Notre Balance humanitaire, ou compte rendu de l'emploi de notre temps à partir du 26 Juillet 1870 jusqu'au 1 Juin 1871, soit sur le champs de bataille, soit dans les ambulances*, Montdidier, Imprimerie de A. Radenez, 1872.

Auzias-Turenne, Joseph-Alexandre, *La Syphilisation, publication de l'oeuvre du Dr Auzias-Turenne faite par les soins de ses amis*, Germer Baillière, 1878.

Bader, Émile, *Mars-la-Tour et son monument national*, Mars-la-Tour, Ritter-Roscop, 1893.

Bagehot, Walter, *Lois scientifiques du développement des nations dans leurs rapports avec les principes de la sélection naturelle et de l'hérédité*, G. Baillière, 1873.

Bainville, Jacques, *Bismarck et la France d'après les mémoires du Prince de Hohenloe*, Nouvelle Librairie Nationale, 1911.

Ballot, Charles, *Des Effets de la guerre à Paris et en France sur le louage, la propriété et les divers contrats*, A. Maresq aîné, 1871.

Bancel, Émile, *Relation médico-chirurgicale du siège de Toul, août–septembre 1870*, Nancy, Berger Levrault, 1873.

Baron, Léon, *Le Petit Alsacien, poème patriotique*, E. Dentu, 1885.

Baron, Louis, *Sous le drapeau rouge*, Nouvelle Librairie Parisienne Albert Savine, 1889.

Bastard, Georges, *La Défense de Bazeilles*, P. Ollendorff, 1884.

Bataille, Alexandre and Eugène de Barins, *Nouveau Mémorial français historique et complet de la guerre 1870–1871, des deux sièges de Paris et de la Commune*, Pick de l'Isère, Librairie Nationale, 1880.

Bavoux, Évariste, *Les Causes de la guerre. Solution à la crise actuelle*, A. Sauton, 1871.

Baye, Hippolyte, *La Frontière, essais de poésie, les juvéniles, fragments*, A. Lacroix, Verboeckhoven and Cie, 1871.

Beaufort, François Louis Charles Amédée, Comte de, *Recherches sur la prothèse des membres*, P. Asselin, 1867.

Beaufort, François Louis Charles Amédée, Comte de, *Étude sur la Société française de secours aux blessés des armées de terre et de mer et sur la convention de Genève*, Imprimerie Administrative de Paul Dupont, 1870.

Beaufort, François Louis Charles Amédée, Comte de, *Questions philanthropiques – transport des blessés – hôpitaux – appareils. Assistance aux mutilés pauvres, etc*, Imprimerie Nationale, 1875.

Beaufort, François Louis Charles Amédée, Comte de, *La Cécité par fait de guerre (le soldat aveugle) conférence faite par le Comte de Beaufort*, Imprimerie Nationale, 1887.

Beaujort, Eugène, *L'Héroïne d'Alsace, récit en vers*, E. Lachaud, 1871.

Beaunis, Henri Étienne, *Impressions de campagne, 1870–1871, siège de Strasbourg, campagne de la Loire, campagne de l'Est*, Félix Alcan and Berger Levrault et Cie, 1887, reprinted from the *Gazette médicale de Paris*.

Beaunis, Henri Étienne, *L'École du Service de santé militaire de Strasbourg et la faculté de médecine de Strasbourg de 1856 à 1870*, Berger Levrault, 1888.

Bégin, Louis Jacques, *Études sur le Service de santé militaire en France: son passé, son présent, son avenir*, J. B. Baillière, 1849, reprinted V. Rozier, 1860.

Belin, Léon, *Le Siège de Belfort, siège et bombardement*, Paris and Nancy, Berger Levrault, 1871.
Belleval, René, Marquis de, *Les Souvenirs de guerre d'un intendant militaire*, Calmann Lévy, 1886.
Bellina, A. de, *Les Polonais et la Commune de Paris*, n.p., 1871.
Bellina, E., *I Treno-ospedali della Germania nella guerra de 1870–1871*, Florence, 1872.
Benedetti, Comte Vincent, *Ma Mission en Prusse*, H. Plon, 1871.
Béraud, Edmond, *Gambetta dictateur*, Poitiers, H. Oudin, 1881.
Béraud, Edmond, *La République c'est la guerre*, n.p., 1885.
Béraud, Régis, *Les Filles publiques de Paris et la police qui les régit*, J. B. Baillière, 1839.
Berenger-Féraud, Laurent Jean-Baptiste, 'Des Blessures de l'abdomen observées dans la deuxième division des blessés du Val-de-Grâce pendant le siège de Paris', *Montpellier médical*, XXVII, 1871.
Berenger-Féraud, Laurent Jean-Baptiste, *Étude sur les blessures du poignet, du métacarpe et des doigts dans la deuxième division des blessés du Val-de-Grâce pendant le siège de Paris*, A. Hennuyer, 1872.
Berenger-Féraud, Laurent Jean-Baptiste, et al., *Discours prononcés le 18 octobre 1895 aux funérailles du baron Hippolyte Larrey*, Librairies-Imprimeries Réunies, 1895.
Berenger-Féraud, Laurent Jean-Baptiste, *Le Baron Hippolyte Larrey, 1808–1895*, Fayard Frères, 1899.
Bergerat, Émile, *Les Cuirassiers de Reischoffen*, A. Lemerre, 1870.
Bergerat, Émile, *Le Petit Alsacien, poème*, A. Lemerre, 1871.
Bergerat, Émile, *Poèmes de la guerre*, A. Lemerre, 1871.
Bergerat, Émile, *Strasbourg, ode*, A. Lemerre, 1871.
Berkeley-Hill, Matthew, *Treatment of the Sick and Wounded: Illustrated by Observations Made at the Seat of War*, James Walton, 1870.
Bernard, Claude, *Introduction à l'étude de la médecine expérimentale*, 1865, reprinted Flammarion, 1984.
Bernhardt, Sarah, *Ma double vie*, 2 vols, Des Femmes, 1910, reprinted 1980.
Berte, Aîné, *Les Menus d'un restaurant de Paris durant le siège, préface d'analogie passionnelle sur les malheurs de la France*, Toulon, Tardy, 1872.
Bienaymé, Gustave, *Le Coût de la vie à diverses époques*, Nancy, Berger Levrault, 1896.
Billroth, Theodor, *Chirurgische Briefe aus den Kriegs-Lazarethen in Weissenburg und Mannheim, 1870, ein Beitrag zu den wichtigen Abschmitten der Kriegschirurgie mit besonder Rücksicht auf Statistik*, Berlin, A. Hirschwald, 1872.
Billy, E. de, *Rapport à la commission des finances à l'assemblée générale des fondateurs de la Société de secours aux blessés des armées de terre et de mer*, Imprimerie Nationale, 1873.
Bingham, D., *Recollections of Paris*, 2 vols, Chapman and Hall, 1896.
Biotière, Francisque de, *Paris dans les caves, épisodes du siège de 1870–1871*, Saguier, 1872.
Bitterlin, Dr G., *La Croix Rouge aux avant-postes de la Marne, 1870–1871*, St Maur, Vigot-Frères, 1912.
Blanchaud, Charles, *Étapes du 71e mobiles, impressions et souvenirs*, Limoges, V. Ducourtieux, 1872.
Blandeau, H. R., *La Dictature de Gambetta*, Amyot, 1871.

Blandeau, H. R., *Patriotisme du clergé catholique et des ordres religieux pendant la guerre de 1870–1*, Lecoffre, 1873.
Bode, Samuel Harris, *The War between Germany and France: A Sermon in Aid of the Fund for the Sick and Wounded*, 20 November 1870, n.p., 1870.
Boguslawski, Albrecht von, *Physionomie du combat d'infanterie pendant la guerre de 1870–1871*, C. Tanera, 1872.
Boguslawski, Albrecht von, *Tactical Deductions from the War of 1870–1871*, trans. Colonel Lumby Graham, Tyndall and Co., 1872.
Boguslawski, Albrecht von, *Considérations générales sur la manière de diriger les troupes*, C. Tanera, 1873.
Boisseau, Edmond, *Des Maladies simulées et des moyens de les reconnaître*, J. B. Baillière et Fils, 1870.
Bonjean, Jean Henry, *L'Emploi de l'ergotine sur les malades et les blessés de l'Armée du Rhin comme homéostatique, cicatrisant et antiputride*, Germer Baillière, 1870.
Bonnal, M. de, *Une Agonie, roman Darwinien*, Angoulême, Luzol, 1877.
Bonnard, Arthur de, *Organisation de la vraie république, première mesure, les dossiers sociaux, le livre d'or du bien*, Berthélémy, 1870.
Bonnard, C., *1870–18??, Vichy ambulance; son rôle pendant la prochaine guerre*, Vichy, C. Bougarel, [1872], 1890, 1891.
Bonnefont, J. P., *Du Fonctionnement des ambulances sur le champ de bataille*, Baillière, 1870.
Bonnefont, J. P., *Ambulances internationales et privées*, Bureau de *l'Union Médicale*, 1871.
Bopierre, A., *Pourquoi la France n'a pas trouvé d'hommes supérieurs au moment du péril? Réponse à M. Pasteur, de l'Institut*, Masson, 1871.
Borel d'Hauterive, André François-Joseph, *Les Sièges de Paris, annales militaires de la capitale depuis Jules César jusqu'à ce jour*, E. Dentu, 1871.
Boucabeille, Vincent, *Jours de marche : journal de guerre d'un soldat de 1870, juillet–octobre*, reprinted Épigones, 1992.
Boulanger, Léon, *Compte Rendu des travaux du comité de secours de la Sarthe*, Le Mans, Imprimerie E. Monnoyer, 1871.
Bournand, François, *Le Clergé pendant la Commune, 1871*, Tolra, 1891, 2nd edn 1892.
Bournand, François, *Les Soeurs martyres, les soeurs Augustines, les soeurs des hôpitaux pendant la guerre (1870–1871) ; dévouements ; témoignages des contemporains ; les soeurs récompensées*, Tours, A. Cattier, 1894.
Boyland, George Holstead, *Six Months under the Red Cross with the French Army*, Cincinnati, Robert Clarke and Co., 1873.
Brackenbury, Henry, *Les Maréchaux de France, étude de leur conduite dans la guerre de 1870*, Lachaud, 1872.
Bréjean, Jules and Joseph Humblot, *Les Mairies de Paris, organisation – attributions – fonctionnement*, Chaix, 1907.
Brice, Marie-Raoul and Capitaine Bottet, *Le Corps de santé militaire en France, son évolution, ses campagnes, 1708–1882*, Paris and Limoges, Berger Levrault, 1907.
Brierre de Boismont, A., 'A lunatic asylum during the siege of Paris', *The Lancet*, 4 March 1871, vol. 1, pp. 301–2, also published in *L'Union médicale*, 24 June 1871.
Bron, Dr Félix, *Histoire d'une ambulance sur le champ de bataille*, Lyons, A. Vingtrinier, 1872.

Brouardel, Paul Camille Hippolyte, 'Pathogénie de quelques unes des maladies qui ont régné pendant les blocus de Metz et de Paris', *Revue scientifique*, 49 (1/06/1872) 1165–8.
Brouardel, Paul Camille Hippolyte, *De l'Exercice de la médecine et de l'enseignement de la médecine, rapport fait au nom du conseil général de l'Association des Médecins de France sur la révision des lois de l'an XI sur l'exercice de la médecine et de la pharmacie*, Malteste, 1873.
Brouardel, Paul Camille Hippolyte, *L'Exercice de la médecine et le charlatanisme*, J. B. Baillière et Fils, 1899.
Brouardel, Paul Camille Hippolyte, *La Profession médicale au commencement du vingtième siècle*, J. B. Baillière et Fils, 1903.
Broussière, François, *Lettre à Monsieur le Major Général de l'armée du Rhin relative au pansement des blessés sur le champ de bataille*, Marseilles, Imprimerie Commerciale Doucet, 1870.
Bruno, J., *Les Reptiles prussiens ou les crimes des espions*, Simon et Cie, 1888.
Bucher de Chauvigné, Anselme and M. Collet, *Rapport sur le service de l'évacuation des militaires blessés et malades présenté à Mr l'Intendant de Première Classe Guérin*, Lefebvre, 1875.
Buret, François, *Syphilis Today and Among the Ancients*, 3 vols, Philadephia and London, Baillière, 1889–92.

Casimir, Prosper, *Les Pages douloureuses de la guerre, l'hôpital-hospice de Niort en 1870–1871*, Niort, L. Favre, 1872.
Cattelain, Paul Peltier, *Souvenirs inédits du chef de la sûreté sous la Commune*, Juven, 1900.
Cavaniol, Henri, *L'Invasion de 1870–1871 dans la Haute-Marne*, [1871] Chaumont, C. Cavaniol, 1973, reprinted Montreuil, Delbos, 1989.
Cazenove, Léonce de, *Considérations sur les sociétés protectrices des animaux*, C. Jaillet, 1865.
Cazenove, Léonce de, *Compte rendu des travaux du comité sectionnaire lyonnais de la Société française de secours aux blessés et malades des armées de terre et de mer*, Lyons, Imprimerie de Bellan, 1872.
Cazenove, Léonce de, *La Guerre et l'humanité au dix-neuvième siècle*, Arnauld de Vresse, 1869, 2nd edn 1875.
Chalanet, Arthur, *Les Bienfaits de la guerre et les leçons de la défaite*, Lyons, Mérat, 1871.
Chanzy, Général Antoine Eugène, *La Campagne de 1870–1871, la deuxième armée de la Loire*, H. Plon, 1871, reprinted Gautier, 1895.
Chapplain, Léonard, *De l'Intendance du corps médical militaire et de la mortalité dans l'armée, réponse à monsieur le docteur Chenu*, Librairie Jean Dumaine, 1872.
Charcot, Jean Martin, *La Médecine empirique et la médecine scientifique parallèle, entre les anciens et les modernes*, A. Delahaye, 1867, (reprinted from *La gazette des hôpitaux* of May 1867).
Charcot, Jean Martin, *Oeuvres complètes : leçons recueillies et publiées par messrs Bourneville, Bobinski, Bernard, Ferré, Guinon Marie, Gilles de la Tourette, Brissaud, Sevestre*, 9 vols, *Progrès médical*/Lecrosnier and Babé, 1886–93.

Charcot, Jean Martin, *La Foi qui guérit, Progrès médical*, 1907.
Charpignon, Louis Joseph, *Souvenirs de l'occupation d'Orléans par les Allemands en 1870–1871, théorie de l'invasion; les effets, les assassinats; les blessés*, Orléans, H. Herluison, 1872.
Chassagne, Amédée, *Contre le Prussien: I Hier ..., II aujourd'hui ..., III demain ...*, Paris and Limoges, Henri Charles Lavauzelle, 1896.
Chasteau, Paul (ed.), *Recueil des dépêches françaises officielles*, 3 vols, A. Lacroix, 1871.
Chaules, M., 'Résections dans la continuité des os longs des membres à la suite des coups de feu', Thèse de doctorat, Faculté de médecine de Paris, 1872.
Chenu, Dr J. C., *De la mortalité dans l'armée et des moyens d'économiser la vie humaine*, Hachette, 1870.
Chenu, Dr J. C., *Aperçu historique, statistique et clinique sur le service des ambulances et des hôpitaux de la Société française de secours aux blessés des armées de terre et de mer durant la guerre 1870–1871*, 2 vols, Hachette, Dumaine, Masson, 1874.
Chipault, Antoine Adolphe, *Fractures par armes à feu, expectation, résection sous-périostée, évidemment, amputation, armée de la Loire*, G. Baillière, 1872.
Christot, J. M. Félix, *Le Massacre de l'ambulance de Saône-et-Loire, 21 Janvier 1871. Rapport du comité médical de secours aux blessés le 7 juillet 1871*, Lyons, A. Vingtrinier, 1871.
Claretie, Arsène Arnaud dit Jules, *La Débâcle, 4 septembre 1870*, Librairie Centrale, 1870.
Claretie, Arsène Arnaud dit Jules, *Paris assiégé, tableaux et souvenirs, septembre 1870 – janvier 1871*, Alphonse Lemerre, 1871.
Claretie, Arsène Arnaud dit Jules, *Paris assiégé. Journal 1870–1871*, reprinted Armand Colin, 1992.
Clemenceau, Georges, *Le Grand Pan*, G. Charpentier and E. Fosquelle, 1896.
Cluseret, Gustave Paul, *Mémoires du Général Cluseret*, 3 vols, Jules Lévy, 1887–88.
Cochin, Auguste, 'Le Service de santé des armées, avant et pendant le siège de Paris', *Revue des deux mondes* (1/11/1870) 58–136.
Cochin, Auguste, *Le Service de santé des armées, avant et pendant le siège de Paris*, Sauton, 1871.
Cochin, Henry, 'Impressions d'un bourgeois de Paris pendant le siège et la Commune', *Revue des deux mondes* (1/08/1916) 526–5; (15/08/1916) 846–74.
Coignon, Gustave, *État sanitaire de Bitche pendant le siège, campagne de 1870–1871*, Bitche, n.p., n.d., 1871?
Colmar, M. (ed.), *Discours parlementaires de M. Thiers*, 16 vols, Calmann Lévy, 1879–89.
Combe, M. de la, *Souvenirs de l'invasion, l'occupation d'Orléans*, Douniol, 1871.
Combes, Eugène, *De l'État actuel de la médecine et des médecins en France avec un plan de redressement d'une situation qui blesse à la fois les intérêts des médecins et des malades*, A. Delahaye, 1869.
Condé, Hector de, *La Prusse au pilori de la civilisation, crimes et forfaits des Prussiens en France*, Brussels, Devillé, 1871.
Conte, Paul Alfred, *Le Ulhan et le raid, études sur la cavalerie et sur l'armée nouvelle*, E. Dentu, 1871.
Coste, E., *Armée de la Loire (1870–1871) ; Nos étapes, journal de l'ambulance de la Haute-Vienne*, Limoges, A. Ducourtieux, 1872.

Coudray, Louis Désiré, *Défense de Châteaudun dans la journée du 18 octobre 1870, incendies de Varize et de Civry,* Châteaudun, Pouiller Vaudecraine, 1871, 3rd edn, E. Dentu, 1871.
Court, Félicien, *Louis Ormières, 1851–1914, et l'ambulance du Grand Orient de France en 1870–1871,* Imprimerie Nouvelle, 1914.
Cousin, Dr A., *Histoire chirurgicale de l'ambulance des ponts et chaussées service de Monsieur Demarquay, ambulance de la presse française, notes pouvant servir à l'étude de la résection du genou en temps de guerre,* Malteste, 1872.
Cresson, Ernest, *Cent jours à la Préfecture de Police, 2 novembre 1870 – 11 février 1871,* H. Plon, Nourrit et Cie, 1901.
Croix Rouge, France, *Album du matériel d'ambulance de la société de secours aux blessés militaires,* Monrocq, 1888.
Crombrugghe, Baronne Ida de, *Journal d'une infirmière pendant la guerre 1870–1871, Sarrebrück, Metz, Cambrai,* H. Plon, 1872, and Brussels, Claessen, 3rd edn, 1871.

Da Costa, Gaston, *La Commune vécue,* 3 vols, Quantin, 1903–5.
Dauban, Charles Aimé, *La Guerre comme la font les prussiens,* H. Plon, 1871.
Dauban, Charles Aimé, *Le Fond de la société sous la Commune d'après les documents qui constituent les archives de la justice militaire, avec des considérations sur les moeurs du temps et sur les évènements qui ont précédé la Commune,* H. Plon, 1873.
Daudet, Alphonse, *Les Contes du Lundi,* 1873, reprinted Maxi Poche Classiques Français, 1995.
Decaisne, Dr E., 'Le Siège de Paris au point de vue de l'hygiène et de la chirurgie', *Revue scientifique,* 20 (1/11/1871) 468–71.
Delambre, Col. Alfred Philippe, *Étude sur les chemins de fer au point de vue militaire,* Amyot, 1874.
Delessert, Eugène, *Épisodes pendant la Commune, souvenirs d'un délégué de la société de secours aux blessés des armées de terre et de mer,* Charles Noblet, private circulation, 1872.
Delorme, Edmond, *Traité de chirurgie de guerre,* 2 vols, Félix Alcan, 1888–93.
Delpech, Auguste Louis Dominique, *Le Scorbut pendant le siège de Paris, étude sur l'étiologie de cette affection à l'occasion d'une épidémie observée dans la maison de correction de la Santé,* J. B. Baillière, 1871.
Delpech, Auguste Louis Dominique, *Rapport sur les épidémies pour les années 1870, 1871, 1872, présenté à l'Académie de Médecine,* G. Masson, 1875.
Delpit, Martial, *Rapport fait au nom de la commission d'enquête chargée au termes de la loi du 17 juin 1871, de rechercher les causes de l'insurrection du 18 mars et de constater les faits qui s'y rattachent,* 3 vols, Versailles, Le Cerf, 1872.
Deluns-Montaud, Pierre, A. Aulard, Émile Bourgeois and Joseph Reinach, *Les Origines diplomatiques de la guerre de 1870–1871, recueil de documents publiés par le ministère des affaires étrangères,* 10 vols, Gustave Ficker, 1910–15.
Denormandie, M. E., *Le VIIIe arrondissement et son administration pendant le siège de Paris,* Garnier Frères, 1875.
Depaul, Jean Anne Henri, *De la Syphilis vaccinale, communications à l'Académie de Médecine,* J. B. Baillière, 1865.
Déroulède, Paul, *1870, feuilles de route, des bois de Verrières à la forteresse de Breslau,* F. Juven, 31st edn, 1907.

Déroulède, Paul, *Nouvelles Feuilles de route de la forteresse de Breslau aux allées de Tourny*, F. Juven, 1907.
Déroulède, Paul, *Pages françaises*, Bloud, 1909.
Des Cilleuls, Alfred, *Histoire de l'administration parisienne au dix-neuvième siècle*, 3 vols. H. Champion, 1900.
Des Cilleuls, Alfred, *Histoire de l'administration parisienne sous la troisième république*, Picard Fils and Cie, 1910.
Deschaumes, Edmond, *L'Armée du Nord (1870–1871), campagne du général Faidherbe*, La France Moderne, Firmin Didot, 1895.
Deschaumes, Edmond, *Souvenirs d'un lycéen de 14 ans pendant le siège de Paris, 1870–1871*, La France Moderne, Firmin Didot, 1890.
Desgranges, Dr Antoine, *Les Ambulances sédentaires de Lyon pendant la guerre de 1870–1871*, Lyons, Bellon & *Le Salut Public*, 1872.
Dolivet, Charles, *Histoire de la garde nationale et des bataillons mobilisés du IXe arrondissement*, l'auteur, 1872.
Domenech, Abbé Emmanuel, *Histoire de la campagne de 1870–1871, et de la deuxième ambulance dite 'de la presse française'*, Lyons, Imprimerie du Salut Public, 1871.
Doncourt, A. S. de, alias Antoinette J. A. Symon de Latreiche, Comtesse Drohojovska, *Souvenirs des ambulances*, Lille, Lefort, 1872.
Dormoy, P. A., *Les Trois Batailles de Dijon, 30 octobre, 26 novembre, 21 janvier*, Librairie Militaire Dubois, 1894.
Doyon, Adrien, *Notes et souvenirs d'un chirurgien d'ambulance, deuxième ambulance lyonnaise*, Lyons, Imprimerie A. Vingtrinier, 1872.
Dramard, Louis, *Transformisme et socialisme : concordance des principales revendications du socialisme contemporain avec les corollaires de la théorie de l'évolution*, Bureaux du *Prolétaire*, 1882.
Dreyfus-Brisac, Edmond Paul, *L'Université de Bonn et l'enseignement en Allemagne*, Hachette, 1879.
Dreyfus-Brisac, Edmond Paul, *L'Enseignement en France et à l'étranger considéré du point de vue politique et social*, A. Colin, 1880.
du Barail, Général, *Mes souvenirs, 1864–1879*, 3 vols, H. Plon, 1896.
du Camp, Maxime, *Paris, ses organes, ses fonctions et sa vie dans la seconde moitié du XIXième siècle*, 6 vols, Hachette, 1869–75.
du Camp, Maxime, *Les Ancêtres de la Commune, l'attentat Fieschi*, Charpentier, 1877.
du Camp, Maxime, *Les Convulsions de Paris, I les prisons pendant la Commune, II épisodes de la Commune, III les sauvetages pendant la Commune, IV la Commune à l'Hôtel-de-Ville*, 4 vols, Hachette, 1878–80.
du Camp, Maxime, *La Charité privée à Paris, l'orphelinat d'Auteuil et l'abbé Roussel*, Ch. Des Granges, 1881, 2nd edn, Hachette, 1885.
du Camp, Maxime, *La Croix Rouge en France*, Hachette, 1889.
du Casse, Baron Albert, *La Guerre au jour le jour, 1870–1871*, J. Dumaine, 1875.
du Mesnil, Dr Octave, 'L'Hygiène pendant le siège de Paris', *Annales d'hygiène*, 2nd series, 35 (1871) 413–28.
du Mesnil, Dr Octave, *L'Hygiène à Paris, l'habitat du pauvre*, J. B. Baillière et Fils, 1890.
Dubos, E., *La Peste bovine dans le département de l'Oise pendant les années 1870, 1871 et 1872*, Beauvais, Père, 1874.

Ducaine, E., 'Le Siège de Paris au point de vue de l'hygiène et de la chirurgie', *Revue Scientifique*, 20 (11/11/1871) 468–71.
Ducray, Camille, *Paul Déroulède 1846–1914*, n.p., 1914.
Ducrot, Général Auguste Alexandre, *La Défense de Paris, 1870–1871*, 4 vols, E. Dentu, 1875.
Dufour, Général and Gustave Moynier, *Congrès de Genève, rapport addressé au conseil fédéral*, Geneva, n.p., 1864.
Dugast, Dr H., *Souvenirs intimes de l'Ambulance Mobile de la Côte d'Or, Campagnes de la Loire et de l'Est, 1870–1871*, Dijon, Marchand, 1872.
Dunant, Jean Henry, *Convention de Genève : un souvenir de Solférino*, Hachette, 6th edn, 1873.
Dupont, Gustave, *L'Explosion de la citadelle de Laon, épisode de l'invasion allemande avec des pièces justificatives inédites*, Caen, Le Blanc Hardel, 1877.
Dupont, Léonce, *Tours et Bordeaux, souvenirs de la république à outrance*, E. Dentu, 1877.
Dupont, Léonce, *Souvenirs de Versailles pendant la Commune*, E. Dentu, 1881.
Dupuy, E., *De la Situation des invalides en Allemagne et en Autriche Hongrie*, Librairie Jean Dumaine, 1874.
Durand-Fardel, Raymond, *L'Internat en médecine et en chirurgie des hôpitaux et hospices civils de Paris, centenaire de l'internat, 1802–1902*, Steinheil, 1904.

Eichthal, Louis d', *Le Général Bourbaki, par un de ses anciens officiers d'ordonnance*, Plon, Nourrit et Cie, 1885.
Ély, Charles, *Paris, études démographiques et médicales*, Masson, 1872.
Ernouf, Alfred Auguste, Baron, *Histoire des chemins de fer français pendant la guerre franco-prussienne*, Librairie Générale, 1874.
Evans, Thomas W., *La Commission sanitaire des États Unis, son organisation et ses résultats avec une notice sur les hôpitaux militaires aux États Unis et sur la réforme sanitaire dans les armées européennes*, E. Dentu, 1865, five edns up to 1867.
Evans, Thomas W., *Essais d'hygiène et de thérapeutique militaire*, E. Dentu, 1867.
Evans, Thomas W., *Histoire de l'ambulance américaine pendant le siège de Paris*, A. Laugel, 1871.
Evans, Thomas W., *History of the American Ambulances in Paris during the Siege of 1870–1871*, Baillière, 1873.
Evans, Thomas W., *Memoirs of Dr Thomas W. Evans, Recollection of the Second Empire*, ed. E. A. Crane, 2 vols, Fisher Unwin, 1905.
Eyre, V., *A Fortnight's Tour among French Ambulances*, 1870.

Faidherbe, Général Léon, *Campagne de l'armée du Nord en 1870–1871*, E. Dentu, 1871.
Faidherbe, Général Léon, *Note supplémentaire addressée à la commission d'enquête du 4 Septembre sur les opérations de l'armée du Nord*, E. Leroux, 1873.
Favre, Jules, *Gouvernement de la Défense Nationale du 30 juin au 31 octobre 1870*, H. Plon, 1871.
Faze, L., *Histoire de la guerre civile de 1871 ; le Gouvernement de l'assemblée de Versailles, la Commune de Paris*, Charpentier, 1879.
Ferré, T., *Rapport sur les services des ambulances municipales du troisième arrondissement pendant le siège de Paris, 1870–1871*, Rigal, 1872.

Feuillet, Paul, *De l'Assistance Publique à Paris*, Berger Levrault, 1888.
Fiaux, Louis, *L'Hygiène militaire, esquisses historiques et médicales à propos d'un bataillon de la garde mobile de l'armée de Paris*, Victor Rozier, 1871.
Fiaux, Louis, *L'Enseignement de la médecine en Allemagne*, Baillière, 1877.
Fiaux, Louis, *Histoire de la guerre civile de 1871, le gouvernement et l'assemblée de Versailles, la Commune de Paris*, Charpentier, 1879.
Fiaux, Louis, *Jules Ferry, un malfaiteur public*, Librairie Internationale, 1886.
Fiaux, Louis, *Les Maisons de tolérance : leur fermeture*, Georges Carré, 1892.
Fischbach, Gustave, *Guerre de 1870. Le siège et le bombardement de Strasbourg*, Cherbuliez, 1871, and Strasbourg, Libraires, 1870.
Fix, Colonel Théodore, *Souvenirs d'un officier d'état–major*, 2 vols, F. Juven, 1898.
Flach, Jacques, *Strasbourg après le bombardement, 2 octobre 1870 – 30 septembre 1872, rapports sur les travaux du comité de secours strasbourgeois pour les victimes du bombardement*, Strasburg, Imprimerie de Fischbach, 1873.
Flamarion, Dr Alfred, *Le Livret du docteur, souvenirs de campagne contre l'Allemagne et contre la Commune de Paris*, Le Chevalier, 1872.
Fleury, André, 'De l'Assistance Publique à Paris', Thèse de doctorat, Faculté de droit, Rousseau, 1901.
Flévy d'Urville, M., *Les Ordures de Paris*, Sartorius, 1874.
Flourens, Gustave, *Paris livré*, A. Lacroix, 1871.
Foderé, F. E., *Traité de médecine légale et d'hygiène publique ou de police de santé*, De l'imprimerie de Mame, 2nd edn, 1813.
Fontane, Théodor, *Souvenirs d'un prisonnier de guerre allemand*, Perrin et Cie, 1892.
Forbes, Archibald, *My Experiences of the War between France and Germany*, 2 vols, Hurst and Blackett, 1871.
Fouquet, Abbé E., *Balan pendant la guerre de 1870*, Charleville, Imprimerie Anciaux, 1891.
Fouquet, Abbé E., *Bazeilles pendant la guerre de 1870*, Balan-Sedan, Imprimerie du Patronage, 1895.
Fournier, A., *De la Contagion syphilitique*, Delahaye, 1860.
Fournier, A., *L'Hérédité syphilitique*, Masson, 1891.
Frégier, H. A., *Des Classes dangereuses de la population dans les grandes villes*, J. B. Baillière, 1840.
Freycinet, Charles de, *Souvenirs, 1848–1878*, Delagrave, 1912.
Furley, John, *Épreuves et luttes d'un volontaire neutre*, Jean Dumaine, 1874.
Fustel de Coulanges, Denis, *L'Alsace est-elle allemande ou française? Réponse à M. Mommsen, professeur à Berlin*, E. Dentu, 1871.

Gallard, Théophile, *Malades et blessés de l'armée de la Loire, services médicaux supplémentaires créés pendant la guerre*, J. B. Baillière et Fils, 1871.
Gallard, Théophile, *Leçons de clinique médicale*, J. B. Baillière et Fils, 1872.
Gallet, Louis, 'Guerre et Commune. Impressions d'un hospitalier de juillet 1870 à juin 1871', *Nouvelle revue*, 105, 106, 107 (1897) 297–321, 551–75, 717–42, reprinted as *Guerre et Commune 1870–1871, impressions d'un hospitalier*, Calmann Lévy, 1898.
Gallet, Henri, *Les Anniversaires de la guerre de 1870–1871 d'après Français et Allemands*, Garnier Frères, 1895.

Garibaldi, Riciotti, *Souvenirs de la campagne de France 1870–71*, Nice, La Semaine Niçoise, 1899.

Garin, Joseph, *De la Police sanitaire et de l'Assistance Publique dans leurs rapports avec l'extinction des maladies vénériennes*, Rapport à la Société Impériale de Médecine de Lyon, Masson, 1866.

Gaulot, Paul, *La Vérité sur l'expédition du Mexique d'après les documents et souvenirs de Ernest Louet, payeur en chef du corps expéditionnaire*, 3 vols, P. Ollendorff, 1889–90.

Gautier, Émile, *Le Darwinisme social*, Derveaux, 1880.

Gavoy, Émile Alexandre, *Étude de faits de guerre: Le Service de santé militaire en 1870, hier, aujourd'hui, demain*, Paris and Limoges, Henri Charles Lavauzelle, 1894

Gazon de la Peyrière, Comte, *L'Église de France devant l'invasion prussienne*, Régis Ruffet, 1872.

Ginestet, C. Habert de, *Souvenirs d'un prisonnier de guerre en Allemagne*, Flammarion, n.d.

Girard, Dr, *Contribution à l'histoire médico-chirurgicale du siège de Paris, l'ambulance de la rue Violet*, n.p., 1872.

Gircourt, M., 'Plaies et résections de l'épaule', Thèse de doctorat, Faculté de médecine de Paris, 1872.

Glais-Bizoin, Alexandre, *Dictature de cinq mois. Mémoires pour servir à l'histoire du gouvernement de la défense nationale à Tours et à Bordeaux*, E. Dentu, 1873.

Goltz, Baron von der, *Gambetta et ses armées*, Sandoz and Fischbacher, 1877.

Goncourt, Edmond de, *Paris under Siege from the Goncourt Journal*, [1870–71] Ithaca, Cornell University Press, 1969.

Gordon, Charles Alexander, *Le Siège de Paris au point de vue de l'hygiène et de la chirurgie*, J. B. Baillière, 1871.

Gordon, Charles Alexander, *The Siege of Paris: A Medical and Chirurgical Study*, Baillière, Tindall and Cox, 1872.

Gordon, Charles Alexander, *Lessons on Hygiene and Surgery, from the Franco-Prussian War*, Baillière, Tindall and Cox, 1873.

Governmental papers, *Bulletin officiel du ministère de l'intérieur, délégation de Tours et de Bordeaux*, Poitiers, A. Dupré, 1871.

Governmental papers, *Rapports du conseil d'enquête sur les capitulations des places fortes*, Librairie Centrale, 1872.

Governmental papers, *Rapport sur les actes de la délégation du gouvernement de la défense nationale à Tours et à Bordeaux*, Versailles, Le Cerf, 1876.

Grand Orient, *Bulletin du Grand Orient de France, suprême conseil pour la France et les possessions françaises*, 3rd series, 26 (1870) 5–6; 27 (1871) 1–6.

Grandeffe, Arthur Raoul de Guilloteau, Comte de, *Mobiles et volontaires de la Seine pendant la guerre et les deux sièges*, E. Dentu, 1871.

Grandière, A. Benoist de la, *Compte rendu chirurgical de l'ambulance des soeurs de Saint Joseph de Cluny, succursale du Val-de-Grâce*, Baillière, 1871.

Grange, Dr J., *Mort et obsèque de Monsieur le Docteur Arendrup: Médecin Danois, mort au service de la France*, Bureau de l'*Union Médicale*, 1871.

Grange, Dr J., *Rapport à Monsieur le président de la Société française de secours aux blessés, sur l'ambulance de Bougival, projet d'ambulance de perfectionnement*, A. Chaix, 1872.

Grange, Dr J., *Société française de secours aux blessés, compte rendu du service funèbre célébré à Notre-Dame de Paris*, Chaix, 1872.
Granveau, Antoine, *La Prostitution dans Paris*, l'auteur, 1867.
Green, Evelyn E., *Ringed by Fire: A Story of the Franco-Prussian War*, Thomas Nelson and Sons, 1904, reprinted 1914.
Grellois, Eugène, *Histoire médicale du blocus de Metz*, J. B. Baillière, 1872.
Grimaud de Caux, Gabriel, *De septembre 1870 à février 1871 : L'Académie des Sciences pendant le siège de Paris*, Didier et Cie, 1871.
Guéronnière, Comte Alfred de la, *La Prusse devant l'Europe*, Brussels, Office de Publicité, 1870.
Guetton, Joannès, *Six mois de drapeau rouge à Lyon*, P. N. Josserand, 1871.
Guillon, Édouard, *Le Nouveau Soldat du service obligatoire*, n.p., 1873.
Guizot, François, *L'Église et la société chrétiennes en 1861*, Michel Lévy Frères, 1861.
Guldin, A., *Les Monuments des soldats de l'armée de Bourbaki décédés en Suisse en 1871*, St Gall, Imprimerie Merkur, 1898.

H. A. U., *On the New Laws of War and the Succour to the Wounded*, n.p., 1865.
Hale, Colonel Lonsdale, *The 'People's War' in France, 1870–1871*, Hugh Rees Ltd, 1904.
Hardonin (Dick de Lonlay), *Français et Allemand, histoire anecdotique de la guerre de 1870–1871*, 6 vols, Garnier Frères, 1887–91.
Hazier, Captain H. M., *The Franco-Prussian War: Its Causes, Incidents and Consequences*, 2 vols, William Mackenzie, 1873.
Henty, George Alfred, *Single Works: The Young Francs Tireurs and their Adventures in the Franco-Prussian War*, F. V. White, 1872.
Henty, George Alfred, *A Woman of the Commune*, F. V. White, 4th edn, 1895.
Holsbeck, Dr H. Van, *Souvenirs de la guerre franco-allemande considérée au point de vue hospitalier et chirurgical*, Brussels, Muquardt, 1874.
Hooper, George, *The Campaign of Sedan: The Downfall of the Second Empire, August–September 1870*, George Bell and Sons, 1897.
Houzé de l'Aulnoit, Alfred, *Historique et mode de fonctionnement des caisses de secours des bataillons de mobiles et de mobilisés de l'armée du Nord pendant et après la guerre 1870–1871*, Lille, L. Danel, 1871.
Hudig, M. S., *In the Ambulance van het Roode Kruis*, Rotterdam, 1871.
Hugo, Victor, *Carnets intimes, 1870–1871*, ed. Henri Guillemin, Gallimard, 7th edn, 1953.
Husson, Armand, *Les Consommations de Paris*, Guillaumin et Cie, 1856.
Husson, Armand, *Administration Générale de l'Assistance Publique de Paris, exposé des progrès et améliorations réalisées dans les services du 1 janvier au 31 décembre 1867*, Paul Dupont, 1868.
Husson, Armand, *Note sur la mortalité des enfants du premier age*, Librairie Administrative de Paul Dupont, 1870.

Jacqmin, François Prosper, *Les Chemins de fer pendant la guerre de 1870–1871*, Hachette, 1872.
Janicot, J., *Trois Mois d'ambulance aux armées de la Loire et de l'Est ; impressions et souvenirs*, Saint-Étienne, Freydier, 1871.

Jaurès, Jean, *La Guerre franco-allemande de 1870–1871,* Jean Rouff, 1908, reprinted, Flammarion, 1971.
Jeamenet, Georges, *Paris pendant la Commune révolutionnaire de 71,* Neuchâtel, 1871, reprinted Le Guillaume, 1968.
Job, Adolphe, *Malades et blessés, ambulance de l'hôpital Rothschild pendant le siège de Paris, 1870–1871,* A. Delahaye, 1871.
Johnson, J. W. S., 'Relations médicales entre la France et le Danemark', *Bulletin de la société française d'histoire médicale,* 10 (1911) 434–6.
Josat, Dr A., *L'Ambulance municipale du Palais-Royal du 12 septembre au 27 février 1871,* Henri Plon, 1871.
Joubert, P. Ch. and Arnauld de Vresse, *De la défense de Paris pendant le siège au point de vue de l'alimentation,* Arnauld de Vresse, 1871.
Joulin, Dr Désiré-Joseph, *Les Caravanes d'un chirurgien d'ambulances pendant le siège de Paris et sous la Commune,* E. Dentu, 1871.
Jourde, François, *Souvenirs d'un membre de la Commune,* Brussels, H. Kistemaeckers, 1877.
Juguriano, A., 'Des Avantages de l'amputation à la suite des blessures de guerre', Thèse de doctorat, Faculté de médecine de Montpellier, 1872.
Jurgensen, Jules, *Le Soir du combat, récit d'une infirmière, poème,* Geneva, Durafort, 1871.

Kératry, Émile de, *Le 4 septembre et le gouvernement de la Défense Nationale, dépositions devant la commission d'enquête de l'assemblée nationale, mission diplomatique à Madrid,* Librairie Internationale A. Lacroix, Verboeckhoven et Cie, 1872.
Kératry, Émile de, *Armée de Bretagne, 1870–1871,* A. Lacroix, 1873.
Koslwitz, Édouard [sic], *Les Français avant, pendant et après la guerre de 1870–1871 d'après les documents français,* trans. Jules Félix, Leipzig and Werter, 1897.
Kruger, Gustave, *L'Ambulance Kruger,* Pau, Imprimerie Véronnaise, 1871.

Laborde, Jean-Baptiste Vincent, *Les Hommes et les actes de l'insurrection de Paris devant la psychologie morbide,* G. Baillière, 1872.
Lacroix, Clément de, *Les Morts pour la patrie, tombes militaires et monuments élevés à la mémoire des soldats tués pendant la guerre, chronologie historique des événements de 1870–1871,* l'auteur, 1891.
Lancereaux, Étienne, 'De l'alcoolisme et ses conséquences au point de vue de l'état physique, intellectuel et moral des populations', Thèse de doctorat, Faculté de Paris, E. Donnaud, 1878.
Lantier, Dr E., *Conservation des membres blessés par armes à feu perfectionnées,* Asselin, 1872.
Lantier, Dr E., *L'École antiseptique conservatrice, créée publiquement en 1870–1871 à l'ambulance générale de l'administration des Postes,* Moulins, E. Auclaire, 1889.
Larrey, Baron Hippolyte, *Discours prononcé par Monsieur le baron Larrey le 14 juin 1880 au sujet du projet de loi sur l'administration de l'armée,* Librairie des Publications Législatives, 1880.
Laurent, Charles Nicolas, *Histoire de la vie et des ouvrages de P.F. Percy, composée sur les manuscrits originaux,* Versailles, Daumont, 1827.

Laurent, Charles, 'Histoire de deux prisonniers allemands à Paris', *Annales politiques et littéraires* (1911) 304–6, 338–9, 358–9, 378, 404–6.
Le Mansois Duprey, M., *L'Oeuvre sociale de la municipalité parisienne 1871–1891*, Imprimerie Municipale, 1892.
Leboulaye, Edmond, 'De la Médecine militaire en France et aux États-Unis', *Revue des Deux-Mondes* (15/12/1869).
Lecour, Charles J., *La Prostitution à Paris et à Londres, 1789–1877*, Asselin et Cie, 1877.
Lecour, Charles J., *La Campagne contre la Préfecture de Paris, envisagée surtout au point de vue des moeurs*, Asselin et Cie, 1881.
Leeson, Michael A., *Reminiscences of the Franco-Irish Ambulance or our 'Corps' with the Maquarts and on the Loire, 1870–1871*, Dublin, M'Gleshan and Gill, 1873.
LeFort, Léon, 'Le Service de santé des armées dans les nouvelles armées Européennes', *Revue des Deux-Mondes* (1/11/1871) 88–133.
LeFort, Léon, *La Chirurgie militaire et les Sociétés de Secours en France et à l'étranger*, G. Baillière, 1872.
LeFort, Léon, *Oeuvres*, ed. Félix Lejars, 2 vols, Félix Alcan, 1895–96.
Legoyt, A., 'L'Alimentation et les prix pendant le siège de Paris', *Journal des économistes*, 66 (1871) 331–47.
Legrand du Saulle, Dr, 'L'État mental des Parisiens pendant le siège de Paris', *Chronique médicale* (1896) 77–80, 119–21, 147–51.
Leighton, John, *Paris under the Commune, or the Seventy–three Days of the Second Siege*, Bradbury, Evans and Co., 1871.
Lemoyne, Jules Victor, *La Mobilisation. Études sur les institutions militaires de la Prusse*, Notices Militaires, Berger Levrault, 1872.
Lénine, Vladimir Illitch, *La Commune de Paris*, François Maspéro, reprinted 1971.
Leven, Dr, *Une Épidémie de scorbut observée à l'hôpital militaire d'Ivry pendant le siège de Paris*, A. Delahaye, 1872.
Lévy, Michel, *Notes sur les hôpitaux-baraques du Luxembourg et du Jardin des Plantes*, J. B. Baillière, 1871.
Lewal, Général Jules Louis, *La Réforme de l'armée*, Jean Dumaine, 1871.
Lewal, Général Jules Louis, *Études de guerre*, Jean Dumaine, 1873.
Lissagaray, Prosper Olivier, *History of the Paris Commune of 1871*, [1876], New Park Publications, 1976.
Loliée, Frédéric, *Le Duc de Morny: The Brother of an Emperor and the Maker of an Empire*, John Long, 1910.
Lombroso, C., *L'Homme criminel, criminel né, fou moral, épileptique: étude anthropologique et médico-légale*, tr. Régnier and Bournet, Félix Alcan, 1887.
Lombroso, C., *La Femme criminelle et la prostituée*, tr. Meille, Félix Alcan, 1896.
Long, Xavier, *Rapport au sujet de la répartition des secours faite par la Société anglaise des Amis, Quakers, aux victimes innocentes de la guerre en France, 1870–1871*, n.p., 1872.
Loua, Toussaint, *Atlas statistique de la population de Paris*, Dejey, 1873.
Louis-Lande, L., *Réçits d'un soldat, les fusiliers marins au siège de Paris, un invalide, le Sergent Hoff, la Hacienda de Camaron* [sic], H. Lecène et H. Oudin, 1886.
Lüder, Carl, *La Convention de Genève au point de vue historique, critique et dogmatique*, Erlangen, E. Besold, 1876.

Luze, François de and Adolphe Labodie, *Rapport au comité départemental pour la Gironde*, Bordeaux, n.p., 1871.

MacCormac, William, *Notes and Recollections of an Ambulance Surgeon*, J. A. Churchill, 1871.

MacCormac, William, *Souvenirs d'un chirurgien d'ambulance, relation médico-chirurgicale des faits observés et des opérations pratiquées à l'ambulance anglo-américaine*, trans. Dr Morache, J. B. Baillière et Fils, 2nd edn, 1872.

MacLeod, George Husband Baird, *Notes on the Surgery in War in the Crimea with Remarks on the Treatment of Gunshot Wounds*, John Churchill, 1858.

Maffitt, A., *A Manual of Instruction for Attendants on Sick and Wounded in War*, National Society for Aid to the Sick and Wounded, 1870.

Magnan, Ernest, *Angéla ou l'Alsace enchaînée*, Ghio, 1884.

Magnan, Valentin, *De l'alcoolisme, des diverses formes de délire alcoolique et de leur traitement*, Delahaye, 1874.

Maillard, Firmin, *Élections des 26 mars et avril 1871, affiches, professions de foi, documents officiels, clubs et comités pendant la Commune*, E. Dentu, 1871.

Maillard, Firmin, *Les Publications de la rue pendant le siège et la Commune*, Auguste Aubry, 1874.

Malinas, Alfred, 'Conservation dans les fractures des membres', Thèse de doctorat, Faculté de médecine de Paris, 1872.

Mangot, Gédéon, *Mes Campagnes : 1870–1871*, Eklitra, reprinted 1990.

Manoury, G., *Les Hôpitaux-baraques et les pansements antiseptiques en Allemagne*, Delahaye, 1878.

Marchal, de Calvi, Charles Jacob, *La Guerre de 1870, formule du Communalisme*, Pau, Imprimerie Véronèse, March 1871.

Marchal, de Calvi, Charles Jacob, *Lettres à l'Académie de Médecine à propos du procédé dit de syphilisation*, Plon Frères, 1852.

Marchant, Louis, *La Bourgogne pendant la guerre et l'occupation allemande, 1870–1871, d'après la gazette officielle de Carlsruhe*, Dijon, Marchand and Maniere-Loquin, 1875.

Marjolin, René, *Étude sur les causes et les effets des logements insalubres*, Masson, 1881.

Marteau, Amédée, *Le Droit prime la force, page d'histoire de l'empire d'Allemagne*, Librairie Internationale, 1876.

Martens, Charles de, *Causes célèbres du droit des gens*, 2 vols, Leipzig, F. A. Brockhaus and Ponthieu et Cie, 1827.

Marthold, Jules de, *Mémorandum du siège de Paris 1870–1871*, Charovay Frères, 1884.

Martial, A. P., *Les Femmes de Paris pendant le siège*, Codart, 1871.

Martin, A. F., *Les Dernières cartouches, drame historique en cinq actes*, Bordeaux, de Lanefranque, 1875.

Marx, Karl and F. Engels, *La Commune de 1871, lettres et déclarations*, Moscow, Union Générale d'Éditions, 1971.

Marx, Karl, *La Commune de Paris : la guerre civile en France*, reprinted Savelli, 1976.

Maublanc, P., *Nouveau mode de recrutement de la médecine et de la pharmacie militaire*, J. Dumaine, 1871.

Maupas, M. de, *Mémoires sur le Second Empire*, 2 vols, E. Dentu, 1884.

Ménecier, Charles, *Rapport sur les travaux de la première ambulance du Midi, attachée à la 3ième Division du 20ième corps d'armée de la Loire et de l'Est*, Marseilles, Cayer, 1872.

Merchie, Zacharie Zéphirin, *Guerre de 1870–1871, les Secours aux blessés après la bataille de Sedan, avec documents officiels à l'appui*, Brussels, H. Manceaux, Muquardt, Delahaye, 1876.

Michel, Louise, *La Commune histoire et souvenirs*, [1886] 2 vols, Maspéro, 1970.

Michel, Louise, *Souvenirs de ma vie*, [1886] Maspéro, 1983.

Michelet, Jules, *Histoire de la Révolution française*, 2 vols, Robert Laffont, [1847; 1868] 1979.

Michiels, Alfred, *Histoire de la guerre franco-prussienne et de ses origines*, Alphonse Picard, 1871.

Middleton, Robert, *Garibaldi, ses opérations à l'armée des Vosges*, Garnier Frères, 1872, and Brussels, C. & A. Vanderauwera, 1871.

Migon, Adolphe, *Des Principales affections chirurgicales dans l'armée*, Masson, 1910.

Milliot, Benjamin, *De l'extraction des plaies de projectiles en fer, en fonte de fer et acier et des morceaux d'armes blanches au moyen des électro-aimants*, Secrétariat de l'association française pour l'avancement des sciences, 1878.

Mireur, Hippolyte, *La Syphilis et la prostitution dans leurs rapports avec l'hygiène, la morale et la loi*, G. Masson, 2nd edn, 1888.

Moltke, Helmuth Karl von, *La Correspondance militaire du Maréchal de Moltke, guerre de 1870–71*, 5 vols, Henri Charles Lavauzelle, 1899–1901.

Monin, E., *L'Alcoolisme : étude médico-sociale*, Octave Doin, 1889.

Monod, Mme William, *La Mission des femmes en temps de guerre*, Bellaire, 1870.

Monod, Mme William, *Les Héroïnes de la charité, soeur Marthe de Besançon et miss Florence Nightingale*, Bellaire, 1873.

Monod, Henri, *Rapport du comité évangélique auxiliaire de secours pour les soldats blessés ou malades, 1870–1871*, Sandoz and Fischbacher, 1875.

Monteil, Edgar, *Souvenirs de la Commune, 1871*, Charovay Frères, 1883.

Montesquiou, L. de, *1870, les causes politiques du désastre*, Librairie Française, 2nd edn, 1979.

Montesson, Charles de, *Souvenirs d'ambulance, 1870–1871*, Le Mans, Monnoyer, 1885.

Monteuil, Charles, *Helfen den Verwundeten, épisode de l'invasion de Melun*, Melun, Herisé, 1873.

Montrorien, Eugène, *Les Peintres militaires*, A. Laurette, 1881.

Mony, Adolphe, *Notes d'ambulance, août 1870 – février 1871*, Plon, Nourrit et Cie, 1907.

Mordret, Ambroise Eusèbe, *Rapport sur le service militaire de santé, guerre de 1870–1871, dans la ville du Mans, du 19 août 1870 au 20 avril 1871, adressé à M le Ministre de la Guerre le 11 juin 1871*, Le Mans, E. Monnoyer, 1872.

Morel, Bénédicte, *Traité des dégénérescences, physiques, intellectuelles et morales de l'espèce humaine*, J. B. Baillière, 1857.

Morillon, Adolphe, *L'Approvisionnement de Paris en temps de guerre, souvenirs et prévisions*, Perrin, 1888.

Motet, Auguste, *L'Ambulance militaire de Reuilly, annexe du Val-de-Grâce*, A. Delahaye, 1872.

Motet, Auguste, *Lettre sur l'enseignement clinique des maladies mentales*, Imprimerie Cusset, 1876.

Moussy, Charles, *Tableau des finances de la France, années 1869 et 1869 à 1874, avec la situation de la France à l'époque de la guerre 1870–1871*, Lessertisseux, 1874.
Moynac, Léon, *Souvenirs d'un chirurgien d'ambulance*, Vigot, 1912.
Moynier, Gustave, *La Neutralité des blessés et du service de santé*, Geneva, Toinon, 1867.
Moynier, Gustave, *Le Droit des gens, études sur la Convention de Genève pour l'amélioration du sort des blessés dans les armées en campagne*, Cherbuliez, 1870.
Moynier, Gustave, 'Notes sur la création d'une institution judiciaire internationale, propre à prévenir et à réprimer les infractions à la convention de Genève', *Bulletin international*, III (1872) 122–34.
Moynier, Gustave, *Notes sur la création d'une institution judiciaire internationale, propre à prévenir et à réprimer les infractions à la Convention de Genève*, Geneva, Comité International, 1872.
Moynier, Gustave, *La Convention de Genève, ou la guerre franco-allemande*, Soullier et Wirth, 1873.
Moynier, Gustave, 'La Convention de Genève pendant la guerre Franco-Allemande de 1870', *Bulletin International*, IV (1873) 51–104.
Moynier, Gustave, *Les dix premières années de la Croix Rouge, comité international de secours aux blessés militaires*, Geneva, Fick, 1873.
Moynier, Gustave, *La Croix Rouge, son passé, son avenir*, Sandoz et Thuillier, 1882.
Moynier, Gustave, *Essais sur les caractères généraux des lois de la guerre*, Geneva, Eggimann, 1895.

Nadaud, Gustave, *Mes Notes d'infirmier*, H. Plon, 1871.
Nass, Lucien, *Le Siège de Paris et la Commune, essais de pathologie historique*, Plon–Nourrit, 1914.
Nass, Lucien and M. Cabanès, *Les Névrosés de l'histoire*, Librairie Universelle, 1908.
Nass, Lucien and M. Cabanès, *La Névrose révolutionnaire*, Société Française d'Imprimerie, 1906, reprinted A. Michel, 1924.
Naundorff, J., *Onder het Rodde Kruis, uit het hoogdutch door H.W. Leopold*, Amsterdam, 1871.
Némésis, *Crimes, forfaits, atrocités et viols commis par les prussiens sur le sol de la France*, André Sagnier, 1871.
Neumann, Dr Émile, *Odyssée d'une ambulance colmarienne aux environs de Paris (1870)*, Paris and Nancy, Berger Levrault, 1884.
Nevins, Birbeck, *On Hereditary Syphilis*, Liverpool, The Medical Enquirer, 1878.
Nimier, Henri-Jacques, *Les Blessures de l'oeil pendant la guerre de 1870–1871*, Archives de médecine et de pharmacie militaire, 1889.
Niox, Gustave Léon, *La Guerre de 1870, simple récit*, Delagrave, 1896.
Niox, Gustave Léon, *The Hôtel des Invalides*, Delagrave, 1924.
Nisbet, J., *Wounded in War: A Tale of August 1870*, n.p., 1871.

Ollivier, Émile, *The Franco-Prussian War and its Hidden Causes*, Isaac Pitman and Sons, 1913.
Onimus, Ernest, *Conseils hygiéniques aux habitants de Paris pendant le siège, suivis des arrêtés municipaux concernant l'hygiène et la salubrité publique*, Charles de Mourgues Frères, 1870.

Pain, Amédée, *Des divers modes de l'Assistance Publique*, Baillière, 1865.

Palat, Barthélémy Edmond, *Bibliographie générale de la guerre de 1870–1871, répertoire alphabétique et raisonné des publications de toute nature concernant la guerre franco allemande parues en France et à l'étranger*, Berger Levrault, 1896.

Pamard, Alfred, *La Quatrième Ambulance de la Société d'aide et de secours aux blessés des armées de terre et de mer pendant la guerre 1870–1871*, Avignon, Aubanel Frères, 1915.

Papillon, Fernand, 'Hygiène et alimentation de Paris pendant le siège de 1870', *Revue des deux mondes* (1/10/1870) 575–84.

Parent-Duchâtelet, Alexandre, *De la prostitution dans la Ville de Paris, considérée sous le rapport de l'hygiène publique, de la morale et de l'administration*, J. B. Baillière, 1836.

Payen, M., 'L'Académie des Sciences pendant l'armistice et la Commune', *Revue scientifique*, 2 (8/07/1871) 33–47.

Pearson, Emma Maria and Louisa Elizabeth Maclaughlin, *Our Adventures during the War of 1870*, London, 1871.

Peltier, Gustave, *L'Ambulance N°5*, Delahaye, 1871.

Petit, D., *Ma Carte de visite, souvenirs de l'ambulance du Midi*, Marseilles, n.p., 1872.

Piedagnel, Alexandre, *Les Ambulances de Paris pendant le siège*, Librairie Générale, 1871.

Pietrowski, Stanislas, *La Guerre et la société de secours aux blessés militaires des armées de terre et de mer*, E. Dentu, 1870.

Pietrowski, Stanislas, *Rapport général, campagne de 1870–1, armée de Sedan, armée de la Loire*, Imprimerie Centrale des Chemins de Fer, A. Chaix, 1871.

Pignot, Albert Bernard Eugène, *L'Hôpital du Midi et ses origines, recherches sur l'histoire médicale et sociale de la syphilis à Paris*, O. Doin, 1885.

Poncet, Antonin, *Le Siège de Strasbourg (1870) hôpital militaire, service de la première division des blessés*, Montpellier, Boehm et Fils, 1873.

Porter, J. H., *The Surgeon's Pocket Book: An Essay on the Best Treatment of Wounded of War*, Harrison and Sons, 4th edn, 1875.

Porter, J. H., *On Some Forms of Contemporeanous Conveyances for the Sick and Wounded in Peace and War, Read before the General Assembly of the Order of Saint John on June 24, 1878*, Harrison and Sons, 1878.

Pressensé, Francis de, *Journal d'Ambulance, armées de la Loire*, Meyrueis, 1872.

Prolès, Charles, *Les Hommes de la révolution de 1871, Raoul Rigault, la Préfecture de Police sous la Commune, les otages*, Chamuel, 1898.

Quatrefages, Armand de, *Charles Darwin et ses précurseurs*, Bibliothèque Scientifique Internationale, 1870.

Quatrefages, Armand de, *La Race prussienne*, Hachette, 1871.

Quesnay de Beaurepaire, Alfred, *De Wissembourg à Ingoldstat, souvenirs d'un capitaine prisonnier de guerre en Bavière*, La France Moderne, Firmin Didot, 1891.

Quesnoy, Ferdinand Désiré, *Campagne de 1870, l'armée du Rhin, camps de Châlons, Borny, Rezonville ou Gravelotte, St Privat, Blocus de Metz, les Ambulances*, Furne Jouvet et Cie, 1872.

Rabuteau, A., *Des alcools et de l'alcoolisme : extraits des comptes rendus du congrès international de 1878 pour l'étude des questions relatives à l'alcoolisme*, E. Donnaud, 1878.

Reclus, Paul, *Éloge du baron Hippolyte Larrey prononcé à la société de chirurgie dans la séance annuelle du 26 janvier 1898*, Masson, 1898.
Red Cross, British, Boulogne, *Red-Cross Operations in the North of France, 1870–2*, Spottiswoode and Co., 1872.
Red Cross, British, *Report of the Operations of the British National Society for Aid to the Sick and Wounded in War during the Franco-German War, 1870–1871*, 1872.
Red Cross, British, 'Opérations de la société nationale anglaise pendant la guerre franco-allemande 1870–1871', in *Rapport des sociétés étrangères sur leurs activités durant la guerre de 1870–1871*, SSABATM, 1873.
Red Cross, British and German, *Rapports des sociétés allemandes et britanniques*, Comité Français SSABATM, 1873.
Red Cross, France, *Bulletin de la Société française de secours aux blessés militaires des armées de terre et de mer*, 10 (1871).
Red Cross, France, *Documents relatifs à l'organisation de la société internationale et des comités nationaux de secours aux blessés*, Grenoble, n.p., 1872.
Red Cross, France, *Comité Central de Chartres pour le secours aux victimes de la guerre 1870–1871, pour les départements de l'Eure et Loir*, Chartres, n.p., 1873.
Red Cross, France, *La Société française de secours aux blessés des armées de terre et de mer, comité de Versailles 1870–1871*, Versailles, n.p., 1874.
Red Cross, France, *Recueil des décrets et statuts, règlements et instructions concernant la société de secours aux blessés militaires, au siège*, 1936.
Red Cross, France, Tours, *Bulletin de la Société française, délégation du conseil central de la société à Tours*, Versailles, n.p., 1871.
Red Cross, France, Comité Central des Ambulances de la Loire, *Rapport général des médecins*, Saint-Étienne, Théolier, 1872.
Red Cross, France, Comité de Secours aux Blessés du Nord, *Notes sur les caisses de secours des bataillon de mobiles et de mobilisés dans le Nord de la France*, Lille, n.p., 1871.
Red Cross, France, Comité Départmental de l'Allier, *Rapport général*, Moulins, Desrosiers, 1871.
Red Cross, France, Versailles, *Rapport du comte de Beaufort secrétaire général de la Société de secours sur son administraion du 14 avril au 31 mai 1871*, Librairie Administrative Paul Dupont, 1871.
Red Cross, France, Versailles, *Compte rendu des opérations du conseil d'administration siégeant à Versailles et du comité d'action depuis le 15 avril jusqu'au 31 mai*, SSABATM, 1872.
Red Cross, Comité International de Genève, *Listes des blessés français recceuillis par les troupes Allemandes*, Basel and Geneva, Georg, 1871.
Red Cross, International, Comité International de Bâle, *Rapports*, 10/12/1870, 10/01/1871, 10/02/1871, 20/03/1871, Basel, Bonfontini, 1871.
Red Cross, Ireland, *Report of the Irish Ambulance Committee of Dublin, Irish Ambulance Corp for the Service of the French Wounded*, Dublin, Browne and Nobu, 1871.
Riche, Alfred, *Conseils sur la manière de se nourrir dans les circonstances présentes, conférence faite le 11 novembre 1870*, Germer-Baillière, 1870.
Richet, Charles, *Les Guerres et la paix, étude sur l'arbitrage international*, Schleicher, 1899.

Ricord, Philippe, *Les Ambulances de la presse, annexes du ministère de la guerre pendant le siège et sous la Commune, 1870–1871*, J. B. Baillière, 1873.
Riencourt, Anne-Honoré Olivier, Comte de, *Insuffisance des pensions accordées aux militaires blessés*, Lachaud, 1872.
Riencourt, Anne-Honoré Olivier, Comte de, *Les Militaires blessés et invalides, leur histoire, leur situation en France et à l'étranger*, 2 vols, Jean Dumaine, 1875.
Riencourt, Anne-Honoré Olivier, Comte de, *Manuel des blessés et malades de guerre, à l'usage des personnes charitables qui désirent faire valoir les titres de ces militaires et ceux des veuves, orphelins et ascendants aux pensions, gratifications et secours*, J. Dumaine, 1876.
Riencourt, Anne-Honoré Olivier, Comte de, *Les Blessés oubliés, les pensions militaires pour blessures et infirmités*, Abbeville, Paillart, 1882.
Riencourt, Anne-Honoré Olivier, Comte de, *Instructions pour le service de l'oeuvre des pensions militaires, rédigées en 1879 et revues en 1883*, Abbeville, Paillart, 1883.
R. M., *Mémoires sur l'armée de Chanzy, journal du bataillon des gardes mobiles de Mortain (Manche)*, E. Dentu, 1871.
Rochard, Félix, *Projet d'ambulance sur la Seine*, Renou Imprimerie, 1871.
Rochard, Jules E., *Histoire de la chirurgie française au dix-neuvième siècle, étude historique et critique sur les progrès faits en chirurgie et dans les sciences qui s'y rapportent depuis la suppression de l'Académie Royale jusqu'à l'époque actuelle*, J. B. Baillière and Fils, 1875.
Rossel Louis Nathaniel, *Mémoires et correspondance de Louis Rossel*, preface by Victor Margueritte with a biography by Isabella Rossel, P. V. Stock, 1908.
Rothan, Gustave, *Les Origines de la guerre de 1870, la politique française en 1866*, Calmann-Lévy, 1879.
Rothan, Gustave, *Souvenirs diplomatiques, l'affaire du Luxembourg, le prélude de la guerre de 1870*, Calmann-Lévy, 1882.
Rouis, Jean-Louis, *Histoire de l'école impériale du service de santé militaire de Strasbourg*, Berger Levrault, 1898.
Rousset, Léonce, *Histoire générale de la guerre franco-allemande 1870–1871*, 7 vols, La Librairie Illustrée, 1895–96.
Rueil, Durand, *Le Siège de Paris, exposition de peinture des épisodes civils et militaires de la défense*, n.p., 1871.
Rundle, H., *With the Red Cross in the Franco-German War 1870–1871*, Werner Laurie, 1911.
Ryan, Charles, *With an Ambulance during the Franco-German War: Personal Experiences and Adventures with Both Armies*, John Murray, 1896.

Sahler, Auguste, *L'Ambulance de Montbéliard*, Montbeliard, Barbier, 1871.
Saint-Edme, Ernest, *La Science pendant le siège de Paris*, E. Dentu, 1871.
Saint-Victor, Paul de, *Barbares et bandits, la Prusse et la Commune*, Michel Lévy Frères, 1872.
Salomon, Louis, *Le Pauvre et son médecin devant la loi sur l'assistance médicale gratuite*, Chamuel, 1898.
Sansas, Capitaine L., *Rapport du Capitaine Sansas commandant la première compagnie des francs-tireurs de Tours*, Tours, Grassien, 1872.

Sarazin, M., *Récits sur la dernière guerre franco-allemande*, Berger Levrault et Cie, 1887.
Sarcey, Francisque, *Le Siège de Paris, impressions et souvenirs*, Lachaud, 1871.
Sarrepont, Major H. de, *Le Bombardement de Paris par les Prussiens en janvier 1871*, Firmin Didot Frères, 1872.
Saucerotte, Tony, *Lunéville pendant la guerre et le rapatriement*, Gazette médicale de Paris, 1872.
Schneider, G. E. and M. Troussaint, *Pages d'hygiène militaire pour les officiers*, Paris and Limoges, Charles Lavauzelle, 1906, reprinted several times until 1914.
Ségur, Louis Philippe de, *Les Marchés de la guerre à Lyon et à l'armée de Garibaldi*, H. Plon, 1873.
Service Historique du Grand État-Major Prussien, *La Guerre franco-allemande de 1870–71*, Berlin, Ernest Siegfried Mittler, and Paris, J. Dumaine, 1872.
Sorel, Albert, *Histoire diplomatique de la guerre franco-allemande*, 2 vols, H. Plon, 1875.
Soubise, Dr Armel-Auguste, *Compte rendu de la deuxième ambulance volante de Maine et Loire attachée au 75e Mobile 16e Corps*, Tours, Mazereau, 1872.
Spillmann, Eugène, *Études statistiques sur les résultats de la chirurgie conservatrice*, P. Asselin, 1868.
Spillmann, Eugène and Gaujot Gustave, *L'Arsenal de la chirurgie contemporaine, description, mode d'emploi et appréciation des appareils et instruments en usages pour le diagnostic et le traitement des maladies chirurgicales*, 2 vols, J. B. Baillière et Fils, 1867–72.
Steenackers, François-Frédéric, *Les Telégraphes et les postes pendant la guerre de 1870–1871: fragments de mémoires historiques*, G. Charpentier, 1883.
Stoffel, Baron Eugène, *Rapports militaires écrits de Berlin*, Garnier Frères, 1871.
Sueur, Dr Henri, *Étude sur la mortalité à Paris pendant le siège*, Sandoz et Fischbacher, 1872.

Tardieu, Ambroise, *Huitième ambulance de la Société de secours aux blessés, campagne de Sedan et de Paris, août 1870 – février 1871, rapport historique, médical et administratif*, Delahaye, 1872.
Templer, Mrs H., *A Labour of Love under the Red Cross during the Late War*, Guernsey, LeLièvre and London, Simpkin, Marshall and Co., 1872.
Terrot, Eugène, *Paris et ses fortifications, 1870–1880*, G. Baillière, 1880.
Thiers, Adolphe, *Notes et souvenirs de Monsieur Thiers, révolution du 24 Février*, n.p., 1902; Calman-Lévy, 1903.
'The Times Correspondent', *Letters on International Relations before and during the War of 1870*, 2 vols, Tinsley Bros, 1871.
Tollet, Claude, *Les Hôpitaux modernes au dix-neuvième siècle, descriptions des principaux hôpitaux français et étrangers*, l'auteur, 1894.
Trailles, Paul and Henry de, *Les Femmes en France pendant la guerre et les deux sièges de Paris*, F. Polo Libraire, 1872.
Trémeau de Rochebrune, Alphonse, *Essai de statistique médicale suivi d'observations médico-chirurgicales créées à Angoulême pendant la durée de la guerre de 1870–1*, Savy, 1871.
Triare, Paul, *Dominique Larrey et les campagnes de la Révolution et de l'Empire, 1766–1842*, Tours, Alfred Mame et Fils, 1902.

Turqueau, Joseph, *1870–1871 : les femmes de France pendant l'invasion*, Nancy, Berger Levrault, 1893.

Une femme de ménage, *La Cuisinière assiègée*, Laporte, 1871.

Vallès, Jules, *L'Insurgé*, Messidor, reprinted 1990.
Vaslin, Louis, *Étude sur les pansements des plaies et l'hygiène des blessés*, Anger, Germain and Grassié, 1878.
Vavasseur, A., *La Paix honteuse ou le droit des gens selon les prussiens*, Lacroix, Verboeckhoven et Cie, 1871.
Vernes d'Arlandes, Théodore, *La Société française de secours aux blessés des armées de terre et de mer. Délégation de l'Est*, Bureau de la délégation, 1871.
Veuillot, Louis, *Paris pendant les deux sièges*, 2 vols, Librairie de Victor Palmé, 1871.
Veuillot, Louis, *Oeuvres complètes*, 12 vols, Lethielleux Libraire, 1932.
Vidieu, A., *Histoire de la Commune*, Dentu, 1876.
Villiers, A. C. E. Bellier de, *Le Cinquième secteur ou rempart des Thermes, notes sur son organisation, son armement etc*, Bachelin-Deflorenne, 1871.

Wachter, Alphonse, *La Guerre de 1870–71, histoire politique et militaire*, E. Lachaud, 1873.
Washburne, E. B., *Recollections of a Minister to France, 1869–1877*, 2 vols, Sampson Low, Marston, Searle and Rivington, 1887.
Wauthoz, H. A., *Les Ambulances et les ambulanciers à travers les siècles*, Brussels, Lebègue, 1872?
Weille, Jacob, *Souvenirs de la campagne de 1870–1871 par un médecin militaire*, Reims, Molet Droin, 1896.
Woyde, Général de, *Causes des Succès et des revers dans la guerre de 1870*, 3 vols, R. Chapelot, 1899–1900.
Wyrouboff, Grégoire, 'Les Ambulances de la société française de secours aux blessés pendant la guerre de 1870–1871', *Philosophie positive*, 6 (1875) 379–403.

Yriarte, Charles, *Les Prussiens à Paris et le 18 Mars*, Henri Plon, 1871.
Yvaren, Prosper, *Des Métamorphoses de la syphilis*, J. B. Baillière, 1854.

Zola, Émile, *Nana*, Living Library, 1946.
Zola, Émile, *La Débâcle*, La Pléiade, reprinted 1990.

Books, pamphlets and articles written and published since 1914

Ackerknecht, Edwin, *Medicine at the Paris Hospital, 1794–1848*, Baltimore, Johns Hopkins Press, 1967.
Ackerman, Evelyn Bernette, *Health Care in the Parisian Countryside, 1800–1914*, New Brunswick, N.J., Rutgers University Press, 1990.
Acomb, Evelyn M., *The French Laic Laws 1879–1889: The First Anti-Clerical Campaign of the Third French Republic*, New York, Octagon, [1941] 1967.
Adams, Mark B. (ed.), *The WELLBORN Science: Eugenics in Germany, France, Brazil and Russia*, Oxford University Press, 1989.

Ados, Michael, *Machines as the Measure of Men: Science, Technology and Ideologies of Western Dominance*, Ithaca, Cornell University Press, 1989.
Adriance, Thomas J., *The Last Gaiter Button: A Study of the Mobilisation and Concentration of the French Army in the War of 1870*, Westport, Greenwood Press, 1987.
Agulhon, Maurice, 'Esquisse pour une archéologie de la république : l'allégorie civique féminine', *Annales*, 28 (1973) 5–34.
Agulhon, Maurice, *Marianne au combat, l'imagerie et la symbolique républicaines de 1789 à 1880*, Flammarion, 1979.
Aldrich, Robert, *Greater France: A History of French Overseas Expansion*, Basingstoke, Macmillan, 1996.
Allinson, A. R. (ed.), *The War Diary of the Emperor Frederick III, 1870–1871*, Westport, Greenwood Press, 1971.
Aminzade, Ronald, *Ballots and Barricades: Class Formation and Republican Politics in France 1830–1871*, Princeton University Press, 1993.
Anderson, Benedict, *Imagined Communities*, Verso, 2nd edn, 1991.
Anderson, R. D., *Education in France, 1848–1870*, Oxford, Clarendon Press, 1975.
Andrieux, Louis, *A travers la République*, Payot, 1926.
Apple, Rima Dombrow, *Mothers and Medicine: A Social History of Infant Feeding, 1890–1950*, Madison, University of Wisconsin Press, 1987.
Armengaud, André, 'L'Opinion publique en France et la crise nationale allemande en 1866', unpublished thesis, Université de Dijon, 1962.
Armstrong, David, 'Public health spaces and the fabrication of identity', *Sociology*, 27:3 (1993) 393–410.
Arnaud, Pierre (ed.), *Les Athlètes de la république, gymnastique, sport et idéologie républicaine 1870–1914*, Toulouse, Privat, 1987.
Arnaud, Pierre, *Le Militaire, l'écolier, le gymnaste: naissance de l'éducation physique en France, 1869–89*, Lyons, Presses Universitaires de Lyon, 1991.
Arnot, Meg and Cornelie Usborne (eds), *Gender and Crime in Modern Europe*, University College London Press, 1999.
Aron, Jean-Paul, *Anthropologie du conscrit français*, Monton, 1972.
Aron, Jean-Paul and Roger Kempf, *La Bourgeoisie, le sexe et l'honneur*, Brussels, Complexe, 1984.
Aron, Jean-Paul, *Le Mangeur du XIXième siècle*, Petite Bibliothèque Payot, 3rd edn, 1989.
Aron, Raymond, *Penser la guerre, Clausewitz*, 2 vols, Gallimard, 1976.
Astruc, Pierre, 'La Guerre de 1870 et la médecine', *Progrès médical*, 80 (1960) 219–26, 236–46, 256–9, 275–81, 295–300.
Audoin-Rouzeau, Stéphane, *1870, la France dans la guerre*, Armand Colin, 1989.
Audoin-Rouzeau, Stéphane, 'Guerre et brutalité, 1870–1918, le cas français', *European Review of History/Revue européenne d'histoire*, 0 (1993) 95–108.
Aurousseau, Paul, *Les Chiens des dieux, le siège de Paris et la Commune*, P. Saurat, 1986.
Auspitz, Katherine, *The Radical Bourgeoisie: The 'Ligue de l'Enseignement' and the Origins of the Third Republic, 1866–1885*, Cambridge University Press, 1982.

Baguley, David, 'Le Récit de guerre: narration et focalisation dans *La Débâcle*', *Littérature*, 50:2 (1983) 82–90.

Bailin, Miriam, *The Sickroom in Victorian Fiction: The Art of Being Ill*, Cambridge University Press, 1994.
Bapst, Edmond, *Le Siège de Metz en 1870*, A. Lahure, 1926.
Barker, Nancy Nichols, *Distaff Diplomacy: The Empress Eugénie and the Foreign Policy of the Second Empire*, Austin, Texas University Press, 1967.
Barker, Nancy Nichols, 'Napoleon III and the Hohenzollern candidacy for the Spanish throne', *The Historian*, 29 (1967) 421–50.
Barker, Nancy Nichols, *The French Experience in Mexico, 1821–1861: A History of Constant Misunderstanding*, Chapel Hill, N.C., University of North Carolina Press, 1979.
Barnes, David S., *The Making of a Social Disease: Tuberculosis in Nineteenth-Century France*, Berkeley, University of California Press, 1995.
Barnett, L. M., *British Food Policy During the First World War*, Boston, Allen and Unwin, 1985.
Bartow, Omer, 'The conduct of war: soldiers and the barbarization of warfare', Supplement to *Journal of Modern History*, 64 (1992) 32–45.
Bassford, Christopher, *Clausewitz in English: The Reception of Clausewitz in Britain and America, 1815–1845*, Oxford University Press, 1994.
Bazan, Michel, *Les Conscrits, arts et traditions populaires*, Berger Levrault, 1981.
Bernard-Griffiths, M. and Paul Viallaneix (eds), *Edgar Quinet, ce juif errant*, Clermont Ferrand University Press, 1978.
Becker, Jean-Jacques, *Comment les Français sont entrés dans la guerre*, Fondation Nationale des Sciences Politiques, 1977.
Becker, Jean-Jacques, *The Great War and the French People*, Oxford, Berg, 1985.
Béguet, Bruno, *La Science pour tous: sur la vulgarisation scientifique en France de 1850 à 1914*, Bibliothèque du Conservatoire National des Arts et Métiers, 1990.
Benabou, Erica-Marie, *La Prostitution et la police des moeurs au XVIIIème siècle*, Perrin, 1987.
Ben Amos, Avner, 'Molding the national memory: the state funeral of the Third Republic', Ph.D. thesis, University of California, Berkeley, 1988.
Benjamin, Marina (ed.), *Science and Sensibility: Gender and Scientific Enquiry, 1780–1945*, Oxford, Blackwell, 1991.
Berlanstein, Lenard R., *The Working People of Paris, 1871–1914*, Baltimore, Johns Hopkins University Press, 1984.
Bernet, Jean, *La Mutualité et la guerre de 1870*, Étampes, Société Régionale d'Imprimerie et de Publicité, 1962.
Bertocci, Philip A., *Jules Simon: Republican Anticlericalism and Cultural Politics in France, 1848–1886*, Columbia, University of Missouri Press, 1978.
Best, Geoffrey, *War and Society in Revolutionary Europe: 1770–1870*, Leicester University Press, 1982.
Best, Geoffrey, *Humanity in Warfare: The Modern History of the International Law of Armed Conflict*, Methuen, 1983.
Biddiss, Michael D., *Father of Racist Ideology: The Social and Political Thought of Count Gobineau*, Weidenfeld and Nicolson, 1970.
Biddiss, Michael D. (ed.), *Gobineau: Selected Political Writings*, Jonathan Cape, 1970.
Biret, J. L., M. Bui and F. Greffe, 'Les Laboratoires dans les hôpitaux de l'Assistance Publique au dix-neuvième siècle', *Histoire et nature*, 26–27 (1985) 77–84.

Bloesinger, Edmond, *Quelques grandes figures de la chirurgie, de la médecine et de la pharmacie militaire*, 2 vols, J. B. Baillière, 1947.
Blonay, Jean de, *1870 : une révolution chirurgicale, les origines et le développement de la chirurgie civile et militaire moderne*, Geneva, Delta, 1975.
Bohannan, Paul (ed.), *Law and Warfare: Studies in the Anthropology of Conflict*, Austin, University of Texas Press, 2nd edn, 1976.
Boisset, Jean, *Gobineau, biographie, mythes et réalité*, Berg International, 1993.
Boissier, Pierre, *Histoire du Comité internationale de la Croix Rouge, de Solférino à Tsoushima*, Geneva, Institut Henry Dunant, 1978.
Bonduelle, Michel, Toby Gelfand and Christopher G. Goetz, *Charcot: Constructing Neurology*, New York, Oxford University Press, 1995. trans. *Charcot, un grand médecin dans son siècle*, Michalon, 1996.
Bordarier, Paul, 'Le Siège de Paris d'après un recueil de lettres-ballons', *Revue hommes et mondes* (1949) 255–75.
Borel, Jacques, *Du Concept de dégénérescence à la notion d'alcoolisme dans la médecine contemporaine*, Montpellier, n.p., 1968.
Borsa, Serge and Claude René Michel, *La Vie quotidienne des hôpitaux en France au dix-neuvième siècle*, Hachette, 1985.
Boudon, Jacques-Olivier, 'Une Promotion épiscopale sous le Second Empire, l'abbé Darboy à l'assaut de Paris', *Revue d'histoire moderne et contemporaine*, 39:3 (1992) 465–82.
Bouniols, Gaston (ed.), *Thiers au pouvoir, texte de ses lettres, annoté et commenté*, Delagrave, 1921.
Boureau, Dr Eugène, *Bras de travail et mains de travail pour amputés*, Masson, 1919.
Bourgin, Georges, 'Une Entente franco-allemande: Bismarck, Thiers, Jules Favre et la répression de la Commune de Paris', *International Review of Social History*, 1 (1956) 41–53.
Bourgin, Georges and Philippe Henriot (eds), *Les Procès-verbaux de la Commune de 1871*, 2 vols, vol. 1, Leroux, 1924, vol. 2, A. Lahure, 1945.
Bourdieu, Pierre, *La Distinction, critique sociale du jugement*, Les Éditions de Minuit, 1979.
Bourke, Joanna, *Dismembering the Male: Men's Bodies, Britain and the Great War*, Reaktion, 1996.
Boutroux, Bruno, 'Hippolyte Morestin, 1869–1919', Thèse de doctorat d'état, Université de Nancy I, 1978.
Bowler, Peter J., *Charles Darwin: The Man and His Influence*, Cambridge University Press, 1990.
Braudel, Fernand and Ernest Labrousse (eds), *Histoire économique et sociale de la France*, 4 vols, PUF Quadrige, 2nd edn, 1993.
Bridge, F. R. and R. Bullen, The *Great Powers and the European States System 1815–1914*, London and New York, Fontana, 1980.
Brockliss, Laurence and Colin Jones, *The Medical World of Early Modern France*, Oxford, Clarendon Press, 1997.
Broglie, Jacques Victor Albert de, *Mémoires du duc de Broglie*, 2 vols, Calmann Lévy, 1938.
Brown, Frederick, *Père Lachaise: Elysium and Real Estate*, New York, Viking Press, 1973.

Brustein, William, *The Social Origins of Political Regionalism in France, 1849–1981*, Berkeley, University of California Press, 1988.
Buican, Denis, *Histoire de la génétique et de l'évolutionisme en France*, Presses Universitaires de France, 1984.
Bülow, Prince Bernard von, *Memoirs, 1849–1897*, London and New York, Putnam, 1932.
Bury, John Patrick T., *Gambetta and the National Defence: A Republican Dictatorship in France*, Longmans, 1936.
Bury, John Patrick T., *Gambetta and the Making of the Third Republic*, Longman, 1973.
Bury, John Patrick T. and Robert P. Tombs, *Thiers 1797–1877*, Allen and Unwin, 1986.
Busquet, François, 'La Prothèse nasale dans l'oeuvre de Claude Martin', Thèse de médecine, Université de Lyon, 1974.
Bynum, William F., Roy Porter and M. Shepherd (eds), *The Anatomy of Madness*, 2 vols, Cambridge University Press, 1985.
Bynum, William F. and Roy Porter (eds), *Companion Encyclopedia of the History of Medicine*, 2 vols, Routledge, 1994.

Cabanès, Dr, *Chirurgiens et blessés à travers l'histoire, des origines à la Croix-Rouge*, Albin Michel, n.d., 192?.
Cabanis, José, *Michelet, le prêtre et la femme*, Gallimard, 1978.
Camporesi, Piero, *The Land of Hunger*, Cambridge, Polity Press, 1996.
Canguilhem, Georges, *Le Normal et le pathologique*, Quadrige, Presses Universitaires de France, 1991.
Carbonell, Charles-Olivier, 'Les Historiens français chroniqueurs de la guerre franco-allemande et de la Commune, naissance du nationalisme historiographique, 1871–1875', *Bulletin de la société d'histoire moderne*, 13 (1974) 37–56.
Carlton, Eric, *Massacres: An Historical Perspective*, Scolar Press, 1994.
Carol, Anne, *Histoire de l'eugénisme en France, les médecins et la procréation, XIXe–XXe siècle*, Univers Historique Seuil, 1995.
Caron, Jean-Claude, 'L'Impossible Réforme des études médicales, projets et controverses dans la France des notables, 1815–1848', *Sources 31/32, Maladies, médecines et sociétés*, 2 vols, L'Harmattan, 1993.
Caron, Vicki, *Between France and Germany: The Jews of Alsace-Lorraine, 1871–1918*, Stanford University Press, 1988.
Carrot, Georges, 'La Garde Nationale 1789–1871, une institution de la nation', Thèse de doctorat de 3ième cycle, Université de Nice, 1979.
Case, Lynn M., *French Opinion on War and Diplomacy during the Second Empire*, Harrisburg, Pennsylvania University Press, 1954.
Casevitz, Jean, *Une Loi manquée : la loi Niel 1866–1868, l'armée française à la veille de la guerre de 1870*, Presses Universitaires de France, 1959.
Cancian, Francesca M. and James William Gibson (eds), *Making War, Making Peace: The Social Foundations of Violent Conflict*, Belmont, Cal., Wadsworth Publisher, 1990.
Certeau, Michel de, *Heterologies: Discourse on the Other*, Manchester University Press, 1986.
Certeau, Michel de, Luce Giard and Pierre Mayol, *L'Invention du quotidien*, 2 vols, Gallimard, 1994.
César, Marc, *La Commune de Narbonne (mars 1871)*, Presses Universitaires de Perpignan, 1996.

Challener, Richard D., *The French Theory of the Nation in Arms, 1866–1939*, New York, Columbia University Press, 1965.
Charenton, Maurice, 'Le Dr Thomas W. Evans, dentiste de Napoléon III et les dentistes de son époque', Thèse de doctorat, dentaire, Université de Paris, 1936.
Charle, Christophe, *Paris fin de siècle*, Univers Historique Seuil, 1998.
Charlton, Donald Geoffrey, *Secular Religions in France, 1815–1870*, Oxford University Press, 1963.
Chartier, Roger, 'Le Monde comme représentation', *Annales ESC*, 44:6 (1989) 1505–18.
Chartier, Roger, *Cultural History*, Cambridge, Polity Press, 1988.
Chastenet, Jacques, *L'Enfance de la Troisième, 1870–1871*, Hachette, 1952.
Chauvard, Frédéric, *De Pierre Rivière à Landru, la violence apprivoisée au dix-neuvième siècle*, Brussels, Brepols, 1991.
Chevalier, Louis, *Classes laborieuses et classes dangereuses*, Plon, 1958.
Citti, Pierre, *Contre la décadence, histoire de l'imagination française dans le roman, 1890–1914*, Presses Universitaires de France, 1987.
Clark, T. J., *The Absolute Bourgeois: Artists and Politics in France, 1848–1851*, Thames and Hudson, 1973.
Cobb, Richard, *French and Germans, Germans and French: A Personal Interpretation of France under Two Occupations, 1914–1918, 1940–1944*, Hanover, Brandeis University Press, 1983.
Cogny, Pierre, 'Le Discours de Zola sur la Commune : étude d'un problème de réception', *Cahiers naturalistes*, 54 (1980) 17–24.
Coleman, William, *Death is a Social Disease: Public Health and Political Economy in Early-Industrial France*, Madison, University of Wisconsin Press, 1982.
Coleman, William, *Yellow Fever in the North*, Madison, University of Wisconsin Press, 1987.
Coleman, William and F. L. Holmes (eds), *The Investigative Enterprise: Experimental Physiology in Nineteenth-Century Medicine*, Berkeley, University of California Press, 1988.
Collins, Irene, *The Government and the Newspaper Press in France, 1814–1881*, Oxford University Press, 1959.
Combes, André, 'Les Élus francs-maçons de la Commune de Paris', *Chronique d'histoire maçonnique*, 27–28 (1981).
Connol, Malcolm E., 'French public opinion on war with Prussia in 1870', *American Historical Review*, 31:4 (1926) 679–700.
Conry, Yvette, *L'Introduction du darwinisme en France au XIXième siècle*, J. Vrin, 1974.
Contamine, Henry, *La Revanche, 1871–1914*, Berger Levrault, 1957.
Cooter, Roger, *Surgery and Society in Peace and War: Orthopaedics and the Organisation of Modern Medicine, 1880–1948*, Basingstoke, Macmillan, 1993.
Cooter, Roger and Bill Luckin (eds), *Accidents in History*, Amsterdam, Rodopi, Clio Medica, 1997.
Corbin, Alain, *Les Filles de noce, misère sexuelle et prostitution (XIXe siècle)*, Aubier, 1978.
Corbin, Alain, *The Village of Cannibals: Rage and Murder in France, 1870*, Cambridge, Mass., Harvard University Press, 1992.
Corbin, Alain, *Les Cloches de la terre, paysage sonore et culture sensible dans les campagnes au XIXe siècle*, Albin Michel, 1994.

Corbin, Alain, *Time, Desire and Horror: Towards a History of the Senses*, Cambridge, Polity Press, 1997.
Crawford, Elisabeth, *Nationalism and Internationalism in Science 1880–1939*, Cambridge University Press, 1992.
Cronhalen, Börje, 'Phantom limbs in amputees', *Acta Psychiatrica et Neurologica Scandinavia* (Copenhagen, 1951) supplement 72.
Crosland, Maurice, 'Science and the Franco-Prussian war', *Social Study of Science*, 6 (1976) 185–214.
Crosland, Maurice, *Science Under Control: The French Academy of Sciences, 1795–1914*, Cambridge University Press, 1992.
Crouzet, François, 'Essai de construction d'un indice annuel de la production industrielle française au XIXe siècle', *Annales ESC*, 22 (1970) 56–99.
Cunningham, Andrew and Perry Williams (eds), *The Laboratory Revolution in Medicine*, Cambridge University Press, 1992.
Cunningham, Andrew and Harmke Kamminga (eds), *The Science and Culture of Nutrition, 1840–1940*, Amsterdam, Rodopi, Clio Medica, 1995.

Dalotel, Alain, Alain Faure and Jean-Claude Freiermuth, *Aux origines de la Commune : le mouvement des réunions publiques à Paris, 1868–1870*, François Maspéro, 1980.
Dantry, Jean and Lucien Sheler, *Le Comité central des vingts arrondissements de Paris, septembre 1870 – mai 1871, d'après les papiers inédits de Constant Martin et les sources imprimées*, Éditions Sociales, 1960.
Darmon, Pierre, *La Longue Traque de la variole, les pionniers de la médecine préventive*, Pour l'Histoire, Librairie Perrin, 1986.
Darmon, Pierre, *La Vie quotidienne du médecin parisien en 1900*, Hachette, 1988.
Darrow, M. H., 'French volunteer nursing and the myth of war experience in World War One', *American Historical Review*, 91:1 (1986) 80–106.
Dautry, J. and L. Scheler, *Le Comité central républicain des vingts arrondissements de Paris (Septembre 1870 – Mai 1871)*, Éditions Sociales, 1960.
Davis, Gerald H., 'National Red Cross societies and prisoners of war in Russia 1914–1918', *Journal of Contemporary History*, 28:1 (1993) 31–53.
Delahaye, M. C., *L'Absinthe, histoire de la fée verte*, Nancy, Berger-Levrault, 1983.
Delaporte, Sophie, *Les Gueules cassées, les blessés de la face de la grande guerre*, Noêsis, 1996.
Delaume, Thierry, 'Contribution à l'étude de la prothèse totale : son évolution du XVIe au XIXe siècle', Thèse de chirurgie dentaire, Université de Strasbourg I, 1988.
Déloye, Yves, *École et citoyenneté, l'individualisme républicain de Jules Ferry à Vichy – controverses*, Presses de la Fondation Nationale des Sciences Politiques, 1994.
Deschodt, Eric, *Histoire du Mont-de-Piété*, Le Cherche-Midi, 1993.
Dessol, Marcel, *Un Révolutionnaire jacobin : Charles Delescluze (1809–1871)*, Marcel Rivière et Cie, 1952.
Destexhe, A., *L'Humanitaire impossible ou deux siècles d'ambiguïté*, Armand Colin, 1993.
Dhombres, Nicole, *Naissance d'un nouveau pouvoir, science et savants en France 1793–1824*, Payot, 1989.
Didi-Huberman, Georges, *Invention de l'hystérie, Charcot et l'iconographie photographique de la Salpétrière*, Macula, 1982.

Digby, Anne, *Making a Medical Living: Doctors and Patients in the English Market for Medicine, 1720-1911*, Cambridge University Press, 1994.
Digeon, Claude, *La Crise allemande de la pensée française*, Presses Universitaires de France, 1959.
Dominique, Pierre, *La Commune*, Grasset, 1930.
Dommanget, Maurice, *L'Instruction publique sous la Commune*, Editions de l'internationale des travailleurs de l'Enseignement, 1929.
Dommanget, Maurice, *Hommes et choses de la Commune*, Marseilles, Éditions des amis de la coopérative des amis de l'école émancipée, n.d., c. 1936.
Dommanget, Maurice, *Auguste Banqui au début de la Troisième République, 1871-1880, dernière prison et ultimes combats*, Moraton, 1973.
Donzelot, Jacques, *La Police des familles*, Éditions de Minuit, 1977.
Droz, Jacques (ed.), *Histoire générale du socialisme, I, Des origines à 1875*, Presses Universitaires de France, 1972.
Dulieu, Louis, *La Médecine à Montpellier, IV, De la Première à la Troisième République, & V, 1870-1920*, 5 vols, Avignon, Aubanel & Montpellier, Quickprint, 1990-95.
Dumoulin, F., 'Le Débat sur l'alcoolisme après la Commune, 1871-1887', Mémoire de Maîtrise, Paris X, Nanterre, 1979.
Dupâquier, Jacques (ed.), *Histoire de la population française*, Presses Universitaires de France, 1988.
Dupoux, Albert, *Sur les pas de Monsieur Vincent, trois cents ans d'histoire parisienne de l'enfance abandonnée*, Revue de L'Assistance Publique à Paris, 1958.
Dupuy, Aimé, *Sedan et l'enseignement de la revanche*, Institut National de Recherche et de Documentation Pédagogique, 1975.
Durand, Pierre, *Louise Michel : la passion*, Messidor, 1987.
Dwork, Deborah, *War is Good for Babies and Other Young Children*, Tavistock, 1987.

Echard, W. E., *Napoleon III and the Concert of Europe*, Baton Rouge, Louisiana State University Press, 1983.
Echard, W. E., *Foreign Policy of the Second Empire: A Bibliography*, New York, Greenwood Press, 1988.
Edwards, Stewart, *The Paris Commune 1871*, Eyre and Spottiswoode, 1971.
Eginer, Camille, *Philippe Ricord, 1800-1889, sa vie, son oeuvre*, Le François, 1939.
Elias, Norbert, *Über den Prozess der Zivilisation, Soziogenetische und psychogenetische Untersuchungen*, 2 vols, Basel, Haus zum Falken, 1939.
Ellis, Jack D., *The Early Life of Georges Clemenceau 1841-1893*, Lawrence, Regent Press of Kansas, 1980.
Ellis, Jack D., *The Physician-Legislators of France: Medicine and Politics in the Early Third Republic, 1870-1914*, Cambridge University Press, 1990.
Elwitt, S., *The Third Republic Defended: Bourgeois Reform in France, 1880-1914*, Baton Rouge, Louisiana State Univerity Press, 1986.

Fabre, Jules, *La Justice à Paris pendant le siège et la Commune 1870-1871*, Marchal et Godde, 1919.
Fajal, Guy, 'L'Histoire des prothèses et des orthèses, les grandes voies de progrès', 2 vols, Thèse de doctorat de médecine, Université de Nancy I, 1972.

Farge, Arlette, *Fragile Lives: Violence, Power and Solidarity in Eighteenth-Century Paris*, Cambridge, Polity Press, 1993.
Farmer, Paul, *France Reviews its Revolutionary Origins: Social Politics and Historical Opinions in the Third Republic*, New York, Octagon Books, [1944] 1973.
Faure, Olivier, *Genèse de l'hôpital moderne, les hospices civils de Lyon, 1802–1845*, Lyons, Presses Universitaires de Lyon, 1982.
Faure, Olivier, *Les Français et leur médecine au dix-neuvième siècle*, Belin, 1993.
Faure, Olivier, *Histoire sociale de la médecine, XVIIIe–XXe siècles*, Anthropos, 1994.
Fierro, Alfred, *Histoire et dictionnaire de Paris*, Bouquins Robert Laffont, 1996.
Fildes, Valery A., *Breasts, Bottles and Babies: A History of Infant Feeding*, Edinburgh University Press, 1986.
Finlay, Mark R., 'Quackery and cookery: Justus von Liebig's extract of meat and the theory of nutrition in the Victorian age', *Bulletin of the History of Medicine*, 66 (1992) 404–18.
Fleetwood, John, 'An Irish field-ambulance in the Franco-Prussian war', *The Irish Sword*, 18 (1964) 137–48.
Ford, Caroline, *Creating the Nation in Provincial France: Religion and Political Identity*, Princeton University Press, 1993.
Forrest, Alan, *The French Revolution and the Poor*, Oxford, Basil Blackwell, 1981.
Forrest, Alan, *Conscripts and Deserters: The Army and French Society during the Revolution and Empire*, Oxford University Press, 1989.
Förster, Stig and Jörg Nagler (eds), *On the Road to Total War: The American Civil War and the German Wars of Unification, 1861–1871*, German Historical Institute (Washington D.C.) series, Cambridge University Press, 1997.
Foucault, Michel (ed.), *Moi Pierre Rivière ayant égorgé ma mére, ma soeur et mon frère*, Archives Julliard, 1973.
Fouquet, Pierre and Martine de Borde, *Le Roman de l'alcool*, Seghers, Médecine et histoire, 1985.
Fouquet, Pierre and Martine de Borde, *Histoire de l'alcool*, Presses Universitaires de France, 1990.
Fouquet, Pierre and Martine de Borde, *L'Alcool, boire et déboire*, Hachette, 1991.
Fourneron, Isabelle, 'La Décentralisation de l'administration des susbsistances. Pache et la Commune de Paris, février–septembre 1793', *Annales historiques de la Révolution Française*, 306 (1996) 649–74
Fox, Robert, *The Patronage of Science in the Nineteenth Century*, Leyden, Noordhoff International, 1976.
Fox, Robert and George Weisz (eds), *The Organization of Science and Technology in France, 1800–1914*, Cambridge University Press, 1980.
Fryer, W. R., 'The war of 1870 and the pattern of Franco-German relations', *Renaissance and Modern Studies*, 18 (1974) 77–125.
Fuchs, Rachel, 'Morality and poverty: public welfare for mothers in Paris, 1870–1900', *French History*, 2:3 (1988) 288–311.
Fuchs, Rachel, *Abandoned Children: Foundlings and Child Welfare in Nineteenth-Century France*, Albany, State University of New York Press, 1984.
Fuchs, Rachel, *Poor and Pregnant in Paris: Strategies for Survival in the Nineteenth Century*, New Brunswick, N.J., Rutgers University Press, 1992.

Furet, François, *La Gauche et la Révolution au milieu du dix-neuvième siècle*, Hachette, 1986.
Furet, François, *La Révolution 1770–1880*, 2 vols, Hachette, 1988.
Furlough, Ellen, *Consumer Cooperation in France: The Politics of Consumption, 1834–1930*, Ithaca, Cornell University Press, 1991.

Gadille, Jacques, *La Pensée et l'action politiques des évêques français au début de la Troisième République*, 2 vols, Hachette, 1967.
Gaillard, Jean-Michel, *Jules Ferry*, Fayard, 1989.
Gaillard, Jeanne, *Communes de province, Commune de Paris 1870–1871*, Flammarion, Question d'Histoire, 1971.
Gaillard, Jeanne, *Paris la ville 1852–1870*, Lille, H. Champion, 1976.
Garcia, Philippe, 'Les Idées médicales à travers l'oeuvre de Guy de Maupassant', Thèse de doctorat en médecine, Université de Lyon I, 1987.
Gay, Peter, *The Cultivation of Hatred: The Bourgeois Experience, Victoria to Freud*, Harper Collins, 1994.
Gerber, David, 'Anger and affability: the rise and representation of a repertory of self-representation skills in a WWII disabled veteran', *Journal of Social History*, 27:1 (1993) 5–28
Giard, Luce (ed.), *Michel Foucault : lire l'oeuvre*, Jérôme Millon, 1992.
Gilpin, Robert, *France in the Age of the Scientific State*, Princeton University Press, 1968.
Girard, Louis, *Napoléon III*, Fayard, 1986.
Girault, Jacques, *La Commune et Bordeaux (1870–1871) contribution à l'étude du mouvement ouvrier et de l'idéologie républicaine en province au moment de la Commune de Paris*, Éditions Sociales, 1971.
Goetz, C. G., 'Visual art in the neurological career of Jean Martin Charcot', *Archives of Neurology*, 48 (1991) 421–5.
Goldstein, Jan, 'The hysteria diagnosis and the politics of anti-clericalism in late nineteenth-century France', *Journal of Modern History*, 54:2 (1982) 209–39.
Goldstein, Jan, *Console and Classify: The French Psychiatric Profession in the Nineteenth Century*, Cambridge University Press, 1987.
Goldstein, Robert Justin, 'Censorship of caricature in France, 1815–1914', *French History*, 3:1 (1989) 71–107.
Goodman, Jordan, *Tobacco in History: The Culture of Dependence*, Routledge, 1993.
Goodman, Jordan and Paul E. Lovejoy, *Consuming Habits: Drugs in History and Anthropology*, Routledge, 1995.
Gordon, Felicia, *The Integral Feminist: Madeleine Pelletier 1874–1939, Feminism, Socialism and Medicine*, Cambridge, Polity, 1990.
Gouault, Jacques, *Comment la France est devenue républicaine, les élections générales et partielles à l'Assemblée Nationale (1870–1875)*, Armand Colin, 1954.
Gould, Roger V., *Insurgent Identities: Class, Community and Protest in Paris from 1848 to the Commune*, Chicago University Press, 1996.
Greenberg, Louis, *Sisters of Liberty: Marseille, Lyon, Paris and the Reaction to the Centralized State*, Cambridge, Mass., Harvard University Press, 1971.
Greenslade, William, *Degeneration, Culture and the Novel*, Cambridge University Press, 1994.
Grieves, Keith, *The Politics of Manpower, 1914–18*, Manchester University Press, 1988.

Griffin, David Eugene, 'Adolphe Thiers, the mayors and the coming of the Paris Commune of 1871', unpublished thesis, Santa Barbara University, 1971.
Grmek, Mirko D., *Claude Bernard et la méthode expérimentale*, Payot, 1991.
Grumwald, Constantin de, *Bismarck*, Albin Michel, 1949.
Guignard, M., 'Philippe Ricord, sa vie, son oeuvre, 1800–1889', Thèse de doctorat, IHU Lariboisière, 1978.
Guillain, Georges, *J.M. Charcot 1825–1893, sa vie, son oeuvre*, Masson, 1955.
Guillais, Joëlle, *La Chair de l'autre, le crime passionnel au XIXe siècle,* Olivier Orban, 1986.
Guillaume, Pierre, *Du Désespoir au salut: les tuberculeux aux XIXe et XXe siècles*, Aubier, 1986.
Guillaume, Pierre, *Médecins, église et foi depuis deux siècles,* Aubier, 1989.
Guillemin, Henri, *Les Origines de la Commune*, 3 vols, Gallimard, 1973.
Guillemin, Henri, *Nationalistes et nationaux, (1870–1940),* Gallimard, 1974.
Guillermand, Jean, *Histoire des infirmières*, France Sélection, 1988.
Guiral, Pierre, *Prévost–Paradol, 1829–1870, pensée et action d'un libéral sous le Second Empire*, Presses Universitaires de France, 1955.
Gullickson, Gay, *Unruly Women of Paris: Images of the Commune*, Ithaca, Cornell University Press, 1996.

Haik, Patrick, 'L'Histoire de la prothèse en rapport avec l'évolution des techniques et des matériaux', Thèse de doctorat de chirurgie dentaire, Université de Paris VII, 1991.
Hamlin, Christopher, *A Science of Impurity: Water Analysis in Nineteenth-Century Britain,* Bristol, Adam Hilgen, 1990.
Hamon, Leo (ed.), *Les Opportunistes : Les débuts de la République aux républicains,* Maison des Sciences de l'Homme, 1991.
Hamon, Leo (ed.), *Les Républicains sous le Second Empire*, Maison des Sciences de l'Homme, 1993.
Handel, M., *Masters of War: Sun Tzu, Clausewitz and Janini*, Frank Cass, 1992.
Harris, Ruth, *Murders and Madness: Medicine, Law and Society in the Fin-de-Siècle*, Oxford, Clarendon Press, 1989.
Harris, Ruth, 'The "Child of the barbarian": rape, race and nationalism in France during the First World War', *Past and Present,* 141 (1993) 170–206.
Harsin, Jill, *Policing Prostitution in Nineteenth-Century Paris*, Princeton University Press, 1985.
Harsin, Jill, 'Syphilis, wives and physicians: medical ethics and the family in late nineteenth-century France', *French Historical Studies,* 16:1 (1989) 72–95.
Harvey, David, *Consciousness and the Urban Experience: Studies in the History and Theory of Capitalist Urbanization,* 2 vols, Oxford, Basil Blackwell, 1992.
Harvey, Joy, 'Medicine and politics: Dr Mary Putman Jacobi and the Paris Commune', *Dialectical Anthropology,* 15 (1990) 107–17.
Hatton, Helen, *The Largest Amount of Good: Quaker Relief in Ireland, 1654–1921*, Kingston and Montreal, McGill-Queen's University Press, 1993.
Hatzfeld, Henri, *Du Paupérisme à la sécurité sociale, 1850–1940,* Armand Colin, 1971.
Hazareesingh, Sudhir, 'Defining the republican good life: Second Empire municipalism and the emergence of the Third Republic', *French History,* 11:3 (1997) 310–37.

Hazareesingh, Sudhir, *From Subject to Citizen: The Second Empire and the Emergence of Modern French Democracy*, Princeton University Press, 1998.
Hémardinquer, Jean-Jacques (ed.), *Pour une histoire de l'alimentation*, Armand Colin, Cahiers des Annales 28, 1970.
Heywood, Colin, *The Development of French Economy 1750–1914*, Cambridge University Press, 1995.
Hildreth, Martha L., *Doctors, Bureaucrats, and Public Health in France 1888–1902*, New York, Garland, 1987.
Holmes, Richard, *The Road to Sedan: The French Army 1866–1870*, Royal Historical Society, 1984.
Horne, Alistair, *The Fall of Paris: The Siege and the Commune 1870–1*, Reprint Society, 2nd edn, 1967.
Horne, John and Alan Kramer, 'German "Atrocities" and Franco-German opinion, 1914: the evidence of German soldiers' diaries', *Journal of Modern History*, 66:1 (1994) 1–33.
Howard, Michael, *War and the Liberal Conscience*, Temple Smith, 1978.
Howard, Michael (ed.), *Restraints on War: Studies in the Limitation of Armed Conflict*, Oxford University Press, 1979.
Howard, Michael, *The Causes of Wars and Other Essays*, Temple Smith, 1983.
Howard, Michael, *The Franco-Prussian War: the German Invasion of France, 1870–1871*, New York, Dorset Press, 1961, reprinted 1990.
Hublot, Emmanuel, *Valmy ou la défense de la nation par les armes*, Fondation pour les Études de la Défense Nationale, 1987.
Huger, M. and Jean Pictet, *Une Institution unique en son genre : Le Comité International de la Croix Rouge*, Geneva, A. Paten, 1985.
Hughes, Daniel, *Moltke and the Art of War*, Noveto, Periodic Press, 1993.
Hunt, Lynn (ed.), *The New Cultural History*, Berkeley, University of California Press, 1989.
Hutchinson, John F., 'Rethinking the origins of the Red Cross', *Bulletin of the History of Medicine*, 63 (1989) 557–78.
Hutchinson, John F., *Champions of Charity: War and the Rise of the Red Cross*, Oxford, Westview Press, 1996.
Hutton, Patrick H., *The Cult of the Revolutionary Tradition: The Blanquists in French Politics, 1864–1893*, Berkeley, University of California Press, 1981.
Hynes, Samuel, *A War Imagined: The First World War and English Culture*, New York, Atheneum, 1991.

Isser, Natalie, *The Second Empire and the Press: A Study of Government-Inspired Brochures on French Foreign Policy in their Propaganda Milieu*, The Hague, Martinus Nijhoff, 1974.
Isser, Natalie, 'Protestant and proselytization during the Second French Empire', *Journal of Church and State*, 30 (1988) 51–70.
Isser, Natalie, *Antisemitism during the French Second Empire*, New York, P. Lang, 1991.

Jauffret, Jean-Charles, *Parlement, gouvernement, commandement : l'armée de métier sous la Troisième République, 1871–1914*, 2 vols, Vincennes, SHAT, 1987.

Jeismann, Michael, *Das Vaterland der Feinde, Studiem zum nationalen Feindbegriff und Selbstverständnis in Deutschland und Frankreich, 1792–1918*, Stuttgart, Klett-Cotta, 1992.
Jenkins, Brian, *Nationalism in France: Class and Nation since 1789*, Routledge, 1990.
Johnson, Martin Philip, 'Citizenship and gender: the *Légion des Fédérés* in the Paris Commune of 1871', *French History*, 8:3 (1994) 276–95.
Johnson, Martin Philip, *The Paradise of Association: Political Culture and Popular Organization in the Paris Commune of 1871*, Ann Arbor, University of Michigan Press, 1996.
Jones, Colin and Roy Porter (eds), *Reassessing Foucault: Power, Medicine, and the Body*, Routledge, 1994.
Jones, H. S., *The French State in Question: Public Law and Political Argument in the Third Republic*, Cambridge University Press, 1993.
Jones, R. A., 'Monuments as ex-voto, monuments as historiography: the basilica of Sacré Coeur', *French Historical Studies*, 18:2 (1993) 482–502.
Jones, R. A., 'Anxiety, identity and the displacement of violence during the année terrible. The Sacred Heart and the diocese of Nantes, 1870–1871', *French Historical Studies*, 21:1 (1998) 55–76.

Karsten, Peter, *Law, Soldiers and Combat*, Westport, Greenwood Press, 1978.
Kayser, J. (ed.), *Émile Zola, La République en marche*, Fasquelle, 1956.
Kessel, Patrick (ed.), *Gustave Paul Cluseret, la Commune et la question militaire*, Union Générale d'éditions, 1971.
Keylor, William R., *Academy and Community: The Foundation of the French Historical Profession*, Cambridge, Mass., Harvard University Press, 1975.
Knibiehler, Yvonne, 'La Lutte anti-tuberculeuse et la médicalisation des classes populaires', *Annales de Bretagne*, 86:3 (1979) 321–36.
Knibiehler, Yvonne, Véronique Leroux-Hugon, Odile Dupont-Hess and Yolande Tastayre, *Cornettes et blouses blanches, les infirmières et la société française*, Hachette, 1984.
Kselman, Thomas A., *Death and the Afterlife in Modern France*, Princeton University Press, 1993.
Kudlick, Catherine J., *Cholera in Post-Revolutionary Paris, A Cultural History*, Berkeley, University of California Press, 1996.

La Berge, Ann F., *Mission and Method: The Early-Nineteenth-Century French Public Health Movement*, Cambridge University Press, 1992.
La Berge, Ann F. and Mordechai Feingold (eds), *French Medical Culture in the Nineteenth Century*, Amsterdam, Rodopi, Clio Medica, 1994.
Laffin, John, *Surgeons in the Field*, J. M. Dent and Sons, 1970.
Lalouette, J., 'Charcot au coeur des problèmes religieux de son temps. A propos de *La foi qui guérit*', *Revue neurologique*, 150 (1994) 511–16.
Langle, Henry Melchior de, *Le Petit Monde des cafés et débits parisiens au XIXème siècle, évolution de la sociabilité citadine*, Presses Universitaires de France, 1990.
Lapert, Louis, *La Guerre de 1870–1871 à Yvelot et ses environs*, Yvelot, Imprimerie Nouvelle, 1971.
Latour, Bruno, *The Pasteurization of France*, Cambridge, Mass., Harvard University Press 1988.

Lebovics, Herman, *True France: The Wars over Cultural Identity, 1900–1945*, Ithaca, Cornell University Press, 1992.

Lecaillon, Jean-François, *Napoléon III et le Mexique : les illusions d'un grand dessein*, L'Harmattan, 1994.

Leclère, Bernard and Vincent Wright, *Les Préfets du Second Empire*, Fondation Nationale des Sciences Politiques, 1973.

Lefebvre, Henri, *La Proclamation de la Commune*, Gallimard, 1971.

Lénine, Vladmir Illitch, *La Commune de Paris*, François Maspéro, 1971

Léonard, Jacques, *La Vie quotidienne du médecin de province au XIX siècle*, Hachette, 1977.

Léonard, Jacques, 'Religieuses et médecins au XIXe siècle', *Annales ESC*, 29 (1977) 887–907.

Léonard, Jacques, 'La Médicalisation de l'état: l'exemple des premières décennies de la IIIème république', *Annales de Bretagne*, 36:2 (1978) 313–20.

Léonard, Jacques, *La France médicale au XIXe siècle*, Gallimard-Julliard Archives, 1978.

Léonard, Jacques, *La Médecine entre les savoirs et les pouvoirs: histoire intellectuelle et politique de la médecine française au XIX siècle*, Aubier Montaigne, 1981.

Le Quillec, Robert, *La Commune de Paris, bibliographie critique*, La Boutique de l'histoire, 1997.

Leroux-Hugon, Véronique, *Des Saintes laïques, les infirmières à l'aube de la Troisième République*, Sciences en Situation, 1992.

Leseigneur, Louis, *Les Prussiens à Barentin pendant la guerre de 1870–1871*, Res Universis, 1992.

Levillain, Philippe and Reiner Riemenschneider (eds), *La Guerre de 1870–1871 et ses conséquences*, Bonn, Bouvier Verlag, 1990.

Lidsky, Paul, *Les Écrivains contre la Commune*, François Maspéro, [1970] 1982.

Ligou, Daniel, 'L'Évolution des cimetières', *Archives des sciences sociales des religions*, 39 (1975) 61–77.

Linon, Pierre-Jean, *Officiers d'administration du Service de santé, monographie d'un corps, d'une association*, EREMM, 1983.

Lizier, Henri, 'Le Marché noir à Paris pendant le siège', *Histoire locale de Beauce et du Perche*, Chartres, 34 (1971) 27–8.

Llopez, Laurent, 'La Garde Mobile de l'Hérault : défendre le territoire nationale de Paris à l'Algérie', *Histoire et défense*, 33:1 (1996) 31–62.

Locke, Robert R., *French Legitimists and the Politics of Moral Order in the Early Third Republic*, Princeton University Press, 1974.

Löwy, Ilana (ed.), *Medicine and Change: Historical and Sociological Studies of Medical Innovation*, Colloque Inserm 220, 1993.

Lüdtke, Alf, 'Coming to terms with the past: illusions of remembering, ways of forgetting Nazism in West Germany', *Journal of Modern History*, 65:3 (1993) 542–72.

Machelon, Jean-Pierre, *La République contre les libertés, les restrictions aux libertés publiques de 1879 à 1914*, Fondation Nationale des Sciences Politiques, 1976.

Maclaren, Angus, *Sexuality and Social Order: The Debate over Fertility of Women and Workers in France, 1770–1920*, New York, Holmes and Meier, 1983.

McMillan, James F., *Housewife or Harlot: The Place of Woman in French Society, 1870–1940*, Harvester, 1981.

McMillan, James F., *Napoleon III*, Longman Profiles in Power, 1991.
Maillet, Serge, 'Des Origines de la prothèse jusqu'à la prothèse adjointe totale et son évolution jusqu'à nos jours', Thèse de doctorat d'état en médecine, Université de Paris VI, Broussais Hôtel-Dieu, 1986.
Margadant, Jo Burr, *Madame le Professeur: Women Educators in the Third Republic*, Princeton University Press, 1990.
Margadant, Ted W., *Urban Rivalries in the French Revolution*, Princeton University Press 1992.
Marion, Olivier and Luc Perrin, 'La Commune et l'Église', Mémoire de Maîtrise, Université de Paris X–XII, 1981.
Marrus, M. R., 'Social drinking in the belle époque', *Journal of Social History*, 2 (1974) 115–41.
Martin, Benjamin F., *Crime and Criminal Justice Under the Third Republic: The Shame of Marianne*, Baton Rouge, Louisiana State University Press, 1990.
Martinier J. and L. Lessurle, *Prothèses restauratrices bucco-faciale et traitement des fractures des maxillaires*, J. B. Baillière et Fils, 1915.
Massa-Gille, Geneviève, *Histoire des emprunts de la ville de Paris (1814–1875)*, Ville de Paris, 1973.
Maurain, Jean, *La Politique ecclesiastique du Second Empire de 1852 à 1869*, Félix Alcan, 1930.
Maurain, Jean, *Un Bourgeois français au XIXième siècle : Baroche, ministre de Napoléon III d'après ses papiers inédits*, Félix Alcan, 1936.
Mayeur, Jean-Marie, *Les Débuts de la Troisième République 1871–1898*, Nouvelle Histoire de France, Le Seuil, 1973.
Mennell, Stephen, 'On the civilizing of appetite', *Theory, Culture, Society*, 4 (1987) 373–403.
Mepham, T. B., 'Humanizing milk: the formulation of artificial feeds for infants, 1850–1910', *Medical History*, 37:3 (1993) 225–49.
Meron, Theodor, *Human Rights and Humanitarian Norms on Customary Law*, Oxford, Clarendon Press, 1989.
Merriman, John M. (ed.), *Consciousness and Class Experience in Nineteenth-Century Europe*, New York, Holmes and Meier, 1979.
Micale, Mark S., 'The Salpêtrière in the age of Charcot: an institutional perspective on medical history in the late nineteenth century', *Journal of Contemporary History*, 20:4 (1985) 703–31.
Micale, Mark S., *Approaching Hysteria: Disease and its Interpretation*, Princeton University Press, 1995.
Millman, Richard, *British Foreign Policy and the Coming of the Franco-Prussian War*, Oxford, Clarendon Press, 1965.
Ministère de la Guerre, *Aperçu statistique sur l'évolution de la morbidité et de la mortalité générales dans l'armée et sur l'évolution de la morbidité et de la mortalité particulières à certaines maladies contagieuses de 1862 jusqu'à nos jours*, Imprimerie Nationale, 1932.
Mitchell, Allan, *The German Influence in France after 1870: The Formation of the French Republic*, Chapel Hill, University of North Carolina Press, 1979.
Mitchell, Allan, 'Crucible of French anti-clericalism: the Conseil Municipal of Paris, 1871–1885', *Francia*, 8 (1980) 395–405.

Mitchell, Allan, *Victors and Vanquished: The German Influence on Army and Church in France after 1870,* Chapel Hill, University of North Carolina Press, 1984.

Mitchell, Allan, 'An inexact science: the statistics of tuberculosis in late nineteenth-century France', *Social History of Medicine,* 3:3 (1990) 387–404.

Mitchell, Allan, *The Divided Path: The German Influence on Social Reform in France after 1870,* Chapel Hill, University of North Carolina Press, 1991.

Mohert, Michel, *Les Intellectuels devant la défaite, 1870,* Carréa, 1942.

Moison, Claude, 'Le Service pharmaceutique pendant la guerre franco-allemande de 1870–1871', Thèse de doctorat de pharmacie, Cahors, Coueslant, 1965.

Montesquiou-Férensac, Léon de, *1870 : les causes politiques du désastre,* Librairie Française, 1979.

Montroy, Jacques Dumont de, *Napoléon III et la réorganisation de l'armée de 1866 à 1870, la loi Niel mutilée du 1 février 1868,* l'auteur, 1996.

Moses, Claire Goldberg, *French Feminism in the Nineteenth Century,* Albany, State University of New York, 1984.

Mosse, George L., *Fallen Soldiers: Reshaping the Memory of the World Wars,* Oxford University Press, 1990.

Murard, Lion and Patrick Zylberman, 'L'Autre Guerre, 1914–1918 : la santé publique sous l'oeil de l'Amérique', *Revue Historique,* 276 (1986) 367–98.

Murard, Lion and Patrick Zylberman, *L'Hygiène dans la République, la santé publique en France, ou l'utopie contrariée, 1870–1918,* Fayard, 1996.

Nessakh, Nabila, 'Histoire de la chirurgie plastique, reconstructive et esthétique', Thèse de doctorat, Université de Besançon, 1995.

Newman, Lucile F. (ed.), *Hunger in History: Food Shortage, Poverty and Deprivation,* Oxford, Basil Blackwell, 1990.

Nicolet, Claude, *L'Idée républicaine en France, essai d'histoire critique,* Gallimard, 1982.

Noël, Bernard, *Dictionnaire de la Commune,* Fernand Hozon, 1971.

Nora, Pierre (ed.), *Realms of Memory: The Construction of the French Past,* 3 vols, New York, Columbia University Press, 1996–98.

Nord, Philip G., *Paris Shopkeepers and the Politics of Resentment,* Princeton University Press, 1986.

Nord, Philip G., 'The party of conciliation and the Paris Commune', *French Historical Studies,* 15:1 (1987) 1–35.

Nord, Philip G., *The Republican Moment: Struggles for Democracy in Nineteenth-Century France,* Cambridge, Mass., Harvard University Press, 1995.

Nourisson, Didier, 'La France alcoolique des années 1870', *Rapports d'activité,* Centre de recherches d'histoire quantitative, 1984.

Nourisson, Didier, *Le Buveur du XIXe siècle,* Albin Michel, 1990.

Nye, Robert, *Crime, Madness and Politics in Modern France: The Medical Concept of National Decline,* Princeton University Press, 1984.

Nye, Robert, 'Honor, impotence and male sexuality in nineteenth-century French medicine', *French Historical Studies,* 16:1 (1989) 48–71.

Nye, Robert, *Masculinity and Male Codes of Honour in Modern France,* New York, Oxford University Press, 1993.

Octave de Lassard, Jean-Marie, 'Les Membres fantômes des amputés', Thèse de la faculté de médecine de Paris, 1944.
Offen, Karen, 'Depopulation, nationalism and feminism in fin-de-siècle France', *American Historical Review*, 89:3 (1984) 648–78.
Ozouf, Mona, *L'École, l'église et la république (1871–1914)*, Cana/Jean Offredo, 1982.

Paret, Peter, *Clausewitz and the State, the Man, his Theories and his Times*, Princeton University Press, [1976], 1985.
Paul, Diane B., *Controlling Human Heredity: 1865 to the Present*, Atlantic Highlands, N.J., Humanities Press International, 1995.
Paul, Harry W., *The Sorcerer's Apprentice: The French Scientists' Image of German Science (1840–1919)*, Gainesville, University of Florida Press, 1972.
Paul, Harry W., *From Knowledge to Power: The Rise of the Science Empire in France, 1860–1939*, Cambridge University Press, 1985.
Penin, Jean-Pierre, *Valmy, première victoire de la Nation*, Groucher, 1989.
Perett, Diane Beyer, 'Ethics and error: the dispute between Ricord and Auzias-Turenne over syphilization, 1845–1870', unpublished thesis, University of Stanford, 1977.
Petrescu, A. D., 'La Participation des médecins et pharmaciens roumains à la guerre de 1870 et à la Commune', *Revue médicale et pharmaceutique*, 20 (1970) 229–231.
Picard, Jean-François, 'L'Organisation de la science en France depuis 1870 : Un tour des recherches actuelles', *French Historical Studies*, 17:1 (1991) 249–68.
Picard, Jean-François, *La République des savants, la recherche française et le CNRS*, Flammarion, 1990.
Pick, Daniel, *Faces of Degeneration: A European Disorder*, Cambridge University Press, 1989.
Pick, Daniel, *War Machine: The Rationalisation of Slaughter in the Modern Age*, New Haven, Yale University Press, 1993.
Pictet, Jean, *Développement et principe du droit international humanitaire*, Geneva, Institut Henry Dunant, 1983.
Pierret, J., *L'Imaginaire décadent (1880–1900)*, Presses Universitaires de France, 1977.
Piggott, Sir Francis, *The Declaration of Paris*, University of London Press, 1919.
Pilbeam, Pamela M., *Republicanism in Nineteenth-Century France, 1814–1871*, Basingstoke, Macmillan, 1995.
Pillar, Paul R., *Negotiating Peace: War Termination as a Bargaining Process*, Princeton University Press, 1983.
Pinell, Patrice, *Naissance d'un fléau, histoire de la lutte contre le cancer en France, 1890–1940*, Métaillé, 1992.
Plessis, Alain, *De la fête impériale au mur des fédérés 1852–1871*, Nouvelle Histoire de la France Contemporaine, Point Seuil, 1979.
Plumridge, John H., *Hospital Ships and Ambulance Trains*, Seeley, Service and Co., 1975.
Poirier, Jacques and Claude Langlois (eds), *Raspail et la vulgarisation médicale*, Vrin, 1988.
Pomard, Dr, *La Quatrième ambulance de la Société nationale de secours aux blessés pendant la guerre de 1870–1871*, Aubonel Frères, 1915.
Porter, Dorothy (ed.), *The History of Public Health and the Modern State*, Amsterdam, Rodopi, Clio Medica, 1994.

Porter, Roy (ed.), *Rewriting the Self: Histories from the Renaissance to the Present*, Routledge, 1997.
Porter, Roy and Lesley Hall, *The Facts of Life: The Creation of Sexual Knowledge in Britain, 1850–1950*, New Haven, Yale University Press, 1995.
Pottinger, E. A., *Napoleon III and the German Crisis, 1865–1866*, Cambridge, Mass., Harvard University Press, 1966.
Prestwich, Patricia E., *Drink and the Politics of Social Reform: Antialcoholism in France since 1870*, Palo Alto, Cal., Society for the Promotion of Science and Scholarship, 1988.
Prestwich, Patricia E., 'Family strategies and medical power: voluntary committal in a Parisian asylum, 1876–1914', *Journal of Social History*, 27:4 (1994) 779–818.
Proust, Marcel, *Le Temps retrouvé*, Gallimard, folio, [1927] 1984.
Przybos, Julia, *L'Entreprise mélodramatique*, J. Corti, 1987.

Quêtel, Claude, *Le Mal de Naples, histoire de la syphilis*, Seghers, 1986.

Rabinbach, Anson, *The Human Motor: Energy, Fatigue and the Origin of Modernity*, New York, Basic Books, 1990.
Ramsey, Matthew, *Professional and Popular Medicine in France, 1770–1830: The Social World of Medical Practice*, Cambridge University Press, 1988.
Rancière, Jacques, *'The Nights of Labor': The Workers' Dream in Nineteenth-Century France*, Philadelphia, Temple University Press, 1989.
Ratcliffe, Barrie M., '*Classes laborieuses et classes dangereuses à Paris pendant la première moitié du dix-neuvième siècle?* The Chevalier thesis reexamined', *French Historical Study*, 17:2 (1991) 542–74.
Red Cross, *Recueils de décrets, statuts, règlements et instructions concernant la Société de secours aux blessés militaires de la croix rouge française*, Croix Rouge Française, 1936.
Redon, Sylvie Clair, Louis (ed.), *Les Galères de la République*, Presses du CNRS, Singulier Pluriel, 1990.
Reid, Donald, *Paris Sewers and Sewermen: Realities and Representations*, Cambridge, Mass., Harvard University Press, 1991.
Rémond, René, *L'Anti-cléricalisme en France de 1815 à nos jours*, Brussels, Complexe, 2nd edn, 1985.
Rials, Stéphane, *Nouvelle Histoire de Paris: de Trochu à Thiers, 1870–1875*, Hachette, 1985.
Rieux, Jean Baptiste Eugène and Colonel J. Hassenforder, *Centenaire de l'école d'application du Service de santé militaire (1850–1950) : histoire du Service de santé militaire et du Val-de-Grâce*, Paris and Limoges, Charles Lavauzelle et Cie, 1951.
Rifkin, Adrian and Roger Thomas (eds), *Voices of the People: The Social Life of la Sociale at the End of the Second Empire*, Routledge and Kegan Paul, 1988.
Rihs, Charles, *La Commune de Paris, sa structure et ses doctrines, 1871*, Geneva, Librairie Droz, 1955; Seuil, reprint, 1973.
Rioux, Jean-Pierre and Jean-François Sirinelli, *La Guerre d'Algérie et les intellectuels français*, Brussels, Complexe, 1991.
Riviale, Philippe, *La Ballade du temps passé, guerre et insurrection de Babeuf à la Commune*, Anthropos, 1977.

Roberts, J. M. G., *The Paris Commune from the Right*, English Historical Review Supplement 6, Longman, 1973.
Robertson, R., 'Civilization and the civilizing process: Elias, globalization and analytic synthesis', *Theory, Culture and Society*, 9:1 (1992) 211–27.
Robins, Joseph, *The Miasma: Epidemic and Panic in Nineteenth-Century Ireland*, Dublin, Institute of Public Administration, 1995.
Roche, Alphonse V., *Provençal Regionalism: A Study of the Movement in the Revue Félibréenne, Le Feu and Other Reviews of Southern France*, Evanston, Northwestern University Press, 1954.
Rollet, Henri, *L'Action sociale des catholiques en France 1871–1914*, Desclée de Brouwer, 1958.
Rosenberg, Charles E., *Explaining Epidemics and Other Studies in the History of Medicine*, Cambridge University Press, 1992.
Roth, François, *La Lorraine annexée, 1870–1918*, Nancy, Presses Universitaires de Nancy, 1976.
Roth, François, *La Lorraine dans la guerre de 1870*, Nancy, Presses Universitaires de Nancy, 1984.
Roth, François, *La Guerre de 1870*, Fayard, 1990.
Roth, Michael S., 'Remembering forgetting: *les Maladies de la Mémoire* in nineteenth-century France', *Representations*, 26 (1989) 49–67.
Rothney, John, *Bonapartism after Sedan*, Ithaca, Cornell University Press, 1969.
Rougerie, Jacques, *Paris Libre 1871*, Le Seuil, 1971.
Rougerie, Jacques, *Procès des Communards*, Archives Julliard, 1976.
Rougerie, Jacques, *La Commune : 1871*, Presses Universitaires de France, 1988.
Rovitch, Norman, *The Catholic Church and the French Nation, 1589–1989*, Routledge, 1990.
Rozan, Paul, *Blessés de guerre, prothèse et orthèse professionnelles*, Berger Levrault, 1919.
Rudelle, Odile, *La République absolue, aux origines de l'instabilité constitutionelle de la France républicaine 1870–1889*, Publications de la Sorbonne, 1982.
Rufin, Jean Christophe, *Le Piège humanitaire suivi de humanitaire et politique depuis la chute du Mur*, Hachette, 1993.

Sabatier, Robert, *Bataille de Wissembourg*, Association des Oeuvres Scolaires, 1989.
Said, Edward, *Imperialism and Culture*, Chatto and Windus, 1993.
Samuel, Raphael, *Theatres of Memory: Past and Present in Contemporary Culture*, Verso, 1992.
Samuel, Raphael, *Island Stories: Unravelling Britain*, Verso, 1998.
Sanchez, Gonzalo J., 'The challenge of right-wing caricature journals: from the Commune amnesty campaign to the end of censorship, 1878–1881', *French History*, 10:4 (1996) 451–89.
Sanson, William, *Proust*, Thames and Hudson, 1973.
Saumade, Christian, 'Histoire des vaccinations dans les armées françaises', Thèse de doctorat d'état en médecine, Bordeaux II, 1979.
Schiller, Francis, *Paul Broca, explorateur du cerveau*, Berkeley, University of California Press, 1979; French trans. Éditions Odile Jacob, 1990.

Schor, Naomi, *Zola's Crowds*, Baltimore, Johns Hopkins University Press, 1978.
Schlumberger, H. G., 'Rudolph Virchow and the Franco-Prussian war', *Annals of Medical History,* 4 (1942) 253–67.
Schneider, William H., *Quality and Quantity: The Quest for Biological Regeneration in Twentieth-Century France,* Cambridge University Press, 1989.
Schnerb, Robert, *Rouher et le Second Empire,* Armand Colin, 1949.
Schroeder, H. J. (ed.), *Disciplinary Decrees of the General Councils,* Herder, 1937.
Schulkind, Eugene (ed.), *The Paris Commune of 1871: The Point of View of the Left,* Jonathan Cape, 1972.
Schulkind, Eugene, 'Socialist women in the 1871 Paris Commune', *Past and Present,* 106 (1985) 124–63.
Schultheiss, Katrin, 'Gender and the limits of anticlericalism: the secularization of hospital nursing in France, 1880–1914', *French History,* 12:3 (1998) 229–45.
Scott, James Brown, *The Hague Convention and Declarations of 1899 and 1907,* Oxford University Press, 1915.
Scott, John W., *The Glassworkers of Carmaux,* Cambridge, Mass., Harvard University Press, 1974.
Sée, Geneviève, *Aujourd'hui Paris, ou les 133 jours du siège, 1870–1871, par ceux qui l'ont vécu,* Versailles, Les Septs Vents, 1988.
Segesvary, Victor, *La Guerre franco-allemande de 1870–1871, la naissance de la Croix Rouge,* Geneva, L'Age de l'Homme, 1971.
Serman, William, *Les Officiers français dans la nation, 1848–1914,* Aubier, 1982.
Serman, William, *La Commune de Paris : 1871,* Fayard, 1986.
Serman, William (ed.), Aristide Denfert-Rochereau, *Lettres d'un officier républicain, 1842–1871,* Vincennes, SHAT, 1990.
Sesnot, P., *1870–1871, l'année terrible,* Musée d'Orsay, 1994.
Sessions, William K., *They Chose the Star: An Account of the Work in France of the Society of Friends War Victims Relief Fund from 1870 to 1875, During and After the Franco-Prussian War; Together with an Account of Bulgarian Relief Work in the 1870s,* Society of Friends, 1944; 2nd edn, York, Ebor Press, 1991.
Shapiro, Ann-Louise, *Housing the Poor of Paris, 1850–1902,* Madison, University of Wisconsin Press, 1985.
Shapiro, Ann-Louise, *Breaking the Codes: Female Criminality in Fin-de-siècle Paris,* Stanford, Stanford University Press, 1996.
Showalter, Elaine, *Sexual Anarchy: Gender and Culture at the Fin-de-Siècle,* New York, Viking, 1990.
Silverman, Dan P., *Reluctant Union: Alsace Lorraine and Imperial Germany, 1871–1918,* Harrisburg, Pennsylvania University Press, 1972.
Sinding, Christiane, *Le Clinicien et le chercheur, des grandes maladies de carence à la médecine moléculaire (1880–1980),* Presses Universitaires de France, 1991.
Singer-Kerel, Jeanne, *Le Coût de la vie à Paris de 1840 à 1954,* Armand Colin, 1961.
Smith, James L., *Melodrama,* Methuen, 1973.
Smith, Roger, *Inhibition: History and Meaning in the Sciences of Mind and Brain,* Free Association Books, 1992.
Smith, Timothy B., 'Republicans, Catholics and social reform: Lyon, 1870–1920', *French History,* 12:3 (1998) 246–75.

Smith, William H. C., *Second Empire and Commune: Framce 1848–1871*, Longman Seminars in History, 1985.
Sonalet, Jacqueline, *Jean-Marie Charcot et l'hystérie au dix-neuvième siècle*, Alpha FNAC, 1988.
Sontag, Susan, *Illness as Metaphor*, New York, Viking, 1979.
Soubiran, André, *Le Baron Larrey, chirurgien de Napoléon*, Fayard, 1967.
Sournia, Jean Charles, *A History of Alcoholism*, Oxford, Basil Blackwell, 1990.
Spivok, Marcel, 'Education physique, sport et nationalisme en France', Thèse de doctorat, Paris I, 3 vols.
Stanhope, Boynes-Jones MD, *The Evolution of Preventive Medicine in the United States Army 1607–1939*, Washington, D.C., Office of the Surgeon General of the US Army, 1968.
Steefel, Lawrence D., *Bismarck, the Hohenzollern Candidacy and the Origins of the Franco–German War of 1870*, Cambridge, Mass., Harvard University Press, 1962.
Stone, Judith F., *Sons of the Revolution: Radical Democrats in France 1862–1914*, Baton Rouge, Louisiana State University Press, 1996.
Stora, Benjamin, *La Gangrène et l'oubli, la mémoire de la guerre d'Algérie*, La Découverte, 1992.
Stroch, Paul, *Bataille de Froeschwiller*, Association des Oeuvres Scolaires, 1989.
Sukstorf, Lothar, *Die Problematik der Logistik im deutschen Heer während des deutsch-französischen Krieges 1870/71*, Frankfurt am Main, Peter Lang, 1994.
Suleiman, Ezra N., *Private Power and Centralization in France: The Notaires and the State*, Princeton University Press, 1987.
Summers, Anne, *Angels and Citizens: British Women as Military Nurses*, Routledge and Kegan Paul, 1988.
Sussman, George, 'The glut of doctors in mid-nineteenth-century France', *Comparative Studies in Society and History*, 19 (1977) 287–304.
Sussman, George, *Selling Mothers' Milk: The Wet-Nursing Business in France, 1715–1914*, Urbana, University of Illinois Press, 1982.
Swain, Valentine, 'Franco-Prussian war 1870–1871: voluntary aid for the wounded and sick', *British Medical Journal*, 3 (1970) 511–14.

Taithe, Bertrand, 'The Rise and Fall of European Syphilization: The debates on human experimentation and vaccination of syphilis' in L. Hall, G. Hekma *et al.* (eds) *Sexual Cultures in Europe*, Manchester University Press, 1999, 34–58.
Taithe, Bertrand and Tim Thornton (eds), *Prophecy: the power of inspired language in history*, Stroud, Sutton Publishing, 1997.
Taithe, Bertrand and Tim Thornton (eds), *Wars: Identities in Conflicts*, Stroud, Sutton Publishing, 1998.
Taithe, Bertrand and Tim Thornton (eds), *Propaganda: Political Rhetoric and Identity*, Sutton Publishing, 1999.
Teller, Michael E., *The Tuberculosis Movement: A Public Health Campaign in the Progressive Era*, New York, Greenwood Press, 1988.
Termeau, J., *Maisons closes de province, l'amour vénal au temps du règlementarisme à partir d'une étude du Maine-Anjou*, Le Mans, Cénomane 1986.
Thane, Stuart, *The History of Food Preservation*, Pantheon Publishing, 1986.

Thomas, Denis (ed.), *Battle Art: Images of War*, Oxford, Phaidon, 1977.
Thomas, Édith, *Les Pétroleuses*, Gallimard, 1963.
Thomas, Édith, *Rossel, 1844–1871*, Gallimard, 1967.
Thomas, Édith, *Louise Michel ou la vélléda de l'anarchie*, Gallimard, 1971.
Thompson, J. M., *Louis Napoléon and the Second Empire*, Oxford, Basil Blackwell, 1965.
Tombs, Robert, *The War Against Paris, 1871*, Cambridge University Press, 1981.
Tombs, Robert, 'Prudent rebels: the second arrondissement during the Paris Commune of 1871', *French History*, 5:4 (1991) 393–413.
Tombs, Robert, 'L'Année terrible, 1870–1871', *Historical Journal*, 35:3 (1992) 713–24.
Tombs, Robert, *France, 1814–1914*, Longman, 1996.
Tomes, Nancy, 'The private side of public health: sanitary science, domestic hygiene and the germ theory 1870–1900', *Bulletin of the History of Medicine*, 64 (1990) 509–39.
Touati, François Olivier (ed.), *Maladies, médecines et sociétés, approches historiques pour le présent*, 2 vols, L'Harmattan, Histoire au Présent, 1993.
Troinin, I. P., 'Questions of guerrilla warfare in the law of war', *American Journal of International Law*, 11 (1946), 534–62.
Troquet, Claude, *La Banlieue Est pendant le siège de Paris. La vie militaire quotidienne de septembre 1870 à janvier 1871*, Vincennes, l'auteur, 1980.
Troyansky, David G., 'Monumental politics: national history and local memory in French Monuments aux Morts in the Department of Aisne since 1870', *French Historical Studies*, 15:1 (1987) 121–41.
Turner, G. L. E., (ed.), *The Patronage of Science in the Nineteenth Century*, Leyden, Noordhoff International Publishing, 1976.

Valley-Radot, Pierre, *Un Siècle d'histoire hospitalière de Louis-Philippe à nos jours, 1837–1949*, Dupont, 1948.
Vaultier, R., 'La Médecine militaire en 1870', *La Presse médicale*, 65 (1957) 2203–7.
Vess, David M., *Medical Revolution in France: 1789–1796*, Gainesville, Florida State University Book, 1975.
Vichniac, Isabelle, *Croix Rouge : Les stratèges de la bonne conscience*, Alain Moreau, 1988.
Viguier, Georges, 'Rappel historique sur l'épidémiologie des infections typho-paratyphiques', Thèse de doctorat en médecine, Université de Paris, 1960.
Vincent, François, *Histoire des famines à Paris*, Librairie de Médicis, 1946.
Vovelle, Michel, *La Mort et l'occident de 1300 à nos jours*, NRF, Gallimard, 1983.

Wald-Lasowski, P., *Syphilis, essai sur la littérature française au dix-neuvième siècle*, Gallimard, 1982.
Wall, R. and J. Winter (eds), *The Upheaval of War: Family, Work and Welfare in Europe, 1914–1918*, Cambridge University Press, 1988.
Warner, John Harley, 'Remembering Paris, memory and the American disciple of French medicine in the nineteenth century', *Bulletin of the History of Medicine*, 65 (1991) 301–25.
Watteville, C. de, 'Le Siège de Paris et les inventeurs', *La Revue* (1915) 249–62.
Weber, Eugen, *Peasants into Frenchmen: The Modernization of Rural France, 1870–1914*, Stanford University Press, 1976.

Weber, Eugen, *France, Fin-de-Siècle,* Cambridge, Mass., Harvard University Press, 1986.

Weindling, Paul (ed.), *International Health Organisations and Movements, 1818–1939,* Cambridge University Press, 1995.

Weiss, J. H., 'Origins of the French welfare state: poor relief in the Third Republic, 1871–1914', *French Historical Studies,* 13:1 (1983) 47–78.

Weisz, George, *The Emergence of Modern Universities in France, 1863–1914,* Princeton University Press, 1983.

Weisz, George, *The Medical Mandarins: The French Academy of Medicine in the Nineteenth and Early-Twentieth Centuries,* Oxford University Press, 1995.

Welch, David A., *Justice and the Genesis of War,* Oxford University Press, 1993.

Wells, Donald A., *War Crimes and Laws of War,* University Press of America, 1984.

Wheeler, Michael, *Heaven, Hell and the Victorians,* Cambridge, 2nd edn, Cambridge University Press, 2nd edn, 1994.

Willems, Emilio, *A Way of Life and Death: Three Centuries of German Militarism, an Anthropological Approach,* Nashville, Tenn., Vanderbilt University Press, 1986.

Willette, Luc, *Raoul Rigaul: 25 ans, Communard, chef de la Police,* Syros, 1984.

Williams, Elizabeth A., *The Physical and the Moral: Anthropology, Physiology, and Philosophical Medicine in France, 1750–1850,* Cambridge University Press, 1994.

Williams, Roger L., *The French Revolution of 1870–1871,* Weidenfeld and Nicolson, 1969.

Williams, Roger L., *The Mortal Napoleon III,* Princeton University Press, 1971.

Willing, Paul, *L'Expédition du Mexique (1861–1867) et la guerre franco-allemande 1870,* Arceuil, Préal, 1983.

Winter, Jay, 'Military fitness and civilian health in Britain during World War One', *Journal of Contemporary History,* 15:2 (1980) 211–44.

Winter, Jay, *The Great War and the British People,* Basingstoke, Macmillan, 1986.

Winter, Jay, 'Catastrophe and culture: recent trends in the historiography of World War One', *Journal of Modern History,* 64 (1992) 525–32.

Winter, Jay, *Sites of Memory, Sites of Mourning: The Great War in European Cultural History,* Cambridge University Press, 1995.

Woloch, Isser, *The French Veteran from the Revolution to the Restoration,* Chapel Hill, University of North Carolina Press, 1979.

Wright, Gordon, 'Public opinion and conscription in France, 1866–1870', *Journal of Modern History,* 14:1 (1942) 26–45.

Wright, Gordon, *Between the Guillotine and Liberty: Two Centuries of the Crime Problem in France,* Oxford University Press, 1983.

Zeldin, Theodore, *The Political System of Napoleon III,* Macmillan, 1958.

Zeldin, Theodore, *Émile Ollivier and the Liberal Empire,* Oxford, Clarendon Press, 1963.

Index

Abeille médicale 64
Academy of Medicine 48–50, 55–6, 65, 75, 98, 105, 117, 139, 153, 214, 216
Academy of Science 112, 116
Adam, Edmond 118
Agulhon, Maurice 180
alcohol and alcoholism 14, 23, 98, 191, 208–17, 232
Algeria, Algerians, *Turcos* 75, 160, 172
Algerian war 233–4
Alsace-Lorraine 6, 16, 23, 39, 109, 180, 187, 189, 205–6, 237
 deputies 41
ambulances 74, 77, 83–4, 121, 126, 134, 139, 142, 146, 170–3, 215
American ambulance 165
American civil war 79, 90–2, 164
Amiens 39
amputations 23, 180–207, 237
anaesthetic 182
Anderson, Benedict 177, 235
Andersonville confederate prisoner camp 164
Andrieu, Jules 140, 210
Angers 90
anticlericalism *see* religion
antisepsis and Listerian theories 23, 61, 183–5
Arnaud, Commandant Antoine 12, 13
arrondissements 53, 88, 100–29, 134, 140, 173
artillery 31, 47
Asseline, Louis 125
Assistance Publique 20, 52, 55, 63–9, 91, 103, 106, 121, 134, 139, 141, 143–5, 148, 150, 193, 201, 220
 Bureau de Bienfaisance 103, 122–6, 139–40
Association française contre l'abus des boissons alcooliques 212
Association générale des médecins de France 52
Association des soeurs de France 137
ataxia 81
Audoin-Rouzeau, Stéphane 13, 25, 30, 81

bakers 109–10
Banque de France 144

Barrès, Maurice 206
Basel 178, 203
bateaux mouches 94
Baudin, Alphonse 36, 196
Bazaine, Marshall François Achille 31–2, 37
Bazeilles and Balan 6, 34
Beaufort, François Louis Comte de vii, 145, 176, 178, 198–204
Beaunes 36
Beirut 27
Belfort 36, 53
Belgium 55
Berkeley-Hill, M. 59
Bernard, Claude 47, 49
Bernhardt, Sarah 3, 82, 174
Bismarck, Otto von 7, 29–30, 112
Blanqui, Auguste 42, 215
Bloody Week, *semaine sanglante* 12, 19, 43, 135, 146–50
Boer war 21
Bonaparte, Pierre 50
Bonapartism 34, 71, 136, 186, 189, 191, 238
Bordeaux 41, 52, 90, 189–90, 237
Borsa, S. 51
Bottard, Marguerite 152
boucheries chevalines 100
Bourbaki, General Charles Denis Sauter 35, 39, 178
Bourdieu, Pierre 100
Bourke, Joanna 180
bread 9, 107–9, 112, 118–29, 212
Breton soldiers 3, 38, 79–80
breweries and distillers 213
British hospitals 59–60
Broca, Paul 65–6, 88, 139, 141, 143
Bülow, Bernard von 189
Buret, François 218
burials, cremation, funerals 193–6
butchers 117–18

Caisse des offrandes nationales 196–7
Camerone 6
Camporesi, Piero 100
canal St-Martin 105

Carbonell, C.-O. 233
Catholic Church 154, 192, 204; *see also* religion
centralisation 130–2
Cham vii, 132–3
Chamber of deputies 71, 189–90
Chanzy, General Antoine Alfred Eugène 39, 94; *see also* Loire army
Charcot, Jean-Martin 47, 151–4
Charité hospital 151
Charlemagne 27
Chenu, J. C. 59–60, 77–8, 88, 145, 165, 168, 176, 185–6, 215
cholera epidemics 53, 56
Chouan 38
Cité-des-Fleurs 119–20
citizenship 1, 19, 94, 99–129, 158, 174, 215
Claretie, Jules 38, 49
Clausewitz, Karl von 19, 72
Clemenceau, Georges 19, 103–4, 192
Cluseret, Gustave Paul 138, 145
Collins, Wilkie 46
colonial wars 27–8, 31, 77
Combes, Émile 192
Comédie Française 3, 83–4, 86–7
Comité de la presse 167–70
commemorative war medals 23
Commission d'hygiène et de salubrité 68, 74, 105, 107, 210, 212
Commission supérieure des ambulances 87–8
Commune of Paris 1, 2, 8, 11, 15, 19–22, 25, 34, 41–3, 69, 96, 131, 190, 227
    parties 42, 133–5, 215
    policies 99, 132–46, 173
Conférence médicale 50, 54
conscription 10, 32, 72, 105, 168
conseil des hospices 64–7
conseils de révision 105
Cooter, Roger 81, 158, 188
Corbin, Alain 12, 230
cordon sanitaire and quarantine 89–95
Coulmiers, battle of 204
Crawford, Elizabeth 70
cremation *see* burials
Cresson, E. 118
Crimean war 27, 77

Dames du Calvaire 137
Danton, Georges Jacques 38
Darboy, Archbishop Georges 43, 110, 135
Darjou, A. vii
Darwinism and eugenics 14, 60, 98, 229–30
Daudet, Alphonse 206, 215
Débâcle 13, 49, 127, 190–1, 206

decadence, degeneracy and national decline 14, 23–4, 98, 187, 208–10, 225–32, 234
Déroulède, Paul 206
Delescluze, Louis Charles 104, 125, 138
    trial 36
Denmark 26–7
Detaille, Édouard 5
Dijon 36, 39
discipline 89–97
disinfection 96
Dmitrieff, Elizabeth 136
Dominique, Pierre 147
Douglas, Mary 214
Dreyfus affair 237
drunkenness 23, 211–17
du Camp, Maxime 63, 77, 99, 190, 208, 215
Duchâtelet, Alexandre Parent 229
Dunant, Henry 71, 77, 155, 164, 179
Dunkirk 6
Dupouy, Edmond 105

education 14, 49–50, 86, 140, 152
elections (8 February 1871) 40
Ellis, Jack 23, 151, 191
Ems telegram 30
eugenics *see* Darwinism
Eugénie, Empress of the French 28, 64, 125, 138
Evans, Thomas 90, 165
externes 51

facial prosthesis 198–200
Faidherbe, General Louis Léon César 36
Faller, Canon vii, 17
Ferry, Jules 19, 48, 64–6, 69, 86, 88, 103, 117, 139
Fiaux, Louis 225
fin-de-siècle 8, 23, 63, 97–8, 208, 217, 232, 234–8
fires (May 1871) 4, 43, 96, 216
First World War 180, 205, 239
Flaubert, Gustave 63, 226
Flavigny, E. Comte de 176, 190
Flourens, Gustave 104
food 4, 99–129
    adulteration 106, 116
    ersastz 4, 8, 21, 100–29
    prices 9, 107–8
    rationing 4, 21, 106–7, 119–20
    requisitioning 21, 108–12, 127
    see also meat; milk; rice
forbidden weapons 162–3
Foreign Legion 6
Foucault, Michel 9, 89, 209
fourneaux économiques 121
Fournier, Alfred 24, 230–1

INDEX 289

Fox, Robert 69
France médicale 50, 67
francs-tireurs 34, 42, 98, 203–4
freedom of the press 29
Freemasons 103, 117, 145–6, 171
Freycinet, Charles Louis de Saulses de 36
funerals *see* burials
Furet, François 19

Gaillard, Jeanne 41
Gambetta, Léon 8, 19, 35, 38, 40, 73, 102, 188, 208, 214
gangrene, hospital rot 74, 89, 95–6, 181, 183–5
Garde Mobile 31, 33, 35, 37, 55, 79–80, 176, 221–2, 225
Gardes nationaux 33, 35, 37, 40, 64, 67, 68, 77, 79, 82, 110, 113, 176, 222
  medical services 138–9, 142, 145
  mobilisés 33, 37, 80, 94, 215
  sédentaires 33, 79–80, 126, 197, 215, 221–2, 228
Gare de l'Est 109
Garibaldi, Giuseppe 36, 39, 41
Gazette médicale de Paris 67
Gaulois, Le 167–9
Geneva convention 79, 83, 157, 159, 164–5, 171, 175
German medicine 46–51
Germany 55, 159, 181, 194, 236
Gilpin, Robert 130
Girondin ambulance 173
Gobineau, Joseph Arthur Comte de 14–15, 210, 216, 237
Goncourt, Edmond de 10, 115
Gordon, Charles 185
Gould, Roger 80
Goupil, Edmond Alfred 140
Goya's *The Third of May* 160
Grand-Hôtel hospital 3, 86, 91, 215
Greenberg, Louis 41
Guerre illustrée, La 121

Harris, Ruth 97
Haussmann, Georges Eugène 53, 64, 69, 127
Hazareesingh, Sudhir 20–1, 238
health 83
Hébert, Jacques René 108
historiography 1, 25
  Annales and *longue-durée* 1, 16
  Marxist 1, 40, 147, 234–5
  of the body 3, 61, 180–1
Hohenzollern candidacy 26–9
home front 18

hospitals 11, 50–2, 56–61, 81, 109, 117, 135–7
Hôtel de Ville 43, 96, 112
Hôtel-Dieu 60, 148
Hôtel du Louvre hospital 91
Howard, Michael 19, 25, 32
Hugo, Victor 8, 41, 112
humanitarianism and 'war atrocities' 4, 22, 146–7, 155–79, 238–9
Huss, Magnus 211
Husson, Armand 64, 69
Hutchinson, John 155–6, 175
hysteria 153–4

Incurables at Ivry 52, 229
Indo-China 27
infanticide 64
insurrection
  31 October (1870) 19, 37, 112
  22 January (1871) 19, 39, 112
  18 March (1871) 19, 41, 115, 215, 236
Intendance (commissariat) 75, 78–9, 84, 95
internes 51
Irish ambulance 166–7
Italian wars 27, 77, 90

Jones, Stuart 130
Jourde, François 144
Journal officiel de la république 138, 142
June days (1848) 40–1

Kératry, Émile de 118, 215
Keylor, William 233
Krupp gun 31, 47, 70, 162, 236
Kudlick, Catherine 62

La Berge, Ann 47
Laennec hospital 151
laissez-faire 131, 170–4
Lancet, The 46
Lancette française 49
Landwehr 7
Laon 34
Larrey, Dominique 71, 75
Larrey, Baron Hippolyte 55, 71, 77–9, 83–4, 87–9, 90, 94–7, 143, 162, 186, 193, 198
Leboeuf, Marshall Edmond 5, 31
Le Bourget 3, 38
Lecomte, General Claude Martin 41
Lecour, C. J. 221
LeFort, Léon 69, 97, 155, 168
Légion d'honneur 17, 96, 170, 186
Le Mans 172

Léonard, Jacques 98, 151, 191
Leroux, Rosalie 154
Les Invalides 179, 204
Lévy, Michel 92, 97, 105
Libourne 90
Lidsky, Paul 208
Liebig, Justus von 116
Lieux de mémoire 18
ligue du midi 33
Lisbonne, Maxime 148
Lissigaray, Prosper Olivier 147, 216
Listerian theories *see* antisepsis and Listerian theories
Longchamps barracks 92
Loire army 37, 41, 94
Lourdes 154
Luxembourg palace and gardens 147, 149
Lyons 33–4, 36, 39, 53

MacCormac, William 184
MacMahon, Marshall Edme Patrice Comte de 32, 146, 176
Magasins Réunis hospital 91, 142
Maison d'Alfort veterinary school 56, 81
malingering 21, 73, 81–3, 142
Manet's *The Execution of the Emperor Maximilian* 160
Marcel, Étienne 234
Marchal (de Calvi), Charles Jacob 54–5, 76
Marey, Étienne-Jules 107
Marianne 23, 180–1, 188, 190, 192
Marseillaise 189
Marseilles 34, 192
Mars-la-Tour 17
masculinity 12, 190
Marthold, Jules de 177
Marx, Karl 234
Mary, Virgin 192
Maupassant, Guy de 230
  Le Lit 29 230
Maximum laws 108
meat 10, 112–13, 115–18, 132
Médecins du Monde 156
Médecins sans Frontières 156
medical faculty 49–50, 67–8, 139, 141
medical statistics 62–3, 81
medicine
  civilian 46–70, 130–40, 220–6
  military 72–98, 220–6
memory 3, 4, 9
Mennell, Stephen 100
Metz 6, 32–3, 36–7, 53, 90, 162, 177, 193, 203
Mexico 27, 77

miasma 61, 94
Michel, C. R. 51
Michel, Louise 136, 227
Michelet, Jules 188, 214
militarisation 72–3, 89–90
milk 105, 119–20
Millière, Jean-Baptiste Édouard 104
Mitchell, Allan 2, 25, 46, 70, 128
mitrailleuse 31, 163
mobilisation 3, 4, 11, 32, 96, 157, 168, 212, 221; *see also* conscription
modernity 14, 236
Moilin, Tony 146–7
Moltke, Karl von 30
Monod, Henri 172–3
Mont-de-Piété 132–3
Montesson, Charles de 204
Montmartre 41, 192, 236
  Sacré Coeur 152
Montpellier 48
Montrosier, E. vii, 6
Moreau, Jean 192
Morel, Bénédicte 216
Morny, Charles Auguste Louis Joseph Comte de 28
mortality 54–61, 91–3, 120–1
mysticism and prophecies 15, 153–4

Napoleon I, Napoleon Bonaparte 38, 72, 95, 179, 205
  consulate 219
  legend 5, 9, 17, 71, 75, 94
Napoleon III, Louis Napoleon Bonaparte 26, 29, 165–6
  diplomacy 26
national decline *see* decadence
National Defence government 22, 33, 48, 66, 110, 208, 238
Nationalverein 159
Nélaton, Auguste 49, 54, 168
Neuville, A. de vii, 7
Niel, Marshall Adolphe 7
  reform (1868) 7, 31
Nisbet, James 188
Noir, Victor 50, 196
Nora, Pierre 8
Nord, Philip 172
Nord army 41, 76
nosology 62
notaries 130
Notre-Dame of Paris 148–9, 176–7
nurses 136–7, 146, 151, 158
Nye, Robert 12, 97, 208

obsidional fever 63, 190, 213
Oeuvre des amputés de la guerre 197–8
Oeuvre des pensions militaires 204–5
Oeuvre des tombes 194
officiers de santé 51, 68–9, 152, 169
Ollivier, Émile 28–9
Onimus, E. 107, 210
Opinion médicale 49, 67
Orleanism 29, 34, 41, 176
Orléans 39
Oxford English Dictionary 157

Palais de l'Industrie 134
Palais-Royal ambulance 83–4
Palikao government 32
Paré, Ambroise 183
Paris
    Conseil Municipal 66, 129, 150, 196, 225, 234
    mayors 65, 102–4, 140; *see also arrondissements*
    population, size of 3, 8, 101–2, 147
    Préfecture de police 33, 62, 103–4, 118–19, 135, 148, 215, 218–29
Pasteur, Louis and Pasteurian revolution 49, 69, 183
paupers 122–5
Père Lachaise 196
Persigny, Jean Gilbert Victor Fialin Duc de 28
Petits Ménages at Issy 52, 143, 147
phenic acid 61, 107, 116
Pick, Daniel 2, 98, 156
Picpus convent 135
Piétri, Pierre Marie 103
Place de la Concorde 177
pneumatic occlusion 61
Pope, Papal state 28
Porter, J. H. 201
Préfecture de la Seine 64–6, 69, 128
preserved meat 116
press *see* freedom of the press
Prestwich, Patricia 209, 211
Prévost-Paradol, Lucien Anatole 12, 28
Prim y Prats, Juan 29
prophecies *see* mysticism
prostitution and prostitutes 218–28
Protestant churches 171–2, 204, 211; *see also* religion
prostheses 197–203
Proust, Marcel 8, 9, 10
Prussian Crown Prince 38, 162
Pyat, Félix 142

Quakers 155–6
quarantine *see cordon sanitaire*
Quêtel, Claude 209, 230

Ranvier, Gabriel 104
Raspail, François Vincent 50
Rastoul, Paul 138, 145
Razoua, Eugène 64
Reclus, Paul 138
Red Cross 3, 22, 61, 68, 74, 78–9, 85–6, 88, 95–6, 134, 136, 140, 145–6, 149, 155–79, 185–6, 198, 235–6
Red Poster 112
Reichshoffen, charge of 6
religion and anticlericalism 125, 129, 134–46, 153–4, 192
religious orders 136–7, 171
Rennes 90
rent moratorium 127
revanche 15, 177, 206–7, 239
Revolution 4 September 33–4, 39, 63, 99, 129, 214
revolutionary clubs 35, 76, 139, 215
revolutionary myth (1789–93) 10, 17, 33–4, 39, 48, 63, 108, 186, 189, 214, 227, 231
revolutions (1830 and 1848) 67, 69, 76, 195, 203
rice 115
Ricord, Philippe 51, 169, 176, 230
Riencourt, Anne Honoré Olivier Comte de 204–5
rifles (Chassepot and Dreyse) 31, 70, 162–4, 236
Rigault, Raoul 135, 143, 195, 215, 228
Rihs, Charles 42
Rimbaud, Arthur xii
River Seine 94, 106
Rochefort, Henri 50
Rossel, Louis Nathaniel 12, 42, 138
Roth, François 25
Rothschild family bank 126, 171
Roubaud, Félix 49
Rougerie, Jacques 40, 234
Rouher, Eugène 28
Roussel, Adolphe Clémence dit 134

Saarbrücken 32, 162
Sadowa 27–8, 187
Saint-Laurent church 135
Saint-Lazare prison 220, 228
Saint-Sulpice church 147, 172–3
Salpêtrière hospital 162
Samuel, Raphael 2
Sarcey, Francisque 9
scurvy 54, 89, 227
Sebastopol 28

Second Empire 3, 44, 47, 137, 158, 169, 205, 223
   liberal 27–9, 103
Second World War 13, 100
Sedan, battle of 6, 32–3, 34, 79, 206, 212
Seine department 65; *see also* Préfecture de la Seine 65
Serman, William 25
Service de Santé 20–1
Showalter, Elaine 97
Simon, Jules 176
Simpson, James 59
Sinding, Christiane 188
smallpox 4, 53–5, 80, 96, 182, 218
   vaccination 54–7
Société chimique 106
Société internationale de secours aux blessés des armées de terre et de mer *see* Red Cross
Solferino 28, 71, 164
Sontag, Susan 97
sortie en masse 10
Soubirou, Bernadette 154
soup kitchens 121–6; *see also* Assistance Publique; *fourneaux économiques*
Sournia, J.-C. 211
Spain 28–9
Strasburg 32, 36–7, 48, 53, 75, 162, 203
   statue of 9, 177
stretcher-bearers 76–7
Suleiman, Ezra 130
surgery 182–93, 213
Switzerland 39, 55, 178, 203
syphilis 14, 23, 191, 210, 217–29
   hereditary 24
   treatment of 220–9

Thiers, Adolphe 13, 22, 40, 41, 42, 66, 95, 177, 189–93
Thiers, Mrs A. 176, 197, 203
Third Republic 13, 19, 43, 129, 132, 150, 152, 191, 205, 217, 234
Thomas, Général Clément 41, 77
time 8, 11, 16, 85
Times, The 86
Tollet, C. 97
Tombs, Robert 42, 95, 145, 147, 217
Toulouse 179
Tours delegation 34, 35, 38
train hospitals 90, 92, 167
Treillard, Camille 134–45
Tridon, Edme Marie Auguste 142
Trochu, General Louis Jules 33, 37, 72, 74, 84, 99, 101, 105, 227
tuberculosis 24, 58, 62–3, 98, 209, 230

Tuileries Palace 43
typhoid and typhus 53–4

Uhlan cavalry 33–4
Union des dames françaises 177
Union des femmes de France 177
Union médicale 68, 70, 149
Universal Exhibitions (1867, 1878) 6, 101, 165–6

Val-de-Grâce, hospital 75, 81, 84, 162
Vallès, Jules 140, 148
Valmy 34
Vermorel, Auguste Jean Marie 142
Versailles, Versaillais 12, 15, 21, 95–6, 131, 141, 143, 145, 150, 190
veterans 205
village of cannibals (Hautefaye) 12–13
Vincennes 148, 225
violence 12, 145–50

war
   à outrance 19, 35, 43, 73, 157, 189, 230
   armistice 39
   causes of 26–8
   meanings of 3, 233–5
   memorials 8, 176–7, 239
   painters 5
   shelling 38, 127–8
   total 4, 19, 72
   victims and wounds 43–4, 127–8, 160–4, 182–207
'war attrocities' *see* humanitarianism
Weber, Eugen 18
Weisz, George 47, 49
Wilhelm, king of Prussia 29–30, 32
wine 210–17
winter (1870–71) 58, 111
Winter, Jay 180
Wintz, Henry 164
Wissembourg 32, 160

Zola, Émile 13, 15, 16, 18, 189, 206, 210, 215, 217–18, 230; *see also* Débâcle
   L'assommoir 217
   Nana 217–18
   Ventre de Paris 116
zouaves pontificaux 38

Lightning Source UK Ltd.
Milton Keynes UK
16 May 2010

154229UK00002B/5/P